African Civilizations

This major new revised edition of African civilizations re-examines the physical evidence for developing social complexity in tropical Africa over the last four thousand years. Graham Connah focuses upon the archaeological research of two key aspects of complexity, urbanism and state formation, in seven main areas of Africa: Nubia, Ethiopia, the West African savanna, the West African forest, the East African coast and islands, the Zimbabwe Plateau and parts of Central Africa. The book's main concern is to review the available evidence in its varied environmental setting, and to consider possible explanations of the developments that gave rise to it. Extensively illustrated, including new maps and plans, and offering an extended bibliography, this book provides essential reading for students of archaeology, anthropology, African history, black studies and social geography.

GRAHAM CONNAH, Emeritus Professor of Archaeology at the University of New England, Australia, is a Visiting Fellow at the Australian National University, Canberra. He has extensive academic and field experience of both African and Australian archaeology, and is widely published. His earlier book *Three thousand years in Africa* (1981) won the Amaury Talbot prize. Recent publications include *Transformations in Africa* (1998), *Kibiro: the salt of Bunyoro, past and present* (1996) and *The archaeology of Australia's history* (1993). He was awarded the Order of Australia in 2000, for his contributions to African and Australian archaeology.

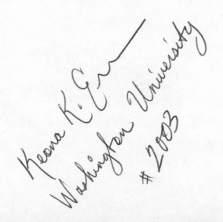

By the same author

The archaeology of Benin: excavations and other researches in and around Benin City, Nigeria (Oxford University Press, 1975)

Three thousand years in Africa: man and his environment in the Lake Chad region of Nigeria (Cambridge University Press, 1981)

Edited. *Australian field archaeology: a guide to techniques* (Australian Institute of Aboriginal Studies, 1983)

Of the hut I builded: the archaeology of Australia's history (Cambridge University Press, 1988). Paperback edition: *The archaeology of Australia's history* (Cambridge University Press, 1993)

Kibiro: the salt of Bunyoro, past and present (British Institute in Eastern Africa, 1996)

Edited. *Transformations in Africa: essays on Africa's later past* (Leicester University Press, 1998)

African civilizations

An archaeological perspective

SECOND EDITION

Graham Connah
Australian National University
Canberra

DRAWINGS BY DOUGLAS HOBBS

CAMBRIDGE
UNIVERSITY PRESS

PUBLISHED BY THE PRESS SYNDICATE OF THE UNIVERSITY OF CAMBRIDGE
The Pitt Building, Trumpington Street, Cambridge, United Kingdom

CAMBRIDGE UNIVERSITY PRESS
The Edinburgh Building, Cambridge CB2 2RU, UK
40 West 20th Street, New York, NY 10011-4211, USA
10 Stamford Road, Oakleigh, VIC 3166, Australia
Ruiz de Alarcón 13, 28014 Madrid, Spain
Dock House, The Waterfront, Cape Town 8001, South Africa

http://www.cambridge.org

First published 1987
Reprinted 1989, 1990, 1991, 1992, 1993, 1994, 1995, 1996, 1998, 2000
Second edition 2001

Printed in the United Kingdom at the University Press, Cambridge

Typeface Sabon MT 10.5/13.5 pt.   *System* QuarkXPress™ [SE]

A catalogue record for this book is available from the British Library

ISBN 0 521 59309 3 hardback
ISBN 0 521 59690 4 paperback
(ISBN 0 521 31992 7 1st edition paperback)

To Nora Fisher McMillan

Contents

Figures

Preface to the first edition

In the last quarter of a century there has been a great number of publications concerned with the archaeology of tropical Africa over the last 3000 years or so. Most of these publications have been highly specialized, however, and it has been apparent to me, as a researcher and teacher in archaeology, that a large part of the reading public of the English-speaking world still has little understanding of the achievements of precolonial tropical African societies. One of the longest-lived and most inaccurate stereotypes has been the vague general notion that such societies consisted only of scattered groups of people living in small villages of grass or mud 'huts'. This book has been written as a synthesis of some of the main archaeological evidence that shows that this was not the case. The much debated word 'civilization' is used in its title as a reminder that tropical Africa *also* attained cultural complexity of a high order. The book is about the material evidence for cities and states, because it is on these that discussion can be most readily focused. Its aim is to reach a wide range of readers and yet also to be of help to students and teachers of later African archaeology. With these intentions in mind, this book has been substantially illustrated and it is also fully referenced. Working from a base in Australia, my main difficulty has been obtaining the more recently published research results but everything possible has been done to ensure that the book was up to date at the time of going to press.

The book was written between June 1983 and March 1985 and revised in November 1985. It was written on the suggestion of Dr Jeremy Mynott and Dr Robin Derricourt of Cambridge University Press and I am particularly grateful to the latter for his encouragement and help throughout its preparation. I am also grateful to Dr David Phillipson of the University of Cambridge who read and commented on the first draft of the book and to the following scholars who were similarly helpful with respect to the chapters indicated: Professor Bill Adams of the University of Kentucky (Chapter 3); Professor J.W. Michels of Pennsylvania State University (Chapter 4); Drs R.J. and S.K. McIntosh of Rice University, Houston, Texas (Chapter 5); Professor Nicholas David of the University of Calgary (Chapter 6); Dr John Sutton of the British Institute in Eastern Africa, Nairobi (Chapter 7); Professor T.N. Huffman of the University of the Witwatersrand, Johannesburg (Chapter 8); Dr Pierre de Maret of the Musée Royal de l'Afrique Centrale, Tervuren, Belgium (Chapter 9); Professor Thurstan Shaw of Cambridge,

England (Chapter 10). To all these people I owe an enormous debt of gratitude for their assistance in correcting errors and filling in gaps. Any shortcomings which remain in the book are entirely my responsibility.

There are many others whose help has been essential. Douglas Hobbs of the Department of Prehistory and Archaeology, University of New England, prepared the line drawings and Rudi Boskovic and Steve Clarke of the Department of Geography of the same University did the photography of those drawings. Mrs Gibbons of Cambridge typed the first draft of the book and Noelene Kachel, of the University of New England, put the whole thing onto a word processor to allow for its subsequent revision. Di Watson, Secretary to the Department of Prehistory and Archaeology, University of New England, did more things to help than I can remember. Sue Pearson of Tamworth, NSW, assisted with the checking of the typescript.

Acknowledgement is also due to Dr A.T. Grove of the African Studies Centre, University of Cambridge, for providing working space when I was on study leave in Cambridge in 1983. My time as a Research Associate of that Centre was most important for the early stages of the writing of this book. During that same period I was also greatly helped by Dr John Alexander of the Department of Archaeology, University of Cambridge, to whom I am indebted for many discussions and for numerous loans of relevant publications.

Similarly, I am grateful to Professor Francis Van Noten of the Musée Royal de l'Afrique Centrale, Tervuren, Belgium, who made me welcome during a brief visit I made to Tervuren in search of reference material. His hospitality and that of Dr Pierre de Maret and his wife is remembered with great pleasure.

I would like to add a special word here for the Interlibrary Loan Service of the Dixson Library in the University of New England. Without the consistent efforts of its staff, I could not have obtained much of the published material that was used. They got it from all over Australia, from Britain, from Germany, from America, from Zimbabwe, and from quite a few places that I have forgotten. In particular, Luise Wissman of that service earned my gratitude many times over.

As stated above, the line illustrations were drawn by Douglas Hobbs but in a book of this nature such illustrations have had to be based in the main on material already published. The source of each line drawing is given in the caption. Some were heavily based on one source only, others on several sources, but almost all of them are modified by additions or simplifications or changes in lettering to render them more suitable for the purposes of this book. I acknowledge the original authors and artists concerned, for providing such a rich resource of illustration material. The photographs in the book come from a variety of sources. The Cambridge University Library provided Figs. 3.4, 6.1, 6.2, 7.9, 9.1 and 9.2. The British Museum provided Figs. 4.6 and 6.8. Dr Pierre de Maret of the Musée Royal de l'Afrique Centrale, Belgium, provided Figs. 9.4 and 9.5. Professor T.N. Huffman of the University of the Witwatersrand provided Figs. 8.3 and 8.7. Professor Frank Willett of the Hunterian Museum, Glasgow, provided Fig. 6.3. The Department of Photography of the University of New England provided Fig. 5.6, which was rephotographed from *Man*, Vol. 43, 1943. The same Department also provided Fig. 5.7, which is rephotographed from *National Geographic*, September 1982. All these photographs are reproduced with permission and details are given in the captions.

I would also like to record the fact that I dedicate this book to Nora Fisher McMillan of the Merseyside County Museums, Liverpool, England, who many years ago introduced me to the world of scientific research.

Finally, to my wife Beryl I owe an enormous debt of gratitude that cannot be measured but must be recorded.

Graham Connah
Department of Prehistory and Archaeology
University of New England
Armidale, NSW, Australia
March 1986

Preface to the second edition

The first edition of this book remained in print for over twelve years, during that time achieving ten reprints and a Japanese translation. However, new archaeological field research, changing interpretations of the evidence and an increasing amount of published material had rendered it sadly out of date. In preparing this new edition, therefore, it has been necessary not only to add to and update much of the content but also to rewrite some sections of the book and to restructure some of the chapters. In addition, both the illustrations and the bibliography have been revised and augmented.

The necessary work was carried out during 1998 and the first half of 1999 and could not have been completed without the assistance of a number of institutions and individuals. In particular I would like to acknowledge the hospitality of the Department of Archaeology and Ancient History at Uppsala University, Sweden, where I spent five months as a STINT-funded Visiting Scholar during 1998 gathering relevant source material. This was made possible by the generosity of the Swedish government and the kindness of Professor Paul Sinclair. Similarly I would like to thank the Humanities Research Centre and the Department of Archaeology and Anthropology, both at the Australian National University, Canberra, for a series of appointments as a Visiting Fellow from 1995 to the present time, which gave me much-valued access to necessary library facilities. Writing about Africa from a base in Australia has never been easy and it has been necessary to take every possible opportunity to keep in touch with relevant archaeological developments. In this connection, I would like to place on record my debt to a number of conferences in recent years: notably those of the Society for Africanist Archaeologists, the British Institute in Eastern Africa and the School of Oriental and African Studies at the University of London; also the Eighth International Conference for Meroitic Studies, the Pan African Congress at Harare in Zimbabwe, the Urbanism in Africa Conference in Mombasa, and the City Walls Conference at the the University of Minnesota. Similarly, of great importance have been the opportunities to conduct field research in Uganda, and to visit sites in Ethiopia, Kenya and Zimbabwe of which I previously had no firsthand knowledge.

As with the first edition, each of the chapters in this new edition has been read and commented on by a colleague and I am most grateful to all those concerned for their help and advice. They are: Chapters 1 and 9, Associate Professor Roland

Fletcher of the University of Sydney; Chapter 2, Dr David Edwards of the University of Leicester; Chapter 3, Dr David Phillipson of the University of Cambridge; Chapter 4, Dr Kevin MacDonald of the University of London; Chapter 5, Associate Professor Christopher DeCorse of Syracuse University, New York State; Chapter 6, Professor Paul Sinclair of Uppsala University; Chapter 7, Robert Soper of the University of Zimbabwe, Harare; and Chapter 8, Dr Peter Robertshaw of California State University, San Bernardino. In addition, Dr Laurel Phillipson of Cambridge has kindly read the entire text.

I am also much indebted to a number of people who have provided new illustration material: Professor Francis Geus of the University of Lille, Dr David Phillipson of the University of Cambridge, Dr Andrew Reid of the University of Botswana and Dr Thomas Wilson of Beloit College, Wisconsin. Detailed acknowledgements will be found in the figure captions. Otherwise the illustration material is from the sources indicated in the first edition, or from my own work or that of Douglas Hobbs, who has revised every one of his drawings as well as converting them to an electronic format. Reproduction of the illustrations used in Figs. 2.7, 5.1 and 8.1 is by permission of the Syndics of Cambridge University Library.

There are so many people who have helped in so many ways with my preparation of this new edition that they cannot all be mentioned. I ask their forgiveness. Nevertheless, I do have to extend my particular thanks to Jessica Kuper of Cambridge University Press, who has had to wait so long for me to complete this work. Finally, as on so many occasions over the years, I would like to acknowledge the support and assistance of my wife Beryl Connah, who has now so graciously accepted that some academics never actually retire. If this book has any merit, it is she who deserves the credit.

Graham Connah
Department of Archaeology and Anthropology
Australian National University
Canberra
June 1999

Chapter 1
The context

Find a map of Africa's physical geography and another of its vegetation. Coded into those two maps is important information that you will need to understand before reading this book. To begin with, Africa is huge; it is so big that you can put the United States of America and the Australian continent into it and still have a bit of space left over. It extends from about 37° North to about 35° South, and has an altitudinal range from depressions that are below sea level to mountain peaks that exceed 5000 metres. As a result it has an incredible diversity of environments. It contains some of the driest deserts in the world, and yet has three of the world's major rivers: the Nile, the Niger and the Zaïre (Congo). Some of the hottest places on earth are in Africa, and yet there are glaciers on its highest mountains. There are steaming rainforests and dry savanna grasslands, low-lying river valleys and high plateaux, extensive deserts and gigantic lakes, mangrove coasts and surf-pounded beaches. This is to give only an impressionistic picture of the very large number of differing environments to be found in the African continent. In reality the major zones merge into one another, so that there is an even greater variety of conditions. Add to this the effects of climatic variation through time and you have an infinitely complex environmental situation.

Into this environmental kaleidoscope introduce human beings and remember that they have been in Africa longer than in any other part of the world. For at least 2 million years (depending on how humanity is defined), people have been learning how to get the best out of African environments. Those environments have not determined what men and women could do, nor have the latter been able to ignore the environments in which they have lived. Instead there has been a dynamic relationship between the two, in which human beings have sought to turn to their advantage the opportunities offered by each environment and to come to terms with its constraints. This relationship can be traced throughout the long course of human history in Africa. First as hunters, gatherers and fishers who gradually intensified their exploitation of available resources; then as pastoralists and cultivators; eventually as city dwellers, artisans and traders: men and women have continued to interact with their environment, retaining this remarkable variety of strategies for doing so. Geographical location; seasonality of climate; water availability; soil fertility; plant species; access to resources such as timber, stone, clay, minerals and animal products; and disease vectors. These are merely some of the factors that have helped to shape human culture and which in many cases have themselves been affected by human activity. If you seek to study the history of Africa, you must understand human ecology.

Without doubt, you must also understand archaeology, which is a major source of information about Africa's past. Documentary sources for African history are limited: their coverage is often chronologically patchy and tends to be geographically peripheral. For large areas of Africa, particularly tropical Africa, their time-depth is restricted to the last century or two. In addition, many of the documentary sources that we do have are based on the observations of outsiders; such people as explorers, traders, missionaries, colonial officers and others, who did not always understand what they observed and were sometimes prejudiced in their assessment of it. Such documentary evidence that does exist is often invaluable but Africanist historians themselves have acknowledged its shortcomings for many areas, by giving considerable attention to oral sources of history. Extensive research has been conducted into oral traditions in many parts of the continent and our knowledge of African history has been greatly enriched by these endeavours. However, although it is a matter of some dispute, it seems unlikely that oral sources can throw much light on periods more than say 500 years ago. Indeed, Jan Vansina (1973: xiv) thought that 250 years was often the maximum. In these circumstances, scholars interested in Africa's past have turned to a variety of other information sources. Thus, art history and linguistics have contributed useful information (the latter particularly so, e.g. Ehret 1998), as have ethnographic and anthropological investigations. In addition, a number of other disciplines have been of assistance, such as investigations of DNA, blood group studies, plant genetics, and faunal research of one sort or another. It is in these circumstances that the archaeological evidence for Africa's past has assumed the very greatest importance.

Many people who are not archaeologists are uncertain about what archaeology is. As for archaeologists themselves, they have spent a lot of time over the last few decades arguing about it. Basically, however, the subject is concerned with the study of the physical evidence of past human activities, in order to reconstruct those activities. Such a reconstruction, it is hoped, will enable us to understand the undocumented past or to increase our understanding of inadequately documented periods of the past. Archaeological evidence, however, has its own strengths and weaknesses and we are still learning ways of gaining the maximum reliable information from it. Perhaps its greatest advantage is that it enables us to examine things that were actually made by people in the past and to investigate the impact that those people had on their environment. We can discover what human beings actually did, not merely what they or others said that they did. The main disadvantage of archaeological evidence is that it is almost always partial evidence, reflecting only part of the activities of past men and women. The differential effects of human behaviour, of climate and soil chemistry, and of subsequent disturbance by either natural or human agencies, cause most archaeological evidence to be rather like a jigsaw puzzle from which two-thirds of the pieces are lost, whilst the rest have the picture worn off or corners missing. These strengths and weaknesses of archaeological evidence can be seen in this book. On the middle Nile and in the Ethiopian Highlands we have the remains of stone-built cities and clear indications of centralized authority and we would not know much about this if we were dependent on historical sources alone. In Central Africa, on the other hand, archaeology has contributed much less information on urban settlements that were constructed in grass, wood and other organic materials and occupied by people who did not express their sense of nationhood in such a material fashion. Unfortunately, however, archaeological evidence has another drawback: it results from human endeavour, and archaeologists (just like other human beings) tend to vary in the amount of effort that they expend on different problems. Thus it is easy to search for settlement sites in the open grasslands of the African savanna but extremely difficult to do so in the tangled undergrowth of the rainforest, where in places one has to chop out a path even to walk through it. Similarly, it is easier to locate the sites of stone ruins than those of timber buildings and it is easier to excavate mud-brick structures than those of pisé. As a result, archaeological distribution maps of Africa tend to show the distribution of archaeological research, rather than that of archaeological evidence. Indeed, for extensive areas of the continent one might as well write the word 'unexplored' across such archaeological maps, just as was done a couple of centuries ago with so many maps of Africa.

Despite these problems, archaeology is very good for certain things. No longer merely concerned with studying artefacts, archaeologists have turned their attention to the study of human behaviour and its change through time. This is as it should be, for over a long time-scale it is probably only they who can throw much light on when and how and why human societies changed in the way that they did. In this book, for instance, an attempt is made to assess how much archaeology can tell us about two aspects of the development of social complexity in tropical Africa: the growth of cities and the appearance of states. The purpose is not to dispute with historians or social anthropologists or sociologists or geographers, who already have their own ideas, but to evaluate the archaeological data and to determine what it has to contribute to the debates on these issues. In doing this, it will also become apparent that future archaeological fieldwork will need more carefully thought-out research designs than has sometimes been the case in the past.

As has already been stated, human beings have been in Africa for at least 2 million years but for most of that time they scavenged, collected, hunted and fished for their food and there were probably few of them, widely scattered across the landscape. From the available archaeological evidence (Phillipson 1993a), it was only about 100,000 years ago that human societies were able to diversify in ways that allowed them to adapt to virtually all the varied African environments. As a result, it is likely that the size of some groups increased and that overall population levels rose. This led to increasing pressure on food resources, which during the period between about 18,000 and about 7000 years ago resulted in an intensification of exploitation strategies, such as the harvesting of grass seed, the manufacture of specialized fishing equipment, and possibly the development of management techniques over herds of wild animals. These changes did not take place everywhere, nor did they all take place at the same time but they are known to have occurred at various dates during this overall period, in parts of what is now the Sahara, in parts of the Nile Valley, and in some areas of the East African savanna. It seems likely that it was these changes that then led to the development of food production, which was well under way in the northern half of Africa by about the sixth millennium BC. Thus Africans have been farmers for less than half of one per cent of their history but the development of farming has had a major accelerating effect on the evolution of human culture and particularly on social organization. The domestication of sorghum, millet, teff, African rice, wheat, barley, yam, and a host of plants of lesser importance, plus the domestication of cattle, sheep and goats, has had the most profound effect on the growth of human populations, on the densities of population that could be maintained and on the growth of human sedentism. This is not the place to discuss the extent to which the development of food production in Africa resulted from local experimentation and the extent to which it was stimulated by influences from South-West Asia. However, the evidence available seems to indicate that plant domestication was generally an indigenous achievement but that most animal domestication, at least of sheep and goats, resulted from Asiatic initiatives. Whatever the truth of the matter, it is in the context of the development of African farming that all subsequent changes in the continent must be seen.

One of the most important of these changes was the adoption of iron metallurgy, which in Africa was taking place from about the middle of the first millennium BC. So great was the impact of this development on both the means of production and the means of destruction during the last two millennia in Africa, that archaeologists have tended to emphasize it almost to the exclusion of other considerations. Thus has come into use the phrase 'the African Iron Age', terminology that is difficult to apply chronologically and which distracts attention from other important changes that were occurring in some African societies. We still do not know enough about these but it would seem that over the last 3000–4000 years or more there was a rapid growth of interation between groups. This was probably brought about by a combination of population growth, increasing sedentism, ecological diversity, and an uneven distribution of resources. Certain animal and plant products, salt, copper, iron and other commodities were increasingly exchanged between different population centres and it was into such exchange networks that long-distance trade, both within and outside of Africa, was eventually able to tap. At the local level, such intergroup dependence encouraged a complex interaction between individual settlements, so that some became larger and more important than others and in time came to control all the other settlements in their immediate region. At the same time there was increasing specialization and social stratification amongst the people living in the larger settlements. In certain instances elite groups gained control of crucial resources, which became the basis of political power over the rest of the population. It was in some such manner that there emerged in particular parts of Africa the cities and states that were the principal manifestation of social complexity and which form the subject of this book. For such there were in tropical Africa before the advent of nineteenth-century colonialism. Neither urbanization nor the idea of the state was grafted onto Africa from modern Europe, as some might think. Particularly was this not so for tropical Africa and this book is an archaeologist's attempt to explain how and why this came to be the case.

Scholars considering the origins of cities and states as global phenomena have tended to see them as components of what they have called the emergence of civilization and have generally concentrated on West Asia, India, China and America, with Egypt being the only part of Africa to which attention has been given (Daniel 1968). The basic reason for this has been the concept of 'civilization' itself, which to Gordon Childe and many of his generation implied the existence of writing (Childe 1951: 161; 1957: 37), and which subsequently continued to attract prescriptive definition, although this became broader as time went on (for example, Kluckhohn 1960: 400; Renfrew 1972: 11; Redman 1978: 218–20). In general it seems to have been thought that 'civilization' implied cities, and vice versa, and inevitably this led to a debate about the definition of the word 'city', in which a list of ten criteria by Childe long remained influential (Childe 1950: 3, 9–16). The latter clearly reflected the circumstances of city development and state formation in South-West Asia, and, like Childe's definition of 'civilization', they were, as a result, of only limited value in other parts of the world. As with the term 'civilization', subsequent attempts to define the term 'city' became increasingly generalized (for example, Sjoberg 1960; Mumford 1961: 85; Jones 1966: 5; Beaujeu-Garnier and Chabot 1967: 30; Redman 1978: 215–16) and by 1981 Adams could comment that: 'Urbanism, to be sure, denotes no set of precise, well understood additional characteristics for societies so described' (R. McC. Adams 1981: 81).

Implicit in these attempts at definition was a concern with process, that is to say: how did states emerge, how did cities develop? It has been these questions that have increasingly attracted attention, resulting in a large and sophisticated literature. Investigations have concentrated on what has often been called 'the rise of complex society' and there has been a tendency to separate the study of urbanization from that of state formation. Indeed, the rise of the state has been seen as central to the emergence of 'complex societies', which some anthropologists would prefer to call 'stratified societies' or even 'pluralistic societies' (the latter as defined by Kuper and Smith 1969: 3–4). There has been much discussion of what has been called 'the anthropology of political evolution' (for example, Cohen and Service 1978; Claessen and Skalník 1978; Claessen and van de Velde 1987; Eisenstadt, Abitbol and Chazan 1988; Claessen and Oosten 1996) but its emphasis has tended to be on theoretical considerations and much of the evidence used has been drawn either from historical sources or from ethnographic and anthropological observations in the recent past. It has been difficult to relate such theories to archaeological evidence, although Jonathan Haas (1982) made an important attempt to do this, just as Roland Fletcher (1995) has constructed a theory of urbanization on a similar basis.

After reviewing the literature of state-formation theory, Haas presented a modified theory of his own and discussed how it might be used in the interpretation of archaeological data. He defined a 'state' as being 'a society in which there is a centralized and specialized institution of government' (Haas 1982: 3) and examined the various ways in which scholars have attempted to explain the emergence of such societies. He grouped these explanations into two schools of thought: the 'conflict' school and the 'integration' school (p. 15): the former arguing that 'the state evolved in response to conflict between unequal social classes' (p. 34) (for example, Fried 1967), and the latter arguing that the state evolved when 'social groups voluntarily came together and submitted to a governing authority in order to gain the military and economic benefits of centralization' (p. 61) (for example, Service 1975). Haas suggested that a more useful theory could be produced by 'introducing major integration elements directly into a broadened conflict model' (p. 129). Examining the main specific theories for the emergence of state societies, he identified three different groups (pp. 132–52): (1) warfare theories (for example, Carneiro 1970); (2) trade theories, either (a) interregional (for example, Rathje 1971; 1972) or (b) intra-regional (for example, Wright and Johnson 1975); and (3) an irrigation theory (Wittfogel 1957). Haas argued that in spite of differences between them, 'All the theories begin with stratification and outline alternate ways by which certain members of a society may gain differential access to basic resources' (Haas 1982: 150). In all the theories, he observed, 'This differential access is based on *control over the production or procurement* of the resources in question' (p. 151; italics in original). It is that control, according to Haas, that gives rulers power and he has advanced what might be called 'the power theory of state formation'. Indeed, others have also recognized the importance of power in the development of social complexity (for example, Earle 1997).

6

Haas understood power to be the capacity to oblige somebody else to do something that he would not otherwise do, through the application, threat or promise of sanctions (p. 157). He identified nine variables that could be used to measure power in social relationships and demonstrated how each of these could be recognized in the archaeological record (pp. 159–71): (1) power base; (2) means of exerting power; (3) scope of power; (4) amount of power; (5) extension of power; (6) costs of power; (7) compliance costs; (8) refusal costs; and (9) gains. Redefining the word 'state' in terms of power, Haas called it 'a stratified society in which a governing body exercises control over the production or procurement of basic resources, and thus necessarily exercises coercive power over the remainder of the population' (p. 172).

Although Haas attempted to relate some of the anthropological ideas about state formation to archaeological data, he made little mention of precolonial African states, drawing all his archaeological evidence from Mesopotamia, China, Mesoamerica and Peru. Like many anthropologists who have written about state formation theory, he restricted his discussion to what have been called 'pristine' states. These are states which arose so early or in such isolation that there can be no question of their being influenced by other states, as may have been the case with what have been called 'secondary' states. Thus, Haas ignored the archaeological evidence from precolonial African states, presumably because he considered them to be 'secondary' in origin, even excluding the early Egyptian state on this basis. It seems strange that so much sophisticated theoretical work should have gone into attempting to understand 'pristine' state formation when, in fact, the greater number of states were inevitably 'secondary' in their origins. Indeed, Barbara Price (1978: 161) commented that there had been 'almost no systematic theoretical treatment of the secondary state'. However, Renfrew referred to the whole idea of a division into 'pristine' and 'secondary' 'civilizations' as 'unacceptably diffusionist', offering, he claimed, 'a facile taxonomy in place of serious analysis' (Renfrew 1983: 17). Many archaeologists would agree with Renfrew that 'to understand the origins and development of any civilization, it is necessary to look at the local conditions of its existence: at its subsistence, at its technology, at the social system, at population pressures, at its ideology, and at its external trade' (p. 17). This is the approach adopted in this book because, important though state formation theory and urbanization theory might be, it is also important to examine the actual physical evidence that we have on and under the ground.

The ground in question is African ground and it is therefore appropriate to consider the ideas of the Nigerian geographer Akin Mabogunje (1968), on the subjects of urbanization and state formation. Reviewing 'the functional specialization theory of urbanization', he pointed out that the mere existence of specialists within a community need not give rise to urbanization. For that to happen, anywhere in the world, it was essential that functional specialization should take place

7

under three 'limiting conditions': (1) the existence of a food surplus to feed the specialists; (2) the existence of a small group of people able to exercise power over the food producers and ensure peaceful conditions; and (3) the existence of traders and merchants to provide raw materials for the specialists (Mabogunje 1968: 35).

Mabogunje defined urbanization as simply 'the process whereby human beings congregate in relatively large number at one particular spot of the earth's surface' (p. 33) and rejected the ethnocentric notions that the presence of writing or the absence of agricultural workers could be used to distinguish between those communities that were urbanized and those that were not. He appears to have been convinced that it was the development of long-distance trade that led to the growth of cities in both East and West Africa (p. 45). On the other hand, the general process of state formation, in his opinion, originated in the necessity to defend urban centres against external aggression, resulting in the extension of control over neighbouring cities (p. 37). Explanations of this sort belong to what may be called the 'conquest hypothesis' of state formation in Africa, such as that favoured by Jack Goody (1971). Concerned mainly with West Africa, he distinguished between what he called the 'horse states of the savannahs' and the 'gun states of the forest' (Goody 1971: 55). To Goody, it would appear that the crucial factor in state emergence was the actual means of destruction and their ownership.

Such an hypothesis is only one of a number that have been advanced by both anthropologists and historians to explain the development of states in Africa, but because of the greater time-depth of their evidence it is perhaps those from historians which are the more useful. John Lonsdale (1981) reviewed the historiography of states and social processes in Africa, commenting on the range of conventional explanations that: 'The point of all these hypotheses was that something rather exceptional was needed to explain any concentration of power in a logically tribal Africa' (Lonsdale 1981: 172). Lonsdale identified the following hypotheses: (1) imposition 'by an autonomous will with a political vision'; (2) the conquest hypothesis, already mentioned, which Lonsdale called 'a favourite explanation'; (3) the demographic pressure hypothesis, 'with the appropriation of power growing out of conflict over resources'; (4) the managerial hypothesis, with the 'articulation of two or more forms of subsistence, typically farming and herding' or the existence of 'deposits of scarce but necessary minerals' providing the basis of power; (5) the long-distance trade hypothesis, as Lonsdale says, the 'most popular explanation for the rise of state power . . . the Pirenne thesis of medieval Africa' (pp. 171–2); and (6) 'Drought . . . as a major explanation of state formation' (p. 175). These hypotheses were not seen as mutually exclusive, Lonsdale accepting that combinations of them might be used in an explanatory role in particular instances. Nevertheless, he stressed that most of these hypotheses originated at a time when there was relatively little known about African state formation. Lonsdale thought that three things had since become apparent. First, state formation was a very slow process: 'it was frequently botched and started again', so that 'the decay and fall of kingdoms is as important a process as their rise'. Second, a great deal more had become known about the politics of state formation and state collapse (for subsequent discussion of the latter, see Tainter 1988). Power seems to have been decentralized in early kingdoms with their kings acting as mediators rather than autocrats. State emergence involved centralization of that power and this was achieved by coercion not by consensus. Third, it was more useful to explain the rise of particular states in terms of local politics, rather than to hypothesize about 'the idea of the state' and the diffusion of political ideas (Lonsdale 1981: 172–3).

The foregoing discussion has considered only a small sample of the extensive theoretical literature on these complex subjects, drawing mainly from the work of anthropologists, historians and geographers. So, what about the archaeology of precolonial cities and states in tropical Africa, which is the subject of this book? There is obviously a need for theory, but what about the physical evidence that might be used to test some of those theories? Two things are immediately apparent: first, that there seems to have been less general writing on the archaeological evidence than on explanatory theories; and, second, that so limited is our knowledge of the later archaeology of tropical Africa that it is unwise, if not impossible, to consider the archaeological evidence without also considering ethnohistorical and historical evidence. Clearly, there are dangers here, for we may 'allow the ethnographic present and the historically constructed past to exercise tyranny over our perception of past human behaviour' (Fletcher 1995: 212).

The scarcity of general studies concerned with the archaeology of precolonial cities and states in tropical Africa results in part from the relatively limited amount of excavation and other field research that has been carried out and from its uneven geographical distribution. It also results from the fact that archaeological research projects in tropical Africa have rarely been designed specifically to throw light on the origins and development of cities and states. Nevertheless, scattered through the archaeological literature there is much relevant information that can be garnered by the would-be synthesizer. An early attempt to do this was Margaret Shinnie's book *Ancient African kingdoms* (1965), which was so widely used that seventeen years after its publication it was still in print. This was an important book but unfortunately it was pitched at too popular a level to achieve the notice from scholars that it probably deserved. A similar fate had overtaken an earlier general study that covered a comparable range of subject matter: Basil Davidson's *Old Africa rediscovered* (1959). Nevertheless, Davidson's book was so widely read that over a decade later a second edition was published in the United States, under the title *The lost cities of Africa* (Davidson 1970).

After Margaret Shinnie's book, the most significant contribution to the general archaeological literature on cities and states in tropical Africa was Peter Garlake's

The kingdoms of Africa (Garlake 1978a). This had a wide geographical coverage and also examined the archaeological background of the emergence of African kingdoms. Again, an attempt at popularization weakened its impact but it provided numerous black-and-white and colour illustrations of relevant archaeological material. In addition, it was noteworthy for Garlake's insistence on the indigenous evolution of African states, although he also stressed the importance of external trade, whereby a small group could monopolize not the resources but the outlets by which they could be converted into a useful surplus. Thus, in Garlake's view: 'centralized authority grew from a monopoly of foreign trade' (p. 24).

Another general work that made an important contribution to this subject, although it ignored archaeological evidence almost totally, was Richard Hull's *African cities and towns before the European conquest* (1976a). Hull also outlined his approach to this subject in a paper published at the same time (Hull 1976b). His main interest was the history of African settlement planning and architecture, and his starting point was that: 'Scholars in the past have either neglected or grossly underestimated the urban factor in African history' (Hull 1976a: xix). Most relevant to the present discussion were the parts of the book concerning the origins of cities and towns and their decline and disappearance. Hull identified five main types, assuming that major function explained origin but emphasizing that most cities and towns served a combination of such functions. The types were: (1) spiritual and ceremonial centres; (2) commercial centres; (3) centres of governance; (4) centres of refuge; and (5) 'cities of vision' (pp. 120–1). Hull also outlined what he saw as the prerequisites for the growth of cities and towns in Africa: (1) government had to be sufficiently developed to exert control over the agricultural surplus; (2) leaders had to have enough power to demand labour from their people for the construction of public works; (3) specialist craftsmen had to be present; and (4) government had to have an ideological power-base (p. 2). So far as decline and disappearance were concerned, Hull suggested four main causes: (1) environmental deterioration; (2) collapse of political superstructure; (3) revolt of peripheral cities against the mother city; and (4) external military invasion (pp. 114–16). In addition, Hull's book contained useful information about traditional African architecture and building techniques, topics that were also examined by Paul Oliver (1971) and Susan Denyer (1978).

A new publication that contributes significantly to the overall study of African complex societies is a book edited by Susan McIntosh titled *Beyond chiefdoms: pathways to complexity in Africa* (McIntosh 1999).

Studies with a more general relevance to the archaeology of precolonial cities and states in tropical Africa include David Phillipson's *African archaeology* (1993a), which is invaluable for contextual information; the volume edited by Thurstan Shaw *et al.*, *The archaeology of Africa: food, metals and towns* (1993), which consists of specialist papers of which some are relevant; and Joseph Vogel's edited *Encyclopedia of precolonial Africa* (1997) that also contains some pertinent material. At an even more general level but still useful are Roland Oliver's *The African experience* (1993), John Iliffe's *Africans: the history of a continent* (1995) and John Reader's *Africa: a biography of the continent* (1997).

Turning to the archaeological evidence itself, a serious discrepancy immediately becomes apparent. According to historical sources, there was a substantially greater number of cities and states in precolonial tropical Africa than the archaeological literature would suggest. Fage and Verity's *An atlas of African history* (1978) shows numerous cities and states on its maps of which little or nothing is known archaeologically. What about the early-second-millennium AD state of Kanem east of Lake Chad, for instance, of which the capital Njimi has not even been located by archaeologists? Or what about the sixteenth-century state of Kongo with its capital Mbanza Kongo, that (with its environs) was thought by Leo Africanus to have had a population of about 100,000 people (Africanus 1896: Vol. 1, 73)? Virtually nothing is known about its archaeology either. There are other similar examples that could be cited, but these illustrate well enough the two main reasons for the patchy state of archaeological knowledge on this whole subject. First, there is the problem of the archaeological visibility of the actual sites. There is a great range of variation in the archaeological evidence that might be expected; at the one extreme, a long-established, partly stone-built, commercial centre like Kilwa (Chittick 1974b) and, at the other extreme, a short-lived, grass-built, centre of governance like the Bugandan capital at Rubaga visited by Henry Morton Stanley in 1875 (Stanley 1878: Vol. 1, 199–202). It is likely that the pastoralist/shifting cultivator settlements of Kanem, including Njimi, were even more mobile than those of nineteenth-century Buganda and were, as Hull (1976a: 7) has described them, 'tent-cities' that 'could be moved quite easily'.

The second of the main reasons for the patchy state of our archaeological knowledge is the uneven distribution of archaeological field research in Africa, unevenly distributed both in space and time. A relatively large amount of excavation and fieldwork has been carried out, for instance, on settlement sites belonging to the last three millennia along the Sudanese Nile but, in contrast, relatively little such work has been done, for example, on the Mozambique coast. Thus Mbanza Kongo (later called São Salvador) is archaeologically unknown probably because it is situated in northern Angola, where very little work has been done on any later archaeological sites. Of course, the two problems of archaeological visibility and uneven field research should not be viewed in isolation; they frequently compound one another. Quite clearly, only the most intensive field investigations will reveal sites of low archaeological visibility and in tropical Africa such investigations have been rare.

An obvious consequence of the patchy state of archaeological knowledge concerning precolonial cities and states in tropical Africa is that any discussion of the relevant archaeological evidence is in danger of giving a distorted picture or at least an incomplete one. However, some indication that this is probably not as serious as it might be can be gained from Chandler and Fox (1974), who made a world-wide study of the statistics of urbanization over the last 3000 years. They produced a series of maps of African cities in AD 1000, 1200, 1300, 1400, 1500, 1600, 1700, 1800 and 1850. These maps are mainly based on historical sources and, although the distribution of cities is not necessarily a reliable indicator of the distribution of states, it is interesting that they reflect very generally the geographical pattern indicated by the archaeological evidence. Thus they show (Fig. 1.1) that the main areas of urban development in tropical Africa were: in West Africa along the southern edge of the Sahara; in the West African forest west of the lower Niger River; on the middle Nile in the Sudan; and in the Ethiopian mountains. They also record urban centres on the East African coast; on the Zimbabwe Plateau; around the lower Zaïre (Congo); and in the Lake Victoria area. So, however deficient the archaeological evidence might be in *quantity*, it does produce a crude geographical *pattern* comparable to that derived from historical and ethnohistorical evidence. It is this that has prompted my choice of subject matter for the substantive chapters of this book.

The chapters that follow might be regarded as a series of case studies, whose choice has been dictated by the availability of archaeological evidence. In reality, they are probably something more than this and it is hoped that they provide an overall picture, however rudimentary, of the processes of state formation and urbanization in tropical Africa. Chapters 2–8 examine the main areas of archaeological evidence by grouping that evidence both geographically and chronologically (Fig. 1.2). Thus, Chapter 2 discusses the evidence from the middle Nile for the cities and states of Kerma, Napata and Meroë, perhaps the first of such developments in tropical Africa, and also considers the evidence for the successor states of Christian Nubia. This is followed in Chapter 3 by an examination of the evidence for Aksum and Christian Ethiopia, in an adjacent part of the continent. The scene is then changed to West Africa, and Chapters 4 and 5, respectively, look at what archaeology has to tell us of the cities and states of the West African savanna and of the West African forest and its fringes. Chapter 6 takes us across the continent again to examine the archaeological evidence available from the cities of the East African coast. In contrast, Chapter 7 considers the evidence from the Zimbabwe Plateau and related areas in the interior, and Chapter 8 focuses on the Upemba Depression and the Interlacustrine Zone, in the heart of Africa.

A problem with this choice of subject matter is that it excludes North Africa and most of Egypt; areas where the processes of state formation and urbanization predate those of tropical Africa, and which are thought to have influenced to varying extents the developments that took place in the West African savanna, the Sudanese Nile Valley and the Ethiopian Plateau. This exclusion may seem unfortunate but the

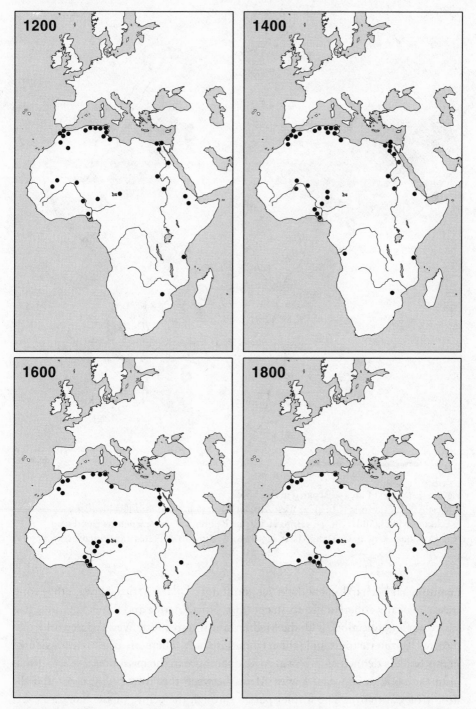

Fig. 1.1 Distribution of African cities with 20,000 or more inhabitants in AD 1200, 1400, 1600 and 1800. After Chandler and Fox (1974: 50, 52, 54, 56).

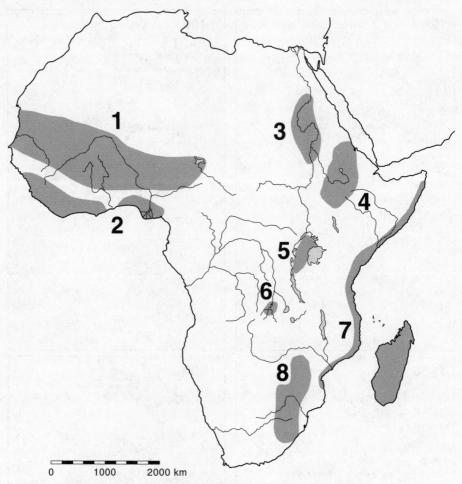

Fig. 1.2 Location of areas discussed in this book.
1: West African savanna (Ch. 4). *2:* West African forest (Ch. 5). *3:* Middle Nile (Ch. 2).
4: Ethiopian Highlands (Ch. 3). *5:* Interlacustrine Region (Ch. 8). *6:* Upemba Depression
(Ch. 8). *7:* East African Coast and islands (Ch. 6). *8:* Zimbabwe Plateau and adjacent areas
(Ch. 7).

intention has been to look at the cities and states of *black* Africa, because they comprise a logically coherent group. In contrast, North Africa and Egypt have long had such diverse connections with the Mediterranean and South-West Asian world, that it seems legitimate to exclude them from this study. Therefore, the area considered in this book is defined as 'tropical Africa', because in the most literal sense of that term the book is concerned with Africa between the Tropic of Cancer and the Tropic of Capricorn. The former passes through the centre of the Sahara Desert and the latter through the Kalahari Desert, so that few of the areas that it is proposed to consider are excluded. The only occasion that the discussion strays outside of the Tropics, in this strict sense, is in Chapter 7 where it is necessary to include some evidence from parts of South Africa.

The subject matter of this book is limited in time as well as in space. The term 'precolonial' has been used to define chronological coverage purely for convenience and without any other intention. The aim has been to find a suitable descriptive term for that complex intermixture of prehistory, protohistory and history constituted by the last four and a half millennia of Africa's past (Fig. 1.3), but prior to colonial take-over and decolonization. The last two millennia or so have often been referred to as 'the African Iron Age' but such techno-epochal terminology has little explanatory value and obstructs rather than aids understanding (Connah 1998b: 5–6). Certainly the period concerned was one of substantial technological change but there were also profound economic and social changes, which it is the purpose of this book to investigate.

This investigation is carried out principally by examining the relevant archaeological evidence for African cities and states. That evidence consists of the material remains of urban settlements and of the culture of their occupants, together with inferences about the relationship of such settlements to the populations of their hinterlands and to the resources available in those hinterlands. In assessing this evidence, it is instructive to test against it some of the theoretical ideas that have been discussed in this chapter. It is important, for instance, to ask how we know that a particular archaeological site represents the remains of a city and how we are able to assume that the area around it constituted a state controlled either from that or from some other city. We can also compare the picture that emerges from the archaeological evidence with the picture that can be reconstructed from any ethno-historical or historical evidence that is available. At the very roots of our enquiry, however, are basic questions around which the whole discussion revolves. When, how and why did cities and states emerge in tropical Africa? In particular, what factors led to their development in some parts of the continent but not in others? Perhaps it is premature to attempt to answer such difficult questions in our present state of knowledge but each of the substantive chapters of this book has been written with these questions in mind. The final chapter, Chapter 9, seeks to identify any 'common denominators' in the different examples of urbanization and state emergence that have been examined. Such common denominators may not answer our questions as satisfactorily as could be wished but they do begin to provide some sort of an answer. They also allow us to assess, principally using archaeological evidence, both the general theoretical explanations of anthropologists like Haas (1982) and the range of explanatory hypotheses advanced by Africanist historians that Lonsdale (1981) has reviewed. In attempting such an assessment, the approach is based on that advocated by Renfrew (1983: 17) that has been discussed above (p. 7). Each set of archaeological evidence for African cities and states is investigated from the point of view of geographical location, environmental conditions,

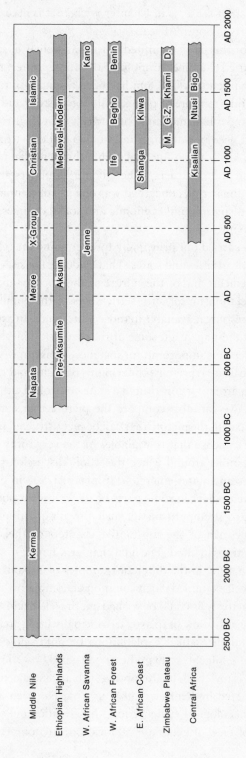

Fig. 1.3 Chronology of urban and state developments discussed in this book. 'M.' = Mapungubwe, 'G.Z.' = Great Zimbabwe, 'D.' = Danangombe (Dhlo Dhlo).

basic subsistence, prevailing technology, social system, population pressures, ideology and external trade. Whatever the many weaknesses of the archaeological evidence for the emergence of cities and states in Africa, that evidence does have the capacity to increase the time-depth of our understanding of these processes and to test and flesh out our knowledge derived from historical sources, where such sources exist. The archaeological evidence reveals a remarkable diversity of both urbanism and state formation in tropical Africa's past, suggesting that a world-wide reappraisal of these aspects of social complexity may be required – a reappraisal that should at last pay proper attention to the physical evidence from previous African civilizations.

Chapter 2

Birth on the Nile: the Nubian achievement

The earliest known cities and states of tropical Africa were situated along the middle Nile, in the region called Nubia. One of the best known of these, Meroë, located about 200 kilometres north-east of the modern city of Khartoum, was mentioned as early as the fifth century BC by Herodotus. Drawing on stories from travellers in Upper Egypt, he recorded the existence of 'a great city, the name whereof is Meroë. And this city is said to be the mother city of the other Ethiopians' (Powell 1949: Vol. 1, 121–2). Meroë, however, was neither the first nor the last example of developing social complexity in this part of Africa. Its antecedents lay in Napata and Kerma, the latter dating back to before 2000 BC; its successors lay in the kingdoms of Christian Nubia, that survived until the early centuries of the second millennium AD, and in the Islamic states that existed until recent times (Adams 1977). Such continuity may be more apparent than real but at least one place saw activity throughout much of this time, and indeed down to the early nineteenth century AD: this was Qasr Ibrim, situated in Lower Nubia, in what is now southern Egypt (Horton 1991: 264).

Why should urbanization and state formation have commenced so early in this area and why should they have lasted for so long? At the beginning of the twentieth century, scholars answered these questions by attributing all such developments to the direct influence of Pharaonic, Ptolemaic, Roman, Byzantine and Islamic Egypt, which is located immediately to the north of the area. Increasing social complexity along the middle Nile was seen as a secondary development, resulting from migrations of people from the more advanced cultures of the north (Trigger 1982). Later the emphasis was changed to one that stressed the indigenous character of these achievements but acknowledged the substantial contributions made to them by northern cultural influences. William Adams, the author of a 1977 monograph on the archaeology of this area, described Nubia as '*the* transition zone, between the civilized world and Africa' and entitled his book: *Nubia: corridor to Africa*. According to Adams, the importance of this narrow corridor through the hot, dry and barren land of Nubia arose from the fact that it was for long the only dependable route across the great barrier of the Sahara Desert. For the ancient world of South-West Asia and the Mediterranean, it was, therefore, the only road that led into the heart of Africa. The African interior contained resources much coveted by this outside world: gold, ivory and slaves, but also a long list of other mineral, animal and vegetable products (Adams 1984: 40). All these could be tapped via the Nubian corridor. Only with the development of Red Sea shipping during the first millennium BC, and of trans-Saharan camel caravans during the first millennium AD, did the middle Nile Valley begin to lose its significance as a major world trade route. That role was finally destroyed by the expansion of maritime trade around all of Africa's coasts in the sixteenth and seventeenth centuries AD.

Both archaeological and documentary evidence support the idea of Adams' trade corridor, and the growth of cities and states in this area was restricted to this corridor, or at least centred on it. This would suggest that this part of Africa can provide us with a very persuasive example of trade as a major stimulus towards the development of social complexity. Perhaps so, but there seems to be more to it than that. These developments took place at the interface of considerable cultural contact, of which trade was only one element, as Adams indeed stressed. People are very likely to meet one another in corridors.

Corridors, however, usually lead somewhere and archaeologists have long debated the extent to which the culture of the inhabitants of the middle Nile Valley might have influenced the rest of Africa. At one extreme, for example, Sayce thought that 'Meroë, in fact, must have been the Birmingham of ancient Africa ... and the whole of northern Africa might have been supplied by it with implements of iron' (Sayce 1911: 55). At the other extreme, Trigger (1969a) wrote about what he called 'the myth of Meroë' and Shinnie (1967: 167) pointed out that 'not a single object of certain Meroitic origin has been found away from the Nile to the west'. Indeed, in the first edition of this book (Connah 1987) it was suggested that the Nubian corridor, in spite of its impressive social developments, was a cultural cul-de-sac, an interpretation also advanced by Alexander (1988). However, the weakness of such a view is that it implies only a passive role for Nubia, suggesting that it was a mere receiver of cultural influences rather than also an initiator of cultural change. Preferably, as Edwards (1996: 5) has put it: 'Meroe, and indeed Kerma before it, should be seen as the early examples of a long and enduring tradition of Sudanic kingdoms.' In the end, Nubia belongs to Africa and so do its achievements. Instead of persisting in a search for Egyptian influences in Africa, it might be more appropriate to seek for African influences in Egypt.

Geographical location and environmental factors

The Nile is a very long river that runs from the Lake Region of East Africa to the Mediterranean Sea, passing in the course of this journey through a number of contrasting environments, some of which are amongst the driest in Africa, if not indeed in the world. It is because it flows through so much arid country that, for much of its length, the river and its narrow valley have played such an important role in human history. Ancient Egypt was, as Herodotus called it, 'the gift of the

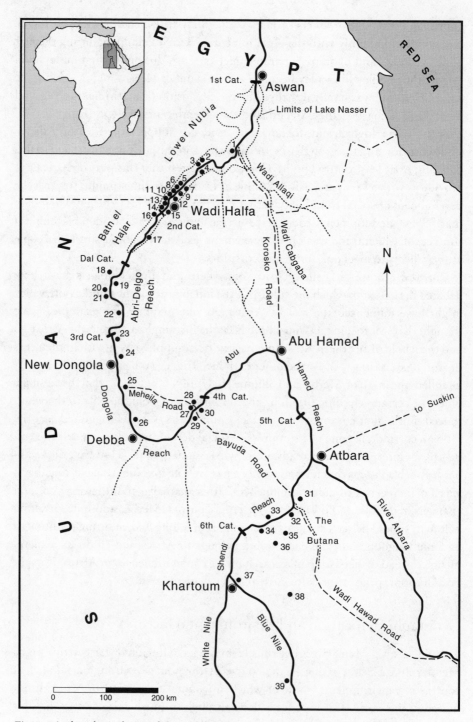

Fig. 2.1 Archaeological sites of the middle Nile.
1: Maharraqa. *2:* Karanog. *3:* Aniba. *4:* Qasr Ibrim. *5:* Arminna West. *6:* Tamit. *7:* Gebel Adda.
8: Abu Simbel. *9:* Qustul. *10:* Ballana. *11:* Faras. *12:* Debeira East. *13:* Debeira West. *14:* Buhen.

river' (Powell 1949: Vol. 1, 111) but if this was true of the lower Nile, it was also partly true of the middle Nile which is our subject here. This is the land of the Nile Cataracts, a series of rocky swift rapids, most of which are conventionally numbered from one to six, that impede or prevent navigation and are set in a landscape of rocky outcrops and narrow canyons. The First Cataract is just south of Aswan, in southern Egypt; the Sixth Cataract is a little way north of Khartoum in the Sudan. It is this very long and very narrow strip that for the last 2000 years or so has been known as 'Nubia' (O'Connor 1993: xii), although, as Adams (1977: 20–1) points out, its southern limits have varied in location over the centuries. For the purposes of this discussion, the 'middle Nile' will be considered to be that part of the Nile Valley between the confluence of the Blue and White Niles at Khartoum, in the south, and the First Cataract at Aswan, in the north (Fig. 2.1). However, it is impossible to consider the valley without some reference to the lands to its east and west, particularly in southern Nubia which does receive a little seasonal rain.

The climate of the more northerly parts of the middle Nile is an extreme one. At Wadi Halfa, in the northern Sudan, the mean daily temperature between May and September is about 32°C but the temperature nearly always exceeds 38°C during the day and may reach above 49°C, although from November to March it is comparatively mild, with temperatures that can occasionally drop almost to freezing. Between Aswan and Dongola, that is to say in the northern half of the middle Nile region, it almost never rains and humidity is usually as low as 15–20 per cent. However in the southern half of the region there is a well-defined wet season of eight to ten weeks, in July and August, but the actual rainfall is very limited, increasing from north to south from about 25 millimetres at Dongola to about 180 millimetres at Khartoum. Another climatic factor of importance is wind, which blows steadily out of the north for the whole year, varying little in direction but rising at times to gale force. This has led to considerable accumulation of desert sand, particularly on the west bank of the Nile, where it has constantly encroached on both settlements and fields. However, with the exception of the reverse bend between Abu Hamed and Debba, it has also made upstream navigation possible on the river, just as the direction of the current has facilitated downstream navigation (Adams 1977: 33–5).

As a result of the climate, the vegetation of the middle Nile region varies from total desert in the north to acacia desert scrub in the south (Andrews 1948: 34). The most important element of the environment, however, is the River Nile itself, rising over 3000 kilometres to the south and bringing to Nubia both the water and

Fig. 2.1 (*cont.*)
15: Meinarti. *16:* Kasanarti. *17:* Duweishat. *18:* Amara. *19:* Sai. *20:* Seddenga. *21:* Soleb. *22:* Sesebi. *23:* Kerma. *24:* Argo. *25:* Kawa. *26:* Old Dongola. *27:* El Kurru. *28:* Jebel Barkal. *29:* Sanam. *30:* Nuri. (Note: Sites 27–30 constitute Napata.) *31:* Meroë. *32:* Shendi. *33:* el Hobagi. *34:* Wad ben Naqa. *35:* Musawwarat es-Sufra. *36:* Naqa. *37:* Soba. *38:* Jebel Qeili. *39:* Sennar. After Adams (1977) with additions.

the soil which are necessary to sustain human settlement. As Adams (1977: 35) has written: 'Nothing is demanded of the local environment except a growing season long enough to take advantage of these exotic resources. Neither Nubia nor Egypt contributes a drop of water to the Nile, nor an acre of their own soil to its banks.' It is paradoxical, therefore, that most published vegetation maps are of too small a scale to show the most important vegetation type of the middle Nile: that of the long, narrow river littoral. So narrow is this strip, that in places it is a mere few hundred metres wide or does not exist at all, but wherever it is present it supports much the same sort of vegetation. One of the most common features of this vegetation is the date palm (*Phoenix dactylifera*). This is really a domesticated tree but date palms are so numerous, fringing the river, separating cultivated fields and in actual groves, that they look like part of the natural vegetation. Other trees also grow along the river littoral, the most important being the *dom* palm (*Hyphaena thebaica*), various acacias, and the tamarisk. Most of the rest of the vegetation consists of cultivated plants, but halfa grass grows wherever it can find moisture, and when the river is low a fringe of papyrus reed can be found in some places at the water's edge (Adams 1977: 37–8).

There is, however, a variety of environments to be found along the narrow littoral of the Nubian Nile. This is because of topographic diversity resulting from differences in geology. From Khartoum to Aswan, the Nile flows alternately over Nubian sandstone and basement complex (which is mostly granite). As a result, it is possible to identify six geographic subdivisions of the middle Nile (Adams 1977: 21–33), their boundaries mostly consisting of the main cataracts of the river, the majority of which have been formed where the river crosses from one geological formation to the other. The most southerly of these physiographic subdivisions is the Shendi Reach, extending from the confluence of the Blue and White Niles to the mouth of the River Atbara (Fig. 2.1). This is an area of Nubian sandstone, although there are also numerous outcrops of granite. Alluvium is found in most places on both banks of the river and there are many farming villages. Beyond the river littoral there is semi-desert grassland and therefore pastoralism is important. Within this reach lay the heartland of the Meroitic state, including the city of Meroë itself. To the north of the Shendi Reach lies the Abu Hamed Reach, a region of barren granite with low productivity. This reach extends as far as the Fourth Cataract and, judging from archaeological evidence, seems never to have been an important area for settlement. Downstream of the Fourth Cataract lies the Dongola Reach, extending as far as the Third Cataract. Again the surface geology is Nubian sandstone, providing an almost featureless landscape that in many places has potentially cultivable land on both sides of the river, as well as in overflow basins that were at one time parts of the bed of the river. It is hardly surprising that it was the Dongola Reach that was the scene of the earliest developments of complex society on the middle Nile: both Kerma and Napata were situated in this region.

From the Third Cataract to the Dal Cataract is the Abri-Delgo Reach, a region of granite and clay plains. There is a wide floodplain in many places, although good land is relatively limited. This reach was particularly important during the period of Egyptian (New Kingdom) colonial expansion, in the second half of the second millennium BC. North of the Abri-Delgo Reach is the *Batn el Hajar*, a name that means 'belly of rock' and is most appropriate for this bare granite landscape, that extends from the Dal Cataract to the Second Cataract. This is a wild and rugged region with only occasional riverside pockets of alluvium that can be irrigated and cultivated, and human settlements seem always to have been limited.

Last of the geographic subdivisions of the middle Nile is Lower Nubia, that stretches from the Second Cataract to the First Cataract. This region is now almost totally submerged beneath Lake Nasser but it was formerly a moderately prosperous region, where the river cut mainly through Nubian sandstone and provided discontinuous alluvial deposits, particularly at the mouths of the larger wadis. In spite of the virtual absence of rainfall, archaeological evidence suggests that it was a significant area of settlement during some periods in the past, and that its proximity to Egypt gave it a particularly important role as a cultural contact zone.

Although the more barren parts of the middle Nile had few resources, its agriculture could support the overall population of the region. Cultivation of seasonally inundated land or of land that could be irrigated, *in recent times* produced sorghum, barley, beans, tobacco, lentils, peas, watermelons, maize and some wheat. Lucerne, dates, mangoes and citrus fruits were also grown. In addition, animal husbandry was important: involving cattle, sheep, goats, donkeys, and – rarely – camels and water buffalo. Chickens, pigeons, ducks and dogs were also kept but horses and pigs were very rare (Trigger 1965: 19–22; Adams 1977: 54). Particularly in Lower Nubia, little of the native fauna seems to have survived to later historical times, and the only part that constituted a continuing important resource was fish, of which there are more than forty species in the Nile, most of which can be eaten. It seems likely, however, that the disappearance of wild game from parts of Nubia resulted from its early exploitation for animal products by the Egyptian trade. At first a primary source of such commodities as ivory, ostrich eggs and feathers, skins and even live animals, Lower Nubia in particular gradually became merely a funnel through which these things passed on their way north.

A longer-lasting Nubian resource consisted of various minerals, including copper, fine-grained igneous rocks and, most important, gold. Gold was scarce but occurred widely, particularly in the desert to the east of the Nile Valley. The most important of the gold mines were situated along the Wadi Allaqi, between Lower Nubia and the Red Sea. A final resource, of considerable importance throughout most of the history of the region, was slaves. Even with this commodity, however, as time went on Nubia became the pipeline rather than the source. One is left with the overall impression that the indigenous resources of Nubia were less important than those which it obtained from further south. Nubia was, it appears, a classic example of an entrepôt: a commercial centre of import, export, collection and distribution (Adams 1977: 41–3).

Most important of the constraints on human settlement in the middle Nile was the level of the river itself (Hassan 1997: 220–2), whose height in the flood season could in some years be too low for irrigation to be possible in particular places and in other years be so high that floodwater swept away both settlements and cultivable alluvium. It also seems likely that there were long-term fluctuations in the average level of the Nile, such as Adams (1977: 242) hypothesized to explain the apparent virtual abandonment of Lower Nubia during the first millennium BC. This region, he claimed, was only reoccupied at the beginning of the first millennium AD, with the advent of the *saqia*, the ox-driven waterwheel, that could raise irrigation water to greater heights than were possible with the man-powered *shaduf* – although it now appears that the abandonment may have been overstated and the *saqia* not introduced until about the fourth century AD (Horton 1991: 273; Edwards 1996: 80–1, 91; Welsby 1996: 156). Even with suitable technology to lift water to the required level, however, there still needed to be alluvium suitable for irrigation, and its distribution varied considerably in the six geographic subdivisions of the middle Nile which have been discussed (pp. 22–3). The second constraining factor was, therefore, the availability of alluvium that could be both irrigated and cultivated. Three sorts of arable land existed: *seluka* land, *saqia* and *shaduf* land, and basin land (Trigger 1965: 19–21). *Seluka* land was situated on the floodplain and was inundated each year when the river was high. When the level of the river fell, the land could produce a crop without further watering and was therefore a type of land that was highly valued. Its exploitation was an example of 'recessional cultivation', that is discussed in Chapter 4 (p. 113). In contrast, *saqia* and *shaduf* land consisted of relatively small areas that had to be watered mechanically but could be cropped almost continuously. *Shaduf* land was land to which water had to be lifted to a height of 3 metres or less, whereas *saqia* land could be situated as much as 8 metres above the source of water. The amount of land that could be irrigated with either of these devices varied according to the height to which the water had to be lifted: the greater the height, the smaller the irrigated area. Basin land, although of importance in Egypt, was more limited in Nubia, and consisted of land lying in natural depressions, adjacent to the river, into which floodwater overflowed, or was channelled by a canal. Basin agriculture could be highly productive but it required co-operation between large numbers of farmers. The availability of these different forms of land, at any point along the middle Nile, was an important factor influencing the location and extent of human settlement.

The life-giving waters of the Nile brought suffering to the inhabitants of Nubia also. Schistosomiasis, a water-borne disease that is common to all of tropical

Africa and is caused by a blood fluke that lives in freshwater snails found in stagnant water, is particularly prevalent in the Nile Valley. Free-swimming at one stage in its life cycle, the fluke gains entry to the human bloodstream usually through breaks in the skin and then attacks the liver and other organs. A gradual deterioration in condition follows and this may continue for over twenty years. Another affliction in parts of the middle Nile region that is associated with water is onchocerciasis, or river blindness, caused by filarial worms transmitted by the minute fly *Simulium damnosum*, found chiefly between the Third and Fourth Cataracts (Manson-Bahr and Apted 1982: 166). Malaria, tuberculosis and trachoma are other diseases which are to be found along the middle Nile and which may have been there for a long time (Adams 1977: 40–1).

A further constraint on settlement has often been the depredations of human beings themselves. Not only has the middle Nile Valley suffered numerous military invasions from the lands to its north, but also the sedentary farmers of the narrow riverine strip have been repeatedly terrorized by the nomadic pastoralists of the vast adjacent deserts. The latter was formerly thought to have been particularly the case after the desert nomads adopted the camel, probably during the last century BC (Trigger 1965: 131), but evidence from Qasr Ibrim that the camel was already in the Nile Valley by the early first millennium BC (Rowley-Conwy 1988) suggests that such attacks were caused by other factors. Whatever the situation, it nevertheless seems that desert pastoralism was so important to the riverine economy (Edwards 1996) that it was essential for people within the valley to control, or at least co-exist with, those from outside it. Circumstances such as these must have been a strong incentive to more powerful political organization and to greater social complexity. It is now appropriate to consider the evidence for these developments.

Sources of information

Present understanding of early cities and states in the middle Nile region is based on two types of evidence: historical documentation and archaeological data (Fig. 2.2). Except for the Islamic period of the second millennium AD, with which this chapter has little concern, the time-span is too great for oral tradition to be able to contribute. Adams (1977: 66–70) identified six groups of historical sources.

The first consists of Egyptian texts in hieroglyphic and hieratic. These cover the period from the first half of the third millennium BC to near the end of the second millennium BC, but there are relatively few which contain more than a passing reference to Nubia and they are primarily intended to record Egyptian exploits.

The second group of historical sources comprises Nubian hieroglyphic texts of the Napatan period, from the eighth to about the fourth century BC. These sources date from after the Nubian conquest of Egypt, where Nubians ruled as pharaohs of the Twenty-Fifth Dynasty during the latter part of the eighth century and the earlier part of the seventh century BC. At that time, and even after they lost control of Egypt, the Nubian rulers had their view of things written down by Egyptian scribes in the Egyptian language and in hieroglyphics. Like the Egyptian texts, these sources have little to tell us about Nubia itself but they do shed valuable light on the political history of the Nubian and Egyptian region as a whole. Because they were written in Egyptian, however, they throw no light on the contemporary Nubian language or languages; so that when in later times Nubians developed their own indigenous 'Meroitic' alphabet, they left texts which are unintelligible to us, largely (it appears) because the language in which they were written bears no recognizable relationship to any other language at present known to scholars (Welsby 1996: 190). Used for texts from about the second century BC to about the fourth century AD, Meroitic writing can be read but the language of the writing cannot be really understood, in spite of extensive study of this problem (e.g. Trigger 1973).

The third group of historical sources is made up of historical and geographical writings by classical authors. One of the earliest of these was Herodotus, who visited Egypt in the fifth century BC and pieced together an account of the lands immediately to its south that still makes an important contribution to our knowledge of the Meroitic state. Other classical writers also contributed information on Nubia and, collectively, these Greek and Latin texts are useful but they are essentially the view of the outsider and written from hearsay evidence. Actual knowledge of the region appears to have been limited, as is suggested by the famous Nile Mosaic at Palestrina, near Rome, which dates from the late second century BC and shows in its upper part 'the landscape of lower Nubia combined with the fauna of upper Nubia' (Meyboom 1995: 50).

The fourth group of historical sources, that of medieval ecclesiastical histories, is comparatively limited in its value. A number of church historians, including John of Ephesus, wrote about the conversion in the sixth century AD of Nubia to Christianity but their accounts conflict with one another depending on their doctrinal background. Also, the information that they give is mainly concerned with the first century of Christian Nubia, because after that the Arab conquest of Egypt cut off Nubia's contact with the rest of Christendom until the end of the medieval period.

The fifth group of historical sources consists of medieval Arab histories and geographies. The most important of these is the fourteenth-century geographer al-Maqrizi, whose writing also preserves part of a tenth-century first-hand account of Nubia. Again, these sources represent the views of outsiders and they are confined to the first half of the second millennium AD, coming to a halt with the Ottoman conquest of Egypt and northern Nubia in the early sixteenth century.

The sixth and last group of historical sources consists of works by European travellers in the early modern period. Their value is very limited for the sixteenth and seventeenth centuries but several eighteenth-century travellers recorded information on Nubia. It is to the nineteenth century, however, that the bulk of this type of source material belongs. Yet again, these are accounts by outsiders but they are an important source of information.

Thus there are nearly 5000 years of historical documentation for the middle Nile. This documentation has three characteristics, however, that considerably weaken its value. First, generally speaking the further up the Nile one goes, the less informative are the historical texts. Second, in total these texts provide only an intermittent recorded history. Third, and perhaps most important, most of the documentation that exists was written by foreigners to Nubia, who were, at best, visitors to the region attempting to understand what they saw and, at worst, distant scholars using information that had already passed through several hands. The situation would be different for part of the time if the numerous Meroitic inscriptions could be properly understood but they cannot.

In such circumstances archaeological evidence has a vital role to play, although neither the historian nor the archaeologist can afford to ignore one another. Nevertheless, studies of ancient Nubia seem to have suffered from something of an historical bias, probably because of the way that archaeological research developed in the area. Although archaeological fieldwork in Nubia commenced at the beginning of the twentieth century with the work of Reisner, Firth, Griffith, Garstang and Wellcome, to be followed in the years up to 1958 by various others (Adams 1977: 78–80), there was an unfortunate tendency for excavations to be tomb-temple-and-palace oriented and for much of the detailed information never to reach publication. Only with the international archaeological campaign of the 1960s, that was made necessary by the construction of the Aswan High Dam and the creation of Lake Nasser, did there develop both an interest in the excavation of settlement sites and a substantial archaeological literature. Despite continuing field research since then, however, there are still large gaps in our knowledge of the archaeology of the middle Nile. This should be kept in mind, when reviewing the major areas of the archaeological evidence.

Some of the earliest archaeological sites relevant to the origins of cities and states in the middle Nile region are Egyptian rather than Nubian. They represent two main periods of colonial expansion, first during the Pharaonic Middle Kingdom, and second during the New Kingdom, although only the more northerly parts of Nubia were affected. The first of these expansions belonged mainly to the Egyptian Twelfth Dynasty of the first quarter of the second millennium BC and resulted in the construction of a series of forts in Lower Nubia, most of them clustered around the Second Cataract (Adams 1977: 175–83). Of at least ten forts in the latter area, Buhen is the best known of those that have been excavated. It consisted of an elaborate series of mud-brick fortifications built on a massive scale. Carefully designed rectangular defences enclosed a small town containing houses, barracks, workshops, a temple and a governor's palace (Emery 1965: 149). Indeed,

African civilizations

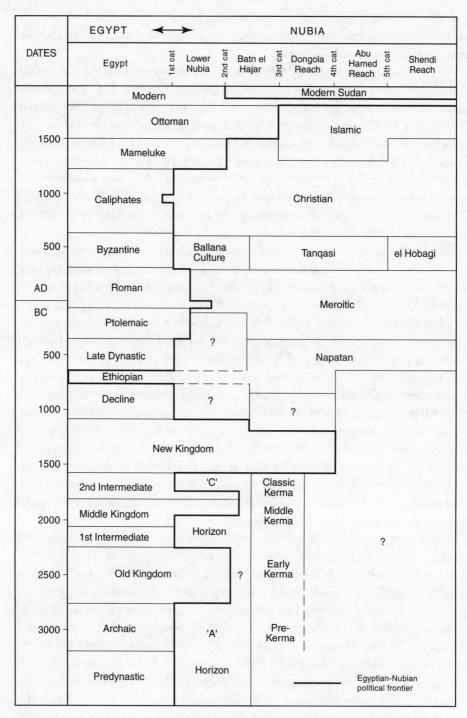

Fig. 2.2 Chronology of Egyptian and Nubian cultural periods. Read time from bottom to top and space from left (north) to right (south). After Adams (1977: Fig. 2) with additions.

28

it appears that this was not the first Egyptian town at Buhen, for during the Fourth and Fifth Dynasties, around the middle of the third millennium BC, and perhaps even earlier, there was already a sizable town surrounded by a stone wall (Adams 1977: 170–4). Evidence for Egyptian occupation as far south as this during the Old Kingdom is rare, however, whereas the Middle Kingdom forts are numerous. This led to an assumption that they were constructed in order to protect Egypt's new southern frontier. Adams questioned this and suggested that their locations indicate that they were primarily intended to protect and control the commerce of the Nile Valley (Adams 1984).

During the Pharaonic Second Intermediate Period, which lasted from about the end of the first quarter of the second millennium BC to about the middle of that millennium, Egyptian political control of Lower Nubia seems to have weakened and the Second Cataract forts may have been abandoned. However, the New Kingdom, of the second half of the second millennium BC, saw a new colonial initiative by Egypt that extended her dominion further up the Nile than ever before, or indeed ever again until the conquests of Mohammed Ali early in the nineteenth century AD.

Egyptian authority was established as far south as the Third Cataract, and perhaps further. The Middle Kingdom forts were restored and enlarged and new fortified towns were built in the Abri-Delgo Reach and in the Dongola Reach. As time went on, the military character of Egyptian settlement diminished and the building of temples replaced the building of fortresses. During the period as a whole, however, colonial settlements of importance grew up particularly in the Abri-Delgo Reach and included such towns as Sai, Amara, Soleb, Seddenga and Sesebi (Delgo), of which the last has been extensively excavated (Fairman 1938). Further south, in the Dongola Reach, there was less Egyptian colonization but towns developed at both Kawa and Napata, possibly to control the Meheila Road, a desert route that cut across the great bend of the Nile in this region. There are also numerous remains of Egyptian temples, of New Kingdom date, in Nubia. Perhaps the most remarkable of these is the temple of Abu Simbel in Lower Nubia but probably the most important from the point of view of the subsequent history of Nubia was that constructed far to the south at Jebel Barkal, where the Temple of Amon, founded by the Egyptian pharaoh Rameses II, was later to become the ideological centre of the indigenous Nubian Napatan state. New Kingdom colonization of the northern parts of the middle Nile terminated towards the end of the second millennium BC, probably because of growing political problems in Egypt itself but possibly also because the level of the Nile was falling. The colonial domination of parts of Nubia by Egypt was over but its consequences for the people of Nubia as a whole were to be far-reaching and long-lasting (Adams 1977: 217–45).

Indeed, Egyptian commercial and colonial involvement in Nubia had already elicited an indigenous Nubian response by the Second Intermediate Period. It was

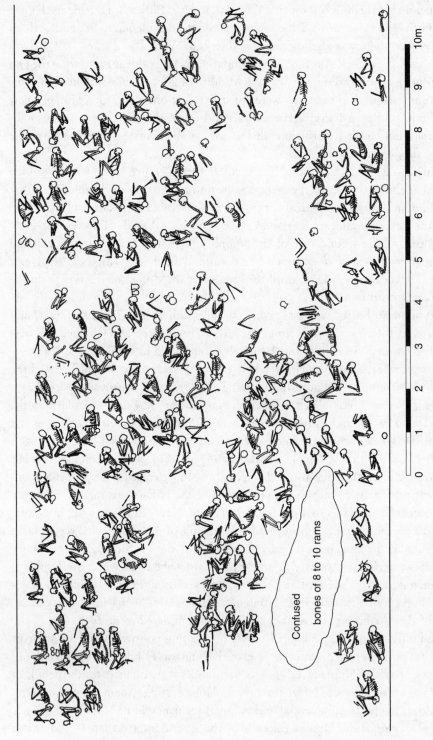

Confused
bones of 8 to 10 rams

Fig. 2.3 Part of the human sacrifices in Tumulus X at Kerma, in Sudan. After Reisner (1923: Part III, Plan XXIV).

at this time, that is to say about the middle of the second millennium BC, that the Nubian kingdom of Kerma was at the climax of its development in the period referred to archaeologically as the Classic Kerma. Prior to that, however, its emergence can be traced back for about 1500 years through the Middle Kerma and the Early Kerma to its origins in the Pre-Kerma before 3000 BC, and there can be no doubt of its indigenous roots (Bonnet 1990; 1992). That these included a substantial pastoralist element is apparent from the sheep and cattle remains with some of the Kerma burials, and MacDonald (1998) has suggested that the socio-political changes indicated by the Kerma evidence originated in what he has termed the 'Mobile Elites', of the African savanna and Saharan margins, from 4000 BC onwards. Nevertheless, Kerma reached its high point at a time of Egyptian weakness during the Second Intermediate Period, when the Second Cataract forts may have been abandoned, and it disappeared at the time of Egypt's colonial expansion during the New Kingdom. This would suggest that Kerma, the earliest example of centralized political authority in Nubia, reached its most developed stage when it had a significant amount of control over Nubian commerce.

Although Derek Welsby has now shown that there was dense Kerma settlement as far south as the Kawa region (Edwards 1999), most of the relevant archaeological evidence for this important development comes from Kerma itself, a complex of sites situated on the east bank of the Nile at the northern end of the Dongola Reach, one of the more fertile regions of the middle Nile. Not only is the floodplain broad at this point but the Kerma Basin, that is flooded each year by the river, permits basin agriculture which is otherwise rare in the Sudan (Adams 1977: 199). Excavations were conducted at Kerma by G.A. Reisner, in 1913–16, and were concentrated on an extensive cemetery containing several thousand graves (Reisner 1923). A substantial number of these were covered by burial mounds, or 'tumuli' as the excavator called them. Of these tumuli, eight were unusually large, the largest of them being about 91 metres in diameter. Like the smaller examples they contained burial chambers, but in the case of the three largest the body of the mound had an internal structure made up of a series of long, straight, parallel, mud-brick walls that seem to have provided a kind of framework for the mound. Part of this internal structure consisted of a corridor which ran right across the mound and the other walls were oriented at right-angles to this corridor. In the main chamber, the principal burial lay upon a bed, accompanied by weapons and personal possessions. The rest of the space, however, was taken up by other human bodies, whose attitudes suggested that they had been sacrificed. A far larger number of sacrifices lay in the transverse corridor, and later subsidiary burials, some also accompanied by human sacrifices, had been inserted in many places between the walls that ran at right-angles to the 'sacrificial corridor', as Reisner called it. In Tumulus X, where the main chamber had been long ago robbed, Reisner found 322 sacrifices in the sacrificial corridor (Fig. 2.3), and estimated that there had originally been as many

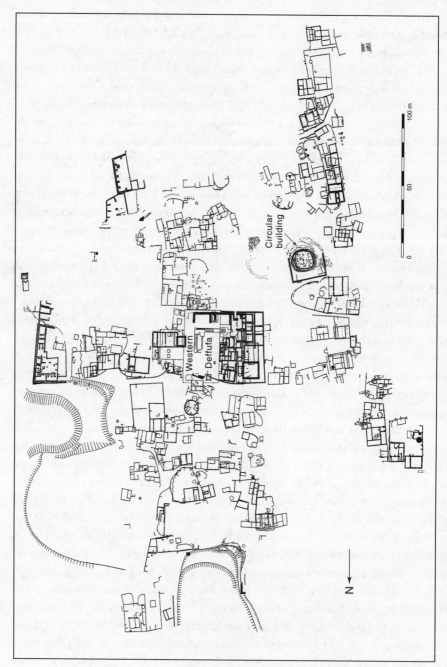

Fig. 2.4 Plan of Kerma during its 'Classic' period, about the middle of the second millennium BC. After Bonnet (1990: Fig. 30).

as 400 before disturbance by tomb robbers (Reisner 1923: Parts I–III, 312). Such evidence suggests a highly centralized political authority and it seems quite justifiable to claim this place as the earliest state in black Africa. Although Reisner thought that the burials were those of Nubianized Egyptians of Middle Kingdom date, and that Kerma had been the headquarters of an Egyptian official, both his dating and Egyptocentric interpretation were later rejected (Adams 1977: 208–10).

Excavations by Charles Bonnet during more recent times have shed much additional light on Kerma (Bonnet 1990; 1992; Bonnet *et al.* 1995). A greater chronological range of burials has now been examined (most of those excavated by Reisner seem to have belonged to the Classic Kerma) and it has been found that the dry climate has preserved bone, leather, hair and feathers, so that a remarkably detailed picture of Kerma society can be reconstructed. For instance, a life expectancy of thirty-one years has been calculated for those who died naturally, although those who were sacrificed were generally younger than this, and some individuals lived until they were eighty years old. In addition, the remains of an extensive and long-lasting settlement have now been uncovered (Fig. 2.4). An excavated area in excess of 400 by 300 metres has revealed an impressive spread of building traces, mainly of rectangular houses of mud-brick or wood, and has provided evidence of an elaborate system of fortification consisting of a mud wall with projecting rectangular towers and a ditch. Naturally there were substantial changes in the plans and layout of structures within the settlement as time went on, and both stone and fired brick were eventually used in the defences, beyond which a secondary settlement also developed. Overall, it seems that this early urban development grew up around a sanctuary that evolved through time into a massive mud-brick temple, locally known as the Western *Deffufa*. This is a solid rectangular mass of mud-brick, measuring about 27 by 52 metres at the base and originally probably far exceeding the height of 19 metres that has survived to modern times (Reisner 1923: Parts I–III, 21–40). A strange structure with no internal chambers, only the remains of a narrow, winding stair that must have led to its top, it has inevitably been the subject of diverse archaeological interpretations. Excavations by Bonnet, however, have shown that it was not originally a solid structure but a temple with interior chambers that were later filled in with brickwork, while at least twelve phases have been distinguished in its masonry (Bonnet 1982; 1992: 613–14). A similar but smaller structure, known as the Eastern *Deffufa*, is situated in the cemetery about 4 kilometres to the east of the settlement and appears to have been some sort of outsize mortuary chapel (Reisner 1923: Parts I–III, 122–34). It is actually one of two such structures in the cemetery but far less has survived of the other (Reisner 1923: Parts I–III, 255–71). Both contain relatively narrow chambers, the insides of which have been painted in an Egyptian style, but their mud-brick walls are over 9 metres in thickness. Attached to one side of the Western *Deffufa* was a building from which Reisner excavated over 500 mud sealings of Egyptian

33

type, which had been affixed to various sorts of containers. There were in addition many fragments of items of Egyptian manufacture and various kinds of raw materials, as well as evidence that some manufacturing was taking place on the spot. This led Adams (1984: 51) to suggest that this was 'a depot where the goods of the south were assembled for shipment to Egypt, and where the manufactures of the north were received (and to some extent produced) in exchange'. However, the discovery by Bonnet of a bronze workshop in the same place, and the argument of Lacovara (1991) that some of the Egyptian material was merely in the process of being recycled, makes it more likely that this was merely an activity area that formed part of the temple complex.

Bonnet's excavations have also shown that by the first half of the second millennium BC the Kerma settlement contained a very large circular building of wood and mud-brick that was at least 10 metres high, probably with a conical roof. Divided inside into several rooms of which one was about 12 metres square, this building was isolated from the neighbouring houses by a large rectangular enclosure, in its final form consisting on three sides of a fired-brick wall and on the fourth of a timber palisade. Clearly an elite structure of some kind, its apparent similarity to much later audience chambers recorded ethnohistorically in other parts of the continent emphasizes the African character of the Kerma development. It contrasts with a rectangular residential or administrative building, at least 26 metres long by more than 10 metres wide, and with an Egyptian-style temple, both dating towards the end of the Kerma sequence and located a kilometre away, closer to the Nile (Bonnet 1992). By this time the Egyptian New Kingdom may have taken control of the area but it seems very likely that prior to this Kerma had already attained urban status and become black Africa's first identifiable state. Apparently David O'Connor has no doubt about this, referring to Kerma as 'the earliest city in Africa outside of Egypt' and concluding that 'the social complexity and the advanced degree of political centralization evoked in the city and cemetery of Kerma would seem to be those of a state, not a complex chiefdom' (O'Connor 1993: 50, 55). Indeed, O'Connor (1991) has also discussed the possibility that Kerma was actually one of several early Nubian states.

The extent of Egyptian influence in the Kerma development will no doubt continue to be a matter of debate. It may be significant, however, that Bourriau (1991: 135–6) has shown that whereas Kerma pottery that occurs in Egypt during the Eighteenth Dynasty is 'tableware or cooking pottery', indicating the presence of Nubians, the Egyptian pottery found at Kerma in the Classic Kerma period 'consists exclusively of medium or large jars with narrow necks, pre-eminently jars for the storage and transport of commodities, and not . . . sufficient evidence for the presence of Egyptians'.

New Kingdom colonization apparently brought Kerma to an end but, when that in turn declined, the next Nubian response to Egyptian influence was that of

Napata, a kingdom that arose on the Dongola Reach during the ninth century BC (Adams 1977: 246–93; Shinnie 1996: 95–105; Welsby 1996). This kingdom, usually known as the Kingdom of Kush, was focused until the fourth century BC on an area extending downstream from the Fourth Cataract for a distance of 24 kilometres or so. It is the whole of this district that is usually referred to as Napata, and it includes major cemetery sites at El Kurru (Dunham 1950) and Nuri (Dunham 1955), a cemetery and temple sites at Jebel Barkal, and a cemetery, temple and town site at Sanam (Griffith 1922). After the fourth century BC, the political focus of Kush seems to have moved south to Meroë on the Shendi Reach of the Nile, although the cultural and chronological relationship of Napata and Meroë is still not fully understood. Napata seems to have had its origins in the power vacuum left by the end of Egyptian colonial domination towards the close of the second millennium BC. As already mentioned (p. 29), the Egyptian colonization of the New Kingdom period had led to the growth of a town at Napata and to the construction of a temple of Amon at Jebel Barkal. With the end of Egyptian control, it seems that power fell into the hands of local rulers who, with the sanction of the priests of Jebel Barkal, went on to control not only much of Nubia but also, for a brief period in the eighth and seventh centuries BC, Egypt itself which they ruled as the Twenty-Fifth Dynasty. Subsequently, Napata gradually became of less importance, but neither its rulers nor those of Meroë, its apparent successor, ever relinquished the style or titles of the Egyptian pharaohs. In particular, the culture of Napata seems to have become strongly imitative of that of Pharaonic Egypt, although it also displayed distinctively Nubian elements. Significantly, Napata remained important to the later rulers of Kush, located at Meroë, who continued to be crowned there and to build temples there. Indeed, it is possible that some of the latest Napatan burials were of rulers whose capital had already been transferred to Meroë.

Archaeological evidence for the Napatan state, if it can be called such, is mainly limited to the sites already mentioned. The cemeteries at El Kurru, Jebel Barkal and Nuri have been interpreted as 'royal' cemeteries, and it is from El Kurru and Nuri, excavated early in the twentieth century by Reisner, that much of our information comes. All three cemeteries are characterized by tombs covered by small, steep-sided pyramids, almost certainly inspired by New Kingdom examples such as those at Aniba in Lower Nubia (Shinnie 1996: 100), and even mummification was practised. However, at El Kurru there are also tumuli and rectilinear stone 'mastabas', which on typological grounds are thought to be of earlier date (O'Connor 1993: 68–9). In addition, temples at Jebel Barkal and Sanam have been excavated and in a number of other places there are the remains of temples constructed by Taharqa, one of the Nubian rulers of Egypt. Nevertheless, there is little known about Napatan settlement sites, in spite of the fact that there appears to have been a very large town at Sanam, which may have been the principal population centre of Napata. Thus, although hieroglyphic inscriptions from excavated tombs have enabled a substantial reconstruction to be undertaken of the Napatan dynastic sequence (Dunham and Macadam 1949; Welsby 1996: 207–9), we have relatively little information about the social and economic organization of the people that these rulers governed. Adams (1977: 293) was of the opinion that this was not a 'complex, urbanized society' but Kendall (1991) has now identified a Napatan palace building at Jebel Barkal and it is also possible that there was a walled town at El Kurru (Welsby 1996: 148). Furthermore, whatever the exact status of Napata, its achievements were clearly important for the subsequent development of the Meroitic state. It is also interesting to note that Napata was at the terminus both of the Bayuda Road, the land route to Meroë, and of the Meheila Road, the land route to Kawa and Argo, which possibly, with Seddenga further to the north, were also Napatan settlements of importance. Napata, it would appear, must surely have been a major staging point in the trade of the middle Nile.

As Napata declined, Meroë rose to prominence and in its case there is abundant archaeological evidence that has been interpreted as suggesting both urbanization and state development. Meroë seems to have been of particular importance during the first century AD but its total life-span probably extended from before the fourth century BC to about the fourth century AD. Excavations at the site of Meroë itself have indeed indicated that its earliest building level could have belonged to the eighth century BC or perhaps even earlier (Shinnie and Bradley 1980: 16; Török 1997: Part I, 15–20). Like Napata, Meroë seems to have been a Nubian response to the classical world to its north. In the case of Napata, it was Pharaonic Egypt that was the main cultural influence; in the case of Meroë, it was Ptolemaic Egypt, which was in turn part of the wider Hellenistic world.

Archaeological evidence for the Meroitic period includes the remains of a number of large settlements, of which Meroë itself is the most important. Situated on the east bank of the Nile, some 200 kilometres downstream from modern Khartoum, Meroë has suffered a chequered archaeological history. Forgotten until its rediscovery at the end of the eighteenth century AD, parts of the site were 'ransacked' by Ferlini in the 1830s (Adams 1977: 295), and early in the twentieth century parts were excavated at various separate times by Budge, Garstang and Reisner. Only Reisner's work was conducted in an adequate fashion and even his excavations had to be published posthumously by Dows Dunham. The extensive excavations by Garstang both were unscientific and remained largely unpublished, until Török rescued them eighty-three years later (Török 1997). At the time only the first season's work was described in any detail (Garstang, Sayce and Griffiths 1911). The rather limited excavations by Peter Shinnie during the 1960s and 1970s remain, in fact, the only archaeological investigations at Meroë to have been carried out and published in a proper scientific fashion (Shinnie and Bradley 1980). Fortunately, prior to those excavations, Shinnie drew together much of what was then known about Meroë and related sites into a monograph, that remained a standard work for some years (Shinnie 1967). More recently he followed this with a more general study (Shinnie 1996) and Derek Welsby has provided a new detailed account (Welsby 1996).

The site of Meroë (Fig. 2.5) appears to cover an area measuring roughly 0.75 kilometre by 1 kilometre (for plans, mostly variants of the same originals, see Shinnie 1967: 76; Adams 1977: 299, 314; Bradley 1982: 164; Shinnie 1996: 107; Welsby 1996: 149; Török 1997: Part II, Figs. 1–3). Within the settlement was a large, stone-walled precinct, more or less rectangular in shape, within which lay a labyrinth of buildings, mostly of monumental character. Many of these buildings, which were usually of mud-brick, often with an external facing of fired brick, were excavated by Garstang who interpreted the area as the residence of the rulers of Meroë, calling it the 'Royal City'. Its buildings were believed to include palaces, audience chambers, stores and domestic quarters for the palace staff, and many of them seem to have been of two storeys (Adams 1977: 314–15; Török 1997). There was also a small temple, in front of which was found a bronze head of Augustus, of Roman manufacture (Shinnie 1967: Plate 28). Perhaps the most remarkable feature of the Royal City, however, was its so-called 'Roman Bath'. This consisted of a large brick-lined tank with water channels leading into it from the Nile. Formerly interpreted as a swimming bath (Shinnie 1967: 79), it is now suggested that it was a water sanctuary associated with Nile floodwater festivals (Török 1992: 117; Welsby 1996: 122–3).

Outside of the Royal City, much of the rest of the site is covered by two extensive occupation mounds and it is possible that Meroë originated as a settlement split between three alluvial islands in a braided channel of the Nile, the course of the river having since changed (Bradley 1982). The south mound remains unexcavated and the only investigations of the north mound have been test excavations by Shinnie. These revealed remains of mud-brick structures serving industrial, domestic and public functions, as well as furnace remains that indicated both iron smelting and iron smithing (Shinnie and Bradley 1980; Bradley 1982; Shinnie and Kense 1982). Other than this, little is known of the ordinary buildings, although Shinnie (1967: 77) described the 'greater part of the town area' as 'consisting of many mounds covered with red [fired] brick fragments' and mentioned 'six large mounds of slag and other debris of iron smelting' on the edges of the site. The significance of these mounds of slag has long been discussed and some idea of their size can be gained from the fact that a railway-cutting has had to be made through one of them to carry the line from Khartoum to Atbara. It is presumed to be this mound into which Arkell excavated an unpublished trial trench in 1940, recording that it consisted of 'solid slag and debris from iron smelting from top to bottom' (Shinnie and Kense 1982: 18).

The site of Meroë is also characterized, however, by the remains of a number of temples and, in contrast with the scant attention given to the residential and industrial areas, the more important of these have been entirely excavated. They include

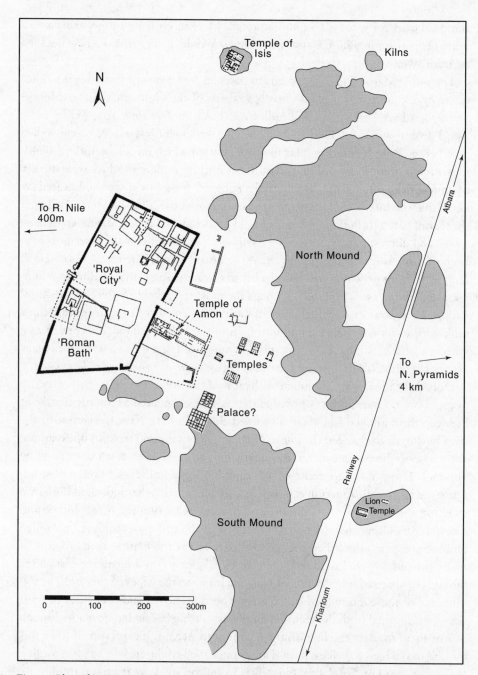

Fig. 2.5 Plan of Meroë, in Sudan. After Shinnie (1967: Fig. 19), Welsby (1996: Fig. 66) and Török (1997: Part II, Fig. 1).

a major temple of Amon, adjacent to the Royal City; a temple of Isis, on the northern edge of the site; the Lion Temple, which stands on top of one of the slag heaps on the eastern edge of the site; and the Sun Temple, which is situated about 1 kilometre east of the site. There is also the Shrine of Apis, located about 2.5 kilometres south of the Royal City, and several lesser temples within the site itself. In addition, archaeological attention has been focused on the cemeteries of Meroë. Just to the east of the settlement site lie three cemeteries which have been entirely excavated and which were found to contain many hundreds of graves, thought to have been occupied by common citizens of Meroë. Some 3–4 kilometres east of the main site, however, lie three other cemeteries. The most important of these is the North Cemetery, which was the main burial place of the rulers of Meroë and their immediate relatives, characterized by the best preserved of the small stone pyramids for which Meroë has become famous (Fig. 2.6). The South Cemetery comprises over 200 graves, most of which were found to contain common citizens, but it also includes a number of mastabas and pyramids belonging both to rulers and (it is thought) to members of the ruling family. In contrast the West Cemetery, which contains about 500 graves, including a number of pyramids, seems to have been intended for less important members of the royal family and also for commoners (Shinnie 1967: 75–87).

In many ways it is most regrettable that the attention of archaeologists has concentrated on the tomb-temple-and-palace aspect of Meroë, rather than on the settlement itself and its apparent urban status. At its peak it may have had a population of 20,000–25,000 people (Grzymski 1984: 289), although Edwards (1999) thought that this estimate was 'more than optimistic'. Nevertheless, such an emphasis has resulted in the discovery of both inscriptions and artistic representations that have made substantial contributions to our knowledge of Meroitic society and history. In particular, we know the names and approximate dates of most of the rulers of Meroë, even though there is still some uncertainty about the details of this dynastic sequence (Shinnie 1967: 58–61; Adams 1977: 251–2; Welsby 1996: 207–9). The inscriptions are in Meroitic, however, rendered either in hieroglyphs or in the distinctive Meroitic cursive alphabet, and because this language cannot be fully understood (p. 26) they can only be read in part. Luckily, the temple and pyramid-chapel reliefs and the small number of pieces of sculpture in-the-round, are more informative: depicting gods, rulers (male and female) and vanquished enemies and generally throwing light on royal dress and regalia and on iconography and religion (Shinnie 1967: 101–9).

There are many other sites along the middle Nile which both culturally and chronologically can be described as 'Meroitic'. Perhaps the most important of these are situated in the western part of the 'Island of Meroë', a name applied to the area known as the Butana, in the triangle formed by the confluence of the rivers Atbara and Nile. Two of these sites are particularly significant: Naqa and

Fig. 2.6 Pyramid N19 in the North Cemetery at Meroë, attributed to King Tarekeniwal, dated to about AD 155–170. Reproduced by permission of Francis Geus (Geus 1991: Plate 5, 2).

Musawwarat es-Sufra (Shinnie 1967: 87–95; Adams 1977: 318–21). At Naqa there are remains of a town nearly as extensive as those of Meroë itself and there are at least seven stone temples, several possible palaces and two large cemeteries. One of the temples, the Lion Temple of Natakamani and Amanitere, has remarkable exterior reliefs depicting the first-century AD king and queen (Fig. 2.7) and the lion-god Apedemak. The reliefs on the two pylons of this temple are a particularly explicit statement of autocratic authority, showing both king and queen brandishing weapons whilst grasping their vanquished foes by the hair. The message could not be clearer! In contrast, the site of Musawwarat es-Sufra has been something of a mystery, consisting principally of a cluster of monumental stone buildings, of which the largest, the Great Enclosure, is a maze of enclosures, corridors, ramps and chambers that has no Nubian or Egyptian parallel. It seems most likely that it was a temple, palace and ceremonial complex, serving as a pilgrimage centre (Welsby 1996: 143–6; Hinkel 1997: 402, 406).

One other site in the Meroë area deserves a mention here. This is Wad ben Naqa on the east bank of the Nile, where there is evidence of a considerable town. Excavations here have revealed the remains of a large square building of at least two storeys, that has been interpreted as a Meroitic palace, apparently similar to others at Meroë, Jebel Barkal and Naqa (Edwards 1999). It was built of mud-brick, its exterior walls faced with fired brick and plastered over with white stucco. Only the lower floor was preserved and this consisted mainly of long, narrow rooms that were probably vaulted storerooms, supporting more important rooms in the storey above. Nevertheless, the plan (Fig. 2.8) is an impressive indication of the development of centralized authority in the Meroitic state (Vercoutter 1962; Adams 1977: 322–3; Hinkel 1997: 395).

Other evidence of Meroitic settlement has been found as far south as Sennar, far up the Blue Nile, and as far north as Maharraqa, in Lower Nubia, a distance of over 1100 kilometres in a straight line (Edwards 1989; 1996). The distance along the river itself is very much greater, of course, but Meroitic settlement on the middle Nile was discontinuous, being concentrated along those stretches of the river that were economically more viable. Adams (1977: 302) identified three main areas of Meroitic culture: the Southern Province, containing Meroë itself; the Napatan Province; and the Lower Nubian Province. The Southern Province, which may be regarded as the Meroitic homeland, was connected to the Napatan Province not by the barren Abu Hamed Reach of the Nile (p. 22) but by the Bayuda Road, a most important desert road that bypassed both the Fifth and Fourth Cataracts and the contrary winds of this part of the Nile. In the Napatan Province there was Meroitic activity at Jebel Barkal, Sanam, Kawa and Argo and (further north) at Seddenga, but the development of the Korosko Road – a desert route leaving the Nile at Abu Hamed that rejoined it far downstream in Lower Nubia – cut this area off from the mainstream of commerce, so that the Napatan Province

Fig. 2.7 Queen Amanitere depicted on the Lion Temple at Naqa, in Sudan. From Budge (1907: Vol. 2, 133).

became something of a cultural and economic backwater. It is possible that the introduction of the camel, probably in the early first millennium BC (Rowley-Conwy 1988), was one of the factors that eventually brought about this change (Adams 1977: 304–5) but far more needs to be known about the early history of this animal. North of the Napatan Province lay the barren and empty *Batn el Hajar* (p. 23) but beyond that was the Lower Nubian Province where substantial Meroitic settlement has been claimed (Adams 1977: 345–81). Because of the extensive excavations carried out in this area during the 1960s, in connection with the construction of the Aswan High Dam, we probably know more about Meroitic life in Lower Nubia than in either of the other two provinces. As already explained (p. 24), it was an area thought to have been virtually uninhabited for some centuries, until resettlement in the second and third centuries AD as a result of the introduction of the *saqia*, the ox-driven waterwheel, but this view has now been challenged. The evidence of both cemeteries and occupation sites indicates that Meroitic settlement in

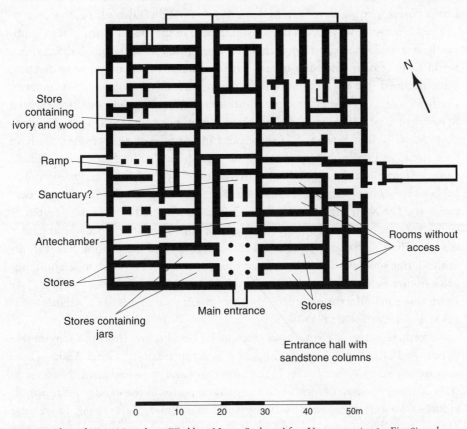

Fig. 2.8 Plan of Meroitic palace, Wad ben Naqa, Sudan. After Vercoutter (1962: Fig. 8) and Hinkel (1997: 395).

43

Lower Nubia was characterized not by large settlements with monumental build-ings, as in the southern provinces, but by what has been assumed to be a nearly con-tinuous line of prosperous farming villages along the Nile, together with a few relatively small administrative centres. The latter are thought to have included Qasr Ibrim, Gebel Adda and Faras, all of them walled settlements, although their Meroitic associations are uncertain (Edwards 1999). Karanog appears to have been another important centre but it consisted of a rather scattered collection of houses without a surrounding wall. Amongst these, however, were two large mud-brick buildings, each apparently of three storeys, that are thought to have been succes-sive palaces of local governors, although their dating remains problematic (Woolley 1911; O'Connor 1993: 100–1; Edwards 1999). Apparent cultural differ-ences between the Meroitic north and south prompted Adams to conclude that in Lower Nubia there had been a secularization of government and that control of trade had passed into private hands, allowing a widespread development of material prosperity (Adams 1974; 1976). Subsequently, however, this interpreta-tion has been questioned and it has also been suggested that the settlement of Lower Nubia may not have been as dense as was thought (Edwards 1996: 50–2).

The Meroitic state seems to have disintegrated in the fourth century AD, signifi-cantly at a time when substantial changes were taking place in the Mediterranean world to the north. Meroitic urban centres were abandoned and long-distance trade declined, but the elite burials in the mounds of el Hobagi, 70 kilometres south-west of Meroë, suggest some continuity of Meroitic traditions along with a re-emergence of older ones (Lenoble 1989; Lenoble and Sharif 1992; Edwards 1996: 92–3; Welsby 1996: 202). Even clearer indications of a successor state have been found in Lower Nubia, where the 'X-Group', called by Adams the 'Ballana Culture' (1977: 392) and by others 'post-Meroitic' or 'Nobatian' (Edwards 1999), suggests the development of an absolute monarchy during the fifth and sixth cen-turies AD. The X-Group was first recognized from scattered burial evidence, but as time went on a number of village sites were identified and it also became apparent that there had been major settlements at Gebel Adda and Qasr Ibrim. Excavations at this latter site have, indeed, revealed the remains of well-built stone and mud-brick houses belonging to this period, and associated evidence suggests that Qasr Ibrim was a manufacturing centre of some importance at this time (Adams 1982: 27–8; Alexander 1988: 81–2).

Nevertheless, the X-Group continues to be best known from the remarkable burials of Ballana and Qustul, situated a little upstream of Gebel Adda. These were excavated by Walter Emery in the early 1930s and produced evidence of a sub-stantial concentration of wealth and autocratic power in the hands of a few indi-viduals, who were interpreted as having been kings (Emery 1938; 1948). There were 122 tombs at Ballana on the west bank of the Nile and 61 at Qustul on the east bank. All 183 of these tombs were excavated, and the size of the structures and richness of contents of perhaps 40 of them may suggest that they contained 'royal' burials. Typically, these larger tombs consisted of a series of brick chambers, constructed at the bottom of a large pit, which was entered by means of a ramp cut into the hard alluvium. The chambers were roofed with barrel-vaulting and in front of them there was often a small open court into which the entrance ramp opened. After the burials and offerings had been placed inside the chambers, in the court and at the bottom of the ramp, both the pit and the ramp were filled with earth and a large earthen mound was raised over them. At Ballana the largest of these mounds measured 77 metres in diameter and 12 metres in height. It was the contents of these tombs that were most impressive, however. The 'king' was buried with his 'queen', with his servants, with his horses, camels, donkeys, dogs, sheep and cows. Also included were furniture, food and drink, cooking utensils, jewels, weapons, tools and all manner of personal possessions.

Many of these tombs had been ransacked by tomb-robbers in the past but some of them had survived intact. One of the more remarkable of these was Tomb 95 at Ballana, the plan of which is reproduced here (Fig. 2.9). Animal burials lay at the bottom of the entrance ramp, beyond which were three sealed burial chambers. Inside the first chamber was the skeleton of the 'king', who had been laid, wearing his silver crown and other finery, on a wooden bier from which he had been displaced soon after burial by the collapse of the chamber roof. Also in the chamber were the skeletons of his 'queen', wearing a silver crown, and of a male servant and of a cow. Weapons and other personal possessions lay in other parts of the chamber. In an adjacent chamber were the skeletons of no less than six additional servants, two of them children, accompanied by more weapons and by lamps, iron ingots, pottery wine jars, drinking cups and several other things. Most of the third and final chamber was packed with more pottery wine jars and drinking cups and with them were numerous bronze cups, a bronze flagon and pan, a stone bowl, a large vessel of green glass, several scarabs and a small gold ingot. In all, the excavator listed 295 objects from this tomb, plus the burials themselves (Emery 1938: Vol. 1, 135–41).

The animals buried in the tombs at Ballana and Qustul had been pole-axed and it was presumed that the human beings, other than the main burial in each tomb, had met their deaths either by the cutting of their throats or by strangulation. The combination of monumental tomb, of wealth and of human sacrifice, for the burial of crowned individuals, is surely indicative of some form of absolute monarchy in Lower Nubia during the time to which the X-Group belongs?

Reisner, who first identified the X-Group, thought that it represented an invasion of a new people. With such an interpretation, the burials of Ballana and Qustul might suggest a nomadic pastoralist origin for the deceased. There is, however, increasing evidence that the X-Group evolved within the Nile Valley, where both settlement and burial evidence suggest that it was a direct successor culture to the Meroitic state, with similar subsistence strategies and with characteristics comparable to those indicated by the el Hobagi burials far to the south. Then, with the conversion of the people of the middle Nile to Christianity in the sixth century AD, a new period of state development and urbanization was inaugurated (Adams 1977: 421–2, 429; Trigger 1969b; Welsby 1996: 205).

The Christian kingdoms of Nubia (Adams 1977: 433–546; Shinnie 1996: 119–34) existed from the sixth century to about the fourteenth century AD, their last remnant actually disappearing at the end of the fifteenth century. The two major states were Makouria, to the north, and Alwa, to the south, and they have left a large quantity of archaeological evidence. There are, for instance, the remains of many churches built of mud-brick and stone. There is also evidence of urban centres at Qasr Ibrim, Gebel Adda, Faras, Old Dongola and Soba, as well as

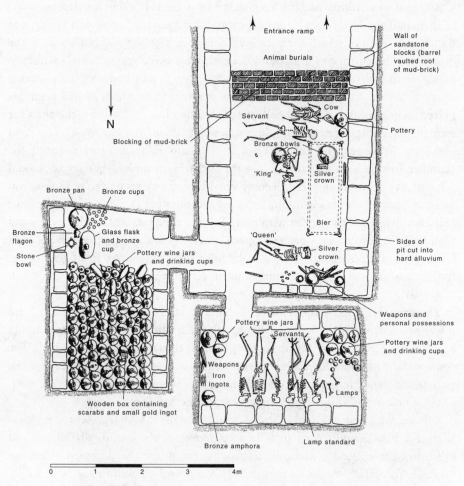

Fig. 2.9 Plan of Tomb 95 at Ballana, Egypt. After Emery (1938: Vol. 1, Fig. 68).

evidence elsewhere of many smaller towns and villages, fortresses, monasteries, industrial sites and cemeteries. The churches of medieval Nubia have attracted archaeological interest for many years (Clarke 1912) but it was not until the 1960s that much work was done on other Christian sites. Study of church architecture has revealed a steady reduction in size and a decline in pretentiousness as time went on, reflecting the gradual decline of Christian Nubia and of its Monophysite, Coptic church. Nevertheless, many of the buildings were impressive structures with stone columns, masonry piers and brick vaults. Most important of those studied so far are the episcopal cathedrals at Qasr Ibrim, Faras and Old Dongola and a possible cathedral at Gebel Adda (Adams 1977: 473–8). The insides of many churches were originally decorated with brightly coloured wall paintings, which achieved artistic expression of a high order. Only fragmentary remains of these were known until the 1960s, when excavations revealed well-preserved paintings in three different churches, of which those discovered in Faras cathedral were quite remarkable. This building (Vantini 1970) had been abandoned after it had become filled with blown sand during the heyday of Nubian Christianity. Within it were numerous large paintings depicting biblical scenes and individuals, as well as Nubian kings, bishops and eparchs (high-ranking government officials), most of whom were identified by name. The Faras paintings have provided an important insight into Christian Nubia.

The archaeological remnants of the churches of Nubia indicate the existence of organized religion and secular authority as separate but interacting entities, each needing the protection of the other. Under their joint umbrella, the society of the middle Nile developed its commercial activities to a high level and became, at least in the northern part of the region, probably more densely urbanized than in earlier periods. Unfortunately, archaeological excavation of the major urban centres has not been as extensive as could be wished, both Faras and Gebel Adda, for instance, being lost beneath Lake Nasser before much could be done. Work has continued at the remarkable site of Qasr Ibrim, however, which was occupied throughout the Christian period and which has survived as an island at the edge of Lake Nasser. Excavations there have demonstrated that the Early Christian period (*c*.500–*c*.800 AD) displayed a remarkable continuity from X-Group times, with many of the same houses remaining in use and manufacturing activities, particularly weaving and wood-working, continuing on a large scale. Only the conversion of Meroitic temples to churches and the building of a cathedral and of a monastery mark the introduction of Christianity. During the Classic Christian period, however, which lasted roughly from *c*.800 to *c*.1200 AD, the city seems to have become primarily a religious and pilgrimage centre, with most of its housing being cleared to provide a large open plaza, perhaps to accommodate the large numbers of religious visitors. Nevertheless, during the Late Christian period (*c*.1200–*c*.1500 AD) the site was again fortified and once more became crowded

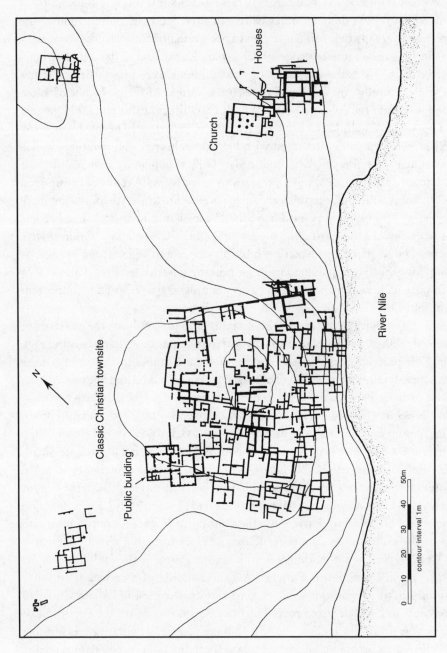

Fig. 2.10 Plan of Arminna West, Egypt. After Weeks (1967: Fig. 1).

with houses, regaining its commercial importance and (according to excavated manuscript material) also becoming an administrative centre (Adams 1982: 28–30; Alexander 1988).

There have also been excavations at the site of Old Dongola, far to the south, which was the capital city of the Christian kingdom of Makouria (e.g. Godlewski and Medeksza 1987; Godlewski 1990; Dobrowolski 1991). Some indication of the standard of living in this city during the Christian period, for some of its citizens, may be gained from the heated bathroom with piped hot water and painted decorations which was found in one supposed house (Jakobielski 1982) and the fragments of pottery toilet seats that were also recovered (Godlewski 1991: 92–3, 97). Even further to the south the site of Soba, the capital of the kingdom of Alwa, has also been partly excavated and has revealed rectangular palatial buildings and churches of mud-brick, fired brick and stone, as well as both rectangular and circular (wooden) domestic structures and many burials. Its overall radiocarbon chronology is from the fifth to the eleventh or twelfth century AD (Shinnie 1955; Welsby and Daniels 1991; Welsby 1998). In addition, some of the smaller settlements in Nubia have been excavated, such as Arminna West (Weeks 1967) and Debeira West (Shinnie and Shinnie 1978), both of which were referred to as 'towns' by their excavators, although Adams (1977: 488) thought that such settlements numbered only 200–400 inhabitants. Nevertheless, the packed houses of Arminna West (Fig. 2.10) give some idea of what urban living must have been like. For instance, many houses in these settlements attempted to deal with one of the perennial problems of such a life-style by providing 'inside' latrines (Adams 1977: 491). Usually these would have required the services of night-soil carriers but at Debeira West there were some latrines that were designed to discharge into individual, vaulted soakaways that were filled with ash and potsherds (Shinnie and Shinnie 1978: 106). Clearly, if people had to live in a crowded situation, they might as well be as comfortable as possible.

One distinctive feature of these Christian Nubian settlements was that they usually lacked fortifications, suggesting a time of peace and stability. The Late Christian period, however, was typified by fortified settlements, which concentrated particularly in the *Batn el Hajar*, in which poor and isolated region much of the Lower Nubian population seems to have sought refuge. There was also a growing tendency to build fortified houses and castles. Christian Nubian civilization was, in fact, disintegrating into a society of peasant farmers gathered around the castles of local rulers. The Christian Church was also in decline and bedouin Arabs from the desert were moving into the region of the middle Nile. With the gradual Arabization and Islamicization that overtook the area by about the fourteenth century AD, central government was replaced by numerous Arab sheikhdoms based only on the tribe. However, eventually a series of loose confederations appeared, the largest and longest-lasting of which was the Fung kingdom of

Sennar, which survived from the sixteenth century to the early nineteenth century AD (Crawford 1951; O'Fahey and Spaulding 1974). Furthermore, the remarkable settlement of Qasr Ibrim, whose occupation dates back to perhaps 1500 BC, was not finally abandoned until the early nineteenth century AD, epitomizing the continuity of the urban and state traditions in the middle Nile region (Adams 1977: 508–636; Alexander 1995). The surprising thing is that those long-standing traditions seem to have had so little influence on the rest of tropical Africa (Shinnie 1989; Alexander 1993a), raising questions about the nature of cultural diffusion between human groups.

Subsistence economy

The archaeological evidence that has been reviewed above is more extensive than any available for the other areas of Africa that are considered in this book. It remains to analyse this evidence to see what it tells us about the origins and development of cities and states in the middle Nile region. The first question that must be asked is about the nature of the subsistence base which supported these developments. Information both from Pharaonic Egypt and from ethnographic sources would suggest that, throughout the period under consideration, a form of mixed farming was practised, depending on the cultivation of both cereals and vegetables and on animal husbandry. The key factor in much of this land must have been the availability of suitable soils that either received seasonal floodwater or could be irrigated mechanically (Trigger 1970: 354). It is interesting to observe that all the developments that have been discussed took place in areas which in one way or another were relatively favoured agriculturally. Of the six geographic subdivisions of the middle Nile that were described at the beginning of this chapter, the barren Abu Hamed Reach and *Batn el Hajar* were ignored, while the remainder, particularly the Shendi Reach and the Dongola Reach, were more than once the scenes of great achievements.

Direct archaeological evidence for details of subsistence economy, at various times during the 3500 or more years that need to be considered, is not as plentiful as could be wished. Many excavators in the past have not given this aspect of their sites the attention that it merited. Fortunately, however, there is good evidence from Kerma for the cultivation of barley and for the herding of cattle, sheep and goats, as well as for hunting, fishing, and the keeping of dogs and donkeys. It is particularly significant that sacrifices of sheep and goats were such a consistent feature of Kerma burial and that in many cases a row of ox skulls was placed around one side of the burial mounds (Bonnet 1990; 1992; Bonnet *et al.* 1995). This would suggest an early importance of animal husbandry in Nubia, and later evidence, from Meroitic times, reinforces this impression. A bronze bowl (Fig. 2.11a) from Tomb G187 at Karanog in Lower Nubia, for instance, is decorated with a charming engraved scene showing a cow being milked and another cow suckling a calf, whilst other calves have been tied to a tree to keep them out of the way. A total of eight cows and two bulls are shown on the bowl, one cow wears a bell, and milk is being presented to a woman seated nearby before a corn-stalk hut. The apex of this hut is decorated with an ostrich egg, and the hut is similar to some that have been made in parts of the African savanna until recent times. This remarkable bowl, which has often been illustrated in publications, is actually one of two, the

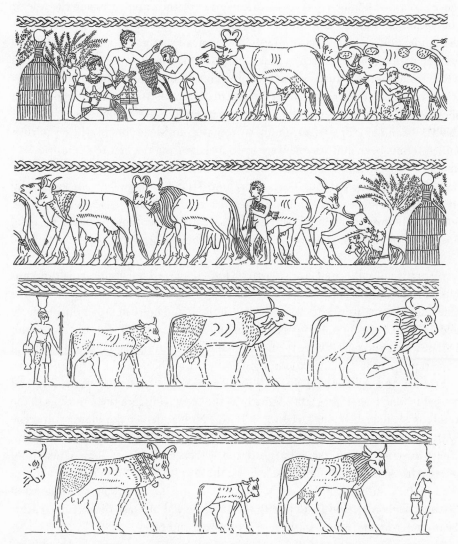

Fig. 2.11 Pastoral scenes engraved on two bronze bowls from Tomb G187 at Karanog, Egypt. The two at the top are on one bowl (a) and the bottom two on another (b). From Woolley and Randall-MacIver (1910: Vol. 4, Plates 27 and 28).

other (Fig. 2.11b) showing a bull, four cows and a calf, as well as a herdsman who carries two pots and what might be a harpoon (Woolley and Randall-MacIver 1910: Vol. 3, 39, 59–61, Vol. 4, Plates 26–8). To these informative rural scenes can be added the fact that the quantities and age structure of cattle, sheep and goat bones excavated from Meroë itself indicate that meat as well as milk was important (Carter and Foley 1980). Indeed, Ali (1972) suggested that the archaeological sites of the Butana region near Meroë reflect its exploitation by semi-nomadic pastoralists, demonstrating the significant role of pastoralism in the Meroitic subsistence economy. Adams (1981) was unconvinced of the latter, stressing the role of cultivation, and in the drier northern Meroitic provinces it does seem likely that the cultivation of either naturally or mechanically irrigated land provided the greater part of the subsistence base. Evidence for the growing of sorghum has come from Meroë, Musawwarat es-Sufra and Naqa, and of barley from early levels at Meroë (Edwards 1996: 22). Particularly good evidence from Qasr Ibrim shows that barley, emmer wheat and common millet were at first important, but that the 'summer crops' of sorghum, cotton, durum wheat, bread wheat, bulrush millet, termis bean and sesame were introduced during the first five centuries AD, about the time that the *saqia*, the ox-driven waterwheel, was being adopted in the area (Rowley-Conwy 1989; 1991). Sorghum seems to have become especially important and it is significant that a relief on a granite boulder at Jebel Qeili, in the southern Butana, depicts the sun god apparently presenting the Meroitic King Sherkarer, of the first century AD, with a number of heads of sorghum (Hintze 1959: Fig. 2; Shinnie 1967: 51, 96).

The range of cultivated crops seems to have remained much the same throughout Christian and Islamic times. At Soba, far to the south, for instance, the excavated cereal remains were dominated by sorghum and bulrush millet during Early and Classic Christian times (van der Veen 1991: 266); and at Qasr Ibrim, sorghum, barley, wheat and pulses were the major plant foods during the Late and Terminal Christian periods (Adams 1996: 100) and during the Islamic period (Adams, Alexander and Allen 1983). In addition, a variety of fruits and vegetables had probably long been important. As early as the New Kingdom the paintings in the tomb of Djehuty-hetep at Debeira, in Lower Nubia, depicted a plantation scene with workers harvesting dates and dom-palm fruit (Säve-Söderbergh 1960: 38–40). The Christian deposits at Soba produced evidence of grapes, figs, dates, dom palm, African fan palm and Christ's thorn; those at Debeira West yielded castor oil seeds, date stones, cucumber seeds, groundnuts and dom-palm nuts (Shinnie and Shinnie 1978: 107); and from late in the same period at Qasr Ibrim came castor bean, water-melon, onion, garlic and probably cucumber.

Nevertheless, Edwards (1989; 1996) has questioned the assumption that cultivation in the Nile Valley was the main subsistence base and has stressed the probable importance of rainfed agriculture along wadi beds and on other suitable alluvial soils, particularly (citing Ahmed 1984) in southern Nubia. Edwards has also emphasized the important and continuing input from pastoralism, an input of which the number of domestic animals buried in X-Group tombs at Ballana and Qustul might serve to remind us. So too may the bones of sheep, goats, cattle and pigs, as well as copious quantities of goat droppings, at the Christian site of Debeira West (Shinnie and Shinnie 1978: 107); and the bones of sheep, goats, pigs, cattle, horses, donkeys and camels, and 'ubiquitous' sheep and goat dung, and horse, donkey and camel dung, in the Late and Terminal Christian deposits at Qasr Ibrim (Adams 1996: 101). For Islamic times Qasr Ibrim continues to be informative, showing sheep, goats and cattle to be common (Adams, Alexander and Allen 1983). That domestic animals were so important even in the rainless north of Nubia may seem difficult to believe, but in 1963 a livestock census, along the Sudanese stretch of the Nile Valley subsequently flooded by Lake Nasser, reported 2831 cattle, 19,335 sheep, 34,146 goats, 86 horses, 3415 donkeys, 608 camels, and large numbers of chickens, pigeons and ducks, in an area which had just over 50,000 people (Adams 1977: 54). These figures demonstrate the carrying capacity even of this dry area, where grazing was limited to the narrow fertile riverine strip, inevitably competing with cultivation. To the south, with seasonal grazing available away from the river, pastoralism must have been even more important.

So far as subsistence economy is concerned, therefore, Nubia clearly had the capacity to support both a sedentary population along the thin ribbon of the Nile, that nucleated at points particularly favoured with water and fertile silt, and a more mobile population dispersed through the savanna lands of the south. In addition, human ingenuity, in the form of mechanical means of irrigation, further increased the agricultural viability of small parts of the region. Thus there was an adequate subsistence base to support a growth of social complexity.

Technology

In contrast with subsistence economy, there is an abundance of direct archaeological evidence that throws light on the technology of the middle Nile during the periods under review. From this, it is apparent that at times this part of Africa reached a high level of technological sophistication. There is, however, a problem in interpreting such evidence: how much of this technological achievement is attributable to indigenous endeavour and how much to exotic sources, be they actual importation or merely the presence of expatriate craftsmen? Because of the repeated cultural contact along the middle Nile, this is a difficult problem to resolve; indeed some aspects of it may be insoluble. Possibly, it is an irrelevant problem, because it may be argued that it matters little what the origin of a technological base may be, so long as the society concerned benefits from its presence. In this discussion, however, we are concerned with causes for growing social complexity, and when evaluating the role of technology in such causes, it is obviously important to identify the indigenous and the foreign import. Here an attempt will be made to do this in general terms, whilst recognizing the difficulties.

Perhaps the most outstanding aspect of middle Nile technology was the area of building and construction. Ashlar masonry, coarser types of stonework, fired brick and mud-brick were all handled with skill to produce structures that were often complex in design and sophisticated in execution. Foreign influence is evident in much of this, from the Temple of Amon at Jebel Barkal, which we know to have been built originally by the Egyptians, to the pyramids of Napata and Meroë, or the churches of Christian Nubia, all of which are examples of buildings of alien inspiration, if not of actual foreign construction. Nevertheless, most of these structures have characteristics which are distinctively Nubian and it is clear that Nubians played a part in the technological achievements that they represent. The *deffufas* and tombs of Kerma and the tombs of Ballana and Qustul were, indeed, completely indigenous in both design and execution and both their size and structural complexity demand admiration. So also does the Great Enclosure at Musawwarat es-Sufra which is both unique and mysterious. Clearly, Nubians expended considerable energy on building, in spite of many of their less important structures probably being of grass and wood. Such examples as the Meroitic palace at Wad ben Naqa, the cities and towns of Meroitic and Christian Nubia, or the water-storage *hafirs* of the dry areas east and south-east of Meroë, are eloquent of effort as well as of building and engineering skills. Furthermore, the heated bathroom of the supposed house at Old Dongola (p. 49), and the numerous latrines in Christian Nubian houses, demonstrate a concern for comfort and convenience as well as for monumental structures.

Associated with building were a number of other skills whose existence can be inferred or for which evidence exists, such as quarrying, stone-dressing, mud-brick making, brick-firing, carpentry, sculpture, wall painting and inscription cutting. A knowledge of surveying and architectural design would also have been necessary, and indeed on the wall of one of the pyramid chapels at Meroë is an architect's elevation drawing at a scale of 1:10, that appears to have been done during the construction of one of the other pyramids in the cemetery (Welsby 1996: 134–5). The question of foreign influence and sometimes even foreign execution inevitably arises in such matters but, again, the end-products usually had a strong Nubian flavour, suggesting a very real local input. It is also relevant that for much of the time under discussion the people of the middle Nile were at least partly literate and during the Meroitic period even developed their own unique alphabet. Moreover, the frequency of graffiti and other inscribed material at Nubian sites indicates that in some periods literacy was fairly widespread. In such circumstances, it seems unnecessary to explain technological sophistication in terms of alien origins.

Another important area of Nubian technology lay in the extraction and manufacturing of metal, especially of iron. It is clear that many items of bronze, of silver and of gold were imported, but the furnace remains and substantial quantities of iron slag at Meroë would suggest that there at least an extensive iron-working industry flourished. Further evidence that this was so is provided by the range of iron weapons and tools recovered from Meroitic sites, including spears, arrowheads, hoe blades, adzes, axes, shears and tweezers (Shinnie 1967: 162–5). Mounds of iron slag, probably of a similar date, have also been reported from Kerma, Kawa and Argo (Shinnie 1967: 182), and the iron objects from the Ballana and Qustul tombs indicate that iron-working skills remained at a high level even after the disintegration of the Meroitic state. Another metal for which Nubia was an important source was gold, much of which came from the desert east of the Nile, north of the Fifth Cataract (Vercoutter 1959: 129). Particularly during the New Kingdom period, this area seems to have been one of Egypt's main suppliers, as the well-known paintings in the Theban tomb of Huy appear to indicate (O'Connor 1993: 63).

In addition, manufacturing along the middle Nile produced pottery, textiles, leatherwork, woodwork, basketry, and even wine. Of these, the pottery is especially deserving of comment. Even during the Kerma period remarkably fine pottery had been made, but exceptionally high-quality wares were produced during Meroitic, X-Group and Christian Nubian times. These were wheel-made, well fired and often had painted decoration. It is apparent that they were fired in specially constructed pottery kilns of brick, of which a number have been excavated at Debeira East which date from late X-Group and Early Christian times (Adams 1977: 402–3). Other kilns have been uncovered at Faras, dating from the Early and Classic Christian periods (Adams 1961; 1977: 496, 498), and kilns are also known from Meroitic contexts at Meroë and Musawwarat es-Sufra and from the Christian period at Old Dongola (Edwards 1999).

Textile production seems also to have been important, largely because cotton was grown in the area, at least by Meroitic times, but textiles found in Meroitic, X-Group and Christian tombs at Ballana and Qustul during the 1960s included cotton, linen and animal fibre from either goats, sheep or camels (Thurman 1979: 36). Clearly, leather-working depended on the widespread animal husbandry, and basketry was based on palm fibres and grasses that were widely available. Only the appearance of wood-working remains difficult to understand in terms of the environment of the region but there is plentiful direct evidence for it in both X-Group and Christian deposits at Qasr Ibrim (Adams 1982: 28–9). As for the wine, a number of supposed wine presses have been found in Lower Nubia and, although the environment was not really suitable for vine cultivation, it does seem as if wine was produced locally whenever the supply of the superior Egyptian product was interrupted (Adams 1966).

Some items in Meroitic, X-Group and Christian sites suggest even more sophisticated technologies than those that have been discussed. Glassware, lamps, furniture, jewellery of gold or silver set with semi-precious stones: these and other things mostly represent imported status symbols that were not part of Nubian technology. There were also some aspects of Nubian technology that resulted from technology transfer. The most important of these was mechanical irrigation. To modern eyes both the *shaduf* and the *saqia* look simple contrivances but their adoption was clearly most important for the development of human societies on the middle Nile. Almost as important was transportation technology, enabling the commerce of the region to exist. The oldest aspect of this was the sailing boat, whose importance on the Nile throughout the period under discussion is so easily forgotten. It was, however, the development of desert transportation systems, particularly that involving the camel, that seems to have had the greatest impact on the commercial life of this region. These aspects of irrigation and transportation technology emphasize the importance of technology to social development on the middle Nile and, together with the other achievements that have been discussed, would suggest that the technological base was clearly adequate to support such development.

Social system

There is abundant indication from the middle Nile region, during the periods under review, of the development of social complexity. Monumental tombs at Kerma, Napata, Meroë, and Ballana and Qustul, in their scale, their sophisticated construction and their contents, show the presence of absolute monarchy at various times. The divinity and/or autocracy of such rulers is demonstrated by the practice of human sacrifice at Kerma, and at Ballana and Qustul, and by the sculptured reliefs of some Meroitic buildings. Just in case the beholder should miss the message, some of the latter reinforce their point with inscriptions, which unfortunately we cannot always fully understand. Interestingly, Meroitic monarchy gave women an important role (Fig. 2.7); indeed sometimes they governed in their own right. Absolute monarchy is also suggested by the existence of large and elaborate domestic buildings interpreted as palaces, of which those at Meroë, Wad ben Naqa and Jebel Barkal are perhaps the most convincing. In addition, numerous temples from various periods represent ideologies in which both spiritual and secular power were intertwined. Indeed, not only is the archaeological record eloquent of the emergence of absolute authority but it also chronicles its dissolution, as indicated by the numerous fortified buildings of Late Christian and Islamic times.

At the other end of the social scale, the archaeological evidence shows us a numerous labouring class that presumably consisted, during most periods, of both free peasants and slaves. Their presence is indicated not only by the clusters of small houses in many settlements and the numerous 'poorer' graves in cemeteries but also by the monumental constructions such as temples, tombs and burial mounds that were the achievement as much of their labour as of the authority of their rulers. The relationship of this lowest level of society, to both the rulers and their associated elite, is on occasion starkly demonstrated by the willing or enforced sacrifice of such lesser human beings at the burial of those to whom they were subservient, as was the case at Kerma and at Ballana and Qustul.

What about the middle of this stratified society? Archaeological evidence for the development of trade and manufacturing, particularly in the Meroitic and Christian periods, would suggest that at times there may have been merchant-entrepreneurs and some skilled craftsmen, as well as various government officials and holders of temple or church appointments. However, direct archaeological evidence is not easy to find or is ambiguous, although some burials at Kerma, Napata and Meroë seem to belong neither to the elite nor to the peasantry. Settlement evidence is slightly better, with Meroitic houses including both 'de luxe' and 'humbler' structures (Adams 1977: 357–8) in locations where one would not expect to find residences of the elite. The houses of some Christian Nubian settlements also suggest that some residents were better off than others. So it does seem that, at least during some periods, there were the beginnings of a third class between the two extremes.

Just as the archaeological evidence suggests the existence of social stratification, so it also indicates the development of functional specialization. Cross-cutting much of the social hierarchy, and indeed contributing to its differentiation, there emerged a variety of specialized occupations. The archaeological evidence indicates that by Meroitic and Christian times, for instance, there were specialist potters making high-quality wheel-formed wares, as distinct from traditional potters who continued to turn out rougher hand-built pottery in their spare time. In addition, there must have been iron-smelters, blacksmiths and perhaps other metal-workers; spinners and weavers; builders, who would have included both masons and brick-makers; leather-workers, carpenters and joiners, basket-makers and boatmen. There would also have been scribes, artists (both sculptors and painters), priests and temple and church officials, some members of the army and merchants.

A level of social complexity conducive to both urbanization and state formation would appear to have been reached during several periods along the middle Nile. It seems likely, however, that the social systems which have been discussed were as much symptomatic as causative of the development of cities and states. It is necessary to look further if this development is to be explained.

Population pressures

The people of the middle Nile were agriculturalists who at best lived in dry savanna and in the north lived in a desert. They were able to do this because of the existence of the river, which provided water for the irrigation of such areas of fertile silts as could be reached either by seasonal flooding or by mechanical means. It also provided them with a base from which, particularly in the south, they could exploit the seasonal grazing and rainfed cultivation of the surrounding areas. However, cultivable land and accessible pasture were limited resources; indeed in some areas they were absent altogether. Yet, where present, they had the potential to yield a surplus and to support population growth. The problem was that if the population grew, there was nowhere to go: there was only a finite amount of land that could be exploited by the means available. As a result, the settlement of the region was restricted to a long, narrow and frequently broken strip of viable agricultural land, with some isolated more fortunate areas, and to such adjacent areas that could support transhumant pastoralism or rainfed cultivation. Theoretically, therefore, the middle Nile constituted a classic example of environmentally induced population pressures. The question is: have we any archaeological evidence that such pressures actually existed?

Unsatisfactory though they might be, there are some archaeological indications of population pressures during certain periods. For instance, the distribution of archaeological sites in Lower Nubia, which is still the best-studied area, seems particularly dense for later Meroitic and Christian times. Although Edwards (1996: 80) has argued that the Meroitic population was actually small, it does seem that this rainless area did support a surprisingly large number of people in later times. Similarly, the existence of Meroitic sites in the dry western Butana, away from the Nile but along wadis that could provide some seasonal cultivation, suggests that the population of that area found it necessary to exploit its available resources to the limit. It is even possible that the tight clustering of houses within some Meroitic and Christian settlements was at least partly caused by a desire to conserve potentially cultivable land, again an indication of a population pressing against the limits of its resources.

The most obvious way that the carrying capacity of the region could be improved was by increasing the available cultivable land, and the only way to do this was to introduce better irrigation technology. Two such improvements are known to have taken place during the periods under review. The first was the introduction of the *shaduf*, an idea imported from Egypt probably during the New Kingdom. Quite possibly it helped to encourage the growing population of that time that has been calculated by Trigger (1965: 156–66). The second was the *saqia*, again a foreign idea, that was adopted in Nubia in about the fourth century AD, during the X-Group period (Edwards 1996: 80–1, 91). In conjunction with the new 'summer crops' introduced around this time (p. 52), it is likely that the improved irrigation that resulted did lead to an increase in population and, indeed, the very fact that the *saqia* and the new crops were adopted would suggest that there was already population pressure in the area.

Thus, although Edwards (1999) remains unconvinced, there is some archaeological evidence that suggests the existence of population pressures on the middle Nile, pressures that would have been accentuated by fluctuations in river level and rainfall. It seems that cultivable land and accessible grazing could indeed have been scarce resources at times, and control of them might have provided a power-base for an emerging elite. The hot-house conditions which could well have resulted must surely have been at least a contributory factor in the growth of cities and states.

Ideology

The Nubian archaeological record is, in general, highly informative on ideological matters. Tombs, temples and churches have much to tell us about the beliefs of those who built them. Their designs, their sculptural and graphic decorations, sometimes even their inscriptions, indicate that, throughout much of the period under review, Nubia was a borrower and adapter of foreign faiths. Until about the middle of the first millennium AD it was the gods of Pharaonic Egypt that dominated the Nubian scene; indeed their observance survived longer on the middle Nile than in Egypt itself. The most important of these seem to have been Isis and Amon, the worship of the latter becoming a state cult for both Napata and Meroë, with their rulers often taking the name of Amon as one element of their throne names, for example Tenutamon, Arkamani, Natakamani. From about the middle of the first millennium AD to about the middle of the second millennium, Christianity became the dominant faith, to be replaced, in its turn, by Islam. Nevertheless, all these faiths developed their own Nubian characteristics and there were also at times separate indigenous beliefs. This would seem to be indicated by the human sacrifices at Kerma and at Ballana and Qustul, and also by the worship of Apedemak, the lion-god of Meroë, who seems to have been a consequence of Egyptian–Meroitic syncretism (Zabkar 1975).

The archaeological evidence also suggests that these different ideologies played a significant contributory role in the development of states and cities. Prior to the arrival of Christianity on the middle Nile, the religious beliefs of Nubia were characterized by that close integration of secular and spiritual authority which was common in the ancient world of South-West Asia and the Mediterranean, and was also frequently present in Africa. In such cases, the ruler became the personification of the god, a notion that sometimes manifests itself archaeologically in monumental tombs and temples, which were an expression at once of both human and divine authority. Thus was provided a legitimization for the rule of an absolute monarch, who could literally claim a divine mandate. In addition, ideas of this sort considerably strengthened the power-base of such a ruler, who was enabled to exert both physical and spiritual force. The state developments of Kerma, Napata,

Meroë and the X-Group all betray the importance of this ideological contribution. With the advent of Christianity, the ruler was no longer a god, even though his rule might be strengthened by being divinely sanctioned. Human and divine authority were separated and 'royal' tombs disappeared from the archaeological record. However, this does not necessarily mean that there was any loss of authority by the temporal ruler who, as the Faras paintings show, could still call on ideological support from a Church that he in turn protected. As a result, the Christian states of Nubia were ruled by both the Crown and the Cross: the one claiming authority over people's bodies, the other over their souls (Adams 1977).

The role of ideology in the process of urbanization was rather different. It is apparent that the construction of an important temple or church at a particular place sometimes led to development of a settlement at that place, or led to increased growth of a settlement that already existed. In this way, some cities came into existence as religious ceremonial centres, or became more important because they assumed such a ceremonial role. It seems likely that Qasr Ibrim was an example of both these processes. Nubian cities also had a more general symbolic role, irrespective of whether religion, administration or commerce was the main activity; each city confered political and ideological legitimacy on the regime that controlled it. Clearly, ideology could have played an important part in the developments that we are investigating.

External trade

All our sources for the period under review indicate that long-distance trade was very important to Nubia. As was discussed at the beginning of this chapter (p. 18), Adams has described Nubia as the only trade corridor into the heart of Africa, so far as the ancient world of South-West Asia and the Mediterranean was concerned. Moving north seem to have been gold and other minerals, ivory, slaves and a whole range of African exotica; going south in exchange was a variety of manufactured goods, including many best described as luxury goods. It was a classic example of that age-old interchange between developed and underdeveloped world: manufactures for raw materials.

Archaeological evidence for this trade is abundant, although it has little to tell us about some aspects of it. Least well represented in the archaeological record are the commodities that were traded north to Egypt but there are some significant pieces of evidence. For example, diorite quarries have been discovered in the Nubian desert west of Abu Simbel; they were being exploited during the Egyptian Old Kingdom and Middle Kingdom. This rock was the favoured material for statues and stelae in Egypt at this time and apparently was transported as far as Giza, near modern Cairo, a distance along the Nile of more than 1200 kilometres (Adams 1977: 169–70). Similarly, copper-smelting furnaces have been found in the

Old Kingdom town investigated at Buhen (Adams 1977: 170–4) and numerous gold mines, that were producing by Middle Kingdom times, are known in the desert east of the Second Cataract area and in the *Batn el Hajar* (Vercoutter 1959). There is archaeological evidence that all these activities were at first in Egyptian hands and, originally at least, their output was probably only intended for Egyptian use. Thus, the trade in gold and other minerals can be shown to have developed at an early date. Evidence for the trade in ivory is less easy to find but it is surely significant that, in the Napatan town of Sanam, one room of a possible storehouse was found by its excavator to have part of its floor 'covered with tusks of raw ivory injured by fire' (Griffith 1922: 117, Plate LIIIb). In addition, ivory tusks were found in one of the storerooms in the palace at Wad ben Naqa (Vercoutter 1962: Plate xxb). Almost invisible in the archaeological record, however, is the trade in slaves, which was probably of substantial importance for much of the time that we are considering. The people sacrificed at Kerma, or Ballana and Qustul, for instance, were not necessarily slaves, although they may well have been. It could be significant, nevertheless, that the relief at Jebel Qeili and those on the pylons of the Lion Temple at Naqa show live rather than dead captives; they were worth more alive. As for the other tropical exotica that were traded north to Egypt, Egyptian documentary and archaeological sources provide details but, amongst other things, they seem to have included ostrich eggs and feathers, various skins from wild animals, live wild animals, ebony, semi-precious stones and incense. A painting in the mid-second-millennium BC tomb of Rekhmire at Thebes actually shows such a range of goods (Kendall 1997: 9). It seems likely that all the commodities sought by Egyptians were collected together at trading stations during earlier times, until their handling came under indigenous control in Napatan and later times. The Second Cataract Forts, for instance, seem to have had some such role.

There is rather better archaeological evidence for the commodities that were traded south into Nubia, although it is not without its own problems. Outstanding amongst these imports were a whole range of manufactured items that, although often common enough in their places of origin, seem frequently to have been prized as status symbols in Nubia and therefore buried in the more important graves. Sometimes these objects can be attributed on the basis of their style to their places of origin, although more commonly their foreign manufacture has merely been assumed because of the sophistication of the technology by which they have been produced. Perhaps the most impressive, by reasons of its fragility and the distances that it nevertheless travelled, is the glassware that has been found in Meroitic, X-Group and Christian Nubian contexts. Shinnie (1967: Plates 82–4) illustrated two glass vessels from Meroitic graves at Faras in Lower Nubia and one from Meroë itself which are remarkable enough, but the most impressive Meroitic collection of glass is perhaps that excavated from tombs at Seddenga on the Abri-Delgo Reach of the middle Nile (Leclant 1973; Wildung 1997: 364–8). In addition to glassware, fine metalwork and jewellery seem also to have figured amongst the imports to Nubia. Thus, for example, a silver gilt goblet, probably of Roman origin, was found at Meroë (Shinnie 1967: Plates 78–81) and a gold ring, also from Meroë, was inscribed in Greek (Shinnie 1967: Plate 61). From various Meroitic contexts have also come an assortment of bronze lamps, bowls, beakers, bottles and vases, whilst the X-Group tombs of Ballana and Qustul produced a bewildering mass of metal goods and other manufactures which seem to have originated in Byzantine Egypt. However, the most common imports in Meroitic Nubia, according to the archaeological record, were beads of glass or stone, so common indeed that Adams (1977: 373) suggested that they may have been used as a medium of exchange.

In addition to the wide range of durable manufactures that were traded into Nubia at various times, it is apparent that the imported goods also included some consumables, and some other commodities that have not usually survived in archaeological deposits. Some of the Meroitic glass vessels, for instance, are of shapes that are known to have been used elsewhere for containing unguents and oils, and it is likely that they were imported for their contents rather than for their own sakes (Shinnie 1967: 130–1). Similarly, some of the imported Graeco-Roman pottery that appears alongside indigenous wares in Meroitic contexts could also have arrived in Nubia as containers for consumables. An Egyptian Old Kingdom text, for example, mentions the Nubians' fondness for Egyptian honey (Adams 1984: 41), and the Egyptian amphorae that are found in Nubian sites of Meroitic, X-Group and Early Christian date seem to have been imported full of either olive oil or wine (Adams 1966; Hofmann 1991). There must also have been other commodities that have left little or no archaeological evidence of their importance as trade goods, such as some of the fine textiles which have been recovered from Meroitic, X-Group and Christian tombs at Ballana and Qustul (Thurman 1979).

Another form of archaeological evidence that throws light on the organization of Nubian trade is the location of some of the major urban sites. All of the cities that survived for any length of time seem to have been at places where the export commodities of the African interior could be collected at the riverbank, ready for shipment to Egypt. As time went on and trade networks expanded ever further into the interior, so these places appeared successively further up the Nile: first there was Buhen, then Kerma, then Napata, then Meroë and finally there were Shendi, Soba and Sennar. Some of these places, and indeed others also, grew particularly important because they were situated at a point where a major route reached the Nile. Thus, Meroë and Napata stood at the southern and northern end respectively of the Bayuda Road, that cut off the great bend of the Nile containing the Fourth and Fifth Cataracts. In turn, Napata and Kawa stood at each end of the Meheila Road, that cut off the next great bend of the river further downstream. These routes were only part, however, of those that seem to have existed by

Meroitic times, including the Korosko Road, that cut off the whole of the Nile bend that contained the Second, Third and Fourth Cataracts; the Wadi Hawad Road that led south-east from Meroë to Aksum; and another route that led north-east from the Atbara–Nile confluence to the Red Sea port of Suakin (Adams 1977). The location of the urban centres that have been mentioned and the existence of these important land routes suggest two things: first, that the external trade of the Nile may have played an important role in urban growth; second, that such trade was only part of a vast network of regional trading links about which little is known. Archaeological evidence from the Gash Delta in the eastern Sudan, suggesting contact with Kerma, and the possibility that the area between the Gash and Baraka Valleys was the location of the Land of Punt, whose trade with New Kingdom Egypt was recorded in a famous carving at Deir el Bahari, are indications of how extensive that network may have been (Fattovich 1990a; 1991; Phillipson 1993a: 151–2).

Until we do have more archaeological evidence that can throw light on regional trading systems in this part of Africa, it is probably premature to assess the actual contribution that *external* trade made to the development of cities and states on the middle Nile. Nevertheless, it could be argued that trade in general provided the main causative factor for these developments and that if there had been no trade centred on the Nile, then there would have been very little social development there either. Perhaps the most important point to recognize, however, is that the external trade was only one aspect of a long-continued cultural interaction between the middle Nile region and the world to its north. It was, as it were, merely one symptom of that interaction that happens to be more susceptible to archaeological study than some others.

Conclusion

Considering its environment, Nubia would seem to have been an unlikely place for the development of states and the appearance of cities. Yet not only did these things happen, they happened here earlier than anywhere else in tropical Africa. It is little wonder that a common historical explanation has been to regard such developments as 'secondary' in character, resulting directly from contact with Egypt and South-West Asia. An examination of the archaeological evidence reveals a very much more complex situation, in which exotic influences undoubtedly played a continuing although fluctuating role but where important contributions and perhaps initial development came from within, so that the resultant social complexity had its own quite distinctive Nubian characteristics.

First of all, Nubia was partly a gift of the Nile, just as Egypt was completely so. Without it, Nubia would have been very different. Water and silt from the Nile allowed the development of a sound subsistence base which in some favoured areas was capable of producing a surplus, especially where seasonal grazing and rainfed cultivation were possible away from the river. It is noticeable that all of the major socio-cultural developments, which have been discussed in this chapter, were located on more favoured parts of the river and not in the less productive areas. Secondly, Nubian technology, although often dependent on foreign ideas and products, was able to extend the cultivated land and to intensify its exploitation, by means of mechanical irrigation. It was also able to provide both land and water transportation systems that could overcome the communication problems of a population strung out along many hundreds of kilometres of river.

It seems likely that cultivable land and accessible grazing rapidly became, and remained, scarce resources, providing a power-base for those who controlled them and creating population pressures that contributed to a tendency for people to gather in urban aggregations. Social stratification followed, with society divided between the rulers and the ruled, and with an increasingly sophisticated technology encouraging the development of functional specialization. Without doubt, however, it was trading and commercial activities, and the general cultural interaction of which they were a part, that became the catalyst of major social development in Nubia. It is quite likely that the middle Nile had long been part of an extensive regional trading system, but from Egyptian Old Kingdom times onwards the demand of the developed world to the north for raw materials and tropical exotica created a major interest in external trade. Nubia became both a pipeline of supply and a successful entrepôt, profiting not so much from its own products but from those that it merely handled on their way north or on their way south. The origins of Kerma can already be discerned at this time, although its socio-political status is uncertain. Subsequently, Egypt controlled this trade herself, extending her authority into Nubia both in Middle Kingdom and, more extensively, in New Kingdom times. When her grip weakened, indigenous control quickly reasserted itself, first of all with Kerma and eventually with the states of Napata and Meroë, and of later times. The earlier of these polities may have been only tentative but by Meroitic times we find evidence of a highly complex stratified society. It is, however, apparent from archaeological evidence that all of these autocratic regimes sought to strengthen and legitimize their control by sheltering behind powerful religious ideologies, the observance of which in turn contributed to the growth of urban centres. The foreign origin of most of those religions indicates the very considerable contribution made to Nubian developments by cultural contacts with the north, but even with religion there was a strong indigenous input that cannot be denied.

The emergence of social complexity on the middle Nile may thus be seen as the result of a complex interaction between local and exotic factors but an interaction in which indigenous people made their own decisions. As Shinnie (1967: 169) wrote of the best known of these polities: 'Meroë was an African civilization, firmly based on African soil, and developed by an African population.' Indeed, the roots of Meroitic achievement can be traced back to Kerma in the middle of the second millennium BC, and the cultural origins of Kerma appear to have been contemporary with those of Pharaonic Egypt. Rather than continuing to see the development of social complexity in Nubia as secondary to that of Egypt, we should perhaps begin to regard them as parallel and interacting African achievements. It is no longer Egypt that can claim Nubia but Africa that should reclaim Egypt. Many years ago Agatha Christie wrote a famous detective story called *Death on the Nile* but, so far as the origins of African cities and states are concerned, archaeologists still have to solve the mystery of birth on the Nile.

Chapter 3
The benefits of isolation: the Ethiopian Highlands

'Rugged escarpments overlooking the Sudan, and desert plains in north-east Kenya, separate the highlands of Ethiopia and the Horn of Africa from the rest of the continent.' It was in such words that the geographer A.T. Grove introduced a discussion of this part of Africa (Grove 1978: 222). For many observers, indeed, it has been the isolation of this region, particularly that of the central highlands of Ethiopia, that has made the greatest impression on them. The core of Ethiopia is a great block of mountains, everywhere over 1000 metres in height, that reaches a general level of 2300 metres and in places exceeds 4200 metres above sea level. At first sight, one could not imagine a less likely setting for state emergence and urbanization. Nevertheless, in the modern countries of Ethiopia and Eritrea there is clear evidence of such developments by the first century AD, and some indication of them as early as the eighth century BC (Fattovich 1990b). Not only are these dates early for the attainment of social complexity in tropical Africa but also these achievements were at a particularly high level of sophistication. Almost 2000 years ago, the state of Aksum, as it became known to the ancient world, boasted urban centres; its own form of writing; coinage in gold, silver and bronze; masonry buildings of a distinctive architectural style; unique monuments that indicate substantial quarrying and engineering skills; extensive trading contacts both within and outside Africa; and a significant role in the international politics of its period. Indeed, Aksum seems to have been one of the first states to adopt Christianity (Phillipson 1998a: 145 note 1). However, the origins of Aksumite success may already be discerned in the mid-first-millennium BC Pre-Aksumite state of *D'mt*, with its towns at Yeha and Matara, its script, its sophisticated stone masonry, sculpture and metallurgy, and its contacts with both South Arabia and the Nile Valley. Far from being isolated, Ethiopia (together with Eritrea) would appear to have formed, at times, a most important zone for cultural integration. Edward Ullendorff summed up the situation eloquently:

> In its long history the country has always formed a bridge between Africa and Asia . . . from which it is separated only by the narrow straits of the Bab-el-Mandeb, a distance of less than twenty miles. With its ancestry astride two continents and its position in the horn of Africa, Ethiopia has always occupied a favoured place at a cross-road of civilizations and a meeting point of many races. (Ullendorff 1960: 23)

On the other hand, after the rise of Islam in the seventh century AD, Ethiopia did become increasingly isolated, leading the eighteenth-century historian Gibbon to make his famous exaggerated remark that: 'Encompassed on all sides by the enemies of their religion, the Aethiopians slept near a thousand years, forgetful of the world by whom they were forgotten' (Gibbon 1952: Vol. 2, 159–60). However, the Ethiopians' struggle to survive through those centuries can hardly be likened to sleep, nor can their success in that struggle. For some form of Ethiopian state did survive down to modern times, albeit one of a mostly non-urban type. In addition, the Christian Church of Ethiopia also survived, leaving as a legacy of those centuries of sleep some of the most remarkable ecclesiastical architecture in the world. As a result, the Ethiopian Highlands provide one of the most impressive examples of cultural continuity in Africa; indeed, until late in the twentieth century Ethiopia could be claimed to be 'the longest-lived independent Christian kingdom in the world' (Buxton 1970: 56).

It might be argued, therefore, that the apparent isolation of this region is like that of a well-planned fortress. In times of peace, it is so placed that it can take full advantage of all that goes on around it and there will be frequent contact between the garrison and the surrounding population. In times of war, however, not only is the fortress able to withstand a protracted siege, while life continues within it, but also it is so designed that the defenders can sally out to smite the attackers. Isolation of such a kind clearly has benefits.

Geographical location and environmental factors

The mountains of Ethiopia are divided into two parts by the northern end of the East African Rift Valley, here occupied by a string of relatively small lakes and by the Awash River (Fig. 3.1). It is the highlands to the north and to the west of this valley that form the heartland of old Ethiopia, formerly called Abyssinia. This huge area of mountains is roughly triangular in shape and the northern end of this triangle lies close to the western shore of the Red Sea (now part of Eritrea). Compared with the surrounding dry, hot plains, either on the African or on the South Arabian side of the Red Sea, the Ethiopian Highlands offer a range of relatively attractive environments. As a result, cultural contact and even movement of people between the lowlands and the highlands might be expected to have taken place from an early date. Because of the narrowness of the Red Sea at this point, the presence in it of numerous islands, and a comparable range of environments in South Arabia, it might further be expected that such contact and movement would have Asiatic as well as African sources. It is of some interest, therefore, to note that both archaeological and historical evidence indicates that social complexity developed first in the northern extremities of the Ethiopian Highlands and only later gradually moved south in response to changed circumstances in international politics.

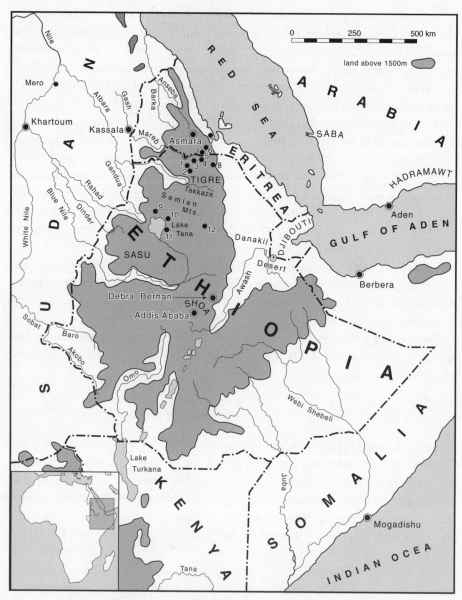

Fig. 3.1 Archaeological sites of the Ethiopian Highlands.
1: Aksum. *2:* Haoulti Melazo. *3:* Yeha. *4:* Debra Damo. *5:* Matara. *6:* Kohaito. *7:* Adulis. *8:* Addi Galamo. *9:* Gondar. *10:* Gouzara. *11:* Lalibela Cave. *12:* Lalibela. Based on Ullendorff (1960).

The proximity of the northern part of the Ethiopian Highlands to the Red Sea had other more important consequences. For the ancient world, as indeed for the modern world, the Red Sea comprised a major shipping route, that connected the Mediterranean with the trade of the Indian Ocean. Ethiopia, able to tap the resources of the African interior, had direct access to this major route, and this was clearly an important contributory element in the rise of the Aksumite state.

The Ethiopian Highlands are the result of Tertiary earth movements and associated volcanic activity and typically consist of basalts and other lavas overlying sandstones and limestones. Most of the region is tilted to the west and therefore drains into the Nile, particularly into the upper Blue Nile which issues from Lake Tana. The drainage pattern has cut deeply into the landscape, carving spectacular gorges, often hundreds of metres deep, that break up the otherwise gently undulating surface of the high plateau. In some cases the walls of these gorges descend in steps that provide habitable areas at very different levels. Similarly the highlands fall away sharply to the east, where a great escarpment drops down to the hot plains below. Parts of the original high plateau have been so eroded that very little level country remains, except in the form of flat-topped *ambas*, isolated hills with precipitous sides (Buxton 1970: 18–20).

The most important environmental factor in the Ethiopian Highlands is altitude. Within about 250 kilometres of each other lie the hot dusty salt-flats of the Danakil Desert and the cool heights of the Semien Mountains that sometimes experience heavy falls of snow (Buxton 1970: 18). Altitude is thus a major determinant of both climate and vegetation. Ethiopians themselves recognize three main climatic zones. These are *dega*, which is land above 2400 metres that has a temperate climate with an average temperature of 16°C; *woina dega*, which is land between 1800 and 2400 metres that has a sub-tropical climate with an average temperature of 22°C; and *kwolla*, which is land below 1800 metres that has a tropical climate with average temperatures of 26°C and over. All three zones can sometimes be found within relatively short distances. However, although temperatures vary greatly with altitude, there is little seasonal variation. The major factor determining seasonality is rainfall. The highlands occasion a somewhat greater rainfall than is usual at this latitude in Africa, but because the rain is brought by winds from the south-west, rainfall is heaviest and the wet season longest in the south-western highlands, and the far north has less rain and a shorter wet season. In general, the main wet season lasts from late June to early September and is followed by a long dry season that lasts until February. The average annual rainfall in the central highlands is about 1000 millimetres. The nearby plains of the Red Sea coast (now mostly in Eritrea) have a comparatively slight rainfall but this occurs in January and February when the highlands are dry, and the coastal plains are at their hottest and driest at the time when the heaviest rain is falling in the highlands. There is thus ample scope for some pastoralists and agriculturalists to exploit this seasonal and altitudinal variation in rainfall (Ullendorff 1960: 26–8; Buxton 1970: 20–1).

Given both the height and the open character of much of the Ethiopian Highlands, it is not surprising that exposure to wind is another environmental factor of significance. Much of the high plateau is sufficiently wind-swept for this to affect its utilization. Thus Buxton (1970: 60) recorded that the population of the Debra Berhan area in Shoa tended to cluster in and around the gorges, rather than on the open plateau itself. Furthermore, Doresse (1959: 162, 203) noted how Menelik II, in the late nineteenth century, first sought to establish his new capital at Entotto but after a few years moved it to a more sheltered site at nearby Addis Ababa because Entotto was so windy.

The wide range of altitude and climate is responsible for a great variety of vegetation. Within the boundaries of the modern states of Ethiopia and Eritrea this extends from desert scrub to rainforest but even within the highlands there was originally an impressive range. Temperate forests of *Podocarpus* sp. occurred below 2200 metres and of *Juniperus* sp. above that level, with some overlap of their distribution. Both have been extensively destroyed by human activity, however, leaving most of the high plateau bleak and empty, but the successful introduction of Australian Eucalyptus trees, at the end of the nineteenth century, has alleviated this situation to some extent. Nevertheless, much of the vegetation cover of the high plateau now consists of short grass, which provides excellent grazing. Finally, at the highest levels of the highlands occurs an 'Afro-Alpine' association, corresponding in general to that of the East African mountains (Buxton 1970: 21–2).

The considerable altitudinal range of the Ethiopian Highlands has thus given rise to very great environmental diversity. Although soil erosion has been a problem (Grove 1978: 224), some 27 per cent of Ethiopian and Eritrean soils have been classified as good agricultural soils and a further 13 per cent as having fairly good but limited agricultural potential (Ethiopian Mapping Authority 1988: 8). Such a combination – a variety of environments and the availability of fertile soils – has enabled agriculture to provide the most important resources of the region. In many places it is possible to obtain two or three crops in the same year, and in some places it is possible to sow and harvest at any time. This is achieved by growing a very great range of crops. Among cereals, for instance, teff, wheat, barley, sorghum and finger millet can all be grown, although it is teff that is most commonly grown in areas of middle and higher altitude. Ethiopia also produces a remarkable selection of vegetables, including chickpeas, lentils, peppers, onions, tomatoes, beans, asparagus, lettuce and artichokes. In addition, many types of fruit can be grown, including bananas, mangoes, lemons, grapefruit, oranges, papaws, guavas, pineapples, peaches and prickly pear. Other agricultural products of importance comprise maize and *ensete* (in the high rainfall areas of the south-west), coffee, cotton, *chat* (a narcotic), *nug* (a source of oil), various medicinal plants and sugar-cane. Some of these plants were obviously introduced in later times but this picture of farming during the second half of the second millennium AD gives some idea of the likely importance of agricultural resources during earlier times. However, those resources also included very large numbers of livestock, particularly cattle (for milk and meat), sheep (not usually with wool) and goats. Working animals included oxen for pulling ploughs, whose use was unique in tropical Africa, horses, asses and mules, the last of these being very important for carrying loads in the often broken landscape. Additional useful animals were chickens, dogs and bees, while civet cats were kept in cages in order to collect the civet that was used as a perfume (Ullendorff 1960: 28–30; Pankhurst 1961: 200–19).

The native fauna of the Ethiopian Highlands provided other resources of significance. Not only could fishing and hunting supplement diet but valuable trade goods could be obtained from some of the numerous wild animals which included elephants, rhinoceros, crocodiles, lions, leopards, giraffes, zebras and many others. Further, traditional resources of significance included minerals, of which gold and iron ore seem to have been the most important, but silver, lead and tin could also be found (Pankhurst 1961: 224–9) and copper is said to occur near Aksum (L. Phillipson 1999). In addition the region produced plentiful supplies of good building stone, and timber only became difficult to find in more recent centuries. Finally, human life, as so often in tropical Africa, provided an important resource in the form of slaves. It will be noticed that, as with Nubia, the non-agricultural resources consisted in the main of commodities much sought after in the ancient Mediterranean world. The Ethiopian Highlands were thus well placed to develop important trade links with the outside world.

The environment of the Ethiopian Highlands was clearly an attractive one for human settlement, much of the region possessing a kind climate and being rather healthier than most of tropical Africa. Nevertheless, constraints did exist. The first and most obvious of these is that extensive areas of the highlands were too rocky, too exposed or too high to have any great agricultural value. In addition, much of the landscape was so rough, and so obstructed by gorges and other natural features, that communication remained difficult down to modern times. A second constraint, surprisingly enough, is that close inspection of historical sources reveals that Ethiopia was not quite as healthy as would at first appear. Thus Pankhurst (1961: 238–47) showed that the highlands have suffered from occasional epidemics of great severity. Some of these cannot now be identified but it is apparent that smallpox, cholera and influenza were amongst them. Dysentery, leprosy, eye diseases, Guinea worm and elephantiasis are also mentioned amongst diseases found in Ethiopia; and in the lowlands (which do not directly concern us here) malaria and other fevers were a serious problem. In the highlands themselves, tapeworm was prevalent, largely because of the long-established practice of eating raw meat, but this affliction has been customarily treated with indifference because of the existence of the *kosso* tree, whose flowers produce a drug that is highly effective in expelling these intestinal worms. Perhaps the most serious constraint in the Ethiopian Highlands, however, has been the periodic recurrence of famine, recorded as early as the ninth century and still a cause of major concern in modern times (Pankhurst 1961: 230–7). Famines could result from crop failure, brought on by inadequate or even excessive rainfall, or by unusually low temperatures. They could also result from crop destruction, caused by swarms of mice, troops of monkeys, or (most important of all) by massive invasions of locusts. Early European visitors in the sixteenth and seventeenth centuries were astounded by the size of these invasions and by the fearful destruction that these insects could bring. Serious as some of these constraints might appear, however, the greater number of them were episodic, so that overall they seem to have had little inhibiting effect on the growth of social complexity in the Ethiopian Highlands. It is to the evidence for that growth that we must now turn.

Sources of information

Oral traditional, historical and archaeological sources all throw some light on the development of urbanization and the process of state emergence in this region but each of these sources suffers from particular limitations. Least valuable of them appears to be oral tradition, much of it preserved in later documentary sources. It attempts to explain the past with fantastic stories, and the Aksumite period, which is the main interest of this chapter, is somewhat beyond its range. Nevertheless, the most famous of Ethiopian oral traditions, that concerning the visit of the Queen of Sheba to Solomon and the consequent birth of the founder of the Ethiopian royal house (Buxton 1970: 34), does perhaps provide further corroboration of the Semitic contribution to Ethiopian developments that is indicated by other sources. It also seems that some of the legends may actually refer, very broadly, to real events and people and, overall, the oral traditions do at least indicate the importance of the remote past to later Ethiopians (Munro-Hay 1991: 9–16).

Historical sources are considerably more important and may be broken up into four different types. First of these are references to Ethiopia by classical writers. Thus Pliny the Younger (about 77 AD) mentioned Adulis (Munro-Hay 1991: 17), and the *Periplus of the Erythraean Sea*, also of the first century AD, mentions Adulis, Koloè and 'the city of the people called the Aksumites' (Kobishchanov 1979: 41; Anfray 1981: 363). Other similar sources are Claudius Ptolemy in the second century AD and Cosmas Indicopleustes of the sixth century AD (Kobishchanov 1979: 42). These and further classical sources give us a picture of a powerful Aksumite kingdom that was able to conquer parts of South Arabia in the sixth century AD and, before that, was already partly urbanized and exporting ivory, rhinoceros horn, tortoiseshell and obsidian through Adulis (Anfray 1981: 363). To these classical sources may also be added some early Islamic sources, that tell us a little more of Aksum's relationship with the outside world.

The second type of historical sources consists of inscriptions on stone found in Aksumite contexts, and inscriptions and representations on Aksumite coins. These constitute historical documents even though their discovery is the result of archaeological endeavour. They are particularly valuable because they are the only internal historical data that exist for the Aksumite period. Unlike Meroitic inscriptions, those from Aksumite or Pre-Aksumite times can be read, being written in Ge'ez (the old Ethiopian language), or in Sabaean (South Arabian) or even sometimes in Greek. Although seemingly intended as propaganda, and therefore of uncertain reliability, the inscribed stones provide information about important military exploits, such as King Ezana's apparent expedition to Meroë in the fourth century AD and King Kaleb's campaigns in South Arabia in the sixth century AD (Munro-Hay 1991: 228, 230). In addition they tell us the names and titles of some of the rulers of Aksum, as do the coins that may record as many as twenty-four different Aksumite kings (Pankhurst 1961: 401). The coins are also informative in other ways, recording, for instance, the fourth-century acceptance of Christianity, by replacing the pagan crescent and disc with the cross (Fig. 3.11). Nevertheless, this internal historical source material is very limited in what it can tell us about the Aksumite state and cities: so much so that scholars have even disagreed as to whether Ezana, one of the best known of Aksumite kings, was actually one king or two different kings (Munro-Hay 1980).

Few of these inscriptions are later than the fourth century and probably none is later than the ninth (Buxton 1970: 119). The Aksumite kingdom finally disappeared sometime between the seventh and the tenth century AD (Munro-Hay 1991: 93–4; Negussie 1994: 27–9) and there followed a period of some centuries for which there is very little historical source material, either internal or external. Occasionally, Arab or Western European authorities have something to say about Ethiopia but there is little of real value. It is not until the end of the fifteenth century that there is again a substantial body of external sources and these constitute the third type of historical data (Munro-Hay 1991:19–25). These writings, this time by European visitors, throw a great deal of light on traditional Ethiopian society from the sixteenth century onwards. Amongst these accounts, those by the Portuguese Francisco Alvares, relating to 1520–6, and by the Scotsman James Bruce, relating to 1768–73, stand out as remarkable but there were many other writers who made significant contributions (Pankhurst 1961: 100). Overall, these external sources of the second half of the second millennium AD provide one of the richest sources of ethnohistory available in any part of Africa. Because they are accounts by outsiders, however, they must always be treated with caution.

The fourth and final type of historical sources consists of writings by Ethiopians themselves. The oldest surviving manuscripts date from the thirteenth century but the greater part of Ethiopian writing was on religious subjects and provides little information on secular matters. However, royal chronicles were also written from the fourteenth century onwards and these form the principal source for later Ethiopian history, although their value is considered to be variable (Buxton 1970: 129; on Ethiopian history in general, see also Sergew 1972 and Taddesse 1972).

Rich though the historical sources are, therefore, it is apparent that many of them consist of observations by outsiders, and in addition they are frequently difficult to interpret. Furthermore, there are substantial periods and numerous subjects on which both outsiders and insiders have little to say. So far as the development of cities and states is concerned, it is clearly necessary to draw also on such archaeological data as are available.

There is, in fact, no shortage of archaeological evidence in Ethiopia. What is perhaps deficient is its investigation and publication. In particular, excavation has tended to concentrate on sites with Aksumite masonry structures and publication has been inclined to be descriptive, rather than concerned with analysis and synthesis. Perhaps the best of the older introductions to the subject of Aksumite archaeology is that by Joseph W. Michels, inserted at the beginning of his English edition of Yuri Kobishchanov's book on Aksum (Kobishchanov 1979: 1–34). In common with other scholars, Michels emphasized the importance of the pioneering work of the German Aksum expedition of 1906 and of the research programme of the Ethiopian Institute of Archaeology from the 1950s to the early 1970s. After the early 1970s, however, political events in Ethiopia prevented further archaeological fieldwork until the beginning of the 1990s. The resumption of such work, particularly by David Phillipson of the University of Cambridge, has added substantially to our knowledge of ancient Aksum (Phillipson 1994; 1995; 1996; Phillipson and Reynolds 1996). Furthermore, at about the same time, several important publications appeared which made the results of earlier research more accessible (Munro-Hay 1989a; 1991; Anfray 1990; Phillipson 1997).

Ethiopian archaeological evidence that is relevant to the present discussion can be divided into three main periods: Pre-Aksumite, Aksumite and medieval–modern Ethiopian. Their chronology remains uncertain but, roughly speaking, these periods represent the eighth century BC to the first century AD, the first century AD to the seventh–tenth centuries AD and the seventh–tenth centuries AD to the present. So far as the theme of this chapter is concerned, it is the first two of these which are of greatest importance and it is indeed these periods that have attracted most archaeological attention. Francis Anfray, who was responsible for much of the excavation in Ethiopia during the 1960s and early 1970s, suggested a further subdivision of these two periods. He divided the Pre-Aksumite into a South Arabian period, lasting from the fifth to the fourth century BC, and an Intermediate period, lasting from the third century BC to the first century AD. He saw the Aksumite period as continuing until the late ninth century AD, and divided it into two at the fifth century (Anfray 1968: 355–8). Similarly, Michels (1988; 1994) also argued for this long chronology, although his extended from 700 BC to AD 1000, differed in some other details, and was divided into seven phases. Indeed, Fattovich (1990b: 14–15) suggested a start for the Pre-Aksumite as early as the eighth or ninth century and possibly even the tenth century BC. In contrast, Munro-Hay (1991), considering only the Aksumite period and drawing heavily on his studies of Aksumite coinage, preferred a short chronology. This consisted of six phases commencing in the first century AD and terminating in the early seventh century, with the later seventh to the twelfth centuries placed in a Post-Aksumite period. To add to the confusion, a comparison of the stratigraphic evidence from Aksum and Matara led Negussie (1994) to conclude that (for the Aksumite period) a long chronology was indicated for Aksum itself but only a short one for Matara!

Setting aside these chronological difficulties, the best known of the Pre-Aksumite sites is that of Yeha, situated in the northern end of the Ethiopian Highlands, where the Aksumite state was to develop. In this place are the remains of a temple (Fig. 3.2) built of ashlar sandstone masonry set on a stepped base. Parts of this ruin still stand to a height of about 9 metres and the German Aksum expedition of 1906 was able to produce a remarkable reconstruction of the building (Buxton 1970: 88), which is thought to date from the sixth to fifth century BC and to have similarities to contemporary South Arabian buildings. According to Fattovich (1990b: 4) originally at least 13 metres in height, and measuring approximately 19 by 15 metres in area, the size and quality of masonry of the Yeha temple are very impressive indeed. When it is considered that it is probably roughly contemporary with the Parthenon in Athens, the implications of its existence for understanding the society that constructed it become extremely important. Yeha has also produced a number of inscriptions which are written in a South Arabian language and in a South Arabian script. There is, in addition, a cemetery of subterranean tombs (which has yielded a large collection of distinctive artefacts, including very fine objects of bronze) and the site of a stone building which excavation has shown to have been destroyed by a violent fire. Anfray, who excavated a part of this latter structure, which is known as Grat-Be'al-Guebri, was of the opinion that it was a palace. Yeha also seems to have other occupation deposits and it appears reasonable to conclude that it was an early urban centre. It should be noticed that iron was already in use and that amongst the bronze objects recovered from Yeha are some curious 'identification marks', consisting of openwork geometrical or animal designs which often incorporate alphabetical characters. These appear to have been a type of personal seal and their impressions have been found on pottery (Buxton 1970: 36–7; Anfray 1972a; 1990: 26–7; Michels, in Kobishchanov 1979: 10–12; de Contenson 1981).

The strong South Arabian influence seen at Yeha is also apparent in the two localities of Haoulti-Melazo, situated in the same general area as Yeha, where several sites have produced Pre-Aksumite material. There is some dispute over the interpretation of the stratigraphic contexts of this evidence but it includes

Fig. 3.2 Inside the Pre-Aksumite temple at Yeha, Ethiopia. Parts of this ruin are 9 metres in height. Photographed 1996.

numerous fragments of dressed stone with South Arabian inscriptions, two limestone statues of seated female figures and a sophisticated limestone throne decorated with low-relief carving. It also includes symbolism associated with the
moon-god, Almouqah, who was apparently venerated in the northern part of
Ethiopia as well as in South Arabia. The statues are comparable with one of
similar date found accidentally at a place on the eastern edge of the Ethiopian
Highlands known as Addi Galamo, but formerly referred to as Azbi Dera, or
Haouilé Assaraou. This was found with a number of other things, including a
broken altar showing the crescent and disc of Almouqah. South Arabian influence
has been seen in all of this evidence (Doresse 1959: 42; de Contenson 1962; 1963b;
van Beek 1967; Pirenne 1970; Michels, in Kobishchanov 1979: 12–13; de Contenson
1981; Fattovich 1990b).

Pre-Aksumite material is known from a total of about ninety sites, extending
from northern Eritrea into Tigray (Fattovich 1990b: 3), although many of these
sites are in the area between Aksum and Yeha, having been identified during a
uniquely detailed surface survey conducted by Joseph Michels (Michels 1988;
1994). There seems little doubt that the earliest Pre-Aksumite culture was strongly
influenced by South Arabia; this is indicated by both stylistic and linguistic evidence. Nevertheless, from the beginning, Pre-Aksumite culture showed signs of
originality and gradually it developed distinctive characteristics of its own, while
those of South Arabia slowly faded. In particular, the language and script used for
inscriptions grew less and less like the South Arabian from which it had originated,
and more and more like Ge'ez, the ancestor of the Eritrean and Ethiopian languages Tigré, Tigrinya and Amharic. At first a consonantal syllabary, it was not
until the fourth century AD that a system of vocalization was introduced and this
was clearly an Ethiopian development (Buxton 1970: 30–1, 178).

Overall, the Pre-Aksumite period deserves far more attention from researchers
than it has yet been given. Its formative role, so far as later developments were concerned, was probably so important that it would be appropriate to give its archaeological manifestations a more distinctive name, such as 'Yehan'. The South
Arabian influences seem to have been from the kingdom of Saba, which may have
originated as early as the late second millennium BC, and Pre-Aksumite inscriptions in Sabaean indicate the existence of a state known as *D'mt* by the mid-first
millennium BC. Located in Tigray and adjacent parts of Eritrea, this development
was associated with modest urban growth at least at Yeha and Matara.
Disintegration seems to have followed during the last two or three centuries BC,
however, and it remains difficult to relate the Pre-Aksumite socio-political situation to that of the subsequent Aksumite period (Fattovich 1990b).

Nevertheless, it seems probable that the Aksumite culture was a development
from the Pre-Aksumite, although in time it came to be characterized by quite
unique qualities. Archaeological evidence for the Aksumite period is more

common than for the Pre-Aksumite, and while Pre-Aksumite evidence suggests that urbanization and state formation may have been at an early stage, Aksumite evidence clearly indicates a society in which these processes had reached a relatively mature stage. Some suggestion of continuity between the two has been provided by excavations at Bieta Giyorgis, just to the north-west of Aksum, which have revealed late Pre-Aksumite occupation overlain by early Aksumite deposits (Bard *et al.* 1997).

Undoubtedly the most important and most thoroughly researched of the Aksumite sites is Aksum itself. It is justly famous for its stelae, tall, thin, standing stones of which the largest have been carefully carved to represent multi-storeyed buildings, although many stelae are small and undressed. Such standing stones are also known at other Aksumite sites, and indeed are a widespread phenomenon in north-east Africa (Fattovich 1987), but none of them has such enormous proportions or such careful finishing and decoration as some of those in the main stelae group at Aksum. One of the larger ones of that group still stands and it consists of a single block of granite 21 metres high (plus about 3 metres underground), carved to represent nine storeys, with a false door at its base (Fig. 3.3). The fallen pieces of a taller one (about 28 metres long and carved to represent ten storeys) were taken to Rome in 1937 and re-erected there, although in the late 1990s arrangements were being made for its return. The largest of all, however, lies broken on the ground at Aksum (Fig. 3.4) and was nearly 33 metres in length, being carved to represent twelve storeys (on the counting of storeys on Aksumite stelae see Buxton and Matthews 1974: 57). Phillipson (1994: 192) described this monster stela as 'a strong candidate for consideration as the largest single monolith which humans have ever proceeded to erect'. Indeed, van Beek suggested that perhaps it fell while being erected (van Beek 1967: 117). Over 140 of these curious archaeological phenomena are known from four main groups in Aksum, although most are far smaller than those just described. In addition, 'well over 100 stele [*sic*] (possibly up to 300)', both Pre-Aksumite and early Aksumite in date, are thought to have existed at the Ona Enda Aboi Zague site on the northern side of Bieta Giyorgis hill (Bard and Fattovich 1993: 17).

Excavations amongst the main stelae group at Aksum have addressed both the question of their purpose and the problem of their date. Work by Chittick (1974a; Munro-Hay 1989a) and Phillipson (1994; 1995; 1996; Phillipson and Reynolds 1996) revealed extensive, subterranean, multi-chambered Aksumite tombs, so that it seems that the area was intended to serve as a cemetery. In particular, the largest stela appears to have been intended to be a marker for two monumental underground tombs: a stone-built 'Mausoleum' to its west, over 16 metres long and with no less than ten side-chambers, and a possibly similar structure to its east that has been only partly investigated and which may never have been completed. Indeed, it now seems that van Beek may have been correct in his suggestion that this giant

Fig. 3.3 Granite Stelae 3 and 6 at Aksum, Ethiopia. Stela 3, which still stands, is the third largest of the storeyed stelae and Stela 6 the smallest. Stela 3 after Krencker (1913: Tafel VI) as reproduced in van Beek (1967: Plate 2); Stela 6 after Krencker (1913: Tafel II) as reproduced in Phillipson (1997: Fig. 13).

stela fell and broke during the process of erection. Only 2.8 metres of its 33 metre
length was intended to be set into the ground, there is no sign of base-plates such as
were fitted to the other large stelae after erection was completed, and it is possible
that the Mausoleum was never actually used for burial. This stela probably represents the last of a series of storeyed stelae, each having been taller than its immediate predecessor until the inevitable disaster occurred. Significantly, no attempt
seems to have been made to clear up the debris or to replace the stela, suggesting
that the whole project might have been abandoned after it fell. Phillipson provisionally dated this event to the fourth century AD and Munro-Hay (1991: 68) put it
at approximately 400 AD. Broadly coinciding with the official adoption of
Christianity at Aksum by King Ezana, which Munro-Hay (1991: 78) put at around
333 AD, it might have been this ideological change that led to the project's abandonment. Certainly, the form of elite tombs seems to have changed at this time; the
nearby 'Tomb of the False Door', discovered and named by Chittick in the early
1970s, consists of a subterranean granite-built chamber covered by a squat surface
structure which appears to have been intended to represent a temple or palace.
Lacking an associated stela but retaining a carving of a door similar to those on the
storeyed stelae, it appears that this represents an early stage in the Christianizing of
the burial tradition, dating to perhaps the fifth century AD. A little to the north of
Aksum lie twin subterranean tombs traditionally attributed to the sixth-century

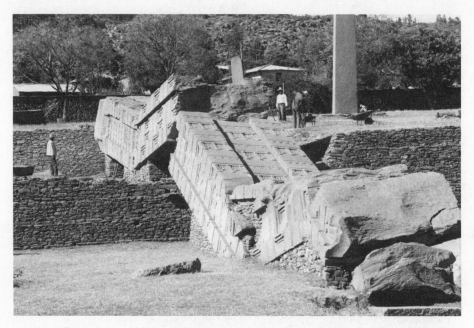

Fig. 3.4 Fallen Stela 1 at Aksum. Nearly 33 metres in length, it is the largest of the stelae and
probably fell while being erected. Reproduced by permission of David Phillipson.

kings Kaleb and Gebra Maskal, which appear to mark a further stage in this process.

Other than the largest stela, it is often difficult to associate these standing stones with specific tombs and in many cases impossible, but it does seem as if they were primarily intended to act as tomb-markers. It is apparent that the area of the main stelae group at Aksum was used for burial from at least the first or second century AD. A series of terraces and platforms was gradually built up, on what originally must have been a gentle slope. Stelae were erected on these platforms, beneath which were subterranean tombs. So long did this process continue that a number of stelae of rougher, earlier type were actually buried upright by later deposits and some of the later carved stelae also had their lower parts covered (Munro-Hay 1989a: 330). In addition to the tombs already mentioned, the main stelae area contained several shaft tombs and an extensive rock-cut tomb called the 'Tomb of the Brick Arches' (Fig. 3.5), which was discovered and named by Chittick. Probably dating to the late third century AD, this latter tomb had not suffered quite so much from robbers as most of the others investigated, and excavations within it by both Chittick and Phillipson produced substantial amounts of important cultural material. More difficult to understand is the curious structure known as the Nefas Mawcha, which is situated adjacent to the main stelae group, and which seems also to have been a tomb. This consisted of a giant granite slab, 17.3 metres long, 6.5 metres wide and 1.1–1.7 metres in thickness, that rested on supporting slabs and walls. This enormous slab is thought to weigh about 360 tonnes and its suppporting structure had collapsed in antiquity owing to its being struck by the largest of the stelae when it fell, weighing as it probably did some 517 tonnes (Chittick 1974a: 183–6; Phillipson 1994: 192, 197). The Nefas Mawcha must, therefore, pre-date the fall of the largest stela; Munro-Hay (1989a: 120) suggested that it belongs to the third century AD. It seems probable that it was originally underground, covered by rubble and soil, although it is possible that it was still unfinished when it was wrecked by the falling stela (Phillipson 1999).

Ancient tombs also exist in other parts of Aksum, usually associated with stelae. To the south-east of the city, for instance, is the large rock-cut tomb known as the 'Tomb of King Bazen', so completely robbed that it is undatable, but traditionally attributed to the legendary King Bazen who was supposed to have been contemporary with the birth of Christ (Munro-Hay 1991: 13). Potentially more informative, however, is the so-called 'Gudit Stelae Field', south-west of Aksum, which seems to have been a cemetery for 'middle-class' Aksumites, rather than for the rulers and other members of the elite for whom the other tombs were constructed (Tarekegn 1996: 614). Nevertheless, modest though the Gudit Stelae Field tomb known as 'GT II' was, Chittick's excavations recovered mid-third-century glassware of high quality, in spite of the previous depredations of tomb-robbers (Munro-Hay 1989a: 143–6, 190–1).

Fig. 3.5 View up the stairway of the Tomb of the Brick Arches at Aksum. Reproduced by permission of David Phillipson.

In addition to stelae and tombs at Aksum, there are a number of stone platforms which have been interpreted as the bases of thrones (Phillipson 1995: 33–5). Such thrones seem to have been important in Aksumite culture: one existed also at the site of Matara, they are mentioned in two inscriptions of King Ezana, and in the sixth century Cosmas Indicopleustes saw one close to a stela at Adulis. Ezana's inscriptions also say that he erected metal statues and although none of these has been found, a stone slab was discovered in Aksum at the beginning of the twentieth century that had hollowed-out footprints 92 centimetres long. If this slab really was the plinth for a statue, as has been claimed, then the statue must have been of enormous size (Anfray 1981: 372; Phillipson 1998a: 30).

Aksum is also notable for the discovery of several Greek, South Arabian and Ge'ez stone-cut inscriptions of the fourth-century King Ezana, in whose reign Christianity appears to have been adopted (Pankhurst 1961: 28–30; Munro-Hay 1991: 224–9). These inscriptions, already referred to several times, are of very great historical significance. It is rare indeed that African archaeological evidence can speak to us so directly: 'I will rule the people', claims Ezana, 'with righteousness and justice, and will not oppress them, and may they preserve this Throne which I have set up for the Lord of Heaven' (Pankhurst 1961: 30).

Similarly of great interest, Aksum has produced some extraordinary residential building evidence, that throws a remarkable light on Aksumite society. At the beginning of the twentieth century, the German Aksum expedition excavated three multi-roomed structures of monumental scale, that were provisionally identified as palaces. These are known, respectively, by the names Enda Mika'el, Enda Semon and Ta'akha Mariam (Phillipson 1997: 93–120). An attempt was made by the German expedition to produce architectural reconstructions of these buildings, using both the excavated archaeological evidence and evidence from ancient church construction still observable in the area. The result for the central part of Enda Mika'el was a castle-like structure of four square towers, standing four storeys high on a stepped base. In the case of Ta'akha Mariam the reconstruction was even more impressive, producing a huge complex of courtyards and towers and connecting buildings, that measured overall 80 by 120 metres and was of two storeys and, in places, three storeys in height (Buxton 1970: 93; Michels, in Kobishchanov 1979: 6; Phillipson 1998a: 84–6). A careful reconsideration of the evidence led Buxton and Matthews (1974: 55, Figs. 6–8) to suggest that the Enda Mika'el was of only three storeys and of a somewhat different design, but their suggested reconstruction still indicated the former existence of a most impressive structure (Fig. 3.6).

These buildings, in common with other major Aksumite buildings now known, were of a quite distinctive architectural style (Buxton 1970: 91–102; Buxton and Matthews 1974). They were built on a massive masonry podium or base with stepped sides, a feature of Pre-Aksumite and South Arabian origin that must have

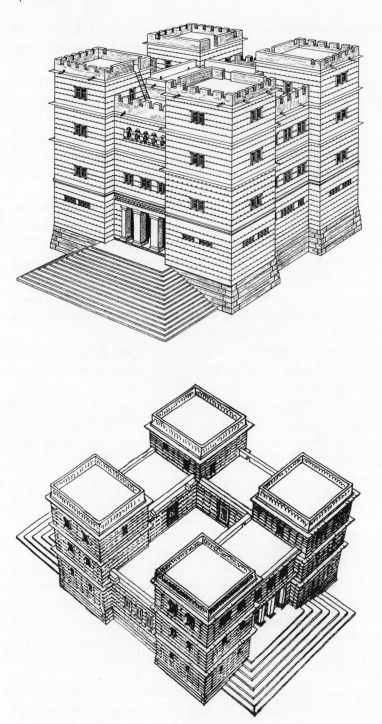

Fig. 3.6 Alternative reconstructions of Enda Mika'el at Aksum. The one above, based on Krencker (1913: Abb. 245), is probably less accurate than that below, which is based on Buxton and Matthews (1974: Fig. 8).

increased a building's apparent height. They were also built with a characteristic 'indented' plan, that is to say both the podium and the wall surfaces above were alternately recessed and projecting, a design that must have given the buildings an appearance of great strength. The upper storeys are thought to have been built of mud-mortared rubble reinforced with timber, a type of construction that left the ends of some timbers projecting from the walls at the corners of windows and doors and at intervals along the wall surfaces. This constructional method (Fig. 3.7) is known from excavated archaeological evidence (e.g. Chittick 1974a: 190–1; Munro-Hay 1989a: 138, Plate 8.8), from its representation on the largest examples of the stelae (Buxton and Matthews 1974), and from the tenth- or eleventh-century church of Debra Damo, studied by the German Aksum expedition but also by Matthews and Mordini (1959). With evidence from Debra Damo and elsewhere, Matthews was even able to attempt several reconstructions of Aksumite interiors (Buxton 1970: 94–5; Buxton and Matthews 1974: Figs. 12, 18, 28). However, Anfray (1981: 370) questioned whether the walls of such structures would have been strong enough to support more than two storeys. He conceded that it was just possible, but rather unlikely, that some of these elite buildings had three storeys 'but to imagine more than that seems far-fetched'. Nevertheless, Anfray goes on to point out that in the sixth century AD Cosmas Indicopleustes wrote that in Ethiopia he saw a 'royal dwelling with four towers'. Whatever the exact details, therefore, it does seem that these monumental residential structures were attempting to achieve the impression of great height. After all, even two storeys, set on a solid masonry base, would have the appearance of a three-storey building. That

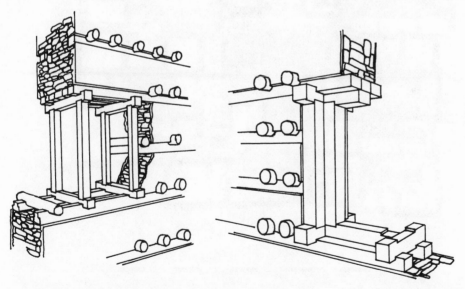

Fig. 3.7 Aksumite constructional method: window to left, doorway to right. After Krencker (1913: Abb. 9, 15) as reproduced in Gerster (1970: Fig. 25).

African civilizations

they were in all probability quite imposing buildings has, in fact, been demonstrated again in more recent times with the excavation by Anfray himself of the so-
called 'Dongur Mansion', on the western side of Aksum. Excavated in 1966–8, this
proved to be a forty-room complex occupying an area of approximately 3000
square metres and with its remains still standing in places to a height of 5 metres.
The stone-built complex comprised a central structure and a series of interior
courtyards that created separate blocks of rooms (Fig. 3.8). It was thought by its
excavator to date to about the seventh century AD. Rather smaller than Ta'akha
Mariam, Anfray interpreted it as a villa of a member of the elite, not a royal palace
(Anfray 1968: 360–3; 1972b: Plate I for plan; 1981: 365–6; 1990: 97, 100–3; Michels,
in Kobishchanov 1979: 7–8). With its numerous rooms and its various courtyards,

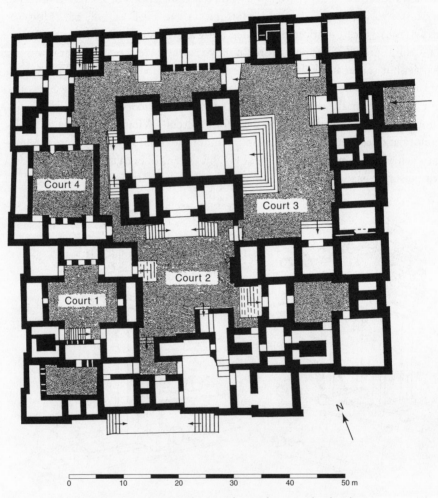

Fig. 3.8 Plan of 'Dongur Mansion' at Aksum. After Anfray (1972b: Planche I).

the Dongur Mansion could have housed numerous retainers, craftsmen, servants and slaves, as well as an elite extended family. It may also have provided storage for agricultural produce and trade goods. Indeed, Munro-Hay (1991: 49) has suggested that this and similar complexes may have been 'local village centres surrounding landlord's [*sic*] houses'.

Excavations elsewhere in and around Aksum have indicated the existence of other stone buildings, some of which must have had more humble purposes than those discussed above. Phillipson and Reynolds (1996: 142–3), for instance, have uncovered the remains of roughly built, stone domestic buildings, about a kilometre north of Aksum, which have been interpreted as part of a 'middle-rank settlement'. It seems likely, indeed, that Aksum was a fairly extensive city of some importance during the first millennium AD. Excavations by Chittick at the base of the hill behind the main stelae group at Aksum (Chittick 1974a: 191) have also provided some indication of the impact of such a city on its immediate environment. The following erosional cycle has been suggested: (1) felling of trees on the hillside in early Aksumite times; (2) cultivation of the hillside and the construction of houses on its slopes; (3) erosion of the hillside over a comparatively short period, ceasing before late Aksumite times; (4) accumulation of recent colluvium. The hillside in question is now largely rocky, with little soil, leading one to wonder whether the eventual decline and disappearance of the city of Aksum may have been linked to an environmental decline, triggered by a high density of population.

Amongst other Aksumite sites, Matara is one of the most important and certainly one of the most extensively investigated (Fig. 3.9). Now in Eritrea, it lies about half-way between the Aksumite port of Adulis and the Aksumite capital of Aksum and is likely, therefore, to have been a place of economic and political significance. Indeed, the site appears to have been a key urban centre, occupying about 20 hectares, and the deep deposits (up to 5 metres) contain evidence of two main phases of occupation: first a South Arabian period of about 500–300 BC and then (after a long abandonment) an Aksumite period of about AD 700. Tombs, churches and residential buildings were excavated by Anfray, and amongst the latter both elite houses and ordinary dwellings were discovered. Mound B yielded a large, multi-roomed mansion, comparable to those excavated at Aksum and three other similar 'villas' were also uncovered. In addition, however, there were houses of only two or three rooms and others that were intermediate in size between these and the villas, suggesting a social hierarchy. Certainly some of the residents of Matara must have had considerable wealth, because there was recovered from this site a remarkable hoard of goldwork of Roman and Byzantine origin. In addition, some material sophistication is suggested by the presence of a piped water supply, provided by fitting the bodies of amphorae one within the other, that served the baptistery of the principal church discovered. Perhaps the most important thing about Matara, however, is that its excavation provided the best indications presently available of Aksumite urban layout (Anfray 1963; 1967; 1974; 1981: 367–8; Anfray and Annequin 1965; Michels, in Kobishchanov 1979: 14–16).

There are also important urban sites of Aksumite culture at Adulis, on the coast, and at Kohaito, north of Matara, both places now in Eritrea. The remains of

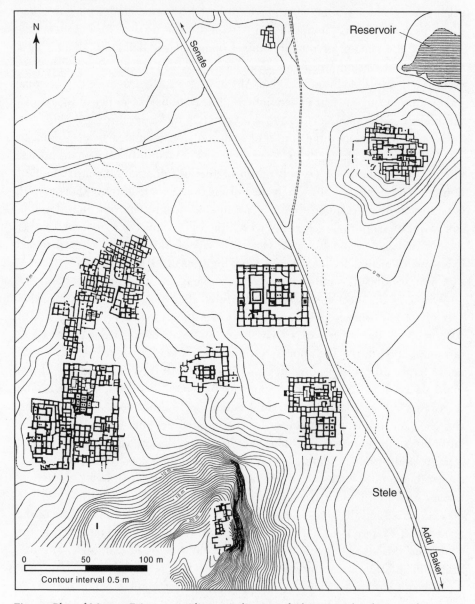

Fig. 3.9 Plan of Matara, Eritrea, providing an indication of Aksumite urban layout. After Anfray (1974: Fig. 7).

stone buildings of Aksumite style have been excavated at Adulis and artefacts of both Aksumite and Mediterranean origin have been found there, indicating its role in long-distance trade (Paribeni 1907; Anfray 1974; Munro-Hay 1989b). Kohaito, like Matara sometimes thought to be the Koloè which is mentioned in the *Periplus of the Erythraean Sea* (p. 72), has not been excavated but is best known for a dam, built of carefully fitted blocks of stone, that is 67 metres long and about 3 metres high (Anfray 1981: 368). This dam was designed to form an artificial reservoir of water, and Pankhurst (1961: 24) has called it 'one of the greatest engineering feats of the Aksumites'. A further Aksumite site worth mention is at Gobedra Hill, about 4 kilometres west of Aksum itself. At this place are quarries from which came the granite used for the dressed stones of local Aksumite buildings and for some of the stelae. There are also traces of a road by which such material was transported to Aksum. In addition, a late Aksumite stone-built structure was excavated at Ouchatei Golo near here by de Contenson, who suggested that it represented a Christian church of a special type, and undressed stelae were found in its vicinity (de Contenson 1961; Michels, in Kobishchanov 1979: 10; Phillipson 1994: 192; 1998a: 92).

There are, however, far more Aksumite sites known than have been excavated or concerning which there are individual published studies. Anfray (1973: 21) published a site distribution map, which showed how the nuclear area of the Aksumite state must have been located in the north-eastern corner of the Ethiopian Highlands, between Aksum and Adulis. Anfray also proposed a distinction between an eastern and a western Aksumite province, the archaeological record suggesting that the eastern province was more prosperous but that the western was the centre of political power. To such traditional archaeological site survey, Michels added a modern touch by carrying out a stratified random sampling procedure of all archaeological evidence in a 40 per cent sample of a 500 square kilometre area, in the Aksum–Yeha region. The result of this work was the discovery and documentation of about 260 sites, ranging from single compounds to large towns, and including temples, stelae fields, tombs and workshops. This survey revealed only a sample of the Aksumite settlement pattern and suggested that much evidence still remained to be located in other areas. However, it did shed some light on Aksumite political organization and demonstrated that the fertile soil of the Aksumite Plain had been a factor in the development of that organization (Michels, in Kobishchanov 1979: 22–4; Michels 1988; 1994).

Before leaving this discussion of Aksumite archaeological evidence, one final point should be stressed. This is that inscriptions, coins and imported items have been found in most of the sites that have been investigated to any extent. Their repeated occurrence emphasizes, if such emphasis is needed, the level of sophistication achieved by Aksumite culture. They also provide important historical data, of which scholars are able to make use.

The chronological problems already discussed (pp. 74–5) make it difficult to date the end of the Aksumite period. Significantly, the issue of coinage ceased early in the seventh century and subsequently there seem to have been few imports or stone buildings. It appears that the economic and political base of the Aksumite state was seriously weakened by the extension of Arab control over the Red Sea trade route to the eastern Mediterranean. Plague, drought and environmental deterioration may also have been factors contributing to Aksumite decline. Then, late in the tenth century AD, according to legend the Aksumite state was finally destroyed by an Agau chieftainess called Gudit from further south. As a result, the political centre of gravity eventually moved south to the Lalibela area, where it was to remain for some centuries (Buxton 1970: 44; Munro-Hay 1990; 1991). An Ethiopian state survived down to modern times but for the earlier part of the second millennium it seems to have lost its previous urban character, with its rulers leading a semi-nomadic life in an unending succession of camps, which Pankhurst (1979) has called 'moving capitals'. Such a camp might consist of as many as 100,000 people and continual movement seems to have been necessitated by the rapid exhaustion in any one area of the supplies of food and firewood. As a result, visible archaeological evidence for the first half of the millennium is dominated by ecclesiastical structures, for not only did Christianity survive and flourish but it also constituted almost the only static element of importance in Ethiopian society. Some remarkable 'built-up' churches from this period have been studied, including Debra Damo, which has already been mentioned. Rock-hewn churches are more numerous, however, having survived rather more readily. These have a very long history but mainly date from about the tenth to about the fifteenth or early sixteenth century, the most remarkable of them apparently belonging to around the thirteenth century (Buxton 1970: 97–115). Best known of the rock-hewn churches are those of Lalibela but there are also many in Tigray Province and others scattered widely across the Ethiopian Highlands. They provide remarkable evidence of technical skill and of an ability to marshal the material resources implied by these often vast undertakings. The church of St George at Lalibela, for instance, is a complex and sophisticated 'building' entirely carved, inside and out, from one gigantic block of stone (10.6 metres high) that had first to be isolated in a huge quarry-pit (Phillipson 1998a: Plate 10). Published accounts of Ethiopian rock-hewn churches include Buxton (1947; 1971), Gerster (1970), and Plant (1985).

In the latter half of the second millennium AD, 'static capitals', as Pankhurst (1979) has called them, tended to replace the frequently moved camps, although even these more stable settlements were shifted periodically or used only seasonally. Beginning in the late sixteenth and early seventeenth century there grew up a practice of constructing stone castles, which formed the nuclei of capitals. It was one of these castles that was studied at Gouzara by Annequin (1965), but the most successful of these castle-based capitals was that at Gondar, north of Lake Tana, where no less than twenty successive emperors made their capital prior to the nine-teenth century. In the meantime, churches continued to be built. Right down to modern times Aksum, much reduced in size, has continued to be important as a religious centre. It is popularly believed by Ethiopians that the true Ark of the Covenant is kept there and such emperors as were able to do so went there for their coronation (Pankhurst 1979: 4–6). It could be argued that this typifies the continu-ity that has so often been claimed to be characteristic of Ethiopian culture. Indeed, archaeological evidence supports the idea of such continuity: some ecclesiastical buildings make use of Aksumite ruins as foundations, such as the 'Old Cathedral' of Maryam Tsion at Aksum (Phillipson 1995: 31–2), and some rock-hewn churches have Aksumite architectural features. Unfortunately, however, archaeologists have paid little attention to the last thousand years of Ethiopia's past, so that the iden-tification and excavation of sites of both 'static' and 'moving' settlements from these centuries remains one of the archaeological challenges of the future.

Subsistence economy

What light does archaeological evidence in Ethiopia and Eritrea throw on the origins of cities and of the state in that part of Africa? For instance, what is known of the subsistence economy on which these developments must ultimately have depended? Until the Phillipson excavations of the 1990s, the quick answer was that very little was known, as might be expected of a type of archaeology that had been mainly interested in architecture, sculpture, inscriptions, coins, objects of fine craftsmanship and artefacts generally. Botanical remains and animal bones had not been given the same attention. An indication of the character of much of the earlier archaeological research in Ethiopia may be gained from the fact that Phillipson (1977a: 98) could claim that 'no analysis of food remains from an Axumite site has ever been undertaken'.

Some scholars probably thought that the lack of archaeological data for subsis-tence hardly mattered. Kobishchanov, for instance, was able to reconstruct the Aksumite subsistence base from information taken from inscriptions and other his-torical sources. According to him, both terracing and irrigation were practised and ox-drawn ploughs were in use. Wheat and other cereals were grown, viticulture existed and large herds of cattle, sheep and goats were kept, as well as asses and mules. He also claimed that elephants had been domesticated but were reserved for use by the royal court (Kobishchanov 1981: 383). Subsequently, Phillipson has been able to confirm parts of this picture with archaeological evidence. Excavations in an area of sixth-century AD domestic occupation, a kilometre to the north of Aksum, produced plant remains amongst which were wheat, barley, teff, a range of pulses, grape, gourd, noog (*nug*), linseed, cotton, brassica and nuts (Phillipson and Reynolds 1996; Phillipson 1998b). In addition, a substantial quantity of ivory was found within the Tomb of the Brick Arches (Phillipson 1995). Detailed analysis of excavated faunal material is still awaited, however, although pottery figurines of shorthorn humpless cattle and of a pair of yoked oxen have been described from Chittick's excavations (Munro-Hay 1989a: 240, 256–7). Furthermore, excavations at Bieta Giyorgis have yielded cattle and sheep and/or goat bones, as well as evidence of wheat, barley, teff, lentils and grapes (Bard *et al.* 1997). It is to be expected that direct archaeological evidence will eventually confirm the important role that domesticated livestock seem to have played in the economy. Witness, for instance, the inscriptions of Ezana, recording, as they do, such figures as 31,957 head of cattle, 51,050 sheep and 827 'beasts of burden'; figures remarkable not only for their size but also for an exactitude that suggests that they may have been the result of counting rather than guesswork (Munro-Hay 1991: 227–8). Overall, some indication of the level of development of Aksumite agriculture is surely provided by the number and size of settlements that it was apparently able to support.

Although direct evidence for Pre-Aksumite subsistence is lacking, bronze sickles were found at Yeha and Haoulti; the latter site also yielded pottery models of cattle, sometimes wearing yokes; and grindstones were found at various sites (de Contenson 1963b: Plate 36; 1981: 356–7; Michels, in Kobishchanov 1979: 14; Anfray 1990: 47). This would suggest that cattle breeding, use of the plough and the cultivation of cereals were already of importance in the first millennium BC. Some support for this interpretation was provided by the excavation by Joanne Dombrowski of Lalibela Cave, east of Lake Tana (Phillipson 1977a: 69), which produced evidence of cultivated barley, chickpeas and some unspecified legumes, together with bones tentatively identified as cattle and small stock bones. This evidence was associated with stone artefacts and came from a first-millennium BC context. Indeed, it seems likely that agriculture developed at an even earlier date in Ethiopia. Portères (1970: 54–5) regarded it as one of the 'primary cradles of agriculture of Africa'. Simoons (1965) suggested that cereal–plough agriculture pre-dated the advent of South Arabian migrants in the first millennium BC, to whom its introduction has often been attributed as a modification of earlier cultivation practices. In addition, Ehret (1979; 1998: 10) used linguistic evidence to argue for a substantial antiquity of agriculture in Ethiopia, originating as much as 7000 or more years ago. However, there is a lack of archaeological evidence for this, although undated Ethiopian and Eritrean rock-paintings depict cattle and herdsmen, fat-tailed sheep, and even a man with an ox-drawn plough (Phillipson 1993b: 351–3).

Clearly, by Pre-Aksumite and Aksumite times a strong subsistence base had been developed, consisting of a broad-based mixed agriculture. Within this, it seems likely that wheat and barley played a particularly important part: Munro-Hay (1991: 185–6) has commented on the frequent depiction of ears of wheat or barley framing the royal bust on Aksumite coins, and Phillipson (1993b: 354–5) has concluded that it is specifically emmer wheat that is represented. Pottery items resembling the modern trays on which *injera* (the flat sour bread made from teff) is prepared appear only in the late Aksumite period (Munro-Hay 1989a: 308, 311). This would suggest that this small and hardy cereal, which will grow at higher altitudes than wheat and barley (Phillipson 1993b: 349), and which now forms such an important part of diet in the Ethiopian Highlands, was not of such significance in Aksumite times. In this respect, it is important to stress again the significance of the high fertility of the Aksumite Plain. On the basis of local farmers' opinions, Michels (1994: 62–3) classified its soil as 'good to excellent', supporting 'a full range of cereal crops (teff, wheat, barley, sorghum)' on land whose gradient is 'optimal for plow cultivation' but which 'requires no fertility intervention other than crop rotation, and relies upon seasonal rains'. In short, the heartland of the Aksumite state lay in an area which was particularly advantaged so far as cereal cultivation was concerned, and which almost certainly was capable of producing a storable surplus. Given the range of other plant foods that were also cultivated, and given the substantial numbers of livestock that were raised, Aksumite subsistence economy must have been exceptionally strong.

Technology

In contrast to the situation with subsistence economy, Ethiopian and Eritrean archaeological evidence is highly informative on the technology of the periods under discussion. As with the middle Nile, there exists some difficulty in discriminating between things made in Ethiopia or Eritrea by local craftsmen and those imported from elsewhere or made in Ethiopia or Eritrea by expatriate craftsmen (p. 53). An attempt must be made to separate the indigenous from the foreign, although some uncertainty will remain as to how reliably this can be done. In general terms, however, it does appear that the technological achievements, of the Aksumite period in particular, must rank amongst the most sophisticated to be found in precolonial Africa.

First, some Aksumite sites have provided evidence of remarkable engineering skills. To quarry and transport and attempt to erect such a monolith as the largest of the stelae at Aksum, nearly 33 metres long and about 517 tonnes in weight, must have involved theoretical knowledge, practical skill and good organization. Furthermore, although this was the most outstanding achievement of this sort it was not alone. There is the giant 360 tonne granite slab of the Nefas Mawcha and there are substantial numbers of other stelae that, although smaller, still imply the existence of considerable engineering ability. It also appears that this ability could be directed to practical as well as ceremonial purposes. The dam at Kohaito and the Mai Shum reservoir at Aksum (Butzer 1981: 479), although neither is securely dated (Munro-Hay 1991: 168), suggest that engineering expertise was applied to the task of water storage. Related to this, there was probably in addition extensive practice of both terracing and irrigation, as claimed from historical sources. So far as the archaeological evidence is concerned, however, it was in quarrying and carving and manipulating masses of stone that the Aksumites evinced their main engineering ability. These skills had a long history, from the cutting of Pre-Aksumite subterranean tombs to the quarrying of the medieval rock-hewn churches, and it seems reasonable to claim for them an indigenous origin. It should be no surprise that the inhabitants of an area as rocky as the Ethiopian Highlands should become expert in handling stone.

Aksumite archaeological evidence can, indeed, throw a good deal of light on the details of that expertise (Phillipson 1994). Granite quarries to the west of Aksum still have rows of slots that were cut for the insertion of either iron or wooden wedges, the latter probably tightly driven while dry and then soaked with water, so that their expansion split away the large pieces of stone needed for stelae and other purposes. Indeed, some of the stelae still standing at Aksum have traces of these slots, that were not completely removed by the percussive stone-dressing employed to finish their surfaces. The extent to which such finishing was carried out seems to have varied greatly, no doubt depending on the importance of the client and the cost of the job, but the Aksumite masons were clearly capable of very high quality work. The storeyed stelae, for instance, have dressed surfaces that are both accurate and attractive, with the north face of the one still standing faintly showing the bands of careful tooling that were necessary to achieve this. Furthermore, indented parts of the decoration on the largest stela have their edges elaborately undercut, so that when lit by the sun the resulting shadows enhance the apparent relief. Even with the hardened iron tools that must have been employed, it would have required an extraordinary combination of skill, patience, time-expenditure and sheer determination to produce such results in a material as obdurate as granite (although David Phillipson (1999) tells me that most of what is called granite at Aksum is technically syenite, which is rather softer). In contrast, the archaeological evidence would also suggest that Aksumite knowledge of mechanics was somewhat deficient. With less than a tenth of the length of the largest stela intended to go into the ground, it would appear that the centre of gravity had either not been calculated or had been calculated incorrectly. It is little wonder that it probably fell during the course of erection, although a comment by architect Ruth Plant (1985: 22) raises the possibility that an earthquake could have been responsible, a possibility that Phillipson (1999) thinks unlikely.

Aksumites also handled stone with great skill architecturally, and building construction was an area of technology where Pre-Aksumites, Aksumites and medieval Ethiopians all excelled. Using mud-mortared stonework tied together with timber reinforcements to construct stepped and indented walls, which were strengthened at the corners with dry-laid ashlar masonry, the Aksumites were able to construct monumental elite residences of up to three storeys. It is possible that the architecture of these major buildings was influenced by Roman style, conveyed perhaps via Syria, with which early Christian Ethiopia had connections (Michels, in Kobishchanov 1979: 27), but whatever the source of the style the workmanship was distinctively Aksumite. Building skills also extended to tombs, temples, early churches and structures of lesser importance. In addition to employing stone (of several types) and timber, Aksumite builders learned both to manufacture and to use fired bricks, and the construction of brick arches and of brick barrel-vaulting were both understood. Lime mortar and lime render were also used – although rarely, perhaps because of the quantity of wood needed to burn the limestone raw material (Chittick 1974a: 172, 186; Munro-Hay 1989a: 162–3; Phillipson 1995). So far as ordinary domestic buildings are concerned, the small number of excavated examples of stone houses (Anfray 1974: 756, Figure 7; Phillipson and Reynolds 1996: 142–3) are supplemented by both Pre-Aksumite and Aksumite pottery models. These came, respectively, from Haoulti (de Contenson 1963b: Plates 37–9) and from Aksum (Munro-Hay 1989a: 288; 1991: 254), and provide evidence for both rectangular and round structures, the former with thatched roofs and the latter made entirely of organic materials.

A number of other technical skills were associated with building construction. These included not only the dressing of fine stonework, which has already been discussed, but also the production of stone sculpture and the cutting of inscriptions. Because the latter included, at one time or another, both South Arabian and Greek characters, it seems likely that a foreign hand or at least a foreign-trained hand was sometimes in use here. Nevertheless, the gradual ascendancy of Ge'ez would suggest that even inscription cutting eventually passed into local hands. Another craft or art form associated with buildings was the creation of the fine wall-paintings that were such a feature of the interiors of many Ethiopian churches. Here again, the debt to foreign influences was great but the style that developed was distinctly Ethiopian (Buxton 1970: 136). The origins of Ethiopian wall-painting are not really known but perhaps it may be assumed that the churches of Christian Aksum were already decorated in this way.

Metallurgical technology seems to have developed early in Ethiopia and to have remained at a high level of proficiency. In the first millennium BC there were still stone-using people at Gobedra, near Aksum (Phillipson 1977b), and at Lalibela Cave, east of Lake Tana (Phillipson 1977a: 69), and there is abundant evidence that the making and use of stone artefacts continued into Aksumite times at Aksum and other sites (Munro-Hay 1989a: 186–7; 1991: 176, 242). Nevertheless, by the fifth century BC a literate urban culture using bronze and iron was established at Yeha. This technological transition has been explained in terms of a gradual infiltration of people from southern Arabia, where iron had been in use from about 1000 BC, but it is possible that the use of copper had already reached northern Ethiopia from the Nile Valley (Phillipson 1977a: 91–2). Whatever the mechanism

Fig. 3.10 Ivory carving found in the Tomb of the Brick Arches at Aksum. One of two panels, each measuring 490 by 160 millimetres, which probably adorned the back of a chair or throne. These panels depict vines, grapes and animals, and indicate highly skilled carving of ivory. Reproduced by permission of David Phillipson.

involved, however, it is clear that by Pre-Aksumite times a wide range of iron and bronze artefacts was in use (Phillipson 1993b: 347–8). Certainly, during the Aksumite period metal craftsmanship excelled both in the number of techniques employed and in the variety and the quality of its products, which were made in gold, silver, copper and bronze, and iron (Munro-Hay 1989a: 210–34). Among the more remarkable achievements was the use of mercury-gilding, to inlay gold on selected areas of silver and bronze coins (Munro-Hay 1991: 177, 188). Admittedly some of the metalwork may have been imported from elsewhere, particularly the more decorative items, but mineral resources were such (p. 71) that iron must have been mined and smelted in Ethiopia, as perhaps some other metals were. As for gold, which is known to have been exported from Ethiopia, it could probably have been obtained by panning superficial alluvial sources rather than by mining.

Artefacts and other evidence recovered from Aksumite sites also indicate a variety of other manufacturing skills. Again the difficulty is to untangle the imported items from the locally produced. Most pottery was made locally, and was at times remarkably sophisticated considering that it was formed without the use of a wheel, but a small amount came from the Mediterranean world, particularly from northern Egypt, probably as containers for wine or olive oil (Munro-Hay 1989a: 235–316). Leather-working appears to have been practised (Munro-Hay 1989a: 321) and it is surmised that textile production was important, although textiles of foreign origin were also in use. Carving of high quality was done in ivory (Phillipson 1995: 16, 19–22; Phillipson and Reynolds 1996: 112), bone is known to have been worked (de Contenson 1963a: 12; Munro-Hay 1989a: 321–2), and civet was probably already produced in Aksumite times (von Endt 1978). The depiction of vines and grapes on third-century AD ivory carvings found in the Tomb of the Brick Arches (Fig. 3.10), the recovery of grape seeds from the domestic site north of Aksum, and the existence of several rock-cut tanks at Atsafi, north-west of Aksum, which may have been wine-presses, suggest that wine-making was also practised (Phillipson 1997: 162–5; 1998a: 59–60). From historical and ethnohistorical sources, it seems that salt was probably obtained from the Danakil Desert but there is no archaeological evidence for this. Coins were struck in Ethiopia in Aksumite times, for over 300 years, although some coins were also imported. Finally, there were numerous luxury goods: jewellery, glass and fine metalwork, for instance, that were clearly of foreign origin and therefore have no relevance for Ethiopian technology. Nevertheless, although most of the surprisingly large amount of glass found in Aksum seems to have come from the eastern part of the Roman Empire or beyond, the characteristics of some pieces suggest that they were actually made at Aksum (Munro-Hay 1989a: 208–9).

A final point needs emphasis. This is that the technological base of Ethiopia, in all the periods under discussion, remained agricultural. It could be argued that the most important aspect of Ethiopia's technology was the ox-drawn plough and the terracing and irrigation systems that went with it. Added to these was the use of the mule for transport. Collectively, these and the other technological achievements that have been discussed must have been contributory to the development of social complexity.

Social system

Ethiopian and Eritrean archaeological evidence suggests that at least by Aksumite times a considerable degree of social complexity had been attained. The society which left so much material evidence in the north-eastern corner of the Ethiopian Highlands, and in some adjacent areas, must surely have been a stratified one. At the top was an absolute monarch, frequently depicted on Aksumite coins wearing a crown and in some cases shown seated on a throne (Fig. 3.11). Some of the inscriptions on the coins suggest that these rulers were, nevertheless, concerned about popular opinion: 'May the country be satisfied!' (Kobishchanov 1981: 394) and 'Joy be to the peoples' (Buxton 1970: 39) lack something of the usual tone of true autocracy. However, monarchical government, whatever its exact character, is indicated also by other elements of the archaeological evidence. Thus, some at least of the monumental, multi-roomed, residential buildings of more than one

Fig. 3.11 Aksumite bronze coin of Armah (seventh century AD), showing the king crowned and throned, with the Christian cross on the reverse. Reproduced by permission of the British Museum.

storey must have been royal palaces. At all events, it seems difficult to explain Ta'akha Mariam at Aksum as anything else. In addition, there are monumental tombs that must have been for royal burials and those of other leading members of society. Other sorts of monumental structures also occur that hint at the existence of a monarchical state: temples in earlier periods, churches in later ones and, of course, the storeyed stelae at Aksum. One thing is common to many of these structures: they are large. Kobishchanov leaves us in no doubt of the historian's view of such evidence:

> The mania for the gigantic reflected the tastes of the Axumite monarchy and the monuments were the concrete realization of its ideological purpose, which was to instil awe-inspiring admiration for the greatness and strength of the potentate to whom the monuments were dedicated. (Kobishchanov 1981: 394)

Although the archaeologist might view the evidence with rather more circumspection, Kobishchanov cannot be far wrong. Perhaps it should merely be emphasized that not all the fine mansions or the large tombs may have been intended for royalty; they seem too numerous for that. Certainly stelae of small or medium size are too common for such a conclusion. In addition, the distribution of luxury goods, many obtainable only from trade with the outside world, is too widespread. The conclusion seems inescapable that there was not only a monarchy but also an elite group of leading members of society, of the sort that usually form part of such an institution.

Equally, the archaeological evidence suggests the existence of a numerous mass of peasants and/or slaves. The existence of the latter might be assumed from the long survival of slavery in Ethiopia, condoned as it was even by Ethiopian Christianity (Pankhurst 1961: 372–3). It also seems likely that slaves were one of the exports of the Aksumite state. In any case, whatever the exact status of the sweating humanity that must have toiled and suffered on such tasks as moving and raising the larger stelae, large labour forces must have been involved. Constructional work on the scale frequently achieved in Aksumite times implies a numerous and an obedient labour force. If the modern world was built on machines, the ancient world was built on human backs. Indeed, the necessarily agricultural basis of Aksumite society, and that of earlier and later times, would require the existence of a large peasant class, which during times of war would also have been expected to provide the bulk of the fighting men. As is often the case, such a class is not so well represented in the archaeological record as that of the elite but the smallest houses of those excavated in the urban site of Matara would seem to confirm its existence (p. 87). Furthermore, the large number of small rooms surrounding the central structure at such elite residences as the Dongur Mansion, would suggest that many of the lowest class lived in some sort of client relationship to society's more privileged people. Most, however, were probably scattered through the countryside in villages and hamlets, such as those located in the survey by Michels (1988; 1994).

Intermediate-sized houses excavated at Matara would indicate that there were also people who belonged to neither the elite nor the peasantry, at least in Aksumite times. Some confirmation of this was provided by Phillipson and Reynolds (1996: 143), who interpreted the domestic area that they excavated just to the north of Aksum as representing 'a middle-rank settlement . . . well above that of a peasant farmstead'. In addition, the burials of the Gudit Stelae Field, placed in modest tombs that were nevertheless marked by medium-sized to small stelae and in at least one case contained high-quality grave-goods, have been interpreted as those of 'middle-class' Aksumites (p. 81). It might be expected that such a class would include government officials, scribes, priests of temple or church, middle-ranking members of the army, merchants and perhaps some of the more skilled craftsmen. Amongst such a class there would probably be some foreigners, permitted to live in Ethiopia because of their special skills or attributes.

Thus, in addition to social stratification, the archaeological evidence suggests the existence of functional specialization. In Aksumite times, as well as rulers, government officials and peasant farmers, there were also expert builders, including masons, brickmakers, carpenters and joiners. There must also have been miners, quarrymen, iron-smelters, blacksmiths, other metal-workers, potters, ivory-carvers, workers of leather and transporters of goods. Finally, one would expect that there were merchants, artists, scribes, coiners, some professional soldiers, and temple or church officials. Many of these specialists must have been urban-dwellers, living in towns and cities that apparently did not need protection by surrounding walls. We know little of the layout of these settlements, although Anfray (1974: Fig. 7) threw some light on that of Matara, and Michels (1990: Figs. 3–5) outlined the probable changing form of the city of Aksum during the first millennium AD. Nevertheless, an attempt can be made to reconstruct the society of the Aksumite period, although that reconstruction will no doubt be incomplete. The picture that emerges is one of a degree of social complexity quite compatible with urbanization and state formation.

Population pressures

In general the Ethiopian Highlands were attractive to human settlement, providing climatic conditions and soils conducive to cereal–plough agriculture and stock-raising. True, large areas of the highlands were of limited or no use because they were too rocky, too exposed or too high, but this was probably offset by the considerable benefits accruing from the great altitudinal range. This gave a diversity and a flexibility to the subsistence base that was clearly advantageous, as is indicated by its continuity throughout the periods under consideration. Such other environmental constraints as there were consisted of occasional epidemics of disease and of periods of famine usually brought on by rainfall variability or crop destruction, the latter particularly caused by locusts (p. 72). It has already been suggested that the episodic character of these constraints (serious though they were) would have meant that they had little overall inhibiting effect on the growth of social complexity in the highlands. Indeed, it is possible that one of these very constraints actually stimulated these developments by creating situations of localized and perhaps temporary population pressure.

The Pre-Aksumite and Aksumite culture grew up in a part of the Ethiopian Highlands well placed for contact with the outside world. Indeed, it can be argued that the contribution of South Arabian migrants from that world had a lot to do with the emergence of social complexity in that part of northern Ethiopia. It was, however, a part of the Ethiopian Highlands that in recent times has had less rainfall and a shorter wet season than areas to the south. As a result it was probably particularly prone to drought-induced famine and it is interesting to note that in medieval and modern times Ethiopia's centre of gravity has usually been considerably further south. It is possible to hypothesize a situation in which such an area, normally able to support a substantial agricultural population, suffered from recurrent episodes of population pressure caused by drought. In those circumstances, considerable power would be placed in the hands of those who controlled agricultural land with a potential for irrigation. Furthermore, the long-term effects of tree-clearance, cultivation and periodic drought, particularly on hillsides, could well have resulted in the destruction of some agricultural lands by erosion, another factor that could place pressure on subsistence agriculturalists. It is quite possible that the emergence of an elite was facilitated by such conditions.

Some light was thrown on such matters by Karl Butzer, who in the early 1970s conducted a palaeo-ecological study in the Aksum area (Michels, in Kobishchanov 1979: 21–2). On the basis of geo-archaeological evidence, Butzer suggested that Aksumite culture flourished at a time of better spring rains than at present, and declined when 'Intense land pressure and more erratic rainfall favored soil destruction and ecological degradation during the seventh and eighth centuries' (Butzer 1981: 471). The possibility of such a moister period might also be supported by other evidence. It is thought that during the first century AD the population of Anfray's western Aksumite province (p. 89) gradually moved away from the plateau drainage system onto the broad plains (Michels, in Kobishchanov 1979: 27). It is unknown whether or not there were episodes of drought during this otherwise wetter period, but if so the impact on a population encouraged to increase by the generally more favourable climatic conditions could have been substantial. Significantly, ecological degradation does seem eventually to have become a problem in some areas. There is, for instance, the evidence excavated by Chittick at Aksum, that suggests that serious erosion of a hillside occurred following tree clearance and cultivation (p. 87). Indeed, it seems possible that resources were unequally distributed in north-eastern Ethiopia and that some land was under greater settlement pressure than other land. Partial confirmation of this may be provided by the settlement-pattern survey undertaken by Michels in the Aksum area also in the early 1970s (p. 89). This stratified random sampling survey demonstrated 'an explosive growth in the number of settlements and in the size of the overall regional population' during the period AD 450–800, with 'extraordinary concentrations of population' on the Aksumite Plain, which nevertheless virtually disappeared in the succeeding period of AD 800–1000 (Michels 1994: 67–8). Thus it seems likely that differential access to resources, in both space and time, could have brought about significant episodes of population pressure that played an important part in Ethiopian history.

Ideology

Archaeological evidence from Ethiopia and Eritrea indicates that religion played an important role in the emergence of the Aksumite state and in the continued existence of its medieval successors. The evidence also suggests that religion contributed to the process of urbanization of Pre-Aksumite and Aksumite times and to the eventual reappearance of urban living in the second half of the second millennium AD. For the Pre-Aksumites and early Aksumites, religion consisted of a complex polytheism probably of South Arabian origin, in which the moon-god, Almouqah, and Mahrem, god of war and of monarchy, were amongst the more important deities. From the fourth century AD onwards, for both the later Aksumites and medieval and modern Ethiopians, the principal religion has been Christianity of a distinctive Ethiopian type. Ullendorff (1960: 97) has called Ethiopian Christianity 'the most profound expression of the national existence of the Ethiopians' and it is quite possible that the beliefs that pre-dated it had a similar significance.

The most obvious indication of the role of religion, during the periods under discussion, consists of the numerous and impressive remains of temples and churches. The temple of Yeha was so well built that after approximately 2500 years its ruins still stand to a height of about 9 metres; the surviving churches of medieval Ethiopia appear to constitute the only extant structures of their period. The direction of resources into such buildings must in all cases have been in the hands of the ruler and the elite, who no doubt expected in return an ideological legitimization of their position.

That such a legitimization was claimed by the monarchical Aksumite state is clearly indicated on the coins that were minted. The earlier ones showed the crescent and disc, presumably representing the moon and the sun; the later ones included the cross (Fig. 3.11), among the earliest coins of any country to do so according to Buxton (1970: 40). The stone-cut inscriptions of Ezana also demonstrate the support that the monarchy sought from religion, calling first on pre-Christian deities and later on the Christian god.

In addition there are the stelae, particularly the larger stelae at Aksum. Although their purpose was at one time uncertain, it does now seem that they were intended as grave markers for royal burials (Phillipson 1994). As such, they would appear to have had some sort of religious role as well as being symbols of state authority. Groups of holes at the tops of the storeyed stelae (Fig. 3.3) have been thought to indicate the fixing of religious symbols to the stone: these symbols were probably made of metal, but none of them survives. Consequently there has been some debate as to whether the symbols consisted of the crescent and disc or the Christian cross (e.g. van Beek 1967: 118, 121). More recently, Phillipson has been able to show that these stelae are, in fact, pre-Christian in date, and indeed a stela at Matara does have a crescent and disc carved at its top (Anfray 1963: Plate 63a). However, whatever the religion was at the time of their erection would probably have made little difference to the role that the more important of these monuments played in reinforcing the power of the state.

Perhaps less obvious is the contribution that religion made to urbanization. The temple at Yeha and the tombs and stelae at Aksum suggest that these urban developments were religious centres as well as commercial and administrative centres. The problem is that we do not know what their primary role may have been. Certainly it was as a religious and a ceremonial centre that Aksum survived into modern times, so that Bent (1893) could call it 'the sacred city of the Ethiopians'. Also, in medieval Ethiopia it was religion that maintained almost the only static settlements: Lalibela may have been principally a religious centre but its archaeological remains imply that there must have been quite a number of people in its vicinity. When urban centres appeared again in the second half of the second millennium AD, the Church still played an important role: Gondar, for example, is said to have had no less than forty-four churches (Pankhurst 1979: 5). Clearly, something more than religious fervour was involved; there was the politics of propitiating a powerful clergy and there was prestige.

External trade

Historical and archaeological evidence indicates that Aksum had trading contacts with the Roman provinces of the eastern Mediterranean, with Egypt, Nubia, South Arabia, the Persian Gulf, India and Sri Lanka (Munro-Hay 1996; Phillipson 1998a: 69). Kobishchanov (1979: 175) used both historical and archaeological sources to put together an impressive list of goods imported into the Aksumite kingdom. They consisted of iron and non-ferrous metals, and artefacts made of them; articles of precious metals; glass and ceramic items; fabrics and clothing;

wine and sugar-cane; vegetable oils; aromatic substances and spices. From purely historical sources, Kobishchanov (1979: 172) also reconstructed the exports of Aksum. They comprised ivory, gold, obsidian, emeralds, aromatic substances, rhinoceros horn, hippopotamus teeth and hide, tortoiseshell, slaves, and monkeys and other live animals. These details suggest that Aksumite external trade was extensive and that, like the Nubian trade of the middle Nile, it was basically one involving the exchange of precious raw materials and African exotica for manufactured and luxury articles. It seems unlikely that Pre-Aksumite trade was anything like so widespread and it is apparent that medieval Ethiopia suffered from a comparative trading isolation, although even then contact was somehow maintained with places as far away as Armenia. It is tempting, therefore, to conclude that the Aksumite state was a product of the international trade of its day. If Nubia was the corridor to Africa as Adams thought (Chapter 2), then it might be claimed that for a time Aksum, through its port of Adulis, was a front door to the continent. Kirwan, indeed, was of the opinion that the rise of Adulis must have damaged the Nile Valley trade and contributed to the decline of Meroë after the first century AD (Kirwan 1972: 168). The question is, what light does the archaeological evidence throw on this subject?

As regards the commodities that were imported and exported, archaeology is at the same time informative and disappointing. As is the case with Nubia, exports are not well represented in the archaeological record. However, an elephant tusk was found at Adulis (Anfray 1981: 377) and the Tomb of the Brick Arches at Aksum has yielded evidence not only for Aksumite involvement in the ivory trade but also for fine craftsmanship in its utilization (Phillipson 1995: 21–2). Furthermore, occasional gold artefacts from excavations in Aksum (Munro-Hay 1989a: 210) and the finding of more Aksumite gold coins in South Arabia than in Ethiopia itself (Munro-Hay 1991: 183), are indications of a trade in gold. The problem is that many of the other commodities exported would either not have survived, or would not have survived in their original state and, furthermore, they would need to be identified as of Aksumite origin in the archaeological record of the country to which they were traded. Archaeological evidence for imports is very much better, although durables tend to survive whereas consumables do not. In addition, soil and climatic conditions in the Ethiopian Highlands are not as conducive to the preservation of organic materials as they are in the middle Nile Valley. As a result, most of the evidence for imports is in the form of artefacts of metal, ceramic and glass. For example, Aksum has produced Byzantine bronze weights, and both bronze scales and weights of Byzantine origin have been found at Adulis. From Matara has come a Byzantine bronze lamp, two Byzantine gold crosses, a necklace of Roman silver coins of the second to third centuries AD and an impressive bronze lamp of South Arabian origin depicting a dog in the act of catching an ibex (Kobishchanov 1979: 173–4). Even more remarkable is the hoard of 104 Indian coins of third-century date which were found at Debra Damo (Munro-Hay 1982: 111). Examples of ceramic and glass imports are rather more numerous. Aksum, for instance, has yielded amphorae of Mediterranean origin, pottery imitative of Roman fine ware, and glass ointment flasks of Roman and Egyptian manufacture (Kobishchanov 1979: 173). Such imports as wine and oil, however, which must have been inside some of these pottery and glass containers, have left no trace. Even textiles, which were probably imported in significant quantities, are only represented by occasional discoveries such as that of silk fabrics at Debra Damo, which originated from Coptic, Mesopotamian and Islamic Egyptian sources of sixth- to twelfth-century AD date (Kobishchanov 1979: 174). Nevertheless, although archaeological evidence cannot provide a complete picture of the range of imported commodities, it does give some indication of the geographical reach of Aksumite external trade. Clearly, that trade was of considerable importance.

Some confirmation that this was indeed the case is offered by several other pieces of evidence. Thus, Aksum was the first state in tropical Africa to mint its own coinage, which was produced, at one time or another, in gold, silver and bronze. It may be noticed that the Aksumite monetary system was similar to the Byzantine system, in weight, standard and form (Kobishchanov 1981: 386), and that many of its coins, particularly the gold ones, were inscribed in Greek not Ge'ez (Munro-Hay 1991: 180–95). Therefore, it would seem very likely that coins were only introduced because of Aksum's participation in an international trade which was accustomed to such a means of exchange. The earliest Aksumite coins belong to the third century AD, the latest to the seventh century (Munro-Hay 1991: 67–8) and it is surely significant that they ceased to be issued at a time when Aksum's external trading interests were in decline. Nevertheless, it is a little strange that of the several thousand coins that are known, 90 per cent have been found in northern Ethiopia itself, and consist mainly of bronze coins. A few bronze coins have also been found in Egypt, Meroë, Israel and Aqaba, but most of the gold coins have come from South Arabia and, less certainly, from India (Kobishchanov 1979: 184; Munro-Hay 1991: 184; Phillipson 1998a: 69). It would appear that the coinage of Aksum had a rather limited circulation, although foreign coins were imported into Aksum from South Arabian, Roman and Indian sources.

A further indication of the importance of external trade to Aksum is the geographical location of this state. Situated as it was in the extreme north-eastern part of the Ethiopian Highlands, it was in a decidedly advantageous situation for taking part in the Red Sea trade. It was, in fact, sitting at the side of one of the major sea routes of the ancient world. Just as the coinage died when Aksum was excluded from that route, so too did the Aksumite state fade away. Indeed, during the second millennium AD the political and cultural centre of Ethiopia was located far to the south. By then the need was not for access to the Red Sea but for maximum isolation from the enmity of Ethiopia's neighbours.

The geographical location of Aksum in relation to the network of trade routes in this part of Africa provides still more evidence of the role of external trade in the development of this state and of its cities. According to the *Periplus of the Erythraean Sea*, the journey from Adulis to Koloè (either Kohaito or Matara) took three days and the journey from Adulis to Aksum took eight, as it apparently still did at the beginning of the twentieth century (Kobishchanov 1979: 185). By the standards of ancient trade routes this was a brief journey, and this route from Adulis to Aksum was, in fact, merely the beginning of a route that led from the Red Sea to the Nile Valley, ending near Meroë. Another route ran north-west from Aksum to the Aswan region, across the Nubian Desert, a journey which took thirty days according to Cosmas Indicopleustes. Yet another route ran south from Aksum to Lake Tana and Sasu, the latter reputedly the major source of Aksumite gold. According to Cosmas Indicopleustes this journey took fifty days. Branches from this route led respectively to Shoa and into the region of the African Horn (Kobishchanov 1979: 185–6). Thus Aksum was at the centre of a giant web of trade routes that tapped the resources of the African interior and injected them into the Red Sea trade. It can hardly be doubted that external trade was an important contributory factor in the rise of the Aksumite state and in the growth of its cities.

Conclusion

It would appear that Ethiopian isolation was a relative thing; relative, that is to say, to the circumstances of the surrounding world. The Aksumite state of the first millennium AD was able to benefit from its participation in the Red Sea trade and for a time ruled parts of southern Arabia; the Ethiopian state of much of the second millennium AD was able to isolate itself from hostile neighbours. Situated, as it were, on the roof of the world, the Ethiopians could join or reject that world as they wished. Thus can be explained the paradox of a people who have spent much of their history forgotten by the rest of humanity, but who were, nevertheless, the creators of one of the earliest states and some of the earliest cities in Africa.

In general, therefore, it can be argued that Ethiopia's geographical location and its mountainous environment played a basic role in these developments. In particular, its accessibility to South Arabian settlers during the first millennium BC and the diversity of agricultural systems made possible by its great altitudinal range provided a foundation for what was to follow. This is not to say that the state of Aksum and its cities resulted from an injection of South Arabian migrants, but it is clear that Ethiopian technology, of the last few centuries BC and the first few centuries AD, benefited from alien contributions the source of many of which was Asiatic. Certainly the earliest state and urban developments took place in that part of the Ethiopian plateau most accessible from the Red Sea coast.

Compared with the surrounding lowlands, the Ethiopian Highlands were healthier, and had better soils and a greater range of possible agricultural adaptations, providing, therefore, a fertile seedbed for the growth of social complexity. In particular, the heartland of the Aksumite state lay in an area with a strong agricultural resource base, in both cereals and other crops and livestock. This appears to have triggered localized increases in population and in population density, during a relatively favourable climatic period early in the first millennium AD. In such a situation and given likely rainfall variability, episodes of stress brought on by periodic drought-induced famine would have created temporary population pressures, that could be exploited by those with access to irrigated land. Such land may well have constituted a limited resource, the control of which could have provided a power-base for an emerging elite. On many aspects of these matters, archaeological evidence provides little information; nevertheless it does demonstrate that by Aksumite times there had developed a partly urbanized stratified society consisting of monarch, surrounding elite, 'middle class' and peasant/slave class. It also indicates the presence of a fair degree of functional specialization. Furthermore, it is clear from the material evidence that the social order was confirmed and legitimized by religious dogma. Even the change from pre-Christian to Christian beliefs may be seen as a reinforcement of the prevailing social system.

To all this must be added the impact of external trade: not in itself a cause of social complexity but, nevertheless, a contributory factor of some importance. It is clear that the apogee of the Aksumite state and cities was coterminous with Aksum's involvement in the Red Sea trade but it is equally apparent that the state of Ethiopia, if not its cities, was able to survive many centuries of comparative isolation from international trade during the second millennium AD. The Red Sea trade, conducted by Aksum through its port of Adulis, must not be seen in isolation, however, but as part of a widespread network of trade that Aksum had developed throughout much of north-east Africa. Thus Aksum profited from the role of entrepôt, acquiring wealth and prestige from commodities that were obtained from others. If Ethiopia appears isolated, this is clearly an isolation that has had its own particular benefits.

Chapter 4
An optimal zone: the West African savanna

'Amid all the world's misery, few people are worse off or face a bleaker future than the Sahelians.' This quotation comes from a leaflet circulated in the early 1980s by an organization called 'S.O.S. Sahel International', centred on Dakar, in Senegal. This organization aimed to raise funds to relieve the immediate effects of drought and to support small-scale technological innovations that could mitigate damage caused by future droughts. It defined 'Sahelians' as residents of the states of Mauritania, Senegal, The Gambia, Mali, Burkina Faso, Niger, Chad, Sudan and Ethiopia (although the Sahel is technically only the driest of the savanna zones south of the Sahara Desert). It is worth reflecting on the fact that three of the areas of precolonial urbanization and state formation which are considered in this book are situated within this group of countries. Clearly, their occupants did not always face the bleak future that, rightly or wrongly, was forecast for them in the late twentieth century. Particularly this seems to have been the case in West Africa, where the savanna lands bordering the southern edge of the Sahara were the setting for very important social and political developments during the first and second millennia AD. Some historical sources indicate conditions that were far from being bleak. For example, in the early sixteenth century Leo Africanus had the following to say about Jenné, situated in the Inland Niger Delta on the edge of the Sahel zone: 'This place exceedingly aboundeth with barlie, rice, cattell, fishes, and cotton: and their cotton they sell unto the merchants of Barbarie, for cloth of Europe, for brazen vessels, for armour and other such commodities. Their coine is of gold without any stampe or inscription at all' (Africanus 1896: Vol. 3, 822). This description was given by an outsider, for Leo Africanus came from North Africa. It is instructive, therefore, to see what a local scholar, al-Sa'di, writing in about 1655, had to say on the same subject:

> This city is large, flourishing and prosperous; it is rich, blessed and favoured by the Almighty . . . Jenné is one of the great markets of the Muslim world. There one meets the salt merchants from the mines of Teghaza and merchants carrying gold from the mines of Bitou . . . Because of this blessed city, caravans flock to Timbuktu from all points of the horizon . . . The area around Jenné is fertile and well populated; with numerous markets held there on all the days of the week. It is certain that it contains 7077 villages very near to one another. (al-Sa'di 1964: 22–4, translated by author)

Although Susan and Roderick McIntosh have pointed out that al-Sa'di may have been very biased in favour of Jenné, because he had lived and worked there for ten years (S.K. McIntosh and R.J. McIntosh 1980: Vol. 1, 49), E.W. Bovill (1968: 135) was of the opinion that this was a 'convincing tribute' because al-Sa'di was 'intensely jealous of the reputation of his own city of Timbuktu, of which Jenné was a rival in both trade and culture'. Notwithstanding the problems of interpreting such pieces of evidence, however, it does seem, from historical sources, from oral tradition and from archaeological data, as if the West African savanna was in the past a zone that offered opportunities as well as constraints to the people who lived there. It is probably not too great an exaggeration to say that this was an optimal zone, so far as the attainment of increasing complexity by human cultures was concerned.

Geographical location and environmental factors

Throughout the history of the human race in Africa, the most important single ecosystem in the continent has probably been the savanna. Rich in faunal and floral resources, suitable for both cereal agriculture and livestock rearing, it offered conditions of relatively easy movement in which natural resources and manufactured products could be readily exchanged. The most extensive area of savanna in Africa consists of a broad zone which stretches almost across the continent from the Atlantic Ocean to the Gulf of Aden. This chapter is concerned with the western part of that zone, that is to say with the savanna lands to the west of Lake Chad.

It is important to understand the location of the West African savanna. Consisting of grassland, with varying densities of trees and shrubs, it is situated between the tropical rainforest to the south and the Sahara Desert to the north. In the past the Sahara formed what Bovill (1968: 1) called 'one of the world's greatest barriers to human movement', although, as Bovill was able to show so brilliantly, that barrier was repeatedly bridged by trade. Beyond that barrier lay the lands of the Mediterranean, heart of the Roman and of the medieval world and with contacts deep into Eurasia. To the south of the tropical rainforest, however, lay only the Atlantic Ocean, bordering a coast that until the middle of the second millennium AD was to remain isolated from the rest of the world. This is in such marked contrast to the East African coast, discussed in Chapter 6, where external contact is known to have been present for some two thousand years, that it is worth examining the reasons for this isolation. Much of the coast of West Africa is uninviting when approached from the sea: natural harbours are relatively few and most of the coast is fringed by mangrove swamps or by exposed surf-pounded beaches, or is backed by inhospitable desert. The real problem with this coast, however, is that south of Morocco, along the Saharan coast, the prevailing winds are always from the north. Given the sailing technology of the ships of the ancient and medieval

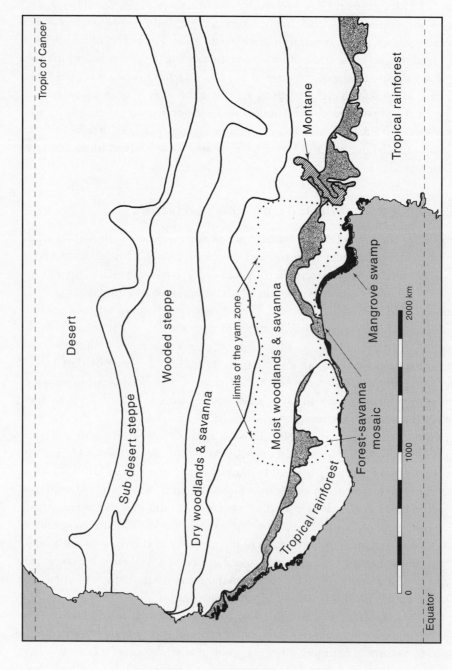

Fig. 4.1 West African environmental zones showing area of major yam cultivation. After Keay (1959) and Coursey (1980: Fig. 1).

worlds, it was possible to sail south but impossible to return (Mauny 1978: 292–3). As a result, Cape Bojador at about latitude 26° North remained effectively the furthest south to which outside ships were able to penetrate until towards the middle of the fifteenth century AD. It was only at that time that circumstances changed, according to Shaw (1975a: 54) because of the adoption of the lateen sail and of the stern-post rudder by seafarers of the western Mediterranean and Atlantic seaboard, which enabled ships to sail into the wind as well as with the wind. Bovill also emphasized the importance of the discovery that it was possible to return from the West African coast, not by fighting contrary winds along the coast but by striking west into the Atlantic for several hundred miles to pick up winds blowing from the south and west. This discovery, discussed in some detail by Crosby (1986: 112–14), occurred about 1440, and was made possible, Bovill suggested, by the Portuguese adoption of the caravel, a vessel that was much more manoeuvrable than earlier ships (Bovill 1968: 115). The caravel, it should be noted, was fitted with both lateen sails and a stern-post rudder.

If the ocean could remain a barrier for so long, it is perhaps surprising that so formidable a barrier as the Sahara Desert should have been successfully bridged by trade at least eight centuries earlier. The fact that it was has often been explained as the result of another cultural innovation: the introduction to Africa of the domesticated camel, as a mode of transport over long distances through arid regions (Bulliet 1975). It will be argued below that the 'ship of the desert', as the camel has so often been called, did not inaugurate trans-Saharan trade but, in the hands of people who knew how best to utilize its peculiar physiology, it undoubtedly led to a very substantial development of that trade. The camel seems to have been brought into use in the Sahara during the first few centuries AD, coming originally from Arabia, although it appears to have been known in Egypt for many centuries previously (Rowley-Conwy 1988). It was not until after the seventh century AD, however, that the coming of the Arabs to North Africa brought about the development of trans-Saharan commerce based on the use of camel transport (Mauny 1978: 286–92).

It would be a mistake, however, to think of the West African savanna as merely a uniform zone, isolated to varying degrees through time by the desert, the forest and the ocean. It was a great deal more than this; it was a world of its own and a highly complex world, richly endowed with resources. Indeed, the West African savanna consists of a parallel series of different environmental zones, running roughly from west to east and forming a part of a greater series of such zones extending from south to north across West Africa. These zones have usually been characterized in terms of vegetation differences and one of the best-known attempts to do this was the map produced by Keay (1959). Thus a hypothetical traveller, journeying due north from the Nigerian coast, could traverse in less than 1500 kilometres a whole range of environments, from coastal mangrove swamp to true desert (Fig. 4.1). On the way he or she would pass through tropical rainforest, forest–savanna mosaic, relatively moist woodlands and savanna, relatively dry woodlands and savanna, wooded steppe, and sub-desert steppe. The close proximity of these different environments must have had an important influence on the development of human culture in West Africa. Because of the range of ecozones and ecotones that they presented, there was both the necessity and the occasion for the exchange of raw materials and products across environmental boundaries. Each environment possessed some resources but lacked others. Thus salt was available in the desert and along the coast but was relatively difficult to obtain in the savanna, where for cereal agriculturalists it was a physiological necessity (Alexander 1993b). Thus the forest was deficient in meat but the savanna supported very large numbers of domestic animals, particularly cattle (Buchanan and Pugh 1955: 120–3). There are many other examples that could be given to illustrate this situation but the important point is that the complexity of the West African environment, as a whole, provided conditions conducive to the development of a complex network of regional trade. Within that network the West African savanna, relatively easy to traverse, played an essential part. It is likely that such trading activity was almost as old as West African food production and, indeed, its remoter origins must have been even earlier. Thus, the beginnings of a trading network were surely already in existence by about 3000 years ago.

It is worth pausing to consider the main resources that would probably have been available in the West African savanna 2000–3000 years ago. Foremost of these would have been agricultural products: cereals such as sorghum, millet, *fonio* and African rice; several indigenous yams; vegetable oils such as those obtained from the shea-butter tree and the oil-palm; two African groundnuts; cowpeas; black beniseed; and other things (Harris 1976: 329–32). Also meat, dairy products and hides and skins from the numerous cattle, sheep and goats. Furthermore, food supplies could have been supplemented by hunting wild animals and by fishing, and such 'wild' resources could in addition have provided ivory. Moreover, a number of wild plants and trees could also have provided human sustenance, particularly in times when cultivated crops failed, while at all times botanical sources would have been able to supply a wide range of useful raw materials, for baskets, canoes, medicines, roofing, and many other purposes (Dalziel 1937; Pullan 1974; Casey 1998). Important inorganic materials would have been available in the West African savanna, as well: particularly iron ore, alluvial gold, rocks suitable for making grindstones, good building earths and potting clays. Lastly, a relatively high population density would have provided a resource in itself that could have been exploited: the slave trade has a history in West Africa which goes much further back than the advent of Europeans on the Guinea Coast.

Nevertheless, the West African savanna was a zone of constraints as well as opportunities. Foremost of these constraints was water availability. The rainfall is markedly seasonal, the amount less and the wet season shorter the further north one goes. Also (the temperature tends to increase as one goes north) leading to a greater loss of surface water to evaporation, so that much of the northern parts of the savanna consists for much of the year of a virtually waterless landscape. Although drinking water for both domestic animals and human beings is usually available by digging wells of varying depths, it is obvious that in such conditions the margins of perennial rivers and lakes must assume an especial attraction for agriculturalists. It is in such areas that 'floodwater farming' in its various forms has been of great importance. Such farming techniques – of which 'recessional cultivation' (the cultivation of naturally watered areas as floodwaters recede) is probably the most common – were one of the principal ways of intensifying African agricultural systems. It is of some significance that such techniques seem to have underlain the growth of social complexity in the Egyptian Nile Valley (Butzer 1976: 19) and that in West Africa they existed (and indeed still exist) both in the Inland Niger Delta in Mali (Harlan and Pasquereau 1969) and around the southern edge of Lake Chad (Connah 1985), as well as probably in other places. Nevertheless, there is a second major environmental constraint in the West African savanna that sometimes discourages human settlement from concentrating around the very bodies of water that attract it. Of the major diseases found in the savanna that can seriously damage human or animal health, sleeping-sickness and animal trypanosomiasis, malaria, schistosomiasis, filariasis, river blindness and a whole range of intestinal parasites are associated in one way or another with water. Clearly the West African savanna was no earthly paradise but it did offer considerable opportunities to human groups that could adapt to its constraints.

Significantly, this interplay of opportunities and constraints was not static through time, because even over the last 3000 years there have been variations in the West African climate which have had profound effects on human societies in the savanna. Although conditions in West Africa were becoming steadily drier from about 4500 years ago, there was a particularly arid period between about 300 BC and about AD 300, a period of increased rainfall from about AD 300 to about 1100, another dry period from about 1100 to about 1500, another period of increased rainfall from about 1500 to about 1630, and yet another dry period from about 1630 to about 1860. Within the savanna, human economic and social responses to these changes have tended to be characterized by stability and growth during moister periods, and instability and decline during drier periods. This is to claim not that climatic change has been deterministic but that such change has been one of the many factors that have helped to shape the complex dynamic relationship of people and environment (Brooks 1998).

Sources of information

Until late in the twentieth century our knowledge of the precolonial cities and states of the West African savanna was mainly based on historical sources. Some of

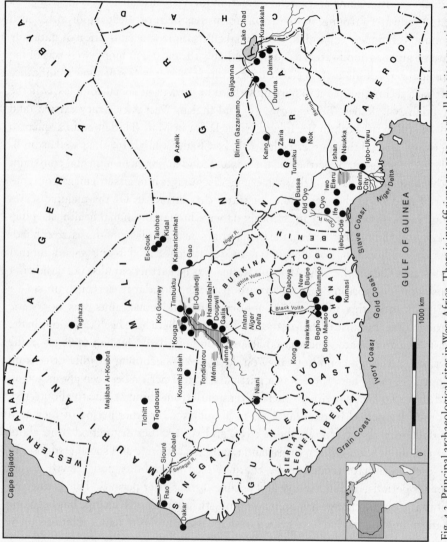

Fig. 4.2 Principal archaeological sites in West Africa. There is insufficient space to mark all the sites mentioned in the text.

these originated as oral traditions, either in the past or in recent times, but most of them consist of documentation, usually in Arabic and mainly written by outsiders who at best had only visited the area. The principal of these authors were al-Masudi, ibn Haukal, al-Bakri, al-Idrisi, Yaqut, al-Umari, ibn Battuta, ibn Khaldun, Leo Africanus, al-Maqrizi, ibn Said, al-Sa'di and ibn Fartua. Collectively they throw light on the period roughly from the tenth century AD to the seventeenth century. Similar sources also provide brief references to the West African savanna back to the eighth century AD. Drawing on all these and other sources (including the writings of mainly nineteenth-century European travellers, such as Park, Denham, Clapperton, Caillié and Barth), modern historians have been able to reconstruct, in varying degrees of detail, the history of the most important states of this area over the last twelve hundred years or so. The old states of Ghana and Mali have been examined, for example, by Nehemiah Levtzion (1973) and those of Songhai, Borno and Hausaland, for example, by John Hunwick (1971). In fact, there exists a very extensive literature on the history of the regions which were known as the Western and Central Sudan and it is not the intention here to attempt to add to it. It is the character of the sources on which that literature is based, however, that for a long time determined the standard explanation of the development of cities and states in the West African savanna. That explanation was, perhaps, most clearly stated by Levtzion. For example:

> *Sahil* is the Arabic word for 'shore', which is well understood if the desert is compared to a sea of sand, and the camel to a ship. Hence, the towns which developed in the Sahel . . . may be regarded as ports. These towns became both commercial entrepôts and political centres. Those who held authority in these strategic centres endeavoured to extend it in order to achieve effective control over the trade. Thus trade stimulated a higher level of political organization, while the emergence of extensive states accorded more security to trade. Political developments in the Western Sudan, throughout its history, are related to the changing patterns of intercontinental and trans-Saharan trade routes. (Levtzion 1973: 10)

In other words, cities and states in this zone developed as a result of external stimulus, in the form of long-distance trade. In addition, this view usually emphasized the role of Islam in these developments. Such an explanation might be expected, of course, if sources are limited to post-eighth-century AD documents written by people of Islamic culture, most of whom belonged to lands beyond the Sahara. As a view of the later developments in the West African savanna, it is no doubt sound enough, but the question is: does it adequately explain the origins of these developments? Fortunately, there is another source of information that can be drawn on, one that has neither the chronological limitations of the historical sources nor their possible prejudices; this source consists of the archaeological evidence, a source not without its own problems but one that deserves more attention than it was formerly given (Fig. 4.2).

Many years ago, G.P. Murdock commented that the archaeologist had 'thus far lifted perhaps an ounce of earth on the Niger for every ton carefully sifted on the Nile' (Murdock 1959: 73). Considering the poor quality of much of the earlier excavation in Egypt and the Sudan, many archaeologists might question his use of the words 'carefully sifted', but otherwise his remark is almost as true at the beginning of the twentieth-first century as it was when he made it. In spite of some remarkable investigations since the late 1970s, our knowledge of the archaeology of the West African savanna is still limited by insufficient fieldwork and excavation. Furthermore, much of the earlier work was technically inadequate even by the standards of its time. In addition, the publication of that work was often poor and some work was never published at all. There was also a tendency to adopt research strategies the main object of which was to throw more light on historically known sites. This earlier work was synthesized by Raymond Mauny in his book *Tableau géographique de l'Ouest Africain* . . . (Mauny 1961). In particular, the historical bias of such work meant that so little was known about the later prehistory of the area that in 1979 S.K. McIntosh and R.J. McIntosh (1979: 227) still called the three millennia immediately preceding the earliest historical documentation, the 'silent millennia'. Similarly, a few years earlier, Mauny himself had used the phrase 'les siècles obscurs' (the obscure centuries) in the title of a general book about the interface of history and archaeology in tropical Africa (Mauny 1970).

Nevertheless, archaeological research in the West African savanna is beginning to throw new light on the origins of cities and states in this area. Perhaps the earliest sign of the emergence of complex societies in semi-arid West Africa is the appearance, from about 4000 BC, of what MacDonald (1998) has termed 'Mobile Elites', based on transitory accumulations of pastoral wealth and power. This development is represented in the archaeological record by evidence for cattle herding, the making of valued objects in polished stone, and the construction of mounds – some for burial and others for the ritual disposal of objects belonging to the deceased. MacDonald has suggested that, in certain favourable regions, additional climatic or cultural stimuli resulted in these Mobile Elites developing into semi-sedentary chiefdoms by about 1500 BC. One of these, he claims, was at Kerma on the middle Nile, which is discussed in Chapter 2. Another was in the Dhar Tichitt-Walata area, in south-eastern Mauritania, where Holl (1985; 1993) studied a large series of drystone-built settlement sites dating from about 4000 to about 2000 years ago, which are strung out along more than 100 kilometres of steep sandstone cliffs. Towards the end of their occupation these sites formed a settlement hierarchy of four ranks: seventy-two hamlets with less than twenty compounds each, twelve small villages with twenty to fifty compounds each, five large villages with 120 to 198 compounds each, and one 'regional center of Dakhlet el Atrous 1, measuring 92.75 ha with 590 compounds, which may be characterized as a city' (Holl 1993: 129). The communities that inhabited these settlements practised mixed farming based on grain cultivation (particularly bulrush millet: *Pennisetum* sp.) and the herding of cattle, sheep and goats. They also exploited wild grains and fruits, fished in the freshwater lakes that then existed, and hunted a range of wild animals. Climatic deterioration almost certainly played a part in concentrating population into this area. It also eventually led to the abandonment of the settlements and indeed to their survival as archaeological sites, providing us with some of the earliest indications of developing social complexity in the West African savanna and the adjacent Sahara (Fig. 4.3).

The ideas of MacDonald and Holl have certainly challenged what Holl (1993: 129) has called 'certain preconceptions concerning the processes and timing of social change in West Africa'. Perhaps the greatest challenge, however, came from the work of Susan and Roderick McIntosh in the late 1970s and early 1980s on the settlement mounds of the Inland Niger Delta of Mali (S.K. McIntosh and R.J. McIntosh 1980; R.J. McIntosh and S.K. McIntosh 1981a; 1983; 1988; S.K. McIntosh 1995; R.J. McIntosh 1998). By combining regional surface investigations with excavations at the sites of Jenné-jeno, Hambarketolo and Kaniana, the McIntoshs were able to trace the emergence of urbanism in this area, from its apparent origins in about the third century BC to the foundation in the early second millennium AD of the nearby historical city of Jenné. At Jenné-jeno the settlement had grown to at least 12 hectares by about the first century AD and it reached its maximum extent of 33 hectares by about the ninth century (Figs. 4.4 and 4.5). At this latter stage it consisted of a packed mass of compounds, containing both round and rectangular mud houses, that was surrounded by a mud-brick city wall some 2 kilometres long. Its population has been variously estimated at between 4800 and 12,800, depending on how it is calculated. Indeed, if the adjacent site of Hambarketolo is included, along with the no less than twenty-five other contemporary satellite sites clustered around Jenné-jeno within a 1 kilometre radius, then a population estimate of 10,000 to 26,700 is achieved. Although such a high density may have been exceptional, this is only a relatively small part of the Inland Niger Delta, suggesting that there was an overall population build-up in the area from late in the first millennium BC to early in the second millennium AD. Excavated evidence from Jenné-jeno suggests that the economic basis for this development consisted of mixed farming on the seasonally inundated floodplain and its margins, particularly involving rice and cattle, but it is apparent that fishing, hunting and the gathering of wild plant food were also important. In addition, both metallurgy and other craftsmanship were well developed and Jenné-jeno participated in a trading network with a radius of at least 350 kilometres. Yet so far as any external stimulus is concerned, such as that suggested by Levtzion, 'Jenné-jeno is too big, too early, and too far south' (S.K. McIntosh and R.J. McIntosh 1980: Vol. 2, 448).

Although the evidence from Jenné-jeno has established a convincing case for the indigenous development of urbanism in the Inland Niger Delta, it has not

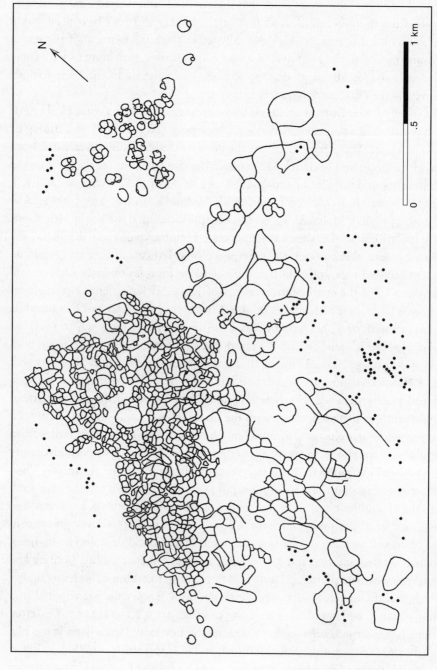

Fig. 4.3 Plan of Dakhlet el Atrous 1, Mauritania, the largest Dhar Tichitt settlement site, 92.75 hectares in size. The dots represent tumuli and the enclosures are stone compound and corral walls not houses. After MacDonald (1998: Fig. 4.5).

demonstrated the existence there of a highly stratified social hierarchy or of a centralized authority (S.K. McIntosh and R.J. McIntosh 1993a), unless it is argued that the construction of the city wall indicates the latter. As a result, the site seems to provide relatively little information about the origins of state formation in the West African savanna. Possibly this should lead us to re-examine some of our theoretical assumptions, as the McIntoshs have suggested, but the fact remains

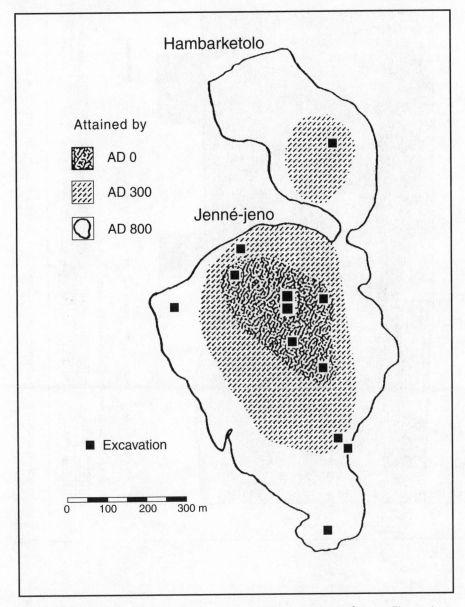

Fig. 4.4 Plan of Jenné-jeno, Mali, showing growth. After S. K. McIntosh (1995: Fig. 10.3).

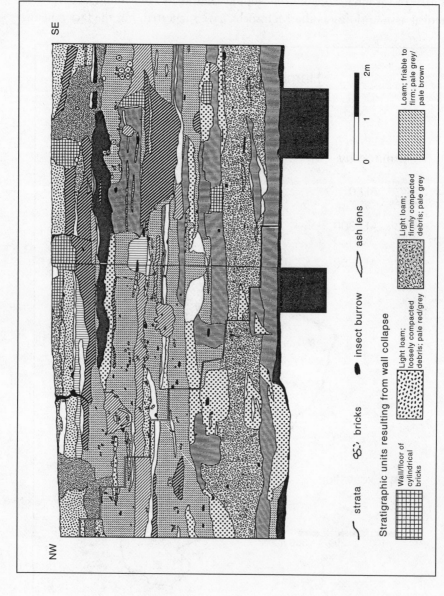

Fig. 4.5 Section through deposits at Jenné-jeno: excavation LX-N in the highest part of the mound. After S. K. McIntosh (1995: Figs. 2.3 and 2.26a).

that the amount of excavation that has been done is still very small considering the size and number of the sites involved. This is a characteristic problem of urban archaeology, although one that systematic multiple coring of deposits might eventually be able to overcome to some extent (R.J. McIntosh *et al.* 1996). Nevertheless, the homogeneity of material culture over a considerable area of the Middle Niger, the existence of a three-tier settlement hierachy in the Jenné-jeno area, and a positive correlation of site size with surface artefact diversity on sites within a 4 kilometre radius of Jenné-jeno, suggest that at its maximum development the city may indeed have formed the centre of a socio-political or economic development larger than its own immediate urban environment (R.J. McIntosh and S.K. McIntosh 1988: 149–51; S.K. McIntosh 1995: 410).

Archaeological field research in other parts of the Middle Niger and in adjacent regions has indicated that past urban development was no isolated phenomenon. In the Timbuktu region, for instance, S.K. McIntosh and R.J. McIntosh (1986a) found surface evidence that indicated both a population peak and site clustering in the later first millennium AD, followed by site abandonment (as at Jenné-jeno) caused by increasing aridity. Much the same seems to have occurred, although from an earlier date, in the Méma area (Togola 1996), and probably also in the Lakes Region of the Middle Niger (S.K. McIntosh 1994: 178). Jenné, Timbuktu and some other urban centres survived into historical times, however, although the chronology of their origins remains uncertain. Significantly, Gao Ancien has been found to have a sequence from the sixth or seventh century to the fifteenth or sixteenth century (Insoll 1996a: 41), and it is possible that some other cities in the area similarly originated in the first millennium AD.

Over 1000 kilometres to the north-west, the Middle Senegal Valley has presented a rather different picture from that of the Middle Niger. Although this is also a floodplain initially colonized only about 2000 years ago, that has a large number of settlement mounds that tend to cluster, the Middle Senegal Valley sites remained uniformly small and the excavated evidence from Cubalel and Siouré indicates a small-scale society that changed little throughout the first millennium AD. Only at the end of that millennium did major changes in scale and complexity take place, at the same time as a sudden expansion of trading contacts, changes that led on to the emergence of the so-called Takrur Empire at the beginning of the second millennium AD. It has been suggested that this contrast in the organization of society, on the Middle Niger and the Middle Senegal, resulted from spatial differences in the distribution of landforms. Evenly distributed subsistence opportunities on the Middle Senegal favoured an even distribution of population in small groups, whereas on the Middle Niger a very uneven distribution of such opportunities encouraged more specialization, and Jenné-jeno and a number of other settlements, such as Kalifa Gallou (40 hectares), Dia (50 hectares), Toladie (85 hectares) and Soy (110 hectares), grew up as urban centres because of their unusually advantageous positions in this respect (S.K. McIntosh, R.J. McIntosh and Bocoum 1992; S.K. McIntosh 1994: 178–9; MacDonald 1999a).

The undoubted success of much of the McIntoshs' research stems at least in part from their early realization that:

> the most effective way to investigate the appearance and development of the pre-colonial town in West Africa is not to excavate only the town site, but to document and explain the evolution of the settlement hierarchy of which the town is the summit. (S.K. McIntosh and R.J. McIntosh 1980: Vol. 2, 346)

Much of the field research done by other archaeologists, particularly the older work, has not used this approach and has tended to focus on the sites of cities or towns which can, with varying degrees of certainty, be identified in the historical sources (Fig. 4.2). For instance, important excavations have been conducted at Tegdaoust, in the Mauritanian desert. Here excavations over a number of years revealed several phases of occupation, the earliest of which was pre-urban, and the entire occupation was thought to extend from the seventh or eighth to the seventeenth century AD and later (Calvocoressi and David 1979: 14–15, 24–5; S.K. McIntosh and R.J. McIntosh 1980: Vol. 1, 18; Devisse 1983: 556; S.K. McIntosh and R.J. McIntosh 1986b: 431, 438). The excavators of the site tentatively identified it with the historically known town of Awdaghust, which was a desert port-of-trade on one of the trans-Saharan trade routes. The excavated evidence certainly indicates that Tegdaoust became a flourishing Islamic town, heavily involved with trade beyond the desert. The investigations at this site have been the subject of a number of publications which discuss them in some detail (Robert 1970; Robert, Robert and Devisse 1970; Robert and Robert 1972; Vanacker 1979; Devisse 1983; Robert-Chaleix 1989 (cited by S.K. McIntosh 1994: 180)). In comparison, the site of Niani, in Guinea, is of uncertain significance. Its excavator claimed it to have been the capital of the old state of Mali but fairly extensive excavations did not reveal the wealth of Arab imports that might have been expected if this had been the case (Filipowiak 1966; 1969). Other writers (for example Hunwick 1973) suggested that the real capital was situated much further to the north-east, David Conrad (1994) arguing that its location changed more than once, during the thirteenth century being at Dakajalan on the Niger, south of Bamako in Mali. The radiocarbon dates for Niani cluster from the sixth to the tenth centuries AD and also suggest a later reoccupation in about the sixteenth and seventeenth centuries (Calvocoressi and David 1979: 15–16, 23; Sutton 1982: 306, 311). The gap in between could be seen as further reducing the likelihood that this was the capital of the state of Mali at the height of its power in the fourteenth century.

In contrast, the site of Koumbi Saleh, in Mauritania, is thought by most scholars to have been the capital city of the old state of Ghana. Excavations have been conducted there on a number of occasions in the past, some of the earliest work being

that of Thomassey and Mauny (1951; 1956). This site, with its stone buildings of
several storeys and extensive cemeteries, is clearly of the greatest importance.
Although Thomassey and Mauny failed to explore its lower occupation levels,
excavations by Serge Robert (Robert and Robert 1972) and later by Berthier have
remedied that omission. There are now radiocarbon dates for this site extending
from about the fourth to about the eighteenth century AD, although it seems to
have reached its maximum expansion from the twelfth to the fourteenth century
(Sutton 1982: 304–5, 311; S.K. McIntosh and R.J. McIntosh 1986b: 429, 438;
Berthier 1997). The problem with Koumbi Saleh, however, is that in the middle of
the eleventh century al-Bakri described it as consisting of two towns: an Islamic
town and, 'six miles away', the royal town (Levtzion 1973: 22–3). It seems likely
that it is the Islamic town that has been excavated; the other town does not seem to
have been located. This is unfortunate because any evidence for indigenous origins
for this urban development would be more likely to be discovered in the native
town than in the strangers' town.

There are many other archaeological sites of cities or towns that can be identified, or tentatively identified, in the historical record. Although excavations have
been conducted at some of these places, they have tended to concentrate on
second-millennium Islamic deposits and, indeed, some of these sites date from
only the last few centuries. In addition, excavations have sometimes been limited in
scale or have not been attempted at all. In one or other of these categories must
fall: Azelik (Niger), possibly the town of Takedda visited by ibn Battuta in 1353
(S.K. McIntosh and R.J. McIntosh 1984: 85; Bernus and Cressier 1991 (cited by
S.K. McIntosh 1994: 180)); Birnin Gazargamo (Nigeria), one-time capital of
Borno but dating only from the fifteenth century AD (Bivar and Shinnie 1962;
Connah 1981); Kong (Ivory Coast), a trading town apparently dating only from the
sixteenth century AD (Sutton 1982: 306–7, 311); Hamdallahi (Mali), which lasted
for only a few decades in the nineteenth century but has been claimed to have been
'the biggest city of precolonial West Africa' (Mayor 1995: 54; see also Gallay *et al.*
1990; Mayor 1996); and a whole collection of other places such as Timbuktu and
Teghaza in Mali and Kano and Zaria in Nigeria.

In addition to historically known sites, there are numerous other large settlement sites which are relevant to our theme. For example, excavations at the settlement mound of Tongo Maaré Diabal, on the eastern edge of the Middle Niger
area, have shown that this 9 hectare 'town' was occupied from about AD 200 to
about AD 1200 (MacDonald 1999b). Also, work by Bedaux and others (1978) on
the two settlement mounds of Doupwil and Galia in the Inland Niger Delta
revealed settlements that were first occupied in the eleventh century AD. Both of the
latter sites were probably about 8 hectares in area, before erosion, and all three sites
may be compared in size to the approximately 12 hectares of Tegdaoust (Robert
1970: 473), a figure which represents the area of stone foundations only and does

not include a much larger surrounding area of mud and other less permanent architecture. Other settlement mounds of importance are those south of Lake Chad, on the *firki* plains of north-east Nigeria (of which Daima is the best known), some of which constitute the remains of quite large settlements whose origins lie in the first millennium BC (Connah 1981). Actually these are only part of a group of 822 known mounds that also extend across northern Cameroon and into south-western Chad (Holl 1996: 581). Although many of the settlements represented by the mounds were probably too small to be considered as urban themselves, they are nevertheless relevant to an investigation of West African urban origins if the McIntosh regional settlement hierarchy approach is employed. Examining the mounds in northern Cameroon, for instance, Holl (1996: 589) has suggested a settlement hierarchy of at least three levels: 'open mounds of different but generally small size; walled sites, former village chiefdoms and later district centres; and finally paramount central settlements'. Examples of the central settlements were from 7 to over 20 hectares in area, and probably represent the origins of the walled cities and small states that were historically recorded in this region from the sixteenth to the nineteenth century AD.

The practice of enclosing settlements with walls of stone or earth, or with banks and ditches, or merely with timber palisades or naturally grown vegetation, seems to have been widespread in Africa over the last 3000 to 4000 years (Connah 2000 ; in press) but became particularly common in West Africa during the second millennium AD. Probably this had to do with increased competition for resources, as populations expanded or environmental conditions deteriorated. In the West African savanna many towns and cities sought to protect themselves in this way, especially with the increasing use of horses in warfare from the thirteenth or fourteenth century onwards (S.K. McIntosh and R.J. McIntosh 1988: 125). As early as about the ninth century, however, Jenné-jeno was already walled, and Koumbi Saleh was partly enclosed probably by a somewhat later date. Although primarily a protective strategy, almost certainly the walling of large settlements had other functions as well; it assisted in the governance of the inhabitants, it made taxation and control of trade easier, it clearly distinguished city-dwellers from outsiders, and it imparted prestige to rulers. It has also provided archaeologists with some important physical evidence that has still not been adequately exploited. The surviving remains of these enclosures should have encoded in them information about many aspects of the societies that constructed them. Archaeological investigation of those remains might be able to throw light on the size and shape of a former settlement, and on changes through time in that size and shape, as well as on such matters as socio-political organization, basic economy, degree of centralized direction or collective effort, labour availability, resource surplus, existence of political stress or conflict, existence of warfare or threat of warfare or fear of warfare, character of warfare, cultural identity and relationships, surveying skills, engineering expertise, building technology, environmental conditions and agricultural practices. Appropriate research strategies would include detailed and accurate mapping of city enclosures, giving particular attention to siting, layout and structural sequence, and the excavation of rigorously controlled sections through the remains of such structures and especially through the accumulated silt of the accompanying ditch or ditches, where present. However, relatively little such work has been done and the evidence is, of course, fast disappearing.

An example that has been investigated to some extent is the formerly massive city wall of Kano in the north of Nigeria, apparently constructed of both mud-bricks and dumped earth. In the mid-1820s Captain Hugh Clapperton recorded it as about 24 kilometres in length, with fifteen entry gates, and with heights of over 9 metres and a dry ditch on both the inner and outer sides (Denham, Clapperton and Oudney 1826, Clapperton's Narrative 50). In 1885 Paul Staudinger claimed the wall to be 'probably twenty metres high' (Staudinger 1889, trans. Moody 1990: Vol. 1, 210), and Frederick Lugard, faced with the task of storming the wall in 1902, admitted: 'I have never seen, nor even imagined, anything like it in Africa' (Lugard 1903: 28). It is therefore most fortunate that we do have a surface archaeological study of the remains of the wall as they were in the mid-1960s, in which they were assessed in the context of the oral and documentary record (Fig. 4.6). This study, by H.L.B. Moody, identified three phases of growth in the Kano wall system: in the eleventh to twelfth century AD, the late fifteenth century and the seventeenth century; a sequence documenting the growing size and importance of the city as the second millennium AD progressed (Moody 1967; n.d. [1970]). Sadly, there have been few attempts to emulate this work, at least so far as accessible published material indicates, although the 6 square kilometre walled site of Turunku, near Zaria in northern Nigeria, has been the subject of a preliminary study (Effah-Gyamfi 1986). The seriousness of this general omission may be judged from the fact that in 1904 Lugard reported that there were forty walled cities within a 48 kilometres radius of Kano alone (Moody n.d. [1970]: 18). Clearly, field survey and excavation of the precolonial city and town walls of the West African savanna has the potential to add significantly to our understanding of the origins and development of urbanization in the region.

In addition to settlement sites, there are also numerous burial sites which can provide information about the growth of social complexity in the West African savanna. Best known of these are tumuli, or burial mounds, which are found particularly in Mali but also occur as far west as the coast of Senegal and as far east as the extreme north of Nigeria. S.K. McIntosh and R.J. McIntosh (1980: Vol. 1, 31–6) distinguished three types of burial mound in Mali: stone tumuli, in the Sahara; earthen tumuli, in the dry savanna to the west and east of the Inland Niger Delta; and tumuli covering rock-cut tombs, in the wooded savanna. The Saharan stone tumuli can belong to any time from about 4000 BC to about AD 500

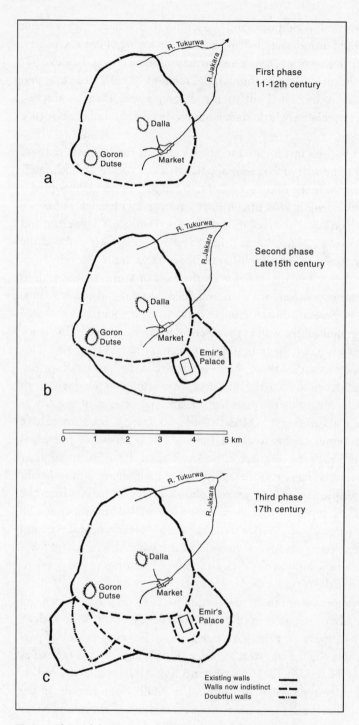

Fig. 4.6 Plans of the Kano city walls, Nigeria, identifying three phases of growth: a, b, and c. After Moody (n.d. [1970]: 39–41).

(MacDonald 1998: 85) and the McIntoshs (1980: Vol. 1, 35) thought that the rock-cut tombs belonged to the first millennium AD. It is the earthen tumuli, however, dating principally to the late first and early second millennium (S.K. McIntosh and R.J. McIntosh 1986b: 428–9, 432; 1988: 116–17) that have provided the most relevant evidence for our inquiry. Both the size of these tumuli and the grave-goods buried with the dead indicate some differences in social status. Indeed, some of the larger earthen tumuli appear to have been quite remarkable structures in a number of ways. Thus some of them have their outer layers of clay baked rock-hard by numerous small fires that were lit on the mound surface. An example of such a tumulus is the 15–18 metre high mound of Koi Gourrey (also known as Killi) in Mali (Desplagnes 1903), where two individuals had been buried with varied grave-goods and with twenty-five to thirty other people, presumably sacrifices entombed at the same time. Still more impressive, perhaps, was the tumulus of El-Oualedji (Fig. 4.7), also in Mali, which was 12 metres high and contained a wooden funerary chamber, in which two individuals had been buried with accompanying objects, and from which a vertical shaft extended to the top of the mound (Desplagnes 1951; R.J. McIntosh 1998: 224–7). These, and perhaps a small number of other tumuli, clearly indicate burial rites of the sort recorded in the middle of the eleventh century, by al-Bakri, for the kings of the state of Ghana:

> When the king dies, they build a huge dome of wood over the burial place. Then they bring him on a bed lightly covered, and put him inside the dome. At his side they place his ornaments, his arms and the vessels from which he used to eat and drink, filled with food and beverages. They bring in those men who used to serve his food and drink. Then they close the door of the dome and cover it with mats and other materials. People gather and pile earth over it until it becomes like a large mound. Then they dig a ditch around it so that it can be reached only from one place. They sacrifice to their dead and make offerings of intoxicating drinks. (al-Bakri, as quoted by Levtzion 1973: 25–6)

Indications of the age of these large earthen tumuli are provided by radiocarbon dates: the early eleventh century AD for El-Oualedji (S.K. McIntosh and R.J. McIntosh 1986b: 428, 439); the tenth to eleventh century for a tumulus at Kouga, in Mali (S.K. McIntosh and R.J. McIntosh 1980: Vol. 1, 31); the eighth to the eleventh century for three tumuli at Toyla, Tissalaten and Kawinza, in the Lakes Region of the Inland Niger Delta (S.K. McIntosh and R.J. McIntosh 1986b: 428–9, 439); and the seventh century for tumuli associated with the Tondidarou standing stones, in Mali (Saliège *et al.* 1980; S.K. McIntosh and R.J. McIntosh 1986b: 428, 439). Some of the grave-goods from these mounds indicate an unusual level of wealth and it has been suggested that this reflects 'the increasing wealth and power of groups controlling the flow of trade goods along the Middle Niger'. It is possible that this increasing social stratification, plus the development of specialized iron production in the Lakes Region and in the adjacent Méma region, and the urban growth

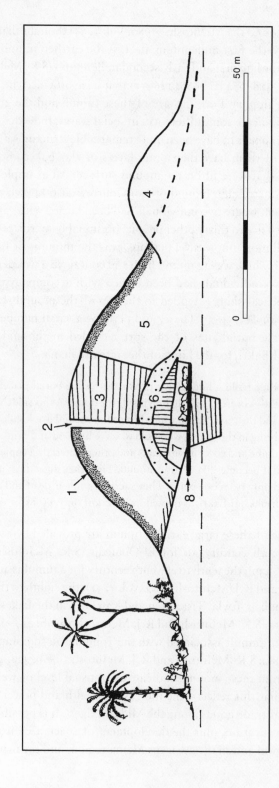

Fig. 4.7 Section through El-Oualedji tumulus, Mali.
1: Fired clay surface. 2: Shaft. 3: Excavated area. 4: Spoil heap. 5: Clay mound. 6: Domed roof of wood and straw. 7: Burial chamber. 8: Layer of sand. Vertical scale double that of horizontal scale. After Desplagnes (1951: Fig. 3).

of Jenné-jeno, were 'all tied in some way to the consolidation of the Empire of Ghana' (S.K. McIntosh and R.J. McIntosh 1988: 116–17).

However, perhaps the most impressive burial evidence comes from a number of tumuli in the Rao region of north-west Senegal. Collectively these mounds yielded a remarkable collection of grave-goods, including jewellery of silver and gold (one item of gold is a decorated disc of exceptional workmanship, of 184 millimetres diameter and 191 grams weight (Fig. 4.8)), an iron sword, beads, and objects of copper (of which two were Moroccan lidded-bowls). When first published, these finds were of unknown age but subsequent attempts to date them have eventually settled on a general period for the northern Senegalese tumuli commencing in the tenth century AD and continuing into the second millennium

Fig. 4.8 Gold disc from Rao, Senegal, diameter 184 millimetres. From Joire (1943: 49).

(Joire 1943; 1955; Posnansky 1973: 152; S.K. McIntosh and R.J. McIntosh 1993b: 104). It is thought that there were until recently over 10,000 tumuli in Senegal, and collective inhumations often with rich grave furnishings have been found in a number of them (S.K. McIntosh and R.J. McIntosh 1983: 247; 1993b: 75). The southern tumuli have been dated to approximately AD 700 to 1000, giving them an earlier origin than those to the north but still making them a later development than the numerous megalithic sites, with which their distribution overlaps (S.K. McIntosh and R.J. McIntosh 1993b: 104–5). Found in both Senegambia and Mali, these arrangements of standing stones, in Senegambia apparently with associated burials and evidence of human sacrifice (Thilmans and Descamps 1974; 1975; Gallay, Pignat and Curdy 1982), have proved difficult to date but radiocarbon dates indicate that they belong principally to the second half of the first millennium AD, although some might be much later (Sutton 1982: 304). Collectively, the wealthy burials and monumental funerary structures of Senegal suggest increasing social differentiation by people who were in touch with both the gold-producing areas to their south and the Arab markets of the Mediterranean world to the north. It seems quite likely that what we are seeing is the archaeological expression of state emergence, in this case of the so-called Empire of Takrur (p. 121) or of some related polity.

All the tumuli discussed above appear to represent non-Islamic burial practices but such practices seem to have been quite varied, so that not only was there inhumation in one sort of tumulus or another but some small earthen tumuli west of the Inland Niger Delta contained cremations in pottery urns (Szumowski 1957). In addition, the usual burial rite in the Inland Niger Delta itself seems to have consisted of inhumation in large pottery urns (S.K. McIntosh and R.J. McIntosh 1980: Vol. 1, 36–7). Nor does this exhaust the variety of non-Islamic burial practices recorded archaeologically from the last three millennia in the West African savanna. However, although many of these burials are probably pre-Islamic in date, some of them could also be later than the introduction of Islam to the area, which was certainly in progress by the eleventh century AD. This is because the replacement of previous practices by Islamic rites is likely to have been a gradual process, rather than an abrupt change. Nevertheless, it is against this general background that the more remarkable burials of Mali and Senegal must be seen, in order to appreciate how exceptional they were.

Subsistence economy

What light does the archaeological evidence outlined above throw on the origins of cities and states in the West African savanna? To begin with one of the easier questions to answer, what does it tell us about the subsistence economy on which such developments must have been based?

Livestock husbandry and cereal cultivation seem to have been firmly established in West Africa by the first millennium BC (S.K. McIntosh 1994: 170; MacDonald and MacDonald 1999). For example, there is evidence for domesticated cattle and small stock, as well as for both domesticated and wild *Pennisetum* sp. (bulrush millet) at Karkarichinkat (Mali) in the second millennium BC (Smith 1992: 73–4). There is also Munson's discovery at Dhar Tichitt, in Mauritania, that *Pennisetum* was being grown by the beginning of the first millennium BC, as part of a mixed farming strategy that included the herding of cattle, sheep and goats (Munson 1976; Holl 1993: 95). Furthermore, from Jenné-jeno itself there is direct evidence for the cultivation of *Oryza glaberrima* (African rice), *Pennisetum* and sorghum from about the third century BC onwards. These were apparently part of a diversified subsistence economy that also included substantial amounts of *Brachiaria ramosa*, a wild millet, and other wild cereals, as well as domesticated cattle, sheep or goats, and hunting and fishing. The occupation of Jenné-jeno lasted till about the fourteenth century AD, and yet the economy remained remarkably stable throughout this long period of approximately 1600 years, although hunting became less important and the breed of cattle changed over time (MacDonald 1995: 313). This general stability was despite marked climatic and demographic changes (S.K. McIntosh 1994: 172–3; 1995: 377–9). The strength of this subsistence base may be judged from the growth of this settlement that was already at least 12 hectares in extent by the beginning of the first millennium AD and reached a maximum area of about 33 hectares towards the end of that millennium (Fig. 4.9). Indeed, the distribution of archaeological sites on the floodplain near Jenné-jeno indicates that towards the end of the first millennium the population density of the Inland Niger Delta was probably greater than it is at present. This was at a time when the climate of this area seems to have been wetter than usual, so that to a large extent this could explain the greater population density (S.K. McIntosh and R.J. McIntosh 1980: Vol. 2, 428; R.J. McIntosh 1983). Another factor of importance, however, may have been the practice of recessional cultivation (the cultivation of naturally watered areas as floodwaters recede), which it is reasonable to assume was used for the cultivation of rice. Elsewhere I have argued that recessional cultivation can constitute a form of agricultural intensification (Connah 1985); so it could perhaps be suggested that urban growth in the Inland Niger Delta was supported by one of the relatively rare examples of African intensive agriculture. Whatever the case, the subsistence economy of the area seems to have been particularly successful. Indeed, the McIntoshs suggest that it was the agricultural surplus of the Inland Niger Delta that provided much of the food for urban centres situated in less fortunate areas such as Timbuktu and Gao and even places further afield. In such movement of foodstuffs, canoe transport on the Niger River seems to have played a major role (S.K. McIntosh and R.J. McIntosh 1980: Vol. 2, 448–50).

Other parts of the West African savanna were probably not quite so fortunate as the area around Jenné-jeno, nor is there much evidence for the subsistence economy of some of them. Nevertheless, it seems that cultivation was already being practised by about 1000 BC both in the Chad basin and in northern Burkina Faso. In particular, the settlement mound of Kursakata, in the Nigerian part of the former area, has produced grains of cultivated *Pennisetum americanum* from the period between about 800 BC and about AD 100, and domesticated cattle and sheep or goat were present at the two settlement mounds of Gajiganna by about 1000 BC (Breunig, Neumann and Van Neer 1996; Neumann, Ballouche and Klee 1996). Significantly the Chad basin is another area where recessional cultivation could have given the inhabitants a distinct advantage, and it seems likely that most cases of increasing social complexity in the West African savanna had an agricultural base that was exceptional in some way, and therefore had the potential to produce a surplus. The probability that such a surplus was frequently in the form of grain, of one sort or another, that could be readily stored or transported, should not be overlooked. This meant that some urban centres strategically situated on trade routes at the edge of the desert could be supported by the surplus produce of more fortunate regions. It also meant that various specialists could be supported within the different urban centres. Furthermore it is becoming apparent that climatic and environmental deterioration may by the twentieth century have rendered the West

Fig. 4.9 Artist's reconstruction of life in the city of Jenné-jeno about 1000 years ago. Photograph from a painting by Charles Santore. Reproduced by permission of the National Geographic Society and of R.J. and S.K. McIntosh.

African savanna less agriculturally viable than it was a thousand years ago. The McIntoshs' evidence for this in the Inland Niger Delta does not stand alone. An overall drop in the level of Lake Chad over the last millennium would indicate that such a deterioration may have been general in the West African savanna (Sutton 1982: 310), in spite of a relatively brief wetter period from about 1500 to about 1630 (Brooks 1998). A similar impression is given by the abandonment of Tegdaoust, after changes in well design which are thought to indicate an increasing water supply problem (Robert 1970).

Technology

It is now apparent that iron technology emerged in West Africa no later than the middle of the first millennium BC. Copper was also being smelted by a similar date (S.K. McIntosh 1994: 173–5; Woodhouse 1998). On the basis of the evidence excavated at Jenné-jeno, it would seem that the occupants of the settlement mounds in the Inland Niger Delta were iron-using from the time of their arrival in the area late in the first millennium BC, in spite of the nearest iron ore being 50 kilometres away (S.K. McIntosh and R.J. McIntosh 1986b: 427; S.K. McIntosh 1995: 380). In addition, the builders of the tumuli and of the megaliths discussed above all seem to have been iron-users. Although the condition of excavated iron is often poor, it is clear that the metal was being used for a variety of purposes by the first millennium AD, ranging from weapons and tools to bracelets and other jewellery. There is also ample evidence that these were indigenous products, in the form of slag and other indications that smelting and blacksmithing were widespread. Indeed, iron production in the Méma region of Mali in the late first millennium and early second millennium AD was on too great a scale for local requirements only (Håland 1980). Similarly, in the Middle Senegal Valley the remains of some 60,000 iron-smelting furnaces have been counted, in only a 15 kilometre portion of the Mauritanian bank of the river, suggesting a substantial level of iron production in the first half of the second millennium AD (Killick and Bocoum 1998).

Judging by the evidence from Jenné-jeno, copper was also reaching the Inland Niger Delta by the middle of the first millennium AD, and crucible and mould fragments as well as metal artefacts indicate that both it and bronze were being worked at Jenné-jeno itself by late in the same millennium, with brass appearing at the end of that millennium. Susan McIntosh has suggested that there may have been 'an in situ evolution of local technology from copper to bronze, with the later introduction of brass from the north' (S.K. McIntosh 1995: 385). Significantly, the early-second-millennium AD tumulus of Koi Gourrey (Killi) produced copper and bronze items, some of which appear to have been made by the lost-wax casting technique (Desplagnes 1903: 165; S.K. McIntosh and R.J. McIntosh 1988: 116). In addition, Bedaux and others (1978) excavated a mould for lost-wax casting from a context dated to the end of the eleventh century and the beginning of the twelfth century, at the settlement mound of Doupwil in the Inland Niger Delta. Thus it does seem likely that items of copper and copper alloys were manufactured locally, although the requisite metals were mined and smelted elsewhere. Less certain in this respect are the occasional items of silver and even gold jewellery that have been recovered from some of the tumulus burials. Gold, which is mentioned so often in the historical sources, is rare in the archaeological record, as might be expected in view of its value in the past as in the present. Nevertheless, a remarkable but apparently undated hoard of gold and silver excavated at Tegdaoust included five gold ingots as well as gold jewellery (Robert 1970), and crucibles with traces of copper and gold, from the same site, possibly belong to the eighth century AD. More satisfactory as evidence, excavations at Jenné-jeno produced a gold earring from a context dated to about AD 850–900 (S.K. McIntosh 1995: 390).

In addition to metal-working of one sort or another, there was probably a fairly wide variety of other technological skills. There must have been miners, particularly of gold (and in this case panners also), but, with the exception of Kiéthéga (1983) archaeology has little to tell us of their techniques. This is in spite of the general location of the gold deposits being quite well known (for example Curtin 1973) and in spite of the existence of ethnohistorical observations of traditional gold-mining methods in West Africa (Addo-Fening 1976). There may also have been specialist builders, because mud architecture dates from the early to middle first millennium AD at Tongo Maaré Diabal and Jenné-jeno, and from a similar date at Daima in north-east Nigeria. Specialization is also possible later in the same millennium at sites in the Inland Niger Delta where mud-bricks rather than merely coursed mud were used for building and occasional fired bricks were employed, while in both the Inland Niger Delta and the Chad basin potsherd pavements were made during the same millennium (S.K. McIntosh and R.J. McIntosh 1980: Vol. 1, 188–9; Connah 1981: 147–9; S.K. McIntosh 1995: 364–5; MacDonald 1999b). Some of the larger megalithic structures and tumuli also suggest the existence of people who had specialized in the necessary construction techniques; particularly is this the case with those tumuli with fire-hardened erosion-resistant clay surfaces, a technique that was at least unusual if not unique.

So far as other crafts are concerned, pottery-making had reached an impressive technical level by the beginning of the first millennium AD. Although hand-made, like most traditional African pottery, it was generally thin-walled, symmetrically shaped in many forms and well fired. It was usually painstakingly decorated, often with impressions and sometimes, in parts of the northern savanna, with painted patterns. Pottery figurines of both animals and humans were also made, particularly in the Chad basin and the Inland Niger Delta, those of the latter area demonstrating considerable artistic skill late in the first millennium and early in the second millennium AD. In addition, from this period at Jenné-jeno there were even pottery drainpipes, that further demonstrate the versatility of fired clay technology (Connah 1981; S.K. McIntosh 1995: 368–9). This technology was part of a long-established and sophisticated tradition of ceramic craftsmanship in the West African savanna, of which the late-first-millennium BC and early-first-millennium AD terracottas from Nok in northern Nigeria are perhaps the most remarkable examples. The production of textiles, on the other hand, as indicated by the archaeological occurrence of spindle-whorls, may not have developed until the end of the first millennium AD, by which time the spinning and weaving of cotton was probably becoming established. However, textile remains (claimed as the earliest known in Sub-Saharan Africa) from Tongo Maaré Diabal have been dated to AD 680–860 (MacDonald 1999b: 41). Previously, such clothing as was worn was probably of leather, and with the longstanding traditions of livestock husbandry in the area, it is reasonable to guess that the working of hides and skins had a long history. Other crafts that must also have been established for many centuries would have included wood-working, bone-working, basketry and mat-making. Although little evidence can usually be expected of these activities, the 8000-year-old dugout canoe from Dufuna in north-eastern Nigeria, Africa's oldest boat and one of the oldest in the world, emphasizes the antiquity of both wood-working skills and water transportation in the West African savanna (Breunig 1996). Equally, the bone tools from the first-millennium BC deposits at Daima and the mat impressions sometimes used as a pottery decoration in the part of Nigeria south of Lake Chad serve as reminders of some of the other less visible crafts (Connah 1981; Wiesmüller 1998). Overall, it does seem that by the first millennium AD there was probably a varied technological base for some of the societies of the West African savanna.

Social system

It is often difficult to determine social organization from archaeological evidence and in the area under discussion it is made the more so by the relatively little fully controlled excavation that has been done until recently. In particular, there has been insufficient area excavation to tell us much about settlement layout or even about house plans. Nevertheless, the apparent density of sedentary settlement in the Inland Niger Delta, or the Middle Senegal Valley, or the plains south of Lake Chad, to name only the better-known areas, suggests the emergence of social complexity before 1000 years ago. So does the growing size of some of these settlements: Jenné-jeno, for example, already of 12 hectares extent by early in the first millennium AD and of 33 hectares towards the end of that millennium. With a population perhaps as large as 13,000 packed into a space enclosed by a 2 kilometre city wall, beyond which perhaps as many people again lived within a distance of 1 kilometre, there must surely have been a development of governmental institutions in order to organize common protection (as the existence of the city wall suggests), maintain law and order, and regulate trade. The McIntoshs question this assumption because of the 'lack of any evidence for chiefly elites' (S.K. McIntosh 1995: 396) and the few indications 'of social or economic differences among the population' (S.K. McIntosh and R.J. McIntosh 1993a: 632), suggesting that this 'challenges many of our assumptions and expectations for early urbanism' (S.K. McIntosh 1995: 397). Perhaps so, but as Peter Breunig has remarked (in a different context): 'In the twentieth century, archaeological research in Africa has repeatedly illustrated the falsity of conclusions drawn from negative evidence' (Breunig 1996: 461). Until far more extensive excavation is done at Jenné-jeno and other early urban sites in the West African savanna, it is probably premature to assume that social stratification and despotic authority were absent, particularly as they do seem to have developed by the time that the state of Ghana first appears in the documentary record in the eighth to ninth century AD. The single gold earring found in the Jenné-jeno excavations appears to be of a similar date and would suggest that there also resources were unequally distributed.

The burial evidence is less problematic: the size and sophisticated construction of some of the larger tumuli, and the wealth of grave-goods sometimes present, are strongly suggestive of the existence of a social hierarchy. The owner of the Rao gold disc, for instance, was no ordinary person (Fig. 4.8). In addition, the presence of human sacrifices in some other burials is also indicative of the special status of the deceased. Overall, it is surely significant that the archaeological evidence, from some of the tumuli, compares so closely with al-Bakri's eleventh-century account of the burial of the kings of Ghana that has already been quoted (p. 127). The Senegambian megaliths also suggest social differentiation, in that like the tumuli they are evidence of the expenditure of considerable effort and resources for the benefit of a select group of people. In general, it seems that during the first millennium AD production and trade in gold and iron, and the presence of an agricultural surplus in some more fortunate areas, were already stimulating social and political changes of which some gave rise to the state of Ghana before the earliest Arab contact. In short, state formation was already in progress before the growth of trans-Saharan trade with Arabic North Africa, and it seems likely that during the earlier first millennium AD ranked chiefdoms, such as may have existed at Dhar Tichitt as early as the second millennium BC, were gradually giving way to stratified societies. At the same time, the development of urban centres was also in progress, as the evidence from Jenné-jeno early in that millennium would suggest. The culmination of such development can be seen in the site plans of Tegdaoust or Koumbi Saleh, the latter with its stone-built houses and tombs, and in the great walled city of Kano, which in 1851 had a population estimated by Heinrich Barth as between 30,000 and 60,000, depending on the time of year (Barth 1857–8: Vol. 2, 124).

As well as social stratification, the archaeological evidence also suggests the development of functional specialization prior to Arab contact. It is apparent from the discussion of technology (pp. 133–5) that a varied range of craftsmen were already present in some West African savanna societies by the first millennium AD. To these should also be added farmers, pastoralists and fishermen; merchants and transporters; religious functionaries and community leaders. Thus the social system in some parts of the West African savanna could have been particularly receptive of Arab and Islamic influences over the last millennium or so. The outcome was a product not simply of those influences but of a complex mixture of the old and the new, of the indigenous and the alien; a mixture that was to evolve over many centuries.

Population pressures

As already discussed in the section on geographical location and environmental factors, the West African savanna is characterized by a dynamic interplay of opportunity and constraint, an interplay that varies through time with fluctuations of rainfall and changes in environment. Not only have human populations had to come to terms with the particular constraints of an area, in order to exploit such opportunities as it offered, but the more productive areas such as the Inland Niger Delta, the Middle Senegal Valley or the plains south of Lake Chad have been bounded by less fortunate areas and have varied in both size and conditions in response to environmental variations, triggered by either climatic change or the impact of human activities such as iron-smelting or the grazing of domesticated animals. Such a situation would have been likely to produce population pressures, not only on the occupants of the advantaged areas by their poorer neighbours, but also within the more productive areas themselves, if a period of environmentally good conditions was followed by a marked environmental deterioration. From the McIntoshs' work, it seems that this is what probably happened in the Inland Niger Delta, where the unusual hydrological conditions allowed the intensification of agriculture by means of the recessional cultivation of rice. Coupled with the availability of other agricultural produce and the movement of commodities both along the Niger River and across it from one environmental zone to another, this could well have encouraged a concentration of population within this area. Certainly the work done by the McIntoshs has revealed an amazing density of settlement by the middle of the first millennium AD. In addition, the area of the Inland Niger Delta is confined and, as the McIntoshs have shown, its complex variety of landforms is highly susceptible to environmental fluctuations, so that by the early second millennium AD many of its settlements had been abandoned. Such an area, richly endowed with resources and yet subject to periodic stress, could well have provided an inception point for social developments in the West African savanna. This is not to say that the Inland Niger Delta was the only place in the West African savanna where this might have taken place, nor is it intended to claim a deterministic role for population pressure so far as increasing social complexity is concerned. Nevertheless, population pressure is surely one of the circumstances that brought about the social changes leading to urbanization and state formation.

Ideology

Historical sources indicate that Islam had an important influence on the course of West African urbanization and state formation. The Islamic world of the early second millennium AD was a world of independent states, in which substantial numbers of people lived in towns and cities that were often the centre of mercantile activities. It was also a proselytizing world, seeking, with fluctuating degrees of enthusiasm, to convert the infidel not only to its religious beliefs but also to its way of life. Archaeology has revealed the remains of early mosques in a number of places: at Koumbi Saleh, Tegdaoust, Es-Souk, Kidal, Talohos and Teghaza (Mauny 1961: 472–6; Robert 1970) and indeed some mosques still in use, such as that at Jenné, are reputed (in origin at least) to be of great age. However, archaeology has also confirmed the historical evidence that indicates that the inhabitants of the earliest cities and states of the West African savanna were definitely not Muslims. The tumuli, in particular, indicate non-Islamic practices, as also do the urn burials of the Inland Niger Delta and the making of clay figurines in that and other areas. Some of this evidence might merely represent a survival of traditional practices after Islam had already been introduced to the West African savanna, and we know from historical sources that this did happen to a considerable extent. Nevertheless, the McIntoshs' evidence of urban development at Jenné-jeno by early in the first millennium would appear to confirm the impression that the origins of urbanization and state formation in the West African savanna *were* pre-Islamic. The people involved with these developments must have been animists of one sort or another and the variety of non-Islamic burial practices in the archaeological record of the West African savanna would suggest that there was considerable diversity of belief between different human groups. It is not known what these beliefs were but the evidence of the tumuli, the megaliths and human sacrifice suggests that funerary cults formed a significant part of them. In such cults, ancestors may have had an important role, so that the monumental character of some of the associated structures may indicate that ideology provided reinforcement for the authority of an elite, as well as part of the cultural identity of a specific group of people.

External trade

Drawing on historical sources, Bovill came to the conclusion that trade was 'a dominant factor in the history of the north-western quarter of the continent'

(Bovill 1968: 236). Indeed, Levtzion, whose opinion has been quoted above (p. 115), clearly saw long-distance trade as a vital stimulus to developments in the West African savanna. What do the archaeological sources have to reveal on the matter? Certainly, evidence of the trans-Saharan trade that Bovill and Levtzion were mainly thinking of has been found often enough. Thus, for example, Koumbi Saleh produced stone plaques with Arabic inscriptions and Islamic decorations painted on them, not to mention stone houses said to show Maghrebian influence (Thomassey and Mauny 1951; 1956). Thus also, Tegdaoust yielded imported pottery, oil lamps, glass vessels, glass weights and ingots of both copper and gold (Robert 1970). Perhaps the most impressive of the archaeological evidence for the trans-Saharan trade, however, is amongst the group of twelfth- and thirteenth-century gravestones found at Sané, near Gao on the Niger in Mali. Some of these are marble gravestones with inscriptions in Kufic, an early angular form of the Arabic alphabet that was often used in decorative work. These inscribed stones have been closely dated to AD 1100–1110 and are thought to have been made to order in Spain and carried by camel across the Sahara (Flight 1975: 82). In fact, there is even archaeological evidence of the difficulties that could assail such trans-Saharan camel transport, in the form of the abandoned loads of a caravan buried in a sand-dune in the lonely Majâbat Al-Koubrâ, halfway across the desert. Dated to the twelfth century AD, these loads consisted of large numbers of brass rods and of cowrie shells of the species *Monetaria moneta* (Monod 1969). The presence of such shells, over 9000 kilometres from their source in the Maldive Islands, south-west of India, is also eloquent testimony to the very extensive trading networks of which the trans-Saharan trade formed a part (Hogendorn and Johnson 1986: 18).

There is, indeed, a considerable amount of archaeological evidence for the trans-Saharan trade. In mentioning some of the more remarkable examples, as has just been done, it should not be forgotten for instance that countless sites in the West African savanna contain beads of glass or semi-precious stones; many of the earlier of these must have originated from that trade. The source and date of manufacture of such beads can be difficult to determine but some may indicate that the Saharan trade is older than has usually been thought. Of six Jenné-jeno glass beads selected for chemical analysis, found in contexts dating from the last two centuries BC to AD 1400, the earliest is likely to have been made in India or East or South-East Asia, while one of the later ones may have come from India, another may have been Roman in origin, from either Egypt or Italy, and only two appear to be from an Islamic source (S.K. McIntosh 1995: 252–6). Furthermore, a rather different sort of evidence for the Saharan trade, consisting of the location of some of the West African cities and towns, should not be overlooked. Pushed well forward of the most viable agricultural lands of the savanna or even into the desert proper, places like Timbuktu, or Tegdaoust, or Teghaza were clearly located at strategic points on the trade-routes, rather than in hinterlands that

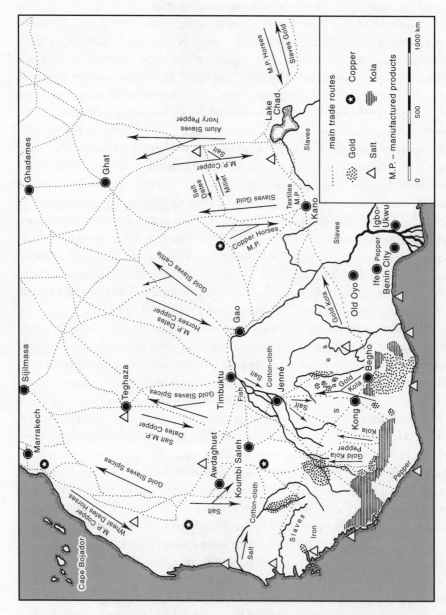

Fig. 4.10 Precolonial trade routes and commodities in West Africa. After Mauny (1961: Fig. 55).

could support them. Also, it is interesting to note that many of the savanna urban centres appear to have grown up at environmental interfaces, between transportation systems. Thus at Timbuktu goods were transferred from camel to canoe and at Kano from camel to donkey. A comparable situation will be seen in Chapter 5: trading centres growing up at the junction of the forest and savanna, where the tsetse fly made it necessary to transfer goods from donkey back to human head.

It may be noticed, however, that archaeological evidence does not give anything like a true picture of the Saharan trade as seen by historians (Fig. 4.10). Where in the archaeological evidence is any indication of the literally millions of tons of salt that must have travelled south from the desert itself to the savanna (Lovejoy 1986)? Similarly, where is the evidence of the cloth that, we are told, was carried south from North Africa, or of the thousands of slaves who were taken north (Meillassoux 1991: 44–64), or of the ivory, ostrich feathers, fine leather and pepper? For that matter, who would realize, from the archaeological evidence, just how important the gold trade was? Clearly, some of the manufactured often inorganic durable commodities, that were traded to the south, had a greater chance of surviving in archaeological contexts than the generally organic consumable raw materials which dominated the trade to the north. Thus there will be a tendency for the West African archaeological evidence to be biased in favour of imports, which makes the discovery at Gao of a tenth- to eleventh-century AD hoard of at least fifty-three hippopotamus tusks, apparently a hidden consignment of export ivory, particularly important (Insoll 1995; 1996a: 38, 40, 98). However, questions about the traded commodities lead on to others. If West African agriculture is at least 3000 years old, as the evidence appears to indicate, then why should we believe that the salt trade developed only towards the end of the first millennium AD with the advent of the Arabs and of their camel caravans? According to Nenquin (1961) it has been calculated that a fully grown person on a mixed diet needs 12–15 grams of salt per day. In the West African savanna, salt could be brought from the coast where it has long been extracted from seawater, or transported from the Sahara where it is quarried from rock-salt deposits, or obtained by filtering plant ashes, which is possible only in certain areas and not very efficient as a source of supply (Bloch 1963). In practice, this leaves extensive areas where the local supply is deficient but where diet and climate make salt a necessity. Implicit in this situation are two probabilities: (1) that trade networks within West Africa are likely to be almost as old as food production, as already suggested on p. 112 and (2) that trading contacts with the desert are likely to be nearer to 3000 than to 1000 years old. In addition, no one has ever suggested that gold-mining in West Africa commenced because of economic or technological stimulus from across the desert. On the contrary historical source after historical source tells us that West Africans were so secretive about the location of the mines that outsiders had very little idea where the gold came from. Furthermore, there is now evidence of gold at Jenné-jeno by AD 800. There thus seem to be several reasons for supporting the McIntoshs' idea that a regional network of trade routes grew up in West Africa before the advent of the Arab trans-Saharan trade. The McIntoshs (1980: Vol. 2, 444–6) pointed out that because Jenné-jeno was iron-using from the time of its earliest occupation, and because there was no iron ore in the vicinity, then supplies of raw materials or of finished iron would have had to be brought from over 50 kilometres away. Also, situated at the interface of the dry savanna and the Sahel, on a fertile alluvial plain, and at the highest point on the River Niger for reliable seasonal river transport, Jenné-jeno was well placed to play an important role in a developing trade network.

That such a network could also have had earlier connections with the desert, and perhaps even beyond it, is suggested by the enigmatic paintings and engravings of horse-drawn chariots and ox-drawn carts on rocks in the Sahara, that have so often been discussed (Mauny 1978; Law 1980a). These are distributed along two main axes across the desert, both of which stretch from North Africa to the Niger, axes which have been called the 'chariot tracks'. It has been assumed that these rock-drawings date from the first millennium BC, more likely from its second half. Most scholars now doubt that these are representations of vehicles used in commerce, however, and Camps (1982) has rejected the idea of 'routes', pointing out that the distribution of this rock art merely reflects the distribution of rock outcrops in the Sahara. Nevertheless, whatever else this art may mean, it is important in indicating that horse and ox traction and wheeled vehicles were known in the desert before the advent of the camel during the first few centuries AD (p. 111). Indeed, Blench has argued convincingly that the small West African ponies, so often mentioned in historical sources, 'were produced by the dwarfing of horses brought across the Sahara in the last three thousand years' (Blench 1993: 103). Even Bovill could admit, with characteristic wisdom, that: 'There is certainly no reason to suppose that caravan traffic in the Sahara only became possible with the arrival of the camel' (Bovill 1968: 17). That such traffic could have been at least pre-Arab in origin has been indicated by Timothy Garrard. He has suggested the existence of a Berber gold trade in the early first millennium AD, between the savanna and the Roman world, because the Carthage mint began issuing gold coins at the end of the third century although it had no local gold source (Garrard 1982). In addition, the McIntoshs (1980: Vol. 2, 445) have commented on the presence of copper at Jenné-jeno from the middle of the first millennium AD; the three closest known sources all being in the Sahara. Overall, the McIntoshs could well have been correct when they argued that 'the rapid establishment and expansion of Arab trade in the Western Sudan was possible because it keyed into an already-extant system of indigenous sub-Saharan trade networks' (S.K. McIntosh and R.J. McIntosh 1980: Vol. 2, 450).

Conclusion

The emergence of urbanism and political centralization in the West African savanna was formerly attributed to contact with the Mediterranean world, resulting from long-distance trade. Suspiciously, the origins of that trade were usually dated to the period of the earliest historical sources that touched on the subject. Archaeology tended to play a confirmatory, some might even say a subservient, role in the stock historical interpretation. It was a case of so much historical information being available that archaeologists failed to ask the sort of questions that they might have asked otherwise. As a result, the quality of the archaeological data available to shed light on the origins of cities and states in the West African savanna was poor. Fortunately, this situation has begun to change, and work at Jenné-jeno and related sites in the Inland Niger Delta, as well as in other parts of the West African savanna, is producing a very different picture. A review of the evidence both new and old makes the long-accepted external-stimulus explanation untenable. It would appear that the West African savanna by the beginning of the first millennium AD already had a sound agricultural base, with the potential for intensification of production in some more fortunate areas, and already had a varied iron-based technology. Developing social complexity is already evident at Dhar Tichitt as early as the second millennium BC, and it seems quite probable that during the first millennium AD, and prior to Arab contact, stratified societies were emerging in the West African savanna, on the basis of resource control stimulated in part by localized population pressures. At the same time those pressures, coupled with increasing functional specialization and expanding local trade, encouraged a growth in size both of individual settlements and of aggregations of settlements, leading to some of West Africa's earliest examples of urbanism. Such developments seem to have taken place before the advent of Islam but, nevertheless, with the ideological support of a variety of probably animistic religions. Finally, although adequately dated evidence is limited, it seems most likely that an extensive trading network existed within West Africa before the Arab trade across the Sahara began and that this network had already developed contacts across the desert. The cities and towns of the savanna were indeed to become 'ports' at the edge of the 'sea of sand', as Levtzion (1973: 10) said (p. 115), but they were ports with a vast trading hinterland that already existed. After all, what ship would ever visit a port unless there was a chance of a cargo to collect?

Chapter 5

Brilliance beneath the trees: the West African forest and its fringes

It was in the second half of the fifteenth century AD that European sailors first set eyes on the southerly coast of West Africa. What they saw was hardly encouraging. From a distance, a vague grey line pencilled in between an immensity of sea and sky. From close-in, either a dangerous, surf-pounded, sandy beach or an uninviting network of mangrove swamp, creek and river mouth. Whatever the character of the shoreline, however, behind it there was nearly always an impenetrable tangle of trees and other vegetation. Experience soon taught such visitors that this was a coast to be reckoned with: ships' crews died of fever, shipworms (*Teredo* spp.) ate the bottoms out of their ships. As the centuries went by, it was this coast that became known as 'The White Man's Grave': a name that to many proved to be no exaggeration. Yet it was neither altruism nor curiosity that tempted most Europeans to such a region, it was profit. The very names that they gave to different parts of this coast indicate their motives: 'The Grain [pepper] Coast', 'The Ivory Coast', 'The Gold Coast', 'The Slave Coast' (Bosman 1967: frontispiece map). For Europeans had quickly discovered that behind the coast itself lay a forested hinterland rich in resources, where the inhabitants were able and willing to trade on a considerable scale. Not only that, but those inhabitants lived in highly organized communities, some of which took on a size and density which left the visitors in no doubt about what they were dealing with. Within some parts of the West African forest there were, indeed, hierarchical states and there were towns and cities. Because of their conspicuousness, it was these large settlements that particularly attracted European attention. Thus, writing in AD 1507–8, the Portuguese Duarte Pacheco Pereira described Ijebu-Ode (in what is now Nigeria) as 'a very large city called Geebuu' (Bascom 1959: 38). Thus also, in about 1600, the Dutchman 'D.R.' (thought to have been Dierick Ruiters) described the main street of Benin City (also now in Nigeria) as 'a great broad street, not paved, which seemeth to be seven or eight times broader than the Warmoes street in Amsterdam' (Hodgkin 1975: 156). In a similar vein, the Englishman Towerson, writing in 1557, could claim, perhaps with some exaggeration, that a town in what is now Ghana, was 'by the estimation of our men, as big in circuit as London' (Blake 1942: Vol. 2, 406).

These quotations have been deliberately selected from *early* in the history of European West African contact. This has been done because state development and urbanization in the West African forest have sometimes been written about as if they were developments resulting from that contact rather than pre-dating it. For instance, this was the impression given by Goody when he discussed what he called the 'gun states of the forest' (Goody 1971: 55, and see p. 8). Although there is no doubt that European seaborne trade did play an important part in the later development of the forest states and their towns and cities, historical sources suggest that some of them at least were in existence before that trade started. In so far as they can be trusted, some oral traditions give a similar impression and, since the middle of the twentieth century, archaeological evidence has become available that points in the same direction. It seems likely that there was increasing social complexity in some parts of the West African forest from late in the first millennium AD onwards. The question is 'why?' Why should such developments take place in the West African rainforest, an environment that to many outsiders has seemed to constrain rather than to encourage human endeavour?

Geographical location and environmental factors

Compared with the West African savanna, discussed in Chapter 4, the tropical rainforest of West Africa occupies a relatively small area. An extension of the equatorial rainforest, it stretches from Cameroon to Sierra Leone but is broken between the western frontier of Nigeria and eastern Ghana by a gap where forest–savanna mosaic and also relatively moist woodlands and savanna reach the ocean. The belt of rainforest is never wider than 400 kilometres and in many places it is far narrower than this. To the south it is bounded by coastal mangrove swamp or by the Atlantic Ocean itself. To the north it merges into forest–savanna mosaic, often called 'derived savanna' because there is a strong suspicion that it results from human agricultural exploitation, over many centuries, of what was originally tropical rainforest. The northern fringes of the forest form, in fact, an ecotone that has been particularly important in the history of the human race in West Africa.

As recently as the middle of the twentieth century the West African forest, where undisturbed, consisted of dense tropical rainforest. A few large trees grew to a height of about 42 metres and many others to a height of about 27 metres, but they protruded above the main leaf canopy that was formed at about 10 metres by most of the trees. Smaller trees and bushes densely occupied the zone below. It is possible that in its natural state the forest often lacked this dense tangle of lower growth and the forest floor may have been relatively easy to traverse (Richards 1952: Fig. 6, pp. 29–31). However, much of the forest has now been taken over by a dense tangle of secondary growth, often of no great height but virtually impenetrable unless one chops a path through with a machete. To some extent, this results from modern timber exploitation but even at the beginning of the twentieth century Thompson (1910–11: 131) recorded that most of the forest consisted of secondary growth. It seems probable that this situation resulted from the long practice of rotational bush-fallow agriculture. In the area around Benin City, for instance, it was shown during the 1960s that most of the apparently 'well-grown forest of considerable age' had probably 'been farmed at one time or another during the past few hundred years' (Allison 1962: 243, 244). Thus, in 1897, Boisragon and Locke, fleeing for their lives after the so-called 'Benin Massacre', found it very difficult to travel through the forest. Boisragon described the tangled vegetation as follows:

> if one tries to imagine a thick wood in which big and little trees all intermingle their branches, with a tremendous dense undergrowth of shrubbery of all sorts, with brambles and various other evildoing thorns, all woven together into a maze so thick that neither man nor beast can press through it, one comes somewhere near the idea. (Boisragon 1897: 94)

It is quite possible that Boisragon exaggerated the difficulties, but an 1817 account of part of the Asante forest, in what is now Ghana, by Bowdich (1966: 20–1), indicated the problems of travel even when fear was not forcing the traveller to attempt to go cross-country. It is descriptions such as these, and illustrations such as that in a late-nineteenth-century French book by Capitaine Binger (Fig. 5.1), that make it so difficult to understand how the West African rainforest could have been the setting for the cultural developments that undoubtedly took place there. In reality, the forest is much more complex and much more varied than descriptions by culture-shocked Europeans, writing to impress other Europeans, have often made it appear. In the area around Benin City, for example, it seems that vegetation on the upper interfluves may originally have been less dense than that of the lower valley slopes and it has been shown that farming has tended to concentrate on those more easily cleared areas (Darling 1982: Vol. 1, 33–48). Darling suggested that the forest environment around Benin varied in part because of the ever-changing mosaic of plant succession following agricultural clearance and fallowing but also in part because of differences in soil characteristics. In addition, if we look at local perceptions of the environment, we find not the European notion of continuous forest broken only by clearings for settlements but a three-part division of the 'forest' itself into farmlands, fallow and 'wild' forest. What Darling found around Benin could in all probability be applied also to other parts of the West African rainforest.

In one important respect the forest has a considerable advantage over the savanna lands to its north: it has more water. Rainfall is higher, the wet season is longer, humidity is greater and evapotranspiration is lower. As a result, the forest is well supplied with rivers and streams, many of which run all the year round. Also as a result, the rate and ease of vegetal growth is phenomenal; even fences take root and grow into thriving hedges or rows of trees. Although fertility is a somewhat subjective concept, it is apparent that many forest soils are moderately fertile, if this is measured in terms of productivity. This is providing that farming practices

Fig. 5.1 Rainforest in the Ivory Coast in the late nineteenth century. From Binger (1892: Vol. 2, 269).

are adopted which minimize erosion and which alternate brief cropping periods with long periods of fallow, during which the 'bush' is allowed to invade the fields.

It is important to note the main resources that would probably have been available in the West African forest some 2000 or 3000 years ago. The most significant of these would have been plant foods, including several species of yam, the oil-palm, kola, coffee, *roselle*, okra, fluted gourd and *akee*. At the western end of the forest belt there may also have been African rice and Melegueta pepper, the so-called 'Grains of Paradise' (Harris 1976: 329–33). So important have introduced plants of South-East Asian and tropical American origin now become in the forest (such as certain yams, plantain, banana, sugar-cane, citrus fruits, cassava, sweet potato, maize, papaw and chili pepper) that it is easy to forget that the West African forest was already well endowed with plant foods before these others arrived. Particularly important amongst the indigenous plants would have been the various West African yams and the oil-palm, the former providing carbohydrates and the latter supplementing these with both fat and vitamin A (Harris 1976: 351). It should be noticed, however, that both yams and oil-palms seem originally to have belonged in the forest–savanna ecotone and must have been introduced to the forest proper by people planting them on cleared land. Thus Coursey's West African 'yam zone' (Fig. 4.1) includes extensive areas of the southern savanna as well as the more northerly parts of the forest (Coursey 1980: Fig. 1). In contrast to the plant food situation, the forest was not so well provided with animal foods as was the savanna. The presence of tsetse flies precluded the keeping of domesticated livestock in the forest, with the exception of small numbers of trypanosomiasis-resistent dwarf goats and cattle (on which see Blench 1993). Furthermore, the forest had fewer wild animals that could be hunted than did the savanna, although a wide selection of those that were present have probably been eaten at various times in the past, including elephants, baboons, monkeys, bats, large rats, the giant land snail (*Achatina* spp.) and anything else that could be caught. In addition, fish from the sea, from coastal lagoons and from rivers have almost certainly been an important source of animal protein for a long time. As well as food, the forest possessed numerous other resources, however. Perhaps most important was the availability of a great many different types of wood, suitable for everything from house-building, to canoe-making, to carving, to firewood. Various sorts of wood could also be burnt to produce such things as charcoal, potash, salt and ashes for 'native soap' and 'native butter' (Darling 1982: Vol. 1, 41). In addition, the forest could supply numerous medicinal substances, beeswax, gum, bark, rope and many other things. There was also ivory, which could be obtained in some quantity, and inorganic raw materials included gold, iron ore, copper, lead, rocks suitable for making grindstones, good building earths and potting clays. Lastly, a population density that in many places was probably higher than could be found in the savanna provided a resource that could be exploited as a source of slaves.

As already indicated in the case of trypanosomiasis, the West African forest zone suffered from constraints as well as benefiting from substantial resources. The most important of these constraints must have been the heavy burden of human diseases. Malaria, in particular, has been so serious a problem for so long a time that some populations in the forest have developed a greater than normal incidence of the sickle-cell gene, a blood anomaly that provides a measure of protection against this disease (Livingstone 1967). Other serious diseases would have included yellow fever, dengue fever, filariasis, yaws and a wide selection of parasitic infections, particularly of the human intestinal tract. This list by no means covers the full range of suffering that was risked by occupants of the West African forest. One suspects that disease levels in the forest may have been higher than those of the savanna, particularly of the drier savanna. Another constraint within the forest was the availability of water during the dry season. For in spite of a more plentiful water supply than in the savanna, a long dry season together with the generally permeable forest soils and high temperatures on cleared surfaces, meant that women and children frequently had to carry water long distances from rivers and streams. Various strategies were used to alleviate this problem, including digging wells, underground cisterns and even artificial ponds. The extent to which dry-season water supply could be a problem, however, particularly for large groups of people on the move, is illustrated by the experience of the British expedition against Benin City in 1897, for which water was a major worry (Home 1982). That same expedition also serves as a reminder of just how difficult communication within the forest could be, with movement restricted to narrow paths and head-loading the only means of shifting burdens. Communication problems have, indeed, been another of the forest's traditional constraints, particularly during the wet season when forest paths are frequently reduced to a sea of mud. Nevertheless, it is possible to exaggerate such difficulties, for the people who lived in the forest adapted well to them. Thus canoe transport on rivers and coastal lagoons was extremely important (Smith 1970) and the very impenetrability of the forest could be turned to good use as a defence by leaving a ring of uncleared land around settlements, as was recorded in the nineteenth century for both the 'war-towns' of Sierra Leone (Siddle 1968) and the towns of the Yoruba (Ajayi and Smith 1971: 23).

It is all too easy for outsiders to underestimate the potential for cultural growth in the West African forest and forest fringes. To people not accustomed to living in such environments and adapted to them, the constraints would seem sufficient discouragement from developing the undoubted resources. However, cities and states did grow up in some parts of those zones and these developments probably commenced without external stimulus, because both distance and environment insulated the forest and its fringes from the communities of the northern savanna. Nevertheless, by the end of the first millennium AD the forest was probably already linked with the savanna in a wide-ranging, regional, trading network (Insoll 1996b:

668). It was only the appearance of European traders on the coast of West Africa that reversed this economic orientation and turned what had been a remote hinterland into a major contact-zone of long-distance trade.

Sources of information

Most of what is known about precolonial urbanization and state formation in the West African forest and its fringes comes from historical sources. These are of two main sorts that give us information on different aspects of the subject: the outsider's view and the insider's view. The outsider's view is represented by the numerous contemporary written accounts of European visitors from the late fifteenth to the late nineteenth century. These visitors included people of different national backgrounds: particularly Portuguese, English, Dutch, French, Danish and German; and with a variety of professional orientations: including sailors, traders, explorers and missionaries. To their number must be added others, who merely stayed at home and compiled books and maps on the basis of information collected from those who had actually visited the Guinea Coast. Some of the principal accounts by outsiders are those by Adams, Barbot, de Barros, Bosman, Bowdich, Burton, Dapper, de Marees, Landolphe and Pacheco Pereira; and this list does considerable injustice to the many it does not mention. Such sources throw a good deal of light on some of the forest societies of West Africa during the 400 years prior to colonial takeover. A.F.C. Ryder, for instance, was able to use them as the main basis for a detailed study of European relationships with the state of Benin (Ryder 1969). They are limited, however, not only by their sometimes imperfect understanding of what they observed but also by their short time range. Whereas external sources for the West African savanna reach back for a little over a thousand years, those for the forest zone cover only half that time. Fortunately, however, they are complemented by the insider's view, represented by the oral traditions of the West African societies themselves. Many of these have been collected by European scholars in recent times but some have actually been recorded by representatives of the people to whom they refer. Perhaps the most notable of these are Samuel Johnson's *History of the Yorubas*, originally published in 1921 (Johnson 1921), and Jacob Egharevba's *Short history of Benin*, first published in 1934 (Egharevba 1968). Such sources do throw a little light on the centuries before the first appearance of the Europeans on the Guinea Coast; they take us back perhaps to the beginning of the second millennium AD. Unfortunately, however, their information on the earlier periods is limited and of doubtful reliability. Their chronologies are particularly uncertain, as Bradbury was able to demonstrate in the case of Benin City (Bradbury 1959). Overall, therefore, the written and oral historical sources have comparatively little to tell us about the *origins* of cities and states in the forest, except that such developments either took place during, or had already taken place by, the first half of the second millennium AD. From such sources, it has sometimes been implied that these developments were generally later than those of the savanna because it took rather longer for long-distance trade routes and postulated migrations to reach so far into the hinterland (for example Oliver and Fage 1962). In other words, as in the savanna, external stimulus has been advanced as an explanation. Clearly, it becomes important to examine such relevant archaeological evidence as we have, in order to see whether this alternative source of information can throw any light on these matters.

Archaeological research, into the last two or three millennia, commenced in the West African forest rather later than in the savanna. As a result, it was spared some of the uninformative destruction that took place further north and was for a time more adequately published. Nevertheless, there has been a similar tendency to pursue research programmes aimed at providing more information on historically known sites. In the case of the forest, however, two particular circumstances have exaggerated this tendency to a marked degree. The first is that archaeological field prospection and survey is so difficult in the forest that sites are not easily found and there has been a disinclination amongst archaeologists even to make the attempt. It is so much easier to excavate sites which are known from documentary sources or from oral traditions to have been important. Patrick Darling's work on the linear earthworks of Benin and Ishan (Darling 1974; 1976; 1982; 1984; 1988; 1998) is one of the rare cases where deliberate, systematic search has revealed previously unknown sites. Second, the remarkable artistic traditions associated with some of the historically known sites of southern Nigeria have tended to concentrate archaeological field research at those sites and to influence the sort of research that is carried out (see for example Willett 1967 on the subject of Ife). The overall result is that archaeological field research, in particular archaeological excavation, has been limited to relatively few sites, although a substantial amount of work has been done at some of those sites. So far as the subject of the present enquiry is concerned, such work has tended to concentrate on Ghana and Nigeria, although there has been some activity in Sierra Leone and the Republic of Bénin. In a number of ways, it is surprising how little these efforts have yet told us.

It is instructive to examine the more important of the archaeological evidence that is relevant to the origins of urbanization and state formation in the forest and its fringes. Perhaps some of the most interesting comes from archaeological investigations into the origins of the Akan states, in what is now Ghana. It is with some justification that James Anquandah (1982: 85–112) wrote of what he called: 'The Akan – "a golden civilization" in the forest', for these states seem to have controlled a part of the gold trade from the forest north to the Inland Niger Delta (Dumett 1979). The Akan states already existed by the late fifteenth century AD, when they were mentioned by the earliest European visitors to the West African coast, and a considerable amount is known about the last major Akan state, that of

Asante, in the eighteenth and nineteenth centuries (McLeod 1981). The earlier of these states were situated on the fringes of the forest, and archaeological investigations at the site of Begho (Fig. 5.2), in this region, have revealed the remains of a large market town made up of four different 'quarters', which were 1–2 kilometres from one another (Posnansky 1987). These constituted a dispersed pattern of residence, probably subject to episodic mobility (Fletcher 1998). According to local traditions they belonged, respectively, to the Akan-speaking Brong, to the Kramo, who were Muslim merchants presumed to have come from Mali to the north-west, to the Tumfour or artisans, and to the Nyaho, who were a mixed group. Each of these quarters consists of a group of mounds, about 1.5 metres high and 30 metres across, which are often L-shaped and which are in most cases the remains of mud-walled houses. Some 1500 of these mounds have been counted, enabling Anquandah (1993a: 648) to estimate that the population of Begho peaked at 10,000 in the seventeenth century AD, when the densest area of settlement covered about 3 square kilometres. At first, oral tradition and radiocarbon dates indicated that the town was occupied between about 1400 and 1725, being most prosperous towards the beginning of the seventeenth century (Posnansky 1976: 51), but radiocarbon dates from subsequent excavations indicated that settlement probably began as early as the eleventh or twelfth century (Crossland 1976; Posnansky and McIntosh 1976: 166, 189). Excavation of some of the house mounds has yielded

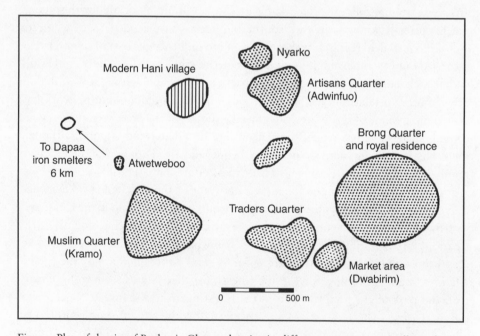

Fig. 5.2 Plan of the site of Begho, in Ghana, showing its different components. Spelling of some names varies in published sources. After Anquandah (1993a: Fig. 38.3).

evidence of a population engaged in metallurgical, textile and ceramic industries, supported by an agricultural subsistence economy that included domestic cattle, sheep, goats and pigs, and by a substantial long-distance trade (Anquandah 1993a: 649).

At Bono Manso (Fig. 5.3), another town site in the same region as Begho, occupation appears to have commenced about the thirteenth century and to have continued until about the middle of the eighteenth century (Effah-Gyamfi 1979; 1985). This seems to have been a more nucleated settlement than Begho and perhaps more homogeneous in its ethnic composition, for there was a separate settlement of aliens (probably Muslim merchants) about 4 kilometres away at Kramokrom. Like Begho, Bono Manso was also characterized by numerous small mounds, most of which represented the remains of houses and from which population estimates could be made. Archaeological investigations, including excavation, showed that Phase I of the settlement had occupied a more extensive area than Phases II and III but that its population, estimated at about 4000, had actually been lower than the approximately 10,000 and 8000 estimated respectively for the two later phases. It thus appeared that a dispersed pattern of residence had changed to a more compact one, perhaps reflecting socio-political changes. As Effah-Gyamfi (1985: 216) suggested:

> between the thirteenth and fourteenth centuries A.D., the inhabitants might have been organized into a loose political unit which developed into a stronger political authority between the fifteenth and sixteenth centuries, a phenomenon which might have affected the morphology of the town.

This contraction to a more densely occupied form of settlement is of considerable theoretical interest because, according to Fletcher's 'Interaction-Communication Model', 'Bono Manso contracted to precisely the maximum areal extent at which it could have been nonliterate and permanently sedentary' (Fletcher 1998: 125).

Thus Begho and Bono Manso do throw some light on the origins of urbanization, and perhaps of state formation, in the fringes of the Ghanaian forest, but there seems to be no evidence of such developments in this area earlier than the beginning of the second millennium AD. Nor is much known of their antecedents, although the second phase of the occupation site excavated some 150 kilometres further north at New Buipe represents an iron-using community and appears to date from late in the first millennium AD. Consisting of three mounds with a total diameter of less than 200 metres, it nevertheless seems to have been part of a larger site complex (York 1973). It may also be significant that the area of the early Akan states on the forest fringes (the centre of Akan power shifted south into the forest proper only after European contact) is the same general area that has provided the bulk of the evidence for the early food-producing Kintampo Culture of the late second millennium BC. In addition, it is an area rich in iron ore and it has produced

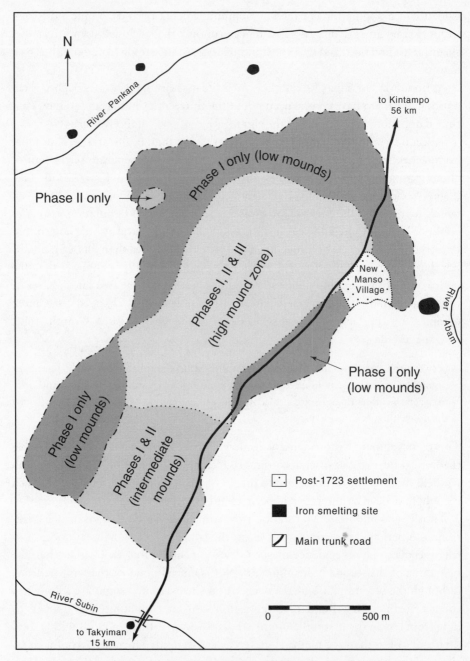

Fig. 5.3 Plan of the site of Bono Manso, in Ghana, indicating a change from a dispersed pattern of residence to a more compact one. After Effah-Gyamfi (1979: Fig. 2).

a second-century AD radiocarbon date for iron-smelting at Hani, near Begho (Posnansky and McIntosh 1976) and a fourth-century radiocarbon date for an iron-smelting site adjacent to Bono Manso (Effah-Gyamfi 1985: 204). The major problem has been the lack of data to link such earlier evidence to the growth of urban communities in the second millennium AD. This is in spite of excavations by Shinnie and Kense (1989) at the town site of Daboya, situated on the White Volta River further north in the savanna, which were able to demonstrate a somewhat shifting pattern of settlement over the last 4000 years or so, with the earliest evidence for iron in about the middle of the first millennium BC. Apparently a source of salt and with the river providing a reliable supply of both water and fish, Daboya probably became a link in a trading network that extended mainly north–south but also east–west. However, investigations at this site have shed relatively little light on the subject of socio-political change.

Other important archaeological evidence relevant to urbanization and the growth of the state in the West African forest and forest fringes relates to the Yoruba people of south-western Nigeria. Yoruba urbanization, in particular, is a subject that has attracted the attention of many scholars. As Bascom could write:

> The Yoruba of Western Nigeria have large, dense, permanent settlements, based upon farming rather than upon industrialization, the pattern of which is traditional rather than an outgrowth of acculturation. They are undoubtedly the most urban of all African peoples, the percentage living in large communities being comparable to that in European nations. (Bascom 1955: 446)

Indeed, as Bascom pointed out, in 1931 nine out of the ten largest cities in Nigeria were Yoruba, the only exception being Kano. Studies of this interesting phenomenon, however, have concentrated on the present time and on historical sources, most of which are of nineteenth-century date (for example Mabogunje 1962; Ojo 1966a; 1966b; Krapf-Askari 1969; but on the archaeology of Nigerian urbanism in general see Okpoko 1998). There has been less concern about remoter origins, except from a theoretical point of view. This is probably because many people are persuaded, like Eades (1980: 43), that 'the impressive scale of urban development' observed by modern scholars 'in most cases does not predate 1800'. Indeed, the early-nineteenth-century Fulani attacks on northern Yorubaland, and the Yoruba civil wars that followed, do seem to have played a substantial part in the development of the urban pattern that now exists. Nevertheless, some large urban centres, such as Ijebu-Ode, clearly did exist amongst the Yoruba at an earlier date (Momin 1989; Fletcher 1998: 128) and archaeological investigations are beginning to give some idea of how they developed. Particularly important were the excavations and survey during the 1970s by Robert Soper at the site of Old Oyo, in the southern savanna, which as the capital of a large Yoruba state was at the height of its power in the seventeenth and eighteenth centuries AD. In common with many Yoruba towns and cities, Old Oyo was surrounded by a complex of earthen banks and ditches, from a study of which Soper and Darling (1980) were able to gain some idea of the shape of the former settlement and to suggest a tentative relative chronology for its development (Fig. 5.4). Soper (1993) also surveyed the site of the ruler's palace within Old Oyo, and showed how closely its plan compared with that of the pre-1979 parts of the palace in the present city of Oyo which lies about 130 kilometres to the south. The excavations at Old Oyo have not been published in detail but radiocarbon dates indicate the existence of a substantial settlement of more than 1 square kilometre as early as the twelfth century AD (and perhaps as early as the eighth century), which apparently pre-dated the earthwork complex (Calvocoressi and David 1979: 19–20, 27; Agbaje-Williams 1990: 369). Old Oyo was, however, only the most important of numerous towns abandoned in the southern savanna as a result of the Fulani attacks and Babayemi located the sites of a substantial number of these in the Upper Ogun area (Babayemi 1974). Near Old Oyo itself, Agbaje-Williams (1990) drew particular attention to the sites of Koso and Ipapo Ile, both of which have defensive earthworks.

It is interesting that even now the greater number of Yoruba towns and cities tend to be concentrated in the transitional zone between grassland and forest (Mabogunje 1962: Fig. 4). From the point of view of our enquiry, the most important of those in the northern part of the forest itself is Ife, where according to Yoruba traditions the world was created. Ife has remained of spiritual and ceremonial importance to the Yoruba, and the remarkable terracottas, copper-based alloy castings and stone sculptures discovered there since the beginning of the twentieth century have focused archaeological activity on this site (Willett 1967). The art itself has been interpreted as evidence of emerging social stratification, for some of it appears to represent personages of importance and, in addition, art on such a scale must surely imply patronage, particularly as the items of copper-based alloys are made from materials that were probably imported to the immediate area (Fig. 5.5). Excavations at various sites in the present city of Ife (which covers the area of the ancient city), by Frank Willett, Ekpo Eyo and Peter Garlake, have produced a radiocarbon chronology suggesting that occupation commenced during the late first millennium AD (Shaw 1980: Fig. 1). Archaeological deposits at Ife have proved technically difficult to excavate and rarely has mud-walling been isolated in the generally shallow deposits. Nevertheless, some indication of the layout of domestic buildings has been provided by the successful excavation of extensive pavements of edge-laid recycled potsherds and small stones (Willett 1967: Figs. 16 and 17, Plate 66; Garlake 1974: Figs. 3 and 4; 1977: Figs. 4 and 8). The main period during which such pavements were made has been dated by radiocarbon to approximately the twelfth to the fifteenth century and both radiocarbon and thermoluminescence dates have been used to suggest that the most important period of the Ife art was in the late fourteenth to early fifteenth century (Shaw 1980: 376). Little, however, can

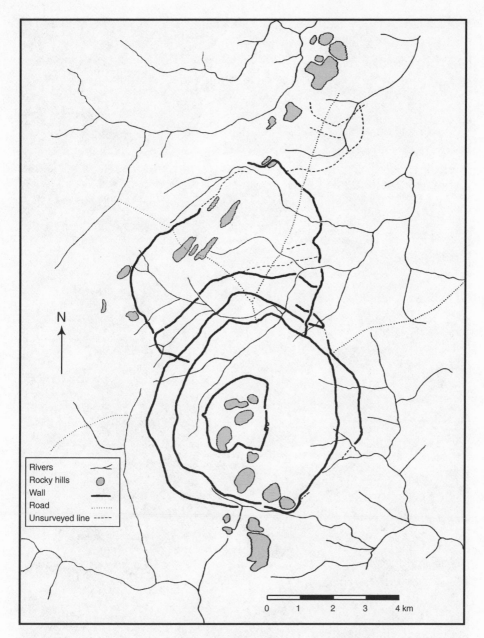

Fig. 5.4 Plan of the city walls of Old Oyo, Nigeria. After Soper and Darling (1980: Fig. 1).

Fig. 5.5 'Bronze' casting of an Oni of Ife. Height 467 millimetres. Reproduced by permission of Frank Willett.

be said of the growth of the city itself, although a series of concentric city walls (Fig. 5.6) suggests a complex series of phases in which the city grew up around the palace of the ruler (Ozanne 1969). Unfortunately these walls have not been adequately dated and it is known that at least some of them belonged to only the last few centuries. It does seem, nevertheless, that the ancient city must have covered a considerable area. Garlake (1977: 92) has suggested that it was probably at least as large as the nineteenth-century walled town, because two of the excavated sites lie outside the western wall of that town while another lies beside and just beyond the

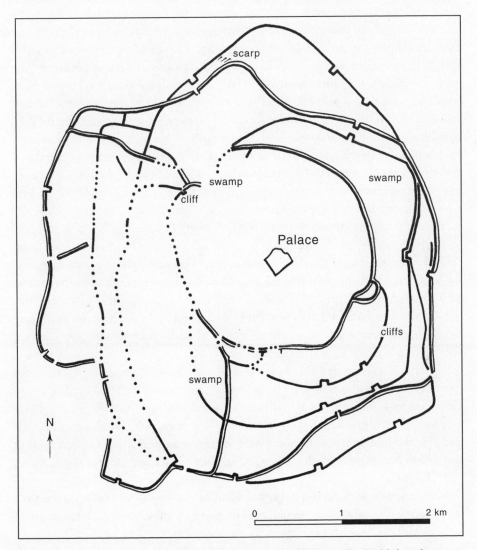

Fig. 5.6 Plan of Ife city walls, Nigeria. Single lines represent earlier walls, double lines later walls. After Ozanne (1969).

159

eastern wall. He has also claimed that: 'There are strong indications that buildings were sufficiently compact and close together for the settlement to be ranked as urban.'

Some of the best-known archaeological evidence relevant to the present discussion comes from Benin City, also in southern Nigeria. Benin (not to be confused with the Republic of Bénin) seems to have mesmerized European visitors for centuries and, indeed, it is archaeologically fascinating not only because it is situated deep in the rainforest but also because its origins are still unclear (in this connection, Andah 1982 should be read with care). Excavations during the 1950s by Goodwin (1957; 1963) and by myself during the 1960s (Connah 1972; 1975) revealed substantial post-European-contact deposits (i.e. dating from after the late fifteenth century AD) on the site of the old palace. However, my own work was also able to demonstrate occupation of the city by about the thirteenth century. The principal evidence for this consisted of radiocarbon dates for a mass burial of at least forty-one young women, who lay at a depth of over 12.5 metres in a narrow well-like cistern (Fig. 5.7). Wearing clothing, bracelets, finger-rings and beads, they appeared to have been dropped down the deep shaft in which they were found and must surely represent ritual sacrifice of a sort indicative of strongly centralized authority, particularly as the shaft lay within the area of the old palace. Good documentary evidence exists for the continued practice of throwing the bodies of sacrificial victims into such pits, as late as 1897 (Roth 1903). Deep beneath the modern, developing city of Benin there must surely be other similar pits, still preserving their evidence of fear and of power, and it is possible that some of them could be earlier in date than the one that was excavated. The excavations of the 1960s also made it apparent that edge-laid potsherd pavements had been made in Benin City during or prior to the fourteenth century AD, and this was a practice that appears to have ended before European contact. In addition to indicating large-scale pottery production, the existence of such pavements suggests formal architecture like that of which Garlake revealed indications at Ife. Indeed, there is ethnohistoric, ethnographic and even a little archaeological evidence for the later (post-contact) existence of a sophisticated architecture in coursed mud in Benin City. This was distingushed by tall, steep-roofed entrances (see Fagg 1963: Plate 35); horizontally grooved, polished red walls (for example Connah 1975: Plates 8 and 17); and a plan in which rooms were arranged around a series of rectangular courtyards left open to the sky (for example Roth 1903: Figs. 180 and 185; Connah 1975: Plate 1).

More important, however, is the evidence of the so-called 'Benin City walls', the innermost of which has been demonstrated by radiocarbon dating, historical documentation and oral tradition to have been constructed before European contact, quite possibly around the middle of the fifteenth century (Connah 1975). Consisting of a massive earthen bank and ditch, with a total vertical height, from

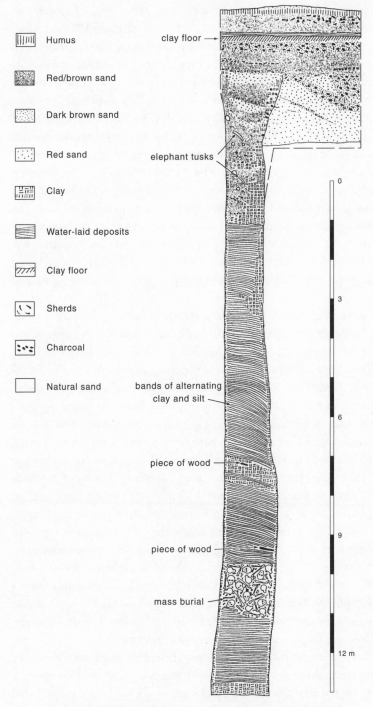

Humus

Red/brown sand

Dark brown sand

Red sand

Clay

Water-laid deposits

Clay floor

Sherds

Charcoal

Natural sand

clay floor →

elephant tusks

bands of alternating
clay and silt

piece of wood

piece of wood

mass burial

0

3

6

9

12 m

Fig. 5.7 Section of shaft containing mass sacrifice, Benin City, Nigeria.
After Connah (1975: Fig. 18).

161

the excavated bottom of the ditch to the top of the surviving bank, of as much as 17.4 metres and a circumference of 11.6 kilometres, this earthwork alone represents an enormous investment of human effort that must clearly have been directed by a powerful centralized authority. Calculations have suggested that its construction would have absorbed 5000 people continuously occupied for ten hours a day, if it had been completed in one dry season. Such rapidity of construction is perhaps unlikely but, even if spread over five dry seasons, a labour force of 1000 would have been necessary. The direction of such a labour force on a massive project of this sort must, indeed, have implications of the very greatest significance for our enquiry into state formation. That is not the whole story, however, because surveys by myself during the 1960s in the tangled vegetation around Benin City revealed a vast network of further interlocking enclosures, consisting of over 145 kilometres of earthworks. These appeared to hint at the process of synoecism ('the union of several towns or villages into or under one capital city' (*Oxford English Dictionary* 1933)) by which a group of villages had developed into a city, at a date prior to the construction of the innermost and most massive of the 'walls'.

Nevertheless, subsequent work by Darling (Darling 1974; 1976; 1982; 1984; 1988; 1998) and by other researchers (Maliphant, Rees and Roese 1976; Roese 1981) showed that even this outer network that was mapped by me (Connah 1975) was only 'a small peripheral part of a much more extensive pattern of rural earthwork enclosures' (Darling 1982: Vol. 1, 387). This overall pattern has been found to cover an area of about 6500 square kilometres, and has been estimated to have a total length in excess of 16,000 kilometres (Fig. 5.8). It is thought to imply at least 150,000,000 person-hours of work over a period of several centuries (Darling 1982: Vol. 1, 392). It is little wonder that the Benin earthworks, or *iya* as they are known locally, have got themselves into the *Guinness book of records* (McWhirter 1980: 125)! As Darling (1982) has shown, they probably have more to tell us about the process of state formation (presumably reflecting power struggles for agricultural land on the interfluves) than about the origins of urban growth that produced Benin City itself. Indeed, on the basis of the distribution and character of the earthworks and of a statistical analysis of surface-collected potsherds, he has proposed a settlement model for both the Benin area and that of Ishan to its north from the late first millennium AD onwards. He has argued that there was 'a strong southward colonization by savannah/savannah–forest ecotone Edo speakers [Edo is the language of Benin] into the rainforest'. Interestingly, the area over which this movement is thought to have taken place has a dense network of enclosures, 'whereas there is an almost total absence of them amongst the Urhobo speakers' just to the south (Darling 1988: 122–3). Thus Darling could well be right but, as he has admitted, his archaeological survey remains 'largely undated' (Darling 1988: 133). It is particularly regretable that a satisfactory series

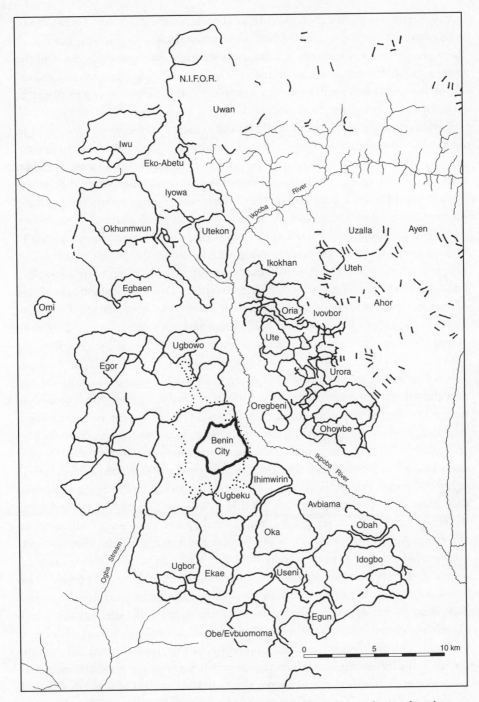

Fig. 5.8 Earthwork enclosures in the Benin City area. Dotted line indicates limits of modern city in 1960s–1970s. After Darling (1982).

of radiocarbon dates for the land surfaces beneath these earthworks has still not been obtained. Six radiocarbon determinations are available, it is true, but two of them give 'modern' dates, one a nineteenth-century date and three dates in the thirteenth to fifteenth centuries (Sutton 1982: 309, 312). Clearly, much more excavation time and money will have to be invested if this enormous complex of earthworks is to be sorted out chronologically.

Indeed, the same might be said also of the artistic use of copper-base alloys in Benin. My own excavations of the 1960s showed that these materials were used artistically as early as the thirteenth century AD but those excavations recovered no evidence of *casting* these metals prior to European contact. In spite of the numerous artistic studies that have been made of the famous Benin castings (for example Forman, Forman and Dark 1960; Dark 1973) we still have very little evidence about their detailed chronology. In view of the implications of these castings, implying as they do both an hierarchical power structure and considerable artistic patronage, it is a great misfortune that so few have ever been recovered from properly controlled and adequately published stratigraphic excavations. However, a small number of Benin castings have been dated on the basis of the thermoluminescence of the fragments of fired clay core remaining within them and it is interesting that they were all found to date from about the fifteenth century AD or later (Willett and Fleming 1976).

It is impossible to leave the subject of archaeological evidence for state formation and urbanization within the West African rainforest without some consideration of a collection of evidence that at first sight might appear irrelevant. This evidence comes from Igbo-Ukwu, east of the River Niger in Nigeria, from an area now occupied by the Ibo people, who have long interested anthropologists precisely because apparently they developed neither cities nor states until recent times, in spite of a high population density. As late as the 1930s the Ibo could still boast that 'there is no one who owns us' (that is to say: we have no rulers) and their society remained characterized by 'a dispersal rather than a concentration of authority' (Green 1947: 145, 73). What, then, is one to make of Igbo-Ukwu, where the burial of a clearly important individual (Fig. 5.9), a repository of sophisticated regalia and a ritual disposal pit produced, amongst other things, 685 copper and bronze objects (many of them highly ornamented) and some 165,000 stone and glass beads? Thurstan Shaw, the excavator of this remarkable site, has suggested that this evidence indicates the former existence of a local 'priest king', who was the holder of the highest politico-ritual title in the democratized title-taking system of the Ibo of this area (Shaw 1970; 1977). There is some ethnohistorical evidence that supports this interpretation, although it is not clear whether this should be applied to archaeological data a thousand years old. This date, at the end of the first millennium AD, is based on a group of radiocarbon dates that were at one time the subject of some argument (Lawal 1973; Posnansky 1973; Shaw 1975b; Onwuejeogwu and Onwuejeogwu 1977) but subsequently there has been a greater

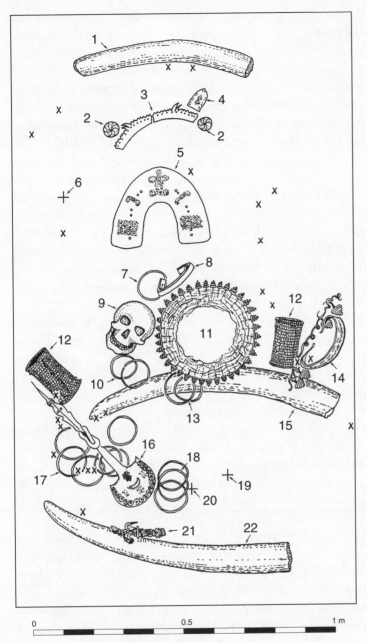

Fig. 5.9 Plan of the burial at Igbo-Ukwu, Nigeria.
1, 15, 22: Elephant tusks. *2:* Decorated copper roundels. *3:* Crown.
4: Decorated copper plate. *5:* Pectoral plate. *6, 19:* Position of point of
bracket. *7, 10, 13, 17, 18:* Copper anklets. *8:* Copper strap. *9:* Skull. *11:*
Spiral copper bosses set in wood: remains of stool. *12:* Beaded armlets.
14: Copper handle for calabash. *16:* Copper fan-holder. *20:* Position of
point of rod supporting bronze leopard's skull. *21:* Bronze horseman
hilt. X: Iron nails and staples. After Shaw (1970: Fig. 14).

readiness to accept them at their face value (Posnansky 1980; R.J. McIntosh and S.K. McIntosh 1981b; Shaw 1993). In my own case I have never doubted the approximately tenth-century date for the Igbo-Ukwu evidence, which is of particular importance not only because of the sophisticated metallurgy and unique art forms but also because it implies early trading connections between the West African rainforest and the Mediterranean world or even India. Analyses have now shown that the copper and copper alloy probably came from the lead-zinc-copper deposits of the Benue Rift, only 100 kilometres to the east of the site (Chikwendu *et al.* 1989), where there is evidence of mining dating to the end of the first millennium AD (Craddock 1991; Craddock *et al.* 1997). However, the glass and carnelian beads must have been the result of trade either across the Sahara or east–west through the Sahel. Indeed, Insoll (1996a: 80) has suggested that elephant ivory was being shipped north up the River Niger to Gao, from where it was transported across the desert by camel caravan. If that was the case, then Gao could have been the immediate source of many of the beads found at Igbo-Ukwu, having been sent south in exchange for the ivory but originating from far more distant locations (Insoll and Shaw 1997).

Clearly there was an early participation in both local and long-distance trade by people living in the Igbo-Ukwu area, and clearly there was some sort of local authority capable of concentrating a considerable quantity of the products of this trade on one individual. Elsewhere, such archaeological evidence would probably be thought suggestive of the sort of social stratification indicative of an emergent state or at least of a ranked chiefdom. In the case of Igbo-Ukwu the ethnohistorical evidence would require considerable qualification of such an interpretation. Until we know far more about the late first millennium AD in this part of Nigeria, there are three tentative conclusions that suggest themselves. First, that we should be very careful when deducing socio-political organization from such archaeological evidence as 'rich burials'. Second, that the social and political organization observed in any area during the last two centuries does not necessarily indicate the situation a thousand years ago: societies are dynamic not static and change exists in forms other than unilinear evolution. Third, that Iboland raises fundamental questions about the nature of West African urbanism. In 1955 this area had one of the densest populations in Nigeria, with estimates for some areas of 'well over 1000 per square mile [259 hectares]', and it was recorded that 'in the densely peopled areas the settlement web is almost continuous, resembling the ribbon development of suburban Europe' (Buchanan and Pugh 1955: 59–60, 76). Perhaps for mainly socio-economic reasons, Ibo settlement was dispersed rather than nucleated like that of the Yoruba, each Ibo farmstead lying in the middle of its own cultivated area near a road or bush path. Given such population densities, it seems pointless to ask questions about the 'absence' of urbanism.

Subsistence economy

What can these rather fragmentary pieces of archaeological evidence tell us about the origins of cities and states in the West African rainforest? To begin with, what about the subsistence economy on which these entities must have been based? It has to be admitted at once that there is very little direct evidence. Forest soils are usually destructive of bone, and the recovery of botanical evidence by means of flotation does not seem to have been adequately attempted as yet. However, the excellent preservation of bones, wood and cloth in the Benin cistern containing the sacrificed women suggests that exceptional conditions do exist if the archaeologist can but find them. Until that happens, the evidence from the second millennium BC Kintampo sites, at the junction of forest and savanna in Ghana, will remain of value even for this later period. From these sites there is evidence of domesticated dwarf sheep or goats and possibly of small domesticated cattle. In addition, cowpeas, oil-palm, and perhaps yam were exploited, although it is unknown whether these were domesticated or not, and several wild plants were also included in the food. Similarly, faunal and artefactual evidence indicates that hunting and fishing remained a significant part of the basic subsistence (Carter and Flight 1972; Flight 1976; Anquandah 1993b; Stahl 1993). From sites of the late first millennium AD, or of the early second millennium AD, there is far less published evidence for subsistence economy. At Daboya the faunal remains indicated the presence of domesticated cattle, sheep or goats, and chicken or guinea fowl, over the last 2000 years or so and showed that wild animals remained an important resource. However, the site provided no direct evidence for domesticated plants (Shinnie and Kense 1989: 223–7). At Bono Manso the faunal material indicated the keeping of goats and chickens, as well as the exploitation of wild species, but only 329 pieces of bone were recovered and 'over 95 per cent of these were either too fragmentary or undiagnostic to be of any use'. Furthermore, most of the bones came from the later phases and, again, there was no direct evidence for cultivated plants (Effah-Gyamfi 1985: 98–9). In the case of Ife there is slight evidence of sheep or goat associated with potsherd pavements (Garlake 1977: 91) and terracottas of a bull and of a ram's head were found at Lafogido (in Ife) in a twelfth-century context (Eyo 1974). As for Benin City, there is no evidence of any value (Connah 1975: 218), and although the ritual disposal pit at Igbo-Ukwu yielded a moderate number of bones they were all of wild though edible fauna, a circumstance perhaps explained by the presumed ritual character of the pit (Shaw 1970: Vol. 1, 247–8).

With so little direct archaeological evidence, it is necessary to fall back on indirect archaeological evidence and on evidence from non-archaeological sources. As already discussed (p. 148), there were substantial plant-food resources in the rainforest and it should be noted that all the sites that have been mentioned are situated within the West African 'yam zone' (Figs. 4.1 and 4.2). Furthermore, those sites tend to be in the more northern parts of the forest or in the southern savanna, where yams and oil-palm originally grew more readily. These, and the complex of other plants already reviewed, would have provided a sound subsistence base. The main deficiency would probably have been animal protein, as in recent times, but small numbers of dwarf goats and cattle, large quantities of fish and extensive hunting in the forest could have rendered this less of a problem than it was with the exploding population of the twentieth century. Overall, this food-production system was almost certainly indigenous in its development and of substantial antiquity. Thus it may be significant that pottery, ground stone axes and possible sickle components appear at the Nigerian rock shelter of Iwo Eleru during the last 5000 years BC (Shaw 1978: 47; Shaw and Daniels 1984: 55) and that during the last few millennia BC many of the stone-using peoples of the forest made pick-like and hoe-like implements, that some archaeologists have interpreted as digging tools for the collection and eventual cultivation of yams. In this connection it is interesting that Sowunmi (1993: 15) has detected a 'sharp rise' in the occurrence of oil-palm at about 2800 BP in a Niger delta deposit, along with the appearance of weeds of cultivation, a situation 'strongly suggestive of clearing of patches of forest by Man for farming purposes'. Furthermore, those trypanosomiasis-resistent goats and cattle must have taken a considerable length of time to acquire the resistence that enables them to survive in the forest.

It would appear that by the end of the first millennium AD, and perhaps 1000 or 2000 years earlier, a sound agricultural system had grown up on the interfluves of the more northerly parts of the forest. This system was based on the rotational bush-fallow cultivation of extensive areas of forest land, that was cleared by slashing and burning and then abandoned to regeneration when soil exhaustion reduced productivity. One of the main crops was probably yams and it should be noted that yams are a food source that can be stored and can be transported. In such circumstances, it seems likely that by the early second millennium AD the subsistence economy of the rainforest was able to produce a surplus and to provide adequate support for the growing social complexity of which the archaeological record provides evidence.

Technology

As stated above (p. 155), iron-smelting was already being practised at Hani in Ghana, just north of the forest, by about the second century AD. Indeed, evidence from Nsukka, in eastern Nigeria, and from Obobogo, in Cameroon, indicates that in the southern savanna such smelting probably commenced in the second half of the first millennium BC, at the latest (Okafor 1993; Woodhouse 1998). At the earliest Nsukka sites, the smelters were already using slag-tapping, forced-draught shaft furnaces that were 'extremely efficient at extracting iron from ore' (S.K.

McIntosh 1994: 174). It seems reasonable to assume, therefore, that the technology of at least some of the occupants of the forest included iron-working from early in the first millennium AD. Certainly the iron-working skills of West African forest peoples grew in time to a high level of sophistication; there is ample evidence of this by the end of the first millennium AD at Igbo-Ukwu (Shaw 1970: Vol. 1, 97–103). Also, ethnohistorical data such as that of Bellamy (1904), who recorded the operation of a most impressive induced-draught furnace near Oyo in Yorubaland, indicate a long-established tradition. The adoption of iron, by people living in and on the fringes of the West African forest, must have made the agricultural exploitation of those zones very much more practicable than previously. Iron tools were almost certainly not a precondition of forest cultivation, as was once thought, but it was probably their existence that made cultivation possible on a scale that could support communities of increasing size.

In addition to the working of iron, copper and copper-base alloys were also being handled with great skill by the close of the first millennium AD. The evidence from Igbo-Ukwu shows that both lost-wax casting and smithing and chasing techniques had been mastered. Indeed, by the second quarter of the second millennium AD, metalsmiths in Ife were producing copper-base alloy castings of a technical excellence and an artistic refinement that is very impressive. A little later, craftsmen in Benin City were excelling in a similar fashion and the Akan were producing their intriguing little copper alloy weights for weighing gold-dust, as well as casting an impressive range of jewellery in gold itself. Only those who have watched a modern West African 'brassworker' attempt to emulate his forebears can appreciate how difficult this craft of casting is and how very skilled were the artisans and artists of the past. The Igbo-Ukwu material, for instance, has been described by modern experts as 'extremely ambitious in design and executed by highly skilled and experienced craftsmen' who were 'masters of all aspects of lost-wax casting technology, and had a good understanding of the necessary alloys' (Craddock and Picton 1986: 4).

Perhaps the most impressive aspect of the forest-dwellers' technology, however, was its diversity. Thus the artists of ancient Ife excelled in the making of terracotta representations as well as ones of copper-base alloy. Furthermore, they also carved hard stone such as granite-gneiss and quartz, to produce accomplished sculptures that included both human and animal figures and ceremonial stools. Some of these sculptures were decorated in a quite distinctive way, by driving iron nails into holes drilled into the stone (Willett 1967: 79–84, Plates 72–4, 77–9). Also at Ife, the complex pavements of potsherds and stones hint at considerable architectural sophistication, a sophistication that can perhaps still be seen in the much later but nevertheless imposing traditional mud palaces of some Yoruba rulers (Ojo 1966b). Indeed, some of the coursed-mud architecture of the West African forest seems to have been quite remarkable. That of the Asante, for instance, with its polished red and white walls decorated with low reliefs (for example McLeod 1981: 56), is still an impressive demonstration of what is possible in this building material, as also is that of Benin, with its polished, fluted red walls. Benin City has, in fact, provided us with a time-capsule of traditional technology, in the form of the massive and varied collection of objects looted from the city at the time of its capture by the British in 1897 (see for example Pitt Rivers 1900). It is apparent that the Bini were proficient not only in iron-working, 'brass-working' and building but also in carpentry, wood-carving, ivory-carving, mud and terracotta sculpture, pottery, leather-working, weaving and beadwork (Dark 1973). In addition, the incredible number of earthworks in the Benin and Ishan areas suggests some understanding of the principles of surveying and civil engineering, as well as a capacity to move monumental amounts of earth.

The full range of technological skills amongst some forest communities, during the last 500–1000 years or so, is too great to discuss in any more detail here. There were, however, two other areas of expertise that particularly deserve a mention. The first is that a number of sites at Ife have yielded evidence of glass-melting, in the form of fragments of crucibles coated with waste glass (see for example Garlake 1977: 89–90). The exact significance of this evidence is not clear, because it might only mean that imported glass was being melted to turn into beads or other small objects (Willett 1977: 22), or it could mean that glass was being made from its basic ingredients. Whatever the case, it is interesting that radiocarbon dates for a site that is described as a glass-bead-making factory, point to a date between the late eleventh and the fourteenth centuries (Sutton 1982: 309, 312). The second area of expertise that deserves special mention is that of mining, particularly of gold-mining in the area of the Akan states in southern Ghana. As stated in Chapter 4, little archaeological research has yet been conducted at West African gold-mining sites but there are some interesting ethnohistorical accounts which indicate that mining in the Akan forest was carried to a depth of as much as 46 metres (Addo-Fening 1976). Clearly, miners who could engage in that sort of enterprise must have known a considerable amount about their craft. Traces of mining have also been reported in the Nigerian lead-zinc-copper deposits east of Igbo-Ukwu, where open-cuts and tunnelling reached depths of about 10 metres below the surface (Chikwendu *et al.* 1989: 31). Importantly, a radiocarbon date in the tenth century AD, for charcoal associated with mining debris, suggests that these mines were in use at the time that the Igbo-Ukwu copper and copper alloy objects were being made (Craddock 1991; S.K. McIntosh 1994: 176; Craddock *et al.* 1997).

Thus it would appear that by early in the second millennium AD, if not before, there was a varied and sophisticated level of technology in at least some of the West African forest communities. There is, in short, good reason to suspect that there would have been a growth in functional specialization amongst the societies concerned.

Social system

Ethnohistorical and oral sources have much more to tell us about social organization in the West African rainforest during the last half millennium than does archaeological evidence. Nevertheless, the latter has an important part to play in amplifying the other sources, and it is our only source of information for the crucial earlier formative periods. From the archaeological data that have been examined, it would appear that by late in the first millennium AD, or early in the second millennium, there was growing social stratification based on the control of trade resources and of agricultural surplus. This took place particularly in the northerly parts of the forest and in the forest-savanna ecotone. It led in some places to increasing centralization of authority, particularly in the form of the much-discussed institution of divine kingship. The copper-base alloy castings of Ife and Benin are eloquent evidence of that institution and, in the case of Benin, of the social and political hierarchy that supported it (Fig. 5.10). In particular, it seems likely that the famous 'bronze' heads of Ife were made for attachment to wooden bodies which, provided with clothing, crowns and/or other appropriate regalia, were carried in funeral processions of rulers, members of their families, and perhaps some of their more important chiefs. Such figures could have represented not only the deceased but also the undying dignity and authority of the office that he or she had held, much as was the case in medieval and early modern Europe where similar practices are well recorded (Willett 1966). Furthermore, the thirteenth-century sacrificial victims at Benin and the scale of the earthworks with which that city and its surrounding settlements were protected give some idea of the power that such authority could wield. In the terms defined by Haas (p. 7), it is possible to see evidence in Benin of the scope, the amount and the extension of power, if not indeed of more of his variables for its measurement. Similarly, whatever the precise socio-political significance of the Igbo-Ukwu evidence, it clearly indicates a concentration of 'wealth' on one individual, an individual who must have held institutionalized power of some sort. The Igbo-Ukwu burial is especially persuasive in this latter respect. As is shown in Caroline Sassoon's careful reconstruction painting (Shaw 1970: Vol. 1, Frontispiece), the deceased sat on an ornamented stool, clothed, crowned, and with both regalia and jewellery. It is quite likely that stools already had a special significance as symbols of authority, as was later to be so famously the case with the Asante of Ghana (McLeod 1981: 112–18). Indeed, some stools of exceptional workmanship from Benin, made of wood or of copper alloy (for example Pitt Rivers 1900: Plate 41; Roth 1903: Figs. 111 and 112; Dark 1973: Plate 40), and from Ife, carved out of stone (for example Willett 1967: Plate 77), must surely have had a similar role. Regrettably we still lack relevant structural evidence such as the layout of palace buildings, other than the much later examples at Old Oyo and Benin City, but nevertheless the material record does provide signs of emergent states in the West African forest by early in the second millennium AD.

There are also clear signs of urbanization by this time; at the very least Begho, Bono Manso, Ife and Benin were already growing communities with tendencies to nucleation, and they are only the ones of which we happen to know something. Although our archaeological evidence for the beginnings of urbanization in West Africa is so poor, as Andah (1976) pointed out, the technological developments

Fig. 5.10 'Bronze' plaque from Benin City, showing a seated Oba with kneeling attendants. Reproduced by permission of the British Museum.

discussed above suggest a growth of specialist crafts and with this a growth in functional specialization within society which, as Mabogunje argued (p. 7), is fundamental to the development of urbanization. Furthermore, it seems that by the early second millennium AD, Mabogunje's 'limiting conditions' (p. 8) for urbanization were also being met in some parts of the West African forest. There was almost certainly a surplus of food production, there were in some areas small groups of people able to exercise power and very likely there was a class of traders and merchants. In some places, however, whether or not these conditions were met, urbanization in the normal sense did not take place. Thus there is the example of the Ibo people of eastern Nigeria who, in spite of what might be assumed on the basis of the recent situation to have been a large population, developed a form of socio-political organization that was dispersed rather than nucleated. The origins of Ibo society would merit careful archaeological examination, for surely it is not enough to explain their case, as Hull (1976a: 25) did, by claiming that 'while the Ibo were urbanites, they were not city dwellers in the classical sense'. If we understood why there were no Ibo cities that could compare with those of the Akan, the Yoruba or the Edo, then we might understand more about the process of urbanization in the West African rainforest.

Population pressures

At first sight, the West African rainforest would seem to be an unlikely place for population pressures to build up. To the outsider, there seem to be almost limitless supplies of unused land and farmers do not have such acute problems of water stress as those that characterize the savanna. Indeed, it is possible that the iron-using farmers of the first millennium AD did enjoy for some centuries a virtual 'frontier' situation, in which there was always sufficient fresh land to meet increases in the population. This might even be the reason why urbanization and state development were conspicuously later phenomena in the forest than they were in the savanna.

It is clear from Darling's work around Benin City, however, that forest soils and environments varied in their attractiveness to farmers. It seems probable that the best farmlands were often situated on the upper interfluves, where the vegetation may have been easier to clear and the soils were better drained. Also there seems to have been a preference for ecotonal environments on the fringes of the forest. Given a rotational bush-fallow agricultural system of the sort that is known to have been practised in the forest during recent centuries, each piece of farmland would have to be fallowed for ten to fifteen years, after only three or four years of cultivation (Grove 1978: 77). During those brief periods of cultivation each piece of land would be relatively productive and capable of producing a surplus of food. Such a surplus might stimulate population growth but a time would come when the best land became harder to find, unless the farmer was willing to reduce the fallowing period, a solution that would be detrimental to productivity and therefore to food supplies. All this is supposition, of course, but it may be significant that, for the area around Benin City, Allison (1962: 244) citing E. W. Jones (1956) was able to produce evidence that most of the forest had been farmed at one time or another. Indeed, surely the vast pattern of earthworks mapped by Darling (1982; 1984) is indicative of an expanding farming population competing for land? Human communities do not indulge in such monumental labour unless there is a very good reason. Whether such competition existed also in other areas of the West African forest remains to be seen. The area occupied by the Ibo, for instance, has been said to have 'among the poorest of Nigerian soils – highly leached, extremely acid, suited only to a limited range of crops and eroding rapidly under conditions of overcropping' (Buchanan and Pugh 1955: 60). It may be that population dispersal was the most appropriate strategy for dealing with such generally poor soils, whereas nucleation on areas of better soils tended to take place in areas with a greater variation in soil quality. Thus it is possible that quite localized population pressure was one of the factors which led to an increasing elaboration of social hierarchies and to an increasing size of human communities, in some areas of the West African forest and its fringes during the earlier part of the second millennium AD.

Ideology

Prior to European contact, the religions of the West African forest peoples seem to have consisted of a very complex and varied collection of beliefs. From ethnohistorical sources and from oral tradition, it appears that whole pantheons of deities as well as worship of the dead played a part in many of these beliefs and that the ruler or leader of a community often fulfilled the function of its chief priest. Thus in Benin City the Oba appears to have been the principal officiant in the most important religious ceremonies, and at least some of these involved human sacrifices in which the victim or victims were asked to carry a message to the gods (Roth 1903: 71–2). Likewise the Oni of Ife was a spiritual leader of importance, and the Akan chiefs seem to have had spiritual as well as temporal powers. Thus it would seem that ideology may have played an important part in the emergence of West African forest states, particularly as a means of legitimizing and reinforcing centralized authority. In view of the importance of a food surplus in the development of both states and cities, it is interesting that in many parts of the forest and its fringes some of the most important ceremonies of the religious year were concerned with the yam harvest.

There is a little archaeological evidence that suggests that the role of religion, indicated by ethnohistory and oral tradition, may have been similar in the early centuries of the second millennium AD. In Ife, for instance, Garlake excavated the remains of fourteenth-century altars built into the edge of potsherd pavements and comparable with those dedicated to past Obas that were still to be seen in the royal palace of Benin late in the twentieth century (Garlake 1977: 69). At Benin itself there is evidence of human sacrifice being practised in the thirteenth century. In addition, many of the Benin copper-base alloy castings of sixteenth- to nineteenth-century date, particularly those in the form of human heads, apparently represented former Obas and originally were important liturgical furnishings of the altars. The 'bronze' and terracotta heads from Ife of fourteenth- to fifteenth-century date were perhaps intended for a similar use or, in some cases, intended to be used in funeral ceremonies. Herbert (1984: 302) suggested that such items were 'actual containers of power', not merely 'passive signifiers' of it, and Bradbury (1973: 251–70), in his discussion of *ikegobo* or Benin shrines for the Cult of the Hand, showed how the objects themselves could be related to the beliefs that they represented. For earlier periods, however, the interpretation of religious symbolism can be extremely difficult, such as with the thousand-year-old Igbo-Ukwu evidence for the existence of what its excavator called a 'priest king' (Shaw 1977). Nevertheless, whatever its precise significance may be, that site does seem to indicate that the combining of spiritual and temporal authority is indeed an ancient practice in the West African forest.

External trade

In Chapter 4 (p. 112) it was argued that the range of environments in West Africa would have provided both the necessity and the occasion for the exchange of raw materials and products across the boundaries between those environments. Thus one might expect an early development of regional trading both within and between the various ecozones and ecotones of West Africa. The forest and forest fringes must have played an important part in such development. Forest products that were probably both exchanged in local markets and traded to greater distances could have included yams, vegetable oils, palm wine, miscellaneous vegetable food, dried fish, salt, Melegueta pepper, kola nuts, dyewoods, various gums, cloth, pots, canoes, charcoal, ivory, gold and slaves. Among these commodities were a number that were sought after by long-distance trade, particularly gold, ivory, slaves, pepper and kola nuts. By the end of the first millennium AD some of these were being carried across the Sahara and by the middle of the second millennium AD seaborne European traders were seeking them on the coast and, in addition, gradually developing what was to become an almost insatiable demand for vegetable oils. In return for their various exports, the forest and forest fringes received an assortment of goods, of which luxury goods that gave status to the recipients formed a substantial part. This is not to deny that regional trade in meat-on-the-hoof from the savanna was important in the forest probably from an early date, or that some of the salt from the trans-Saharan trade must have reached as far south as the forest. Nevertheless, it appears that amongst the most important of the commodities reaching the forest from the Saharan trade were copper-base alloys, either in ingot or in manufactured form. These were much sought after by the peoples of the forest, and from the time of their first arrival on the West African coast European traders were quick to take advantage of this demand. Clearly, copper and its alloys were luxury materials of considerable socio-political and economic importance in the forest (Herbert 1973). In addition, cowrie shells were an important commodity traded into the forest, originally across the Sahara but eventually to the coast on European ships (Johnson 1970a; 1970b; Hogendorn and Johnson 1986). Used both decoratively and as a form of currency, their possession was again an important indicator of status. The same could be said of many of the other imports to the West African forest. As indicated by European records of ships' cargoes, there was a demand for a variety of manufactured goods, particularly glass beads, coral beads, fine cloths, metalware of all sorts (especially iron knives), iron bars, alcohol, tobacco, gunpowder, guns and mirrors; and this is only to name a selection of the goods that were carried at one time or another (Ryder 1969). One of the most remarkable status symbols, however, was the horse. Used in the forest fringes, horses were also known as deep in the forest as Benin City; they were imported there from the savanna and, in later times, occasionally from European traders on the coast (Law 1980b). Given the trypanosomiasis problem in the forest, it is unlikely that horses could have lived very long in such an environment. It would seem that their use in Benin represented a remarkable example of conspicuous consumption.

The above discussion is based on a mixture of ethnohistory and oral tradition, and its major weakness is that so much of the information is drawn from post-European-contact times. Thus, to find evidence of external trade in the forest, from any time before about 500 years ago, we must turn to archaeology. The most obvious of such evidence, and perhaps the earliest, is Igbo-Ukwu. Although it now seems that the metal used in the many items of copper-base alloy at that site came from no great distance (Chikwendu *et al.* 1989; Craddock 1991), the very large number of glass and carnelian beads that were found must imply early trading links. So must the depiction of a mounted horse or donkey on one of the Igbo-Ukwu castings (Shaw 1970: Vol. 2, Plates 365–6) which, even if based on some other work of art rather than on direct observation, indicates a connection with the savanna and perhaps beyond. Sutton (1991) has suggested trading contacts with Egypt and Nubia, and it is relevant to note that, although an Indian origin has often been assumed for the carnelian because of an apparent lack of African sources, it 'occurs abundantly' in Egypt (Lucas and Harris 1962: 391). However, irrespective of whether the beads originated in Egypt or came from India via Egypt or Nubia, the problem is to know what the people of Igbo-Ukwu were giving in exchange. Shaw (1970: Vol. 1, 284–5) suggested ivory, in the form of elephants' tusks, and added that probably slaves and perhaps kola nuts had also been exported from this part of the forest. His suggestions seem reasonable, but the location of Igbo-Ukwu in the northern margin of the forest, near to the Niger River and not very far from the Niger Delta, makes one wonder whether salt, dried fish and perhaps some other Delta products (Alagoa 1970) may not also have been amongst the goods traded to the north. As already mentioned (p. 166), Insoll (1996a: 80) has suggested that some of the ivory was carried up the River Niger to Gao, from where it was fed into the Saharan trade, and that Gao may therefore have been the immediate source of many of the beads found at Igbo-Ukwu, whatever their remoter origin. Indeed, beads excavated from Gao are similar to those from Igbo-Ukwu (Insoll and Shaw 1997). However, Sutton (1991: 154) has pointed out that both elephants (for ivory) and people (for the slave trade) were common enough south of the Sahara a thousand years ago and he has argued that 'to generate so much wealth at so southerly a latitude' as Igbo-Ukwu, there must have been 'some other valued commodity specific to that place'. It is an important point because, whatever else it represents, the collection of objects found at Igbo-Ukwu does indicate a very considerable concentration of wealth, which (so far as present knowledge is concerned) was unique in that region at that time. Sutton has suggested that the special commodity that the people of Igbo-Ukwu might have been trading was silver, which apparently occurs in small quantities in copper ore in south-eastern Nigeria, and of which traces have been found in the copper-alloy objects from Igbo-Ukwu. It is an attractive idea, for here indeed was a rare commodity of considerable international value at the relevant time, particularly sought after for use in the currencies of both the Islamic and Christian worlds.

Further to the west, the location of Begho and other sites thought to relate to the early Akan states is surely indicative of an early trade in gold and other forest commodities. To the south of Begho lay many of West Africa's gold-mines and substantial resources of kola. To the north lay more gold-mines, and the Akan states would seem to have developed astride a major trade-route from the coast, through the forest, up the Black Volta River, to the region of Jenné in the Inland Niger Delta (Wilks 1962). Some confirmation of the importance of this trade exists in the form of a number of copper-base alloy basins and bowls which have survived in eight or more localities in the Akan area. These appear to have had a North African origin; indeed three items from Nsawkaw have Arabic inscriptions and one of those three is thought to be possibly of fourteenth-century date. More remarkable still, perhaps, is the fourteenth-century English bronze jug which was amongst the loot taken by the British from Kumasi in 1896 (Posnansky 1973: 155–6). However, there was probably a far wider range of imports into the Akan area than such items would suggest. Similarly, the commodities exported could well have consisted of things other than just gold and kola. Other likely trade goods would have been ivory, dried fish, slaves and salt. With respect to the latter, it was on this part of the coast of West Africa that an eighteenth-century European visitor recorded salt production (by seawater evaporation) on such a scale that a number of storehouses were seen which each contained about 50 tonnes of good clean salt (Nenquin 1961: 115–16).

At both Ife and Benin City the only really firm archaeological evidence for external trade prior to European contact consists of the presence of items of copper-base alloys. Craddock and Picton (1986: 9) found 'significant analytical differences' between such metal used at these places from the thirteenth to the fifteenth century AD and that which had been used at Igbo-Ukwu, 'showing that new sources of metal, probably imported, were now used'. This very likely reflects the growth of the trans-Saharan trade in brass, that European maritime trade later took over so successfully. As an indication of the range of this pre-European trade, it is interesting that by the fourteenth century objects of copper-base alloys were even getting down into the Niger Delta, implying that canoe-borne trading had already developed (Nzewunwa 1980: 247). In the case of Ife, it has been suggested that a trade-route ran north from Yorubaland to a crossing of the Niger below Bussa, where a remarkable group of copper-base alloy castings known as the 'Tsoede bronzes' were found (Shaw 1973). Significantly, some of these contain a small percentage of zinc, which suggests the use of at least some imported brass from the Saharan trade (Craddock and Picton 1986: 8–9). It seems likely that this could have been an important trade-route into the forest zone, and the most probable commodities traded out of Yorubaland would have been kola nuts (long important in the savanna because kola is the only stimulant permitted by Islam), ivory, salt, dried fish and slaves. Similar trade-goods would probably have been exported from Benin City, although Melegueta pepper was probably more important than kola. Also trade in vegetable oils is likely to have long pre-dated European contact. The location of Benin City seems never to have been adequately explained in terms of trade-routes, however, although it was quite well placed to maintain contact with both the Niger Delta to its south and the Niger River to its east.

Although the direct archaeological evidence is very limited, there seems to be no doubt that external trade was important for the peoples of the West African forest and its margins long before European traders arrived on the coast. It seems probable that such trade had commenced at least by the first millennium AD and its origins may be much earlier. Although long-distance contacts with trans-Saharan trade must have had a stimulating effect on the movement and procurement of certain types of commodities, there seems no good reason why the inauguration of such contacts should be claimed as the beginning of forest zone trade. In Chapter 4 it was argued that a regional network of trade-routes existed in West Africa before the advent of the Arab trans-Saharan trade. It seems logical that such a network must have included the forest and its margins.

Conclusion

Why did cities and states develop in the West African rainforest and its fringes? Why should there have been such apparent cultural brilliance beneath the trees? Inevitably, many explanations have drawn on external trade to explain such developments, and indeed the approximate contemporaneity of these socio-political changes with the appearance of Arab trade across the Sahara has been seen as particularly significant. Such an external stimulus hypothesis remains untested, however, until we know far more about the archaeology of the first millennium AD within the forest. Until then, it seems more likely that the origins of these cities and states lay within the forest and its margins, rather than remote from them. The forest possessed abundant resources and the potential to produce a food surplus. By early in the first millennium AD there existed an iron-based technology sufficiently sophisticated to exploit the forest environment more successfully than ever before. The diversity of this technology in time gave rise to functional specialization and this, probably combined with localized population pressure that may have reflected variations in land productivity, helped to stimulate the growth of larger, more heterogeneous communities. It was possibly population pressure also that in certain areas led to an increasing stratification of society, in which control of resources fell into fewer and fewer hands. In some places this culminated in centralization of authority on one individual, whose power was frequently legitimized and reinforced by the assumption of spiritual as well as temporal attributes. This state of affairs seems to have existed by the early second millennium AD, if not before.

It would be a mistake, however, to ignore the part that trade, both local and external, did undoubtedly play in the development of urbanization and state formation in this zone. Although this role has been frequently overemphasized (see for example Morton-Williams 1972), there is no doubt that it was an important contributory factor in the growth and situation of cities in the West African forest. Thus there was a tendency for such cities to be located in the northern part of the forest or even in the southern savanna, so that they were situated at the interface between donkey transport and human portage. There was also a tendency for them to be located on important trade-routes. In addition, the growth of states within this zone was undoubtedly stimulated by control of trading resources or of the trade-routes. As Law (1978) has shown, for instance, West African rulers in later times drew their incomes both directly and indirectly from trade. Furthermore, imported commodities provided both status symbols to enhance the position of local rulers and a source of movable wealth which could be used to reward supporters. It is little wonder that rulers of the West African forest so often insisted that it was their right to control the trade that was carried on in their territories. Trade, however, was only one factor in the appearance of cities and states in the West African forest and, like the other factors, its origins were probably within that zone rather than external to it.

Chapter 6

The edge or the centre: cities of the East African coast and islands

'Kilwa is one of the most beautiful and well-constructed towns in the world.' It was in such words that the much-travelled ibn Battuta described, first-hand, 'the principal town on the [East African] coast' in 1331. Apparently, Kilwa (properly called Kilwa Kisiwani), situated at 9° South in what is now Tanzania, was no isolated phenomenon. Over 1500 kilometres distant along the same coast, at 2° North in what is now Somalia, was Mogadishu, of which ibn Battuta could write that it was 'a very large town' (Freeman-Grenville 1975: 27–31). Ibn Battuta can be seen as representing the scholarly opinion of the fourteenth-century Islamic world. By the end of the following century, however, there were less scholarly visitors from the Christian world of Western Europe and they also seem to have been impressed with the towns and cities that they saw on the East African coast. Thus in 1498, the unknown author of the *Journal of the first voyage of Vasco da Gama, 1497–1499* could compare 'the town of Malindi' (now in Kenya) with Alcouchette, a town near Lisbon in his native Portugal (Freeman-Grenville 1975: 55–6). Indeed, it is in the account of Vasco da Gama's second voyage (1502) by Gaspar Correa (written long after the event about 1561 but Correa probably visited the East African coast in 1514) that there occurs one of the most detailed early descriptions of an East African coastal city. This again concerns Kilwa and is worth quoting extensively:

> The captain-major told the pilot to show him the port, and that he wished to go to Quiloa, which he did; and on sighting it, he entered the port with the whole fleet, which anchored round the city, which stands on an island which is surrounded and encircled by the sea water, but on the land side there is little water, which at high tide is knee-deep. The city is large and is of good buildings of stone and mortar with terraces, and the houses have much wood works. The city comes down to the shore, and is entirely surrounded by a wall and towers, within which there may be 12,000 inhabitants. The country all round is very luxuriant with many trees and gardens of all sorts of vegetables, citrons, lemons, and the best sweet oranges that were ever seen, sugar-canes, figs, pomegranates, and a great abundance of flocks, especially sheep, which have fat in the tail, which is almost the size of the body, and very savoury. The streets of the city are very narrow, as the houses are very high, of three and four stories, and one can run along the tops of them upon the terraces, as the houses are very close together: and in the port there were many ships. (Freeman-Grenville 1975: 66)

Clearly, the East African settlements would be expected to make a favourable impression on sailors several months outward bound from Portugal, who had just endured a long journey through the eastern Atlantic on a dull if not inadequate diet. Nevertheless, historical sources like those that have just been quoted demonstrate that settlements of considerable size had already developed on the East African coast before the middle of the second millennium AD. Archaeological and oral traditional evidence supports this conclusion. The main problem has been to explain how such a development took place, a development that was limited to a narrow strip comprising 3500 kilometres of coastline, from southern Somalia to southern Mozambique and including various offshore islands, to which should be added the Comoro Archipelago and parts of Madagascar.

The distinctive culture that eventually developed along this coastal strip was at least in part urban, mercantile, literate and Islamic. Modern scholars often refer to it as the 'Swahili Culture', because of the fact that many of the inhabitants of the strip are now speakers of one or another form of ki-Swahili, a north-eastern Bantu language rich in loan-words from Arabic and from a number of other languages; although it is doubtful if the term 'Swahili' should be used in contexts earlier than the last few centuries. Nonetheless, whatever one calls the developments along this coast prior to the arrival of the Portuguese, they were clearly impressive. One can sympathize, although not necessarily agree, with the view that: 'There is little doubt that this civilization, at its zenith in the fourteenth century, was the highest in the material sense that has existed until recent times in Black Africa' (Chittick 1971: 136). Given sentiments such as these, it is not surprising that external stimulus was formerly advanced as the most likely explanation for such developments. Thus we were told that: 'We should picture this civilization as a remote outpost of Islam, looking for its spiritual inspiration to the homeland of its religion' (Chittick 1971: 137). Subsequently, however, this 'colonial-origins interpretation' has been rejected (Allen 1980: 361; see also Allen 1974; 1993), and archaeological as well as other evidence has increasingly suggested that the development of the coastal culture owed far more to its African origins than to any external influences, contributory though these obviously were (Horton 1987a; 1996). The whole debate might be regarded as an interesting case of the edge or the centre: was the East African coast merely the edge of the Islamic world, or was it the centre of an indigenous African development of substantial significance? Viewed simply, the latter now seems to be more likely, but it is also apparent that culture change on this coast was highly complex, as might be expected in such an interaction zone, and did incorporate both local and foreign elements.

Geographical location and environmental factors

The area with which this chapter is concerned consists of a long, narrow coastal strip and a number of adjacent islands. Extending from about 2° North to about 16° South and perhaps to as much as 24° South, this comprises a very large part of the eastern coast of Africa (Fig. 6.1). The cultural developments with which we are

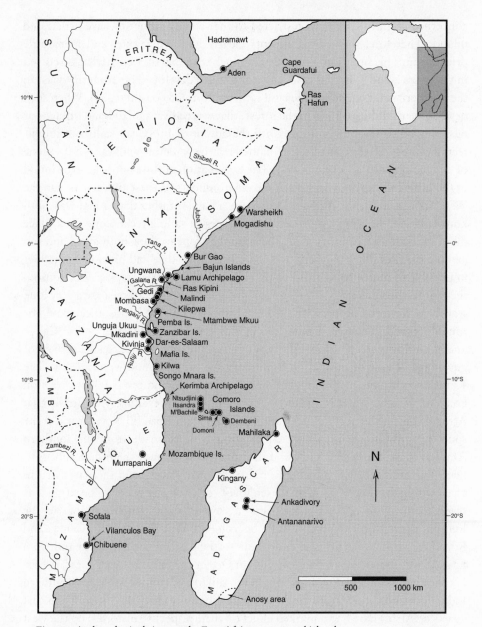

Fig. 6.1 Archaeological sites on the East African coast and islands.

concerned seem to have been restricted to that coast and not to have penetrated inland. Therefore, these developments clearly had a maritime and mercantile orientation. This situation contrasts very much with that of West Africa, discussed in Chapters 4 and 5. In that case, cities and states developed far from the coast in the northern savanna, before they did so in the forested coastal region. When such developments did take place in the forest, they were always inland and often in or near the forest–savanna ecotone. Until the advent of European sailors in the fifteenth century AD the coast itself remained relatively remote and was not the scene of any major cultural developments. The explanation of this contrast can be found in the different locations and maritime environments of these two coasts. On the West African coast, the Atlantic Ocean was a barrier rather than a highway, until knowledge of the winds improved and changes in sailing technology took place during the fifteenth century. Only then could European ships both avoid and sail against the prevailing northerly winds and currents, that had previously made it impossible to return from a visit to this coast (Crosby 1986: 112–14). In addition, the more environmentally attractive parts of the West African coast are a very long way from Western Europe: a voyage from Lisbon to Ghana, for instance, would be roughly 5500 kilometres as indicated by modern marine distance tables (Caney and Reynolds 1976). The East African coast, on the other hand, has the very great advantage of ease of navigation from maritime southern and western Asia. The winds and currents of the Indian Ocean are seasonal and reverse their direction every six months. Thus, from December to March the prevailing wind on the East African coast is the north-easterly monsoon but from April till November it is the south-westerly monsoon. This enables voyages to be made from the southern Arabian coast, the Persian Gulf and the north-west coast of the Indian subcontinent. Furthermore, it is possible to return to such places from the East African coast within the same year. Also, the length of such a voyage need not be so great as those to the West African coast. Thus a voyage from southern Arabia to the Kenyan coast, for example, would be roughly 2800 kilometres (Caney and Reynolds 1976). Currents also contribute to the ease of navigation to and from East Africa. In particular, the main Indian Ocean currents flow east–west, reversing each half year, and thus make it easier to sail to and from western and southern India, Indonesia and South-East Asia. These differences between the west and east coasts of Africa have had a marked effect on their respective histories: on the west coast, seaborne contact with the outside world has existed for only 500 years but on the east coast such seaborne contact has certainly been a reality for over 1000 years (e.g. Ricks 1970) and, judging by the first-century *Periplus of the Erythraean Sea* (Casson 1989: 6–7), there was also such contact during the Roman period. Indeed, Miller (1969: 145–8) argued for the existence at that time of what he called 'the Cinnamon Route', right across the Indian Ocean from Indonesia to Madagascar and East Africa.

As might be expected, the environment varies to some extent within this long coastal strip, although most of it belongs to the vegetational sub-region known as the Zanzibar–Inhambane Mosaic (Sinclair 1991: 181). To its north, the coast of Somalia from Cape Guardafui to round about Mogadishu is open, and has few harbours and an arid hinterland. From Mogadishu to near the present border of Somalia and Kenya, harbours are more numerous but the coast is still exposed, hazardous and somewhat barren. From the Somalia/Kenya border, however, there is a fair rainfall and the coast is frequently broken by drowned valleys that provide natural harbours. Along the northern part of this coast there is also a string of coral islands, close offshore, known as the Bajun Islands. Between them and the mainland is a sheltered channel and at their southern end are the important islands of the Lamu Archipelago: Pate, Manda and Lamu (Fig. 6.2). Only a narrow, mangrove-fringed channel separates these islands from the mainland and from here southwards there is an almost continuous offshore coral reef, providing protected inshore waters along which there are many small creeks and harbours. Much of the mainland coast is fringed with mangrove swamps but there are also stretches of steep sandy beach, the foreshores of which shelve so gradually that at low tide the sea retreats for long distances. The more protected of these beaches provide ideal landing places: the lightly built sewn boats that were used along this coast in the past could be anchored on the high tide and unloaded at low tide while they were high and dry. On the islands along the coast, fresh water could usually be obtained by digging wells and consequently they provided obvious locations for human settlements. To the south, the large ocean islands of Pemba, Zanzibar and Mafia, which are less than a day's voyage from the mainland, are particularly important, but south of them are the inshore islands of Kilwa and Songo Mnara and further south again the Kerimba Archipelago and Mozambique Island, which are the last islands of the coral reef. South of the Zambezi estuary the temperature of the sea is too low for coral growth and beyond Inhambane the coast is not relevant to the discussion here (Chittick 1971: 108–9; Garlake 1978a: 95–6). Both the Comoro Islands and parts of Madagascar are, however, and their inclusion adds further to the range of environments in the overall area. The former are volcanic, tropical and, with the exception of Ngazidja, well watered, whilst Madagascar is characterized by an environmental diversity resulting from altitudinal differences and its oceanic location.

In general, the environment of the coastal strip and adjacent islands from southern Somalia to Mozambique would have been attractive to human settlement. Much of the area has an adequate rainfall of about 1000 millimetres per year and its maritime, tropical climate has encouraged agricultural exploitation in areas where there are suitable soils. The character of the coast and of its inshore waters and their resources, and that of the adjacent islands, would inevitably have stimulated the early development of coastal shipping and, because of the winds and currents of the Indian Ocean, the people of the East African coast and islands were

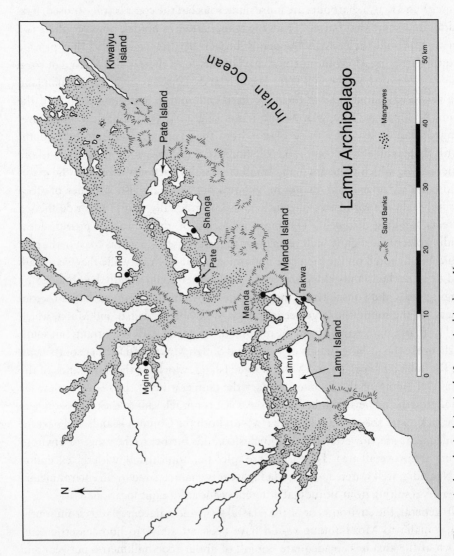

Fig. 6.2 Archaeological sites in the Lamu Archipelago, Kenya.

bound to come into contact eventually with other maritime peoples of that ocean. During the first and early second millennium AD ports in Somalia, Kenya, Tanzania, Mozambique, and the Comoro Islands and northern Madagascar appear to have become part of a vast trading network that extended as far as South-East Asia (Stiles 1992).

In contrast to this narrow coastal strip and its islands, the environment of the interior has often been described as relatively unattractive. According to this view, behind the generally narrow, sandy, often fertile coastal plain, where fresh water could be found in many places, lies a gently rising belt of dry, scrubby, savanna bushland, 100–200 kilometres in width, difficult to penetrate, harbouring tsetse flies and offering little to interest people adapted to a maritime environment. Furthermore, there are few permanent rivers, and of these only the Zambezi, at the southern end of the coastal strip under discussion, is navigable for any distance (Chittick 1977: 185–6). Consequently, it has been assumed that, although there was contact between the coast around Sofala and the Zimbabwe Plateau, there was little between the Kenya/Tanzania coast and the interior until recent centuries. For instance, Posnansky attempted to explain the apparent slightness of contact between the East African lacustrine peoples and the coast (Posnansky 1975: 217). The reality of this situation will be discussed later but it is appropriate to question here the basic idea of an attractive coast and an unattractive hinterland. A closer examination indicates a greater variety of environments, at least in some areas. Thus, in the stretch of coast and hinterland between Bur Gao (Somalia) and Ras Kipini (Kenya) Horton (1983; 1987a: 292) identified a remarkable range of ecological areas. These include: *driest woodland*, the predominant inland vegetation which was exploited by pastoralist groups; *riverine woodland*, where the fertile land of perennial river floodplains has been densely settled by agriculturalists; *lowland wet forest*, along the narrow coastal strip, important both to hunter-gatherers because of the wild animals it contained and to agriculturalists because of its productivity; *coastal swamps*, filled with rapidly growing mangroves that were a source of building timber; *island savanna*, where the soils are poor but fresh water is available at locations close to the sea; and the *reefs and littorals*, which fringe the coast and support rich fishing grounds. Consequently, within relatively short distances are pastoralists, agriculturalists, hunter-gatherers and fishing people, comprising a wide range of ethnic groups of which the pastoralists and some of the hunter-gatherers speak Cushitic languages and the farming and fishing communities speak Bantu languages. Particularly important for East African coastal societies, but formerly overlooked, are the cultivable fertile soils along the lower parts of some of the coastal rivers, such as the Shibeli and Juba in Somalia, the Tana and Galana in Kenya, and the Pangani and Rufiji in Tanzania. Clearly, the environment of this whole region is very much more complex than appears at first sight.

The East African coast possessed a variety of resources that must have played an important part in the cultural developments of the last thousand years or so. To begin with, there was probably substantial food production in some areas. By the middle of the second millennium AD, millet, rice, sorghum, cocoyam, coconuts, bananas, citrus fruits, pomegranates, figs, sugar-cane and vegetables were being grown. Fat-tailed sheep, goats, cattle and chickens were raised, fish and probably other marine foods were extensively exploited and bees were kept in specially constructed hives (Chittick 1971: 136; 1974b: Vol. 1, 236, 248–51; 1977). It should be noted, however, that the list of food plants given here includes a number that were introduced to East Africa from India and South-East Asia at some unknown date before the arrival of the Portuguese on this coast (Gwynne 1975). The most important indigenous African plant foods were probably limited to millet, sorghum and a number of vegetables. Nevertheless, it is apparent that in time food resources became extensive and varied, and that the environmental diversity of this coast must have necessitated the early development of local exchange systems handling these resources. Indeed, by the nineteenth century the East African coast was exporting an increasing quantity of grain, including sorghum, maize and sesame (Spear 1978: 81–2). The last two grains were introduced to Africa and the volume of this trade was probably much greater than in previous centuries but it is probable that grain export to the dry lands of southern Asia had a long history. Thus Chittick (1977: 217) claimed that records in Aden show that rice was imported there from Kilwa prior to Portuguese contact, and he suggested that much of the rice actually came from Madagascar.

It was on the basis of other East African resources, however, that the remarkable export trade of this coast was principally developed. Most important of these seems to have been ivory, already mentioned in the *Periplus of the Erythraean Sea* in the first century AD (Casson 1989: 16, 42) and still important in the nineteenth century (Spear 1978: 81–2). It appears to have been obtainable from areas along the whole coast, from Somalia to Mozambique, but some tusks came from deep in the interior (Ylvisaker 1982: 221). The *Periplus* also mentions rhinoceros horn and tortoiseshell, which actually would have been obtained from sea-turtles, and pearly shell (on the latter see Chittick 1981: 186). At a later date there were, in addition, numerous other resources that became important trade commodities during the first half of the second millennium AD. From Sofala, in the south, came gold and copper, both of which must have been obtained from the interior. From the Horn of Africa, to the north, came frankincense and myrrh, aromatic gum resins much sought after in some parts of the world. From more central parts of the East African coast, mangrove poles, ebony and perhaps other timbers were exported, as was iron, ambergris and sandalwood. Slaves were probably exported from the more northerly parts of the coast (Chittick 1977) but there was no substantial slave trade till late in the eighteenth century. Nineteenth-century exports included other commodities which may or may not have been exported at an earlier date but which are an additional indication of the range of East African resources. Excluding some of obviously late introduction, these comprised copal (a tree resin used in the manufacture of varnish), hides, wax, hippopotamus teeth, coconuts, orchilla (a vegetable dye), beans, shell and livestock (Spear 1978: 82).

Some of these non-food resources would have been important for local use as well as for export. This would have been the case with iron, copper and perhaps ivory. Timber would also have been important, particularly for building construction and shipbuilding. In addition, there were other resources that were of local significance only or formed the basis of production for trade with the interior. Thus the coral reefs and the outcrops of coral on dry land provided important building materials: both stone and lime for mortar and plaster. A considerable amount of cotton was grown on the coast and manufactured locally into cloth. Even silk was produced. Furthermore, the coast probably produced salt and also made use of some of the numerous marine molluscs, either as raw material for beads or, in the case of cowries, perhaps directly for decoration, although in this area not as currency (Hogendorn and Johnson 1986: 102). The various species of coastal palms provided many things, including coconuts, wine, rope, matting and caulking for ships. Finally, the coast had fresh water, so often a problem in the dry hinterland and so crucial both for human settlements of substantial size and for ships' crews anxious to replenish their supplies (Chittick 1977).

With such a diversity of resources, it is difficult to understand why so many settlement sites of the first half of the second millennium AD were abandoned, in some cases prior to the arrival of the Portuguese. What were the constraints that could have operated on this seeming coastal paradise to produce such disasters? The most important was probably dependability of water supply. Horton (1983) has pointed out that in the Lamu Archipelago, for example, the best fresh water is found in wells closest to the sea, where it floats on the heavier, salt water. If the wells are overdrawn or the well shafts made too deep, the supply becomes salty and unusable. In fact, the wells at the abandoned settlements on these islands are today salty. As there is little or no surface water on this coast, the only alternative to such fragile well supply would have been rainwater cisterns: not a very reliable source. Another constraint on this coast would have been soil fertility, which in some places seems to have been poor and may well have been easily damaged by agricultural exploitation. A range of tropical diseases could have provided further problems and one would very much like to know whether or not the extensive maritime contacts of this coast complicated this situation still further, by introducing and reintroducing such diseases as smallpox, cholera and plague. There were also other constraints. Problems of overland communication, particularly with the interior of East Africa, have probably been exaggerated in the past but nevertheless it would have been so much easier to move by boat along the coast that communications would have tended to be concentrated around a coastal axis. The coast-clinging locations of the larger settlements, however, would have rendered them vulnerable to attack, both by those inland peoples over whom they had no control and from the very sea that brought them so much of their livelihood. That vulnerability was clearly demonstrated during the fifteenth and sixteenth centuries AD by the Galla and the Zimba from inland and by the Portuguese from the sea (Chittick 1977: 229–31).

Sources of information

Compared with West Africa, the East African coast is well supplied with sources for the study of its past. Historical documentation is particularly extensive, commencing with the first-century *Periplus of the Erythraean Sea*, which is thought to have been written by an Egyptian Greek merchant from personal experience and includes an account of the East African coast (Casson 1989: 7–10). Another early historical source is Claudius Ptolemy's *Geographia*, originally written in about AD 150 but in its final form probably an edited compilation of about AD 400 (Freeman-Grenville 1975: 3). Both of these sources contain information about the East African coast but it is difficult to use them and there is no further information with which to compare their contents until the ninth and tenth centuries. From then on there is a series of documentary sources, mostly from Arabic authors but with some contributions from Chinese writers, until the arrival of the Portuguese on the East African coast at the end of the fifteenth century. Perhaps the most informative of these historical sources are al-Masudi in the tenth century, al-Idrisi in the twelfth century, and ibn Battuta in the fourteenth century. Only the last of these, however, includes an eyewitness description of some of the East African coastal cities and none of these sources provides the wealth of ethnohistorical evidence to be found in the sixteenth-century accounts of Portuguese writers, such as the anonymous authors of the *Journal of the first voyage of Vasco da Gama, 1497–1499* and *The voyage of Pedro Alvares Cabral to Brazil and India*. Other similarly useful early Portuguese sources include Gaspar Correa's *Lendas da India*, João de Barros' *Da Asia* and an account written by Duarte Barbosa but there are also a number of other sources (Freeman-Grenville 1975). Collectively, these Portuguese sources give us a surprisingly detailed picture of some of the towns of the East African coast in the middle of the second millennium AD. In addition, there is information from a variety of European sources concerning the last few centuries before colonial rule, although the greater part of this dates only from the nineteenth century.

All the historical documentation discussed so far, however, consists of the writings of outsiders, visitors to East Africa who at times either did not understand or did not wish to understand what they had observed, or even writers who had never been there at all and were merely repeating information that was at best second-hand. It is fortunate, therefore, that it is possible to complement such sources with the oral traditions of the people who lived in some of the East African coastal set-tlements. Best known of these is the 'Kilwa Chronicle', available both as a six-teenth-century Portuguese version and as an Arabic version that was copied in Zanzibar in 1862. Collectively, these two versions record the traditions about Kilwa that were current in the earlier sixteenth century and give some account of its origins (Chittick 1974b: Vol. 1, 13–14). There are also a number of other tradi-tional accounts but they seem to have been written down only in the nineteenth or early twentieth century. Perhaps the best known of these is the 'History of Pate', written down about 1910 but covering the period back to 1204 (Freeman-Grenville 1975: preface, 241). Although some of these traditional histories include useful information concerning the life of the coast, much of them consists of a mixture of myth and genealogy which is difficult to use historically. For example, a substantial literature has grown up on the question of how one should interpret the Kilwa Chronicle story of a 'Shirazi' immigration to the East African coast from the Persian Gulf (e.g. Chittick 1965; Allen 1982; Horton 1996: 3). Nevertheless, oral sources do have something to tell us and Thomas Spear with his work on the tradi-tions of the Mijikenda peoples and J. de V. Allen on those about Shungwaya have been able to demonstrate how some of the inland traditions indicate a far greater indigenous contribution to the coastal culture than the better-known oral histories would suggest (Spear 1978; Allen 1983; 1993). The fact remains, however, that his-torical sources, whether oral or documentary, are not able to explain adequately the origins and early development of the coastal cities. To throw more light on that problem, we must turn to the very substantial archaeological evidence that exists.

Archaeological research on the East African coast commenced shortly after the Second World War and it is fortunate that its principal exponents have all been able fieldworkers, most of them excavating extensively. It has also been fortunate that substantial research programmes have been organized by both the British Institute in Eastern Africa, based in Nairobi, and Uppsala University, in Sweden. Nevertheless, until late in the twentieth century work tended to focus on sites with stone ruins, rather than looking at these sites in their overall archaeological context. This resulted from the assumption that the remarkable stone buildings on the coast derived ultimately from the cultural influence of Muslim immigrants from the Persian Gulf and parts of the Arabian coast, an assumption that the emphasis on stone buildings in turn helped to perpetuate. It was admitted that such Arab immigrants had been rapidly integrated with the local people, but it was insisted of the resulting culture that:

> one can detect little in it that appears to have been derived from the indigenous peoples of the continent. On the hinterland of the coast this civilization had little impact, except for the stimulus to trade . . . From the point of view of the homelands of Islam, from which they drew their spiritual inspiration, these cities represented a frontier of the civilized world. (Chittick 1977: 219)

This interpretation of the culture of the East African coast has already been referred to (p. 182). The important point here is to realize that it is this view that shaped much of the archaeological research that has been conducted on this coast. While the coastal cities were thought of as semi-alien trading centres clinging to the edge of the African continent and relevant only as the periphery of an international trading system, there seemed little point in investigating their relationship with the 'indigenous' settlements of the coast or the interior, nor in bothering much about their local antecedents. As a result, much of the archaeological survey and excavation along this coast concentrated on the highly visible stone ruins of mosques, tombs and houses (e.g. Kirkman 1954; 1959; 1963; 1964; 1966; Garlake 1966; Chittick 1974b; Wilson 1978; 1980) and there was relatively little investigation of those parts of settlements built in mud, wood and thatch or of those settlements only built of such materials. In addition, the presence of complex architectural features, of inscriptions, of coins and of imported glazed earthenwares, porcelains, glassware and beads tended to concentrate much of the work on artefact studies and particularly on the detailed chronology that they provided. By the 1970s, however, the emphasis was changing, as some archaeologists came to realize the basically indigenous character of the coastal culture and began to see the cities as part of an ongoing process of African social and economic change, rather than the result of alien colonization (e.g. Allen 1980; Horton 1980; 1987a; 1996; Wilson 1982). These contrasting approaches in East African coastal archaeology must be kept in mind when reviewing the archaeological evidence relevant to the origins of urbanization and state formation.

Allen (1980) listed 173 settlement sites with stone ruins, between Warsheikh (north of Mogadishu) and the Tanzania–Mozambique frontier. In addition, there are sites relevant to our discussion in Mozambique, the Comoro Archipelago and northern Madagascar (Vérin 1976; Duarte 1993; Wright 1993; Chami 1994) and many relevant sites that have no stone ruins have still not received the attention that they deserve. Thus, in total, there must be a large number of sites spread over a great length of coast and its adjacent islands but most of the archaeological investigations that have been carried out have been on the Kenyan or Tanzanian coasts and, indeed, Kenyan sites have had rather more attention than those of Tanzania. One of the first sites to be excavated was the city of Gedi (Fig. 6.3), on the mainland of Kenya, where Kirkman was able to reveal a curiously skeletal city plan (Kirkman 1954: 185). Thus he was able to demonstrate the layout of its city walls, which clearly represented two structural phases: an earlier city of about 18 hectares and a later, smaller city of about 7 hectares (Kirkman 1975a: 239). Within that city were plotted a so-called 'palace', several houses, some of which were concentrated in a group near the palace, and a number of mosques and tombs. The excavations were extensive, but although the Jamia (or main congregational mosque) and the palace were published in detail (Kirkman 1954; 1963), the houses, city walls and other details of this important urban site did not receive the same treatment (Kirkman 1975b). In particular, it is unclear whether Kirkman's city plan shows all the stone ruins or not. If it does, then it must be the case that much of the apparently empty space on his plan was filled with buildings of mud, wood and thatch: that is to say with the houses of the bulk of the inhabitants. Certainly the strange angular outline of the city walls would suggest that they enclosed tightly an irregular mass of houses, similar to that recorded at Shanga (Horton 1996: Figs. 5, 9, 10), where mud and thatch houses partly surrounded a central core of stone structures (compare Fig. 6.3 and Fig. 6.6).

On the basis of the dating of imported ceramics, some of them excavated from beneath a tomb with an inscription containing a date equivalent to AD 1399 (Kirkman 1960), Kirkman suggested that Gedi was founded in the thirteenth century, abandoned in the early sixteenth century and briefly reoccupied in the late sixteenth century, at which time the inner town wall was constructed (Kirkman

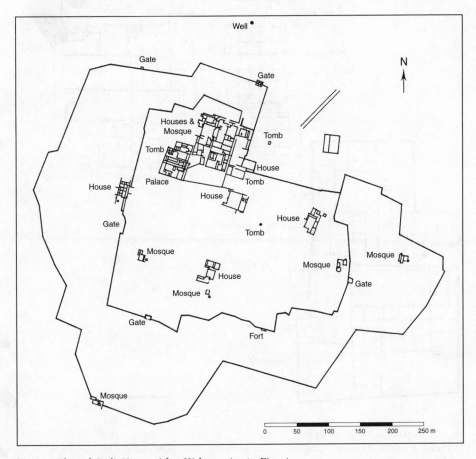

Fig. 6.3 Plan of Gedi, Kenya. After Kirkman (1964: Fig. 7).

193

1975a: 237–9). Most of the buildings that were excavated were, in fact, of fifteenth-century date and the house-plans that were revealed (Garlake 1966: 194) are of particular interest in throwing light on pre-Portuguese social organization. The coral ragstone houses comprised a number of narrow oblong rooms, averaging about 2.4 metres wide, their width dictated by the maximum available rafter span (Fig. 6.4). Although there was some variety of plan at Gedi, the basic house-plan both here and in other coastal settlements consisted of two of these long narrow rooms, one behind the other, with the first one fronting on an enclosed courtyard and the rear

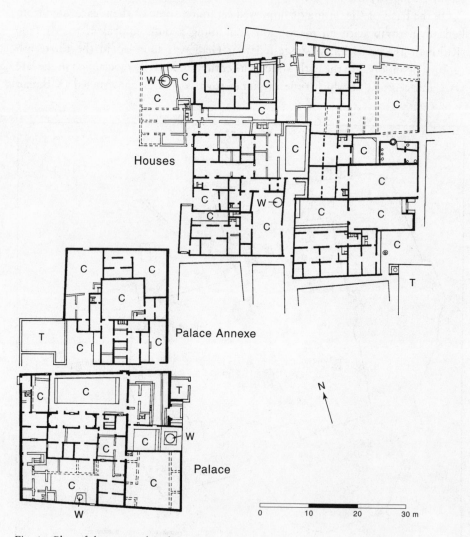

Fig. 6.4 Plan of the centre of Gedi.
C: Court. W: Well. T: Tomb. Original buildings shown solid, alterations in outline. After Garlake (1966: Fig. 76).

one opening into two or three smaller rooms behind. None of these rooms had external windows but sometimes there was another courtyard situated behind the smaller rooms. It seems probable that each house was intended for a separate family, with the rooms providing a graded privacy: most public in the front court-yard, most private in the back rooms. As argued by Allen (1979), the stone houses in archaeological sites such as Gedi are in the same tradition as the mostly eighteenth-century, stone-built mansions of Lamu, some of which are still occupied (Ghaidan 1976; Donley 1987). This would suggest that by the fifteenth century there was already in existence a class of cultured, wealthy, mercantile urbanites (similar to that later known as the *wa-ungwana*) who reinforced their position by reserving to themselves the exclusive right to build their houses in stone, thus making use of what Linda Donley called 'house power' (Donley 1982; Donley-Reid 1990). Looking at the Gedi house-plans, it seems as if a number of such families some-times built their houses in interlocking groups, each group representing a distinct lineage or kin. Certainly such people seem to have lived at a level of material comfort higher than that of most of their contemporaries. Houses had plastered walls, inside toilets, washplaces with bidets, underfloor soakaways and rainwater drains. Indeed, at Gedi one apparent group of houses was identified by Kirkman as a palace. With its monumental arched entrance (Fig. 6.5) and its generous provision of courtyard space, this might well represent the houses of a particular lineage who,

Fig. 6.5 Palace entrance at Gedi, in 1990. Note the high quality of the masonry.

having become the hereditary ruling family, had adapted their dwellings to suit their new duties (Allen 1979: 24).

Kirkman also excavated at a number of other sites in both Kenya and Tanzania. Most significant of them was probably that of Ungwana, on the northern Kenyan coast near the estuary of the River Tana (Kirkman 1966). Here is the remains of a large walled city covering about 18 hectares and occupied from the tenth to the seventeenth century according to the revised dating by Abungu (1990: 212) but Kirkman concentrated on the mosques and the tombs, although the ruins of some stone houses were present. According to his plan, however, extensive areas of this city consisted of empty space (Kirkman 1966: 71) and, as with Gedi, it seems likely that much of this space must have been filled with buildings of mud, wood and thatch. It seems probable that Kirkman's excavation strategy was not designed with this possibility in mind. Thus at Kilepwa, a small thirteenth- to sixteenth-century settlement near Gedi where he also excavated (Kirkman 1952), the remains consisted of a small mosque, two pillar tombs and a group of houses. According to its excavator, this was 'clearly a family unit, corresponding perhaps to the European manor'. Yet we are also told that 'sherds of *sgraffiato* [imported glazed earthenware of eleventh- and twelfth-century date] were found all over the site, so it may have had a large population in the pre-building period' (Kirkman 1975a: 239–40). The last phrase is surely significant: it would appear that, to this excavator, a building that was not made of stone was not a building.

Thus, the first major point that emerges when one begins to examine the settlement archaeology of the East African coast and islands is that buildings of mud, wood and thatch must have constituted a large part of some of these settlements and, if this was the case, then the indigenous African contribution to the growth of these settlements is likely to have been far more important than has sometimes been admitted. For example, the town of Songo Mnara, on the island of that name off the Tanzanian coast, must have consisted of more structures than just a collection of uniformly planned stone houses, a so-called palace and several mosques, loosely distributed within a large walled area. These, after all, appear to have been recorded without resorting to excavation (Garlake 1966: Fig. 74). Similarly, at Kilwa, in the same area, where there have been extensive excavations, it has been estimated that the city site covers about 1 square kilometre but the stone ruins consist of only a scatter of structures. As its excavator admitted: 'Many, and perhaps most, of the buildings at Kilwa, even at the height of its prosperity, were built of mud-and-wattle, evidently in a similar style to that which can be seen on the coast today. The original settlement was probably entirely of such buildings' (Chittick 1974b: Vol. 1, 24). However, it appears that the ratio of buildings of stone to buildings of less permanent materials did vary to a considerable extent from site to site. For instance, the final phases of Shanga, abandoned in the fifteenth century and comprising a town of 8.68 hectares situated on the shore of Pate Island

(Kenya), probably consisted mainly of stone structures, which took up 6.57 hectares of the occupied area (Fig. 6.6). The three mosques, approximately 400 tombs outside the town, other tombs within the town and about 220 houses were all built of stone, leaving some but not much space for buildings of other materials (Horton 1996: 33, 38, 63). A similar but slightly less convincing case might be made for Takwa, a town now thought to have been occupied from the tenth to the seventeenth century (Abungu and Mutoro 1993: 695). Situated near the shore of the Kenyan island of Manda, the final phases of this stone-built walled town of a little over 4 hectares contained a mosque, a well, and 137 other structures, most of which were probably houses (Fig. 6.7). Allowing for open spaces for gardens and markets, there were still some empty areas that could have contained mud, wood and thatch buildings but they were limited (Wilson 1982). In contrast, the stone remains at Dondo, on the coast of the Kenyan mainland close to Pate Island, consist of only two mosques, two wells, two groups of tombs and a building and well suspected to be Portuguese. The excavator of this site has concluded that this unwalled town, which is about 5 hectares in extent, was occupied between the fourteenth and sixteenth centuries by people of sufficient wealth to build lavish tombs and two mosques who were, nevertheless, 'living in non-stone structures' (Horton 1980; 1996: 23–4). Indeed, a comparable site exists at Mgine, on the same part of the Kenyan coast. In this case there are scatters of fifteenth- and sixteenth-century sherds over an area of some 10 hectares but there are no traces at all of stone buildings (Horton 1983). It is difficult to escape the conclusion that mud, wood and thatch buildings, and the African peoples who built them, contributed greatly to the East African coastal settlements.

If mud, wood and thatch buildings meant indigenous contribution, does this imply that stone buildings meant alien contribution? At one time many writers would have answered with a categorical 'yes'; now the question would be considered far more difficult to answer. Garlake, seeking the origins of the architectural styles of the stone buildings, could find various parallels in different parts of South-West Asia but came to the overall conclusion that before the eighteenth century the architectural style of the coast was, 'to a large extent, indigenous to the coast' (Garlake 1966: 116). Clearly, alien influences might be seen in the fourteenth-century palace and commercial centre of Husuni Kubwa, just outside the city of Kilwa, with its audience court, open-sided pavilion, bathing pool, domed and vaulted roofs, and Arabic inscriptions (Fig. 6.8). The same might be said of the nearby site of Husuni Ndogo, a large rectangular enclosure of unknown purpose that could have been a mosque, a market or a barracoon (an enclosure for slaves). These sites, however, are exceptional and the stone buildings of the coast and islands have a far wider range of quality. Thus, Takwa, which Allen called 'the poorest stone settlement so far excavated', consisted mainly of small houses whose 'comfort was little if any greater than that enjoyed by mud and thatch dwellers

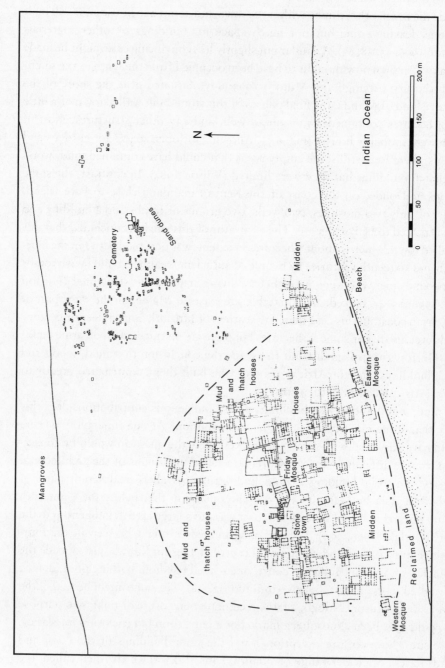

Fig. 6.6 Plan of Shanga, Kenya. The broken line indicates the limits of the settlement: note the areas of mud and thatch buildings as well as those of stone. After Horton (1996: Fig. 5).

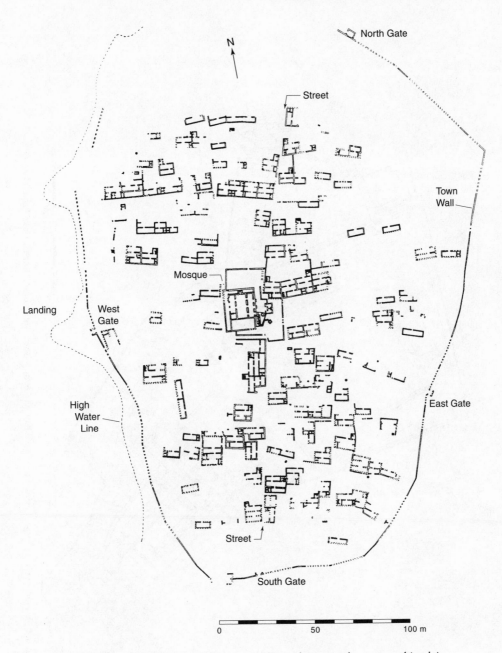

North Gate

Street

Town
Wall

Landing

West
Gate

Mosque

High
Water
Line

East Gate

Street

South Gate

0   50   100 m

Fig. 6.7 Plan of Takwa, Kenya. After Wilson (1982: Fig. 2) but revised to 1999 on his advice.

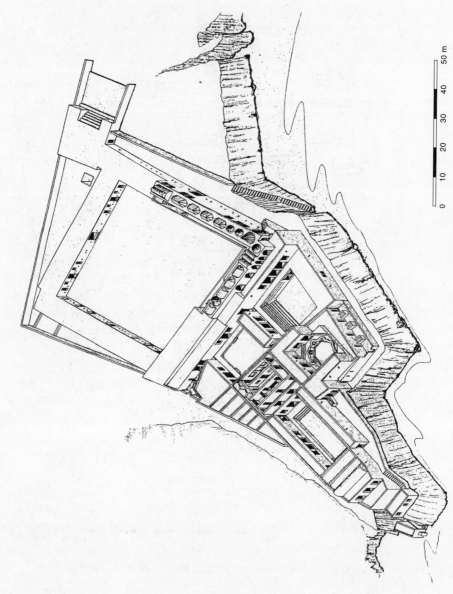

Fig. 6.8 Axonometric reconstruction of Husuni Kubwa, near Kilwa, Tanzania. After Garlake (1966: Fig. 69).

(and well below that enjoyed by some mud and thatch dwellers today)' (Allen 1979: 27). Indeed, as has already been argued, stone buildings, whether houses, mosques, tombs or other structures, were only one aspect of these coastal settlements. Thomas Wilson showed that coastal sites in southern Somalia and Kenya could be subdivided into five classes, based on their size, ranging in area from over 15 hectares to less than 2.5 hectares. Significantly, the smaller sites tended to have fewer buildings built of stone and tended to lack stone-built houses (Wilson 1982). In this way, we begin to see the stone buildings as an integral part of an overall settlement pattern, rather than as the major features of coast-clinging, trading cities of alien merchants, that some might once have thought them. Moreover, when that settlement pattern is analysed for location and date, it appears that this supposedly coast-clinging culture has 30 per cent of the southern Somalian, Kenyan and Tanzanian sites located in places that have 'poor or no harbours' (including six that are actually inland) and it also appears that 'although . . . Swahili society became overwhelmingly sea-oriented, it looks as if it might have been much less so in earlier centuries' (Allen 1980: 362).

In the end, the question of the significance of stone-building is bound up with the question of the origin of these coastal settlements and here the archaeological evidence is becoming increasingly helpful. Ceramics excavated at Ras Hafun, near Cape Guardafui in the far north of Somalia, indicate trading contacts with the Red Sea, the Persian Gulf and perhaps South Asia as early as the first century BC, and with the Persian Gulf and South Asia in the second to fifth centuries AD (Smith and Wright 1988). Nevertheless, the earliest indications of trading settlements further south on the East African coast belong in the main to the last quarter of the first millennium AD. In spite of the mention by the *Periplus of the Erythraean Sea* of an East African port called Rhapta, it has not been possible to identify this early-first-millennium site (Datoo 1970), which was most likely in the Rufiji delta region (Chami 1999a: 210). Although four glass beads of Roman origin have been recovered from an approximately fourth-century deposit at Mkukutu in this area (Chami 1999b) and two sherds of Roman pottery were found in a fifth-century context at Unguja Ukuu on the island of Zanzibar (Juma 1996), none of the supposed discoveries of early-first-millennium coins on this coast is thought to be reliable (Freeman-Grenville 1960; Chittick 1966). Some of the best-published early evidence for a trading settlement is still that from Kilwa, where it is thought that occupation commenced about AD 800. Neville Chittick's excavations at Kilwa are particularly interesting for the light that they throw on the early occupation of this site. The dating of the various excavated 'periods' was partly on the basis of imported ceramics, indicating that the settlement had overseas trading contacts from its very beginning. In Period Ia (ninth century (?) to about 1000) buildings were at first lacking and were then in mud and thatch with a little coral stone used with mud mortar. Similar buildings were found in Period Ib (about 1000 to late

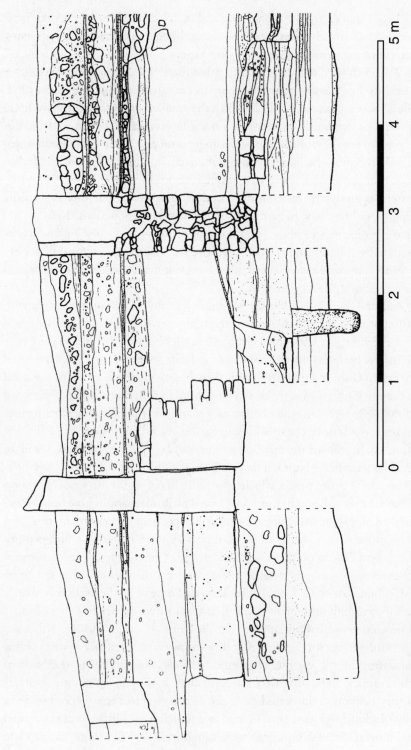

Fig. 6.9 Section through deposits in the prayer hall of the Friday Mosque, at Shanga. See Fig. 6.6 for location. After Horton (1996: Fig. 117).

twelfth century) and it was only in Period II (late twelfth to late thirteenth century) that the first substantial building in lime-mortared stone was found, at the same time that the first coins appeared. It was, indeed, not until Periods IIIa and IIIb (late thirteenth century to about 1400, and about 1400 to about 1500, respectively) that the real floruit of stone-building occurred. Chittick interpreted the evidence as indicating that the earliest settlement was a pre-Islamic fishing village, with Islam beginning to arrive in Period Ib and becoming firmly established by Period II, by which time 'Kilwa had become a substantial and prosperous town' (Chittick 1974b: Vol. 1, 18–19, 28–9, 235–41). Thus the early evidence at Kilwa suggests the gradual development of both building techniques and settlement complexity, rather than any sudden arrival of these cultural characteristics from outside.

Another site with evidence of early settlement is that of Manda, on the island of the same name in the Lamu Archipelago. This was also excavated by Neville Chittick and showed the existence of a flourishing town as early as the ninth century, with occupation continuing until perhaps as late as the nineteenth century. Again, according to the excavator, there was evidence of overseas trade from the beginning of the settlement but in this case buildings of both mud, wood and thatch and of stone were said to have been constructed from the very start, the stonework of the latter sometimes being set in lime mortar, sometimes in red earth. There were also 'sea walls', some of which were of massive masonry that was set without any kind of mortar. In addition, unique for the East African coast, there were structures made of burnt brick set in mud mortar and it was suggested that these bricks could have been imported from the Persian Gulf, perhaps as ships' ballast. From the overall evidence, Chittick deduced that the town was founded by immigrants from the Persian Gulf and that at least some of the inhabitants were Muslim from the settlement's beginning (Chittick 1967; 1971; 1984). This interpretation would make Manda an exception, compared to other similar sites on the East African coast, and Horton (1986) convincingly challenged Chittick's conclusions. The earliest stone buildings were shown to be later than the excavator had thought and to be influenced from the Red Sea rather than the Persian Gulf. Indeed, it seems that the Manda evidence differs little from that from Shanga, only 15 kilometres away on Pate Island. Substantial excavations, during six seasons spread over nine years, have made Shanga (Fig. 6.6) of major importance in any attempt to understand the origins of urbanism on the East African coast. Its excavator, Mark Horton, established a building sequence from mud, wood and thatch to stone, with imported ceramics present throughout (Fig. 6.9). This sequence extends from the late eighth century to the beginning of the fifteenth; mud mortar and stone buildings first appearing in the tenth century and lime-mortared stone buildings not until the twelfth century, becoming more important by the fourteenth century. It seems that the primary occupation at Shanga was non-Islamic but there are the remains of mosques from the end of the eighth century onwards.

Not only does the sequence at this site suggest the indigenous origins of coastal culture, but the ten stages identified during the excavation of its central area (Fig. 6.10) allow us actually to see the evolution of a coastal settlement over a period in excess of 600 years (Horton 1996).

In fact, an increasing number of coastal sites now appear to have had an early origin. Thus, Mogadishu has been shown to have been occupied by the eleventh century AD (Broberg 1995; Dualeh 1996); Mombasa by about 1000 (Sassoon 1980); Pate by about 800 (Wilson 1982: 214–15; Wilson and Lali Omar 1997: 63); and in the Lamu Archipelago alone there are eleven known sites with probable occupation in the ninth century (Horton 1986: 204). Most remarkable of all, Chibuene, an occupation site far away on the southern Mozambique coast, was probably first occupied from the seventh to ninth century and contained imported Islamic glazed wares as well as glass beads and bottle fragments (Sinclair 1982; 1987: 86–91, 168; 1991: 190, 216). It seems, therefore, that early sites are so widely distributed along the coast and on its adjacent islands and so likely, as research progresses, to prove more numerous that one would have to postulate a huge migration from southern Asia to attribute their simultaneous development to external stimulus. Such stimulus doubtless existed to some degree but its relative importance is perhaps indicated by the very small percentage of total pottery in excavated sites that is constituted by imported wares (as little as 0.2 per cent in Period Ia at Kilwa (Chittick 1974b: Vol. 2, 302)). The bulk of the recovered sherds are of indigenous wares and in the earliest periods there is considerable uniformity amongst pottery from widely separated areas. Thus, what is now known as 'Triangular Incised Ware' (often abbreviated to 'TIW') (Chami 1994), but was previously called 'Early Kitchen Ware' (Chittick 1974b: 320–2; 1984: 109–18) or referred to as pottery of 'the Tana tradition' (Horton 1987a: 315–17), has been found on many coastal sites dating to the tenth century and earlier and extending from Somalia to southern Mozambique, as well as on the Comoro Islands and in northern Madagascar. Similar pottery has also been found inland, particularly along some of the river valleys such as that of the Tana River in Kenya, where it has been recorded as much as 250 kilometres upstream (Abungu 1995). In addition, it has been excavated from some of the Mijikenda *kaya* sites of the immediate coastal hinterland in Kenya (Mutoro 1995). There has been some disagreement about the antecedents of this pottery: Horton (1987a: 315–17; 1996: 410–11) and Abungu (1995: 253–5) apparently preferring an ancestry in 'Pastoral Neolithic' pottery made by Cushitic pastoralists of the interior, whereas Chami (1994: 94–8; 1995) has seen its origins in 'Early Iron Age', or what he calls 'Early Iron-Working' (abbreviated to 'EIW'), wares produced by Bantu agriculturalists. Nevertheless, it is clear that the presence of Triangular Incised Ware, in first-millennium AD contexts on the East African coast, argues strongly for an indigenous origin for the settlements concerned. This probability is further strengthened by the work of Chami and Msemwa (1997) on

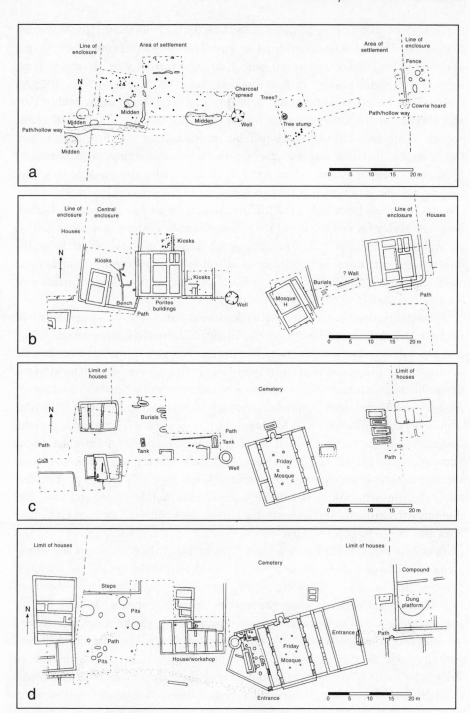

Fig. 6.10 Four of the ten stages in the evolution of Shanga, as identified during the excavation of its central area. *a:* Stage A, c.760–780. *b:* Stage D, c.920–1000. *c:* Stage G, c.1075–1250. *d:* Stage J, c.1375–1400. After Horton (1996: Figs. 296, 299, 302, 305).

the central coast of Tanzania, investigating sites dating from the first to the seventh century AD. They have found evidence of Early Iron-Working farmers both on the coast and islands and in the interior, with Triangular Incised Ware clearly overlying Early Iron-Working pottery at the important site of Kivinja that dates to the fifth and sixth centuries. Also at that site were imported ceramics from the Middle East and glass from the Graeco-Roman world, showing that both local and trans-oceanic trade had already developed by the middle of the first millennium. Confirmation that this was the case is provided by other sites, such as Unguja Ukuu, on Zanzibar Island, where again both forms of indigenous pottery have been found, in conjunction with a wide variety of imports dating to the fifth to seventh centuries, from India, the Middle East and even Roman sources. Indeed, both Triangular Incised Ware and Early Iron-Working pottery were also found at an eighth-century site near Dakawa, some 200 kilometres inland from the Tanzanian coast, along with indications of substantial iron production (Haaland 1995). Increasingly, therefore, archaeological evidence is providing verification of the pre-Islamic origins of the East African trading network.

Significantly, that network eventually embraced not only a substantial length of the East African coast and its immediate islands but also the Comoro Archipelago and Madagascar. In these places archaeological research has made considerable progress since the 1950s, demonstrating the commencement of settlement in the first millennium AD, most likely in about the eighth century (Sinclair 1995: 100–1; Allibert and Vérin 1996). Linguistic evidence indicates that Malagasy, the most commonly spoken language in Madagascar, has its closest relatives in Indonesia (Adelaar 1996) but archaeological research has been unable to confirm the arrival of people from that source (Wright 1993: 659) and it seems likely that settlers from the East African coast were also important (Dewar 1996). By the late first millennium AD, iron-using villages on the Comoro Islands that depended on fishing and domesticated animals and plants were also trading with the Persian Gulf, East Asia and the coast of East Africa, as is shown by the ceramics, glass beads and glass vessels recovered from their sites (Wright 1984). Best known is the site of Dembeni, a large village of mud, wood and thatch buildings on the island of Maore (also known as Mayotte), its earliest occupation dating to about AD 850–880, and a later one to about the tenth to eleventh centuries (Allibert, Argant and Argant 1990). The occupants of such settlements, the larger of which were 3–6 hectares in size, were probably supplying tortoiseshell and marine shell, and perhaps other commodities, for the Indian Ocean trade. The presence of Triangular Incised Ware indicates contact with the East African coast, and items made from chlorite-schist, that must have come from Madagascar, show connections with that island also. Furthermore, the bones of house mice in several Dembeni Phase sites suggest that some of the ships visiting the Comoros were large, long-distance vessels (Wright 1992: 84–5). As Sinclair (1995: 101) has claimed, the Comoro Islands 'were significant hubs of the western Indian Ocean trading systems, articulating Madagascar and the southern coasts of Mozambique with the East African coast, the Gulf and India'. In origin, these developments were pre-Islamic but Islam gradually became established as the settlements increased in size; the towns of Sima and Domoni, on the island of Nzwani, growing to about 8 hectares during the eleventh to thirteenth centuries and to about 11 hectares during the fourteenth and fifteenth centuries (Wright 1992: 124). By the eighteenth century the Comoros seem to have been characterized by fortified towns, like Itsandra and Ntsudjini on Ngazidja Island, which controlled adjacent territories (Damir 1988; Dahalani 1992).

Archaeological research has also been able to trace the socio-economic changes that led to urbanization and state formation in some parts of Madagascar. By the 1850s both processes seem to have been well advanced, as was recorded by the Reverend William Ellis (1859) during his visits to the island (Fig. 6.11). Amongst the most important early archaeological evidence is that from Kingany on the north-west coast of Madagascar, a town site with stone ruins that seems to have been occupied from the ninth or tenth century AD to about the sixteenth century, and some of whose inhabitants participated in the Indian Ocean trade (Vérin 1986: 161–7). Subsequently, a town site on the island of Antsoheribory, in the same area, was occupied from the late sixteenth to the early eighteenth century and has yielded evidence of trading contacts with the Near East, the Far East and Europe (Wright *et al.* 1996: 55–66). Another important early town site is that of Mahilaka, further north along the same coast. Occupied from the tenth to the fifteenth century, this site had a walled area of more than 60 hectares, within which were a few stone structures but many others of less permanent materials (Radimilahy 1992; 1998; Wright 1993: 668). At its greatest extent, the population of Mahilaka has been estimated to have been in the range of 780–3000 and to have had wide trading connections, possibly exporting rock crystal, chlorite-schist and gold, as well as other products such as mangrove wood, copal, tortoiseshell and slaves. Rat bones from the site suggest plague, brought to the island by visiting shipping, as one possible cause of the town's abandonment (Radimilahy 1998: 110, 202–6, 208–11). Radiocarbon dates from sites in the Anosy area in the south-east of Madagascar show that even the more remote parts of the island were occupied by early in the second millennium AD (Rakotoarisoa 1998) but it seems to have been in the central highlands that the most remarkable socio-political developments took place, leading to the emergence of the Merina state by the eighteenth century. Ankadivory, near present-day Antananarivo, is one of many ditched settlements in this area and has been dated to about the thirteenth century. It has also produced evidence that by that time even the inland of Madagascar was in contact with the Indian Ocean trade (Wright and Rakotoarisoa 1990: 28–9; Sinclair 1991: 196–8).

Fig. 6.11 Antananarivo, Madagascar, in the 1850s. Showing a royal procession passing along its eastern side. From Ellis (1859: 365).

Subsistence economy

It remains to examine the archaeological evidence reviewed above, to ascertain what can be learnt from it about the origins of cities and states on the East African coast and islands. The basis of these developments must have been the subsistence economy, so what does the archaeology have to tell us about this? In the past, archaeologists sometimes neglected this subject, probably because the ethnohistorical sources from the end of the fifteenth century onwards are so informative, and indeed it is these which have already been used to discuss the food resources available at the middle of the second millennium AD (p. 188). However, we cannot be sure that the descriptions in such sources can be applied to the end of the first millennium AD, unless we also make use of such archaeological evidence as is available. For example, the cultivation of sorghum in the eleventh and twelfth centuries is presumably attested by the recovery of carbonized sorghum from a layer attributed to Period Ib at Kilwa (Chittick 1974b: Vol. 1, 52–3). Also the early deposits at Kilwa produced plentiful evidence for the eating of fish and shellfish, while the filling of a well dated to the late thirteenth to fourteenth centuries produced the mandible of a very immature camel, an animal not now found on this coast and not recorded there historically (Chittick 1974b: Vol. 1, 28, 43, 98). The evidence from Chibuene is of rather more value, indicating the presence of sheep and cattle and the exploitation of fish and shellfish in the lower occupation level at this site, dating from the middle and late first millennium AD, although there is no direct evidence for plant husbandry (Sinclair 1982: 152, 162; 1987: 88; 1991: 190, 216). Similarly, at Shanga, botanical evidence appears to be lacking but the faunal record is substantial and highly informative. At this site seafood seems to have been particularly important and included fish of reef, inshore and (rarely) deep-sea type, dugong, turtles and shellfish. In addition there were domesticated cattle, sheep and goat, camel and chicken. Cats and dogs were also kept and the hunting of wild animals contributed a small part of the diet. Significantly, the black rat was present throughout the sequence, suggesting relatively dense human occupation and, as a vector of bubonic plague, perhaps one of the causes for the eventual abandonment of the site. It is probable that a mixed economy was practised at Shanga, although the absence of plant food evidence (presumably because of poor conditions of preservation) is a problem and both domestic animals and fish appear to have had only a minor role during the earliest periods (Horton and Mudida 1993; Horton 1996: 378–93). A broadly similar subsistence economy is suggested by the excavations at Manda, which have provided evidence of goat or sheep, of cattle, of domestic fowl and of the domesticated cat. In addition, dugong, turtles and fish were exploited. Camel was present and a small amount of land game was hunted. Again, this site seems to lack evidence for plant food (Chittick 1984: 215).

A more complete insight into diet has been provided by the sites of Dembeni, Old Sima and M'Bachile in the Comoro Islands. Excavations at these sites produced evidence of substantial use of fish, particularly from in or near the coral reefs, the hunting of turtles and of some wild animals and birds, and the keeping of domesticated sheep or goats, most probably goats. Importantly they also yielded botanical evidence for the cultivation of rice (*Oryza sativa*), millet (possibly *Setaria*), coconut (*Cocos nucifera*) and sesame (*Sesamum cf. indicum*) (Wright 1984: 48–54; Allibert, Argant and Argant 1990: 153). The site of Mahilaka, in Madagascar, has also provided a remarkable insight into subsistence, with evidence of rice cultivation and the use of coconut, the keeping of cattle, sheep, goats, pigs, chicken, guinea fowl and ducks, and the hunting of wild animals and birds, as well as fishing, turtle catching and shellfish gathering (Radimilahy 1998: 195–9). Finally, the approximately thirteenth-century site of Ankadivory has produced evidence for the keeping of cattle in the central highlands of Madagascar (Sinclair 1991: 196).

This selection of evidence suggests that by late in the first millennium AD, when the earliest known of the coastal cities and towns were first settled (earlier sites could have been lost owing to coastline changes), there already existed a varied mixed economy in which the resources of both sea and land played a part. Livestock husbandry and fishing could between them have provided ample animal protein and, although the archaeological evidence is often lacking, plant food must also have made a significant contribution to the diet. In particular, it is likely that an important role was played by a number of plants originating in South-East Asia, that were introduced to East Africa possibly about the beginning of the first millennium. It is tempting to see the introduction of Asian rice, coconuts, bananas, sugar-cane and some other plants as a direct result of the settlement of Madagascar by Indonesians at about that time (Shepherd 1982; Ehret 1998: 277–9). In a paper that some regarded as controversial, Shepherd argued that the southern end of the East African coast, particularly the Comoro Islands, played an important early role in the development of the coastal culture. If this was so, then perhaps one may be justified in seeing the enhancement of the coastal subsistence economy by the South-East Asian food plants as a vital factor in the growth of the coastal settlements. As the archaeological evidence is beginning to suggest, rather than being peripheral to the African coast, Madagascar and the Comoro Islands may have been a gateway for new ideas. Whether such a view is justified or not, however, it is clear that by the second half of the first millennium AD, the subsistence economy of the East African coast must have been able to produce a surplus adequate to support a growth in social complexity. In particular, the environmental diversity of the coast, its islands and its hinterland probably allowed, and even encouraged, great flexibility in the subsistence economy. Thus, the camel bones that have been recovered from some coastal sites might be an indication of resource exchange with nomadic pastoralists of the dry interior.

Technology

Archaeological evidence from the East African coastal and island sites clearly indicates considerable technological sophistication. The main problem in interpreting that evidence is to determine how much of it originated from overseas trade, rather than from local expertise. Nevertheless, indigenous technology seems to have attained a remarkably high level. Particularly important were a range of metal-working skills. As might be expected, iron was both smelted and forged and evidence of one or both of these processes occurred, often at an early date, at Kilwa, Manda, Shanga and Chibuene, as well as at Dembeni and Old Sima in the Comoro Islands, and at Mahilaka in Madagascar. In addition, some of these sites produced evidence of working in copper or copper-base alloy, in the form of copper slag or of crucibles containing traces of copper, and there are also indications that gold, silver and lead were sometimes worked (Chittick 1974b; 1984; Wright 1984; Sinclair 1987; Horton 1996; Radimilahy 1998). An impressive variety of metal artefacts seems to have been manufactured on the coast and adjacent islands but it was perhaps the minting of coins that was most notable. These have been recovered from many coastal sites and were produced at Kilwa, Mafia, Zanzibar, Mogadishu and perhaps other places. Usually they were of copper or copper-base alloy, but over half of the coins found at Shanga are of silver (Brown 1996) and most of the over 2000 coins in the eleventh-century hoard found at Mtambwe Mkuu on Pemba Island are of silver (Horton, Brown and Oddy 1986). Also from East African coastal sites there are rather less common coins from other parts of the world of Islam and even from China, most of the gold coins recovered coming from the former source.

The most remarkable aspect of East African coastal technology, however, was undoubtedly seen in building craftsmanship. As well as a continuing tradition of working in timber, mud and thatch, considerable skills were developed in the construction of stone buildings. Coral was quarried, either from the offshore reefs or on land, and Horton (1996: 26–7) distinguishes between well-coursed walls of dressed pieces of *Porites solida*, from the first source, and rougher walls of coral rag from the second. Traces of quarrying for both materials have been found near Shanga and those for the *Porites* coral are of particular interest because they are underwater, implying a specialized knowledge of diving and of underwater quarrying (Horton 1986: 206). Both types of walling could be bonded with either mud or lime-mortar, the latter being obtained by burning coral and mixing sand with the lime produced. The use of lime-mortar seems to have become more common as time went on, and plaster for internal wall surfaces and rendering for external surfaces were also made with a similar lime base. Stone structures were built which were sometimes of considerable height, and scaffolding, presumably with lashed mangrove poles, seems to have been well understood. Roofs consisted usually of a combination of mangrove rafters, stone and lime-mortar but they could also be supported with columns and beams or could consist of vaults or domes (Fig. 6.12). Doors and windows usually had fitted woodwork, most houses possessed internal pit-toilets and washing places, and drainage was provided both inside and outside of some buildings (Garlake 1966). Wells were dug to provide convenient water supplies. All of this implies considerable craftsmanship and specialization: there must have been quarrymen, lime-burners, stone-masons, plasterers and carpenters, to name only the most obvious. In addition, some knowledge of architectural skills was obviously present. Whatever the contributions to this overall expertise from alien sources, the bulk of the actual work must have been done by local craftsmen and it is worth pointing out that the so-called 'pillar tomb', that is so common on the East African coast, has no known parallels elsewhere.

A particularly important part of coastal technology must have been concerned with boat-building, although there is as yet no archaeological evidence to support this claim. Nevertheless, sewn boats were recorded on this coast by the *Periplus of the Erythraean Sea*, nearly 2000 years ago (Casson 1989: 9) and the Portuguese (who knew as much about boats as anybody) noted them with interest at the end of the fifteenth century (Ravenstein 1898: 26). All the materials needed to construct these boats were available on the East African coast and it is likely that the *dau la mtepe* and the *mtepe*, with their sewn hulls and matting sails, were in fact often constructed on this coast. Although we now have very few details of how they were

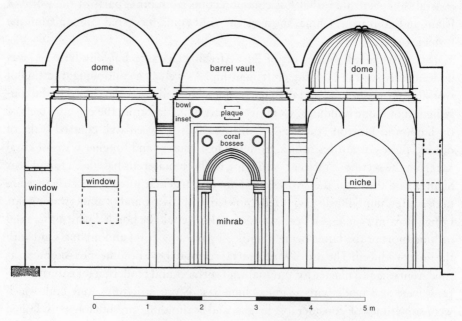

Fig. 6.12 Section through Small Domed Mosque, Kilwa. After Garlake (1966: Fig. 14).

built (Chittick 1980; Prins 1982), the frequent graffiti of such boats, scratched into the wall plaster of houses and mosques up and down the coast, show how important they must have been to many people (Garlake and Garlake 1964; Chittick 1974b: Vol. 2, 266–7). It should be noted that boats constructed in the manner that these were stand up particularly well to the rough treatment of the frequent strandings caused by the character of much of the eastern coast. It is also apparent that some of them were of considerable size: in 1866 David Livingstone was able to have one loaded with 'six camels, three buffaloes, and a calf, two mules, and four donkeys' (Waller 1874: Vol. 1, 9). Furthermore, it seems that the people of the East African coast not only had developed the necessary skills to build these boats but also knew how to use them effectively. The evidence of frequent contact between Madagascar, the Comoro Islands, and the East African coast and islands, not to mention the probability that Indonesian seafarers reached Madagascar, implies a substantial knowledge of seamanship and of winds, currents, tides and weather conditions.

Of the variety of other crafts practised on the coast, probably the most important was the spinning and weaving of cotton cloth, suggested by the number of spindle-whorls which occur in contexts dated to the first half of the second millennium (for example Horton 1996: 337–41). There was also the making of salt by evaporating sea water, for which there is some rather unsatisfactory ninth- or tenth- to late twelfth- or thirteenth-century evidence at Mkadini on the Tanzanian coast (Chittick 1975). In addition, there was carving of ivory and bone, manufacture of shell beads and of semi-precious stone beads using rock crystal and carnelian (for example Horton 1996: 323, 332–3, 346–7, 349–50), and the production of a range of pottery including some with complex painted patterns and including lamps (Chittick 1974b). Of particular interest is evidence from Mahilaka that is thought to indicate glass-bead manufacture, probably by melting broken glass from imported items (Radimilahy 1998: 184, Plate 7.1d, h, j, k), and the possibility exists of similar activity at Shanga (Horton 1996: 332).

It seems that by the end of the first millennium AD there was already a sound technological basis on the East African coast. In the centuries that followed, that foundation was able to support an increasing complexity of technological expertise and this in turn must have led to an increasing functional specialization within coastal society.

Social system

The archaeological evidence on the eastern coast and islands is more explicit on the subject of social organization than is such evidence in some other parts of Africa. We are able to study the plans of a number of settlements, some of them walled, which range in size from villages to cities. The use of stone for some buildings has left us with clear evidence of the progress which urbanization had made in the area prior to Portuguese contact. Apparently, this was a society where many people lived in towns or cities but where many also remained in the rural areas. One suspects that the level of functional specialization was much higher in the larger settlements, with the bulk of the inhabitants of smaller settlements still engaged in primary production. In addition, the degree of social stratification seems to have been greater in the larger settlements. This is suggested by the range in quality and size of the houses, both within the settlements and between different settlements. At the bottom end of the scale were mud, wood and thatch buildings, about which little is known, although the excavations at Shanga have shed some light on the subject (Horton 1996: 235–42). Above these were small stone houses of one to three rooms only but with the larger houses provided with toilets, like those at Takwa (Wilson 1982: Fig. 2). Higher again were multi-roomed houses with an enclosed courtyard, like some of those at Songo Mnara (Garlake 1966: Fig. 74). At the top of the scale were large multi-roomed houses with multiple courtyards and monumental features, such as imposing entrances, like the so-called palace at Gedi (Kirkman 1963: Fig. 2). Surely this is a classic example of social and economic stratification fossilized in archaeological evidence? The various houses suggest a society that ranged from slaves or lowly menials, to successful artisans, to wealthy merchants, to ruling merchant princes. There are also signs that social differentiation became more marked with time. For example, building in mud, wood and thatch was at first the most usual practice but building in stone gradually became more common. Also, the so-called palaces of Gedi and Songo Mnara probably originated as a group of interlocking houses belonging to one extended family. These could have been subsequently transformed into a 'palace', by the addition of monumental features, when the head of that family became the hereditary ruler of the settlement (Allen 1979: 24; also this book, p. 195). An indication of the elevated status to which some of these rulers eventually aspired is given by the coins bearing their names that were issued by various rulers, particularly during the twelfth to fourteenth centuries. Indeed, at least one ruler seems to have been outstandingly ambitious, if the luxury of the 'palace' of Husuni Kubwa at Kilwa is considered. Perhaps of more general importance, however, is the indication, both from the number of medium-to-large stone houses and from the wide use of imported ceramics, that there came into existence a socially superior merchant class comparable to the *wa-ungwana* class of recent Swahili towns and cities (Allen 1979; Donley 1982; Donley-Reid 1990). Indeed, the many stone tombs that were constructed along the East African coast have been interpreted as providing additional evidence of the existence of such a class (Wilson 1979).

It remains to consider the extent to which these social developments along the coast led to state formation. Little has been said on this subject in the present chapter, largely because the available archaeological literature offers comparatively little relevant information. However, the existence of a few much larger settlements, and their geographical relationships to neighbouring settlements of medium or small size, suggest that some cities, for example Mogadishu, Pate, Malindi, Mombasa and Kilwa, controlled the territory around them, a possibility reinforced perhaps by the issue of coinage by some places. Indeed, the considerable prosperity apparent in the early fourteenth century at Kilwa has been interpreted as evidence of an extension of Kilwa's authority at that time, so that it included control of the gold trade from the Sofala area, far to the south in what is now Mozambique (Chittick 1977; on the problematic archaeology of Sofala see Liesegang 1972). A coin minted in Kilwa even got as far as Great Zimbabwe (Huffman 1972: 362 and Plate 1). It seems most likely that some of the east coast cities did function as small city states from early in the second millennium AD and that, as time went on, some of these city states came to dominate others. Documentary sources since the sixteenth century suggest a political pattern of this sort, with Zanzibar, for instance, controlling much of the coast during the greater part of the nineteenth century.

Population pressures

The distribution and density of old settlements and of settlement sites along the East African coast and on its islands suggest that prior to Portuguese contact a long, narrow coastal strip together with its adjacent islands supported a substantial population. Provided with both land and sea resources, with food supplies augmented by South-East Asian domesticated plants, and with fresh water available in many places, the coast and its islands must have contrasted strongly with the dry lands that characterized much of the African interior. Thus the coast could well have provided a stimulus to population growth but with nowhere for excess population to go, other than further along the coast or further out into its islands, for it is difficult to believe that coastal peoples would have been willing to adapt to the dry interior. In this way one can perhaps understand the long, narrow distribution of the East African coastal culture. However, the optimum coastal conditions, that must have been one factor in the development of this culture, were not limitless and to both the north and the south those conditions gradually petered out. In addition, even within the area of optimal attraction, soil character and water availability varied considerably, making some localities more attractive for settlement than others. In such circumstances, population pressures could well have been one of the factors that brought about the development of the coastal cities and city states. Two things suggest that such pressures did indeed exist. First, a significant number of settlements, on the coast itself and also in the Comoro Islands and in Madagascar, were protected by walls, suggesting that population levels had reached a point where competition for resources was causing inter-group conflict or threat of conflict. A particularly remarkable example is the fifteenth- to seventeenth-century fortified site of Pujini, on Pemba Island, Tanzania, whose 'crenelated, fortified surrounding wall appears to have been a manifestation of, and contributor to, island tensions – political, economic, social' (LaViolette 1996: 81). Second, although archaeological evidence is so difficult to identify, the export of slaves from this coast does seem to have had a long although somewhat varied history (Horton 1996: 415–16), implying the existence of excess population that could be exploited as a source. Nevertheless, it is possible that most of the slaves came from inland rather than from the coast itself.

Indeed, the situation was probably more complex than often stated. The hinterland is not all dry, unattractive country. As has been pointed out (p. 187), cultivable fertile soils along the lower parts of some of the coastal rivers must have made important contributions to the coastal economy, so that Mogadishu for instance, although situated on a dry coast mostly unsuitable for cultivation, was largely maintained by the productivity of the Shibeli River area inland to its west (Dualeh 1996). That such interaction of coast and inland riverine plains was important in the past is indicated by the coastal and interior distribution of first-millennium AD Triangular Incised Ware in both Kenya and Tanzania (Abungu 1995; Chami 1995). It was this relationship of coastal and interior peoples that must have formed the basis of the trading networks that provided the commodities sought by the Indian Ocean trade (Mutoro 1998). Like the coast, however, the more productive inland areas were limited in extent and are quite likely to have experienced population pressures, particularly during periods of environmental stress. According to Herring (1979: 48), the eighth and ninth centuries AD could have been a period of severe drought in the interlacustrine regions, and it has also been suggested that there were dry conditions in Ethiopia and Equatorial Africa between about AD 500 and 800 (Hassan 1997: 219–20). Much more information on environmental history is now becoming available and it will be of some interest if it is found that there were indeed periods of reduced rainfall at about the time that the earliest of the settlements that grew into the coastal cities and towns were being established.

Ideology

As with the cities and states of the West African savanna (Chapter 4), Islam was the major ideological factor in the cities and states of the East African coast and islands. At many sites there is at least one stone-built mosque and, significantly, the main congregational mosque usually occupies a central position within each settlement. In addition, the care and expense that was lavished on the building of mosques reinforces the impression that Islam filled an important role in coastal life. The adoption of Islamic beliefs by East African coastal communities was undoubtedly of great significance to those communities. Islam was the faith of urban, mercantile, literate South-West Asia and its adoption brought East Africa into a huge common market; in particular it ensured commercial and cultural intercourse with the Arab lands to the north. It is surely significant that in Swahili the word for 'civilization' is *ustaarabu*, often understood to mean 'becoming like an Arab' (Chittick 1971: 112; Jahadhmy 1981: 10). On the East African coast, to become like an Arab meant to follow Islam, to live in a stone house in a city, and to be involved in trade.

It would be a mistake, however, to imagine that Islam was the primary cause of urbanization and state development on the East African coast, whatever the extent of its later influence on those developments. As in the West African savanna, Islam seems to have arrived after the initial changes had already taken place. Thus, in the fourteenth century when ibn Battuta visited Kilwa, Islam had already been accepted there, but in the tenth century when al-Masudi visited the East African coast some at least of its occupants were clearly animists: 'Every man worships what he pleases, be it a plant, an animal or a mineral' (Freeman-Grenville 1975: 31–2, 16–17). The archaeological evidence now available from some sites confirms that Islam was usually adopted only some time after initial settlement. For example, the primary occupation at Shanga, dated to about AD 760–780, contained no evidence for Islam, although from the late eighth century onwards there was a succession of buildings which have been interpreted as mosques (Horton 1996: 394–406). At Gedi there may have been a much longer pre-Islamic period, because the site of the congregational mosque was probably occupied by houses until as late as the middle of the fifteenth century (Kirkman 1954: 8–9, 14). At Kilwa its excavator thought that Islam began to arrive in the eleventh to twelfth centuries (Chittick 1974b), although at Manda the same excavator thought it probable that some of the inhabitants were Muslim from the time of its earliest settlement in the ninth century (Chittick 1984: 218, but see Horton 1986 concerning the chronology of Manda). Overall, we can conclude that although Islam played a very big part in the developments on the East African coast, it did not necessarily inaugurate them. So far as ideological input was concerned, unknown animistic beliefs probably contributed substantially. The strength of those beliefs may be judged from the fact that East African Islam has remained markedly syncretic until recent times.

External trade

So considerable is the archaeological evidence for long-distance external trade that has been found in the East African coastal and island sites, that it has often dominated discussion of those sites and greatly influenced interpretations. The cities and city states of the East African coast and islands have been seen as a direct response to the growth of that trade. According to this now questioned view, the cities grew up as the trading bases of agents for overseas mercantile interests. As such, they originated as colonial settlements of alien and sophisticated culture, clinging to the coast of a hostile continent, in which they had no interest other than the acquisition of primary products for export. In the long term, the settlements had little influence on the interior of the African continent and themselves were gradually Africanized as intermarriage took place between the colonists and the indigenes. In the process, however, African people adopted some aspects of the alien culture and there evolved that distinctive coastal culture which in recent times has come to be called Swahili.

Such an interpretation is now doubted by many people but it is nevertheless important to examine the extent to which the available archaeological evidence might or might not support it. Certainly, the evidence of long-distance, overseas trade is remarkable. The greater part of this consists of imported ceramics, material that is quite distinct from African potting traditions and can usually be assigned both to an area of origin and to an approximate date. At Kilwa, for example, the earliest deposits of the ninth and tenth centuries contained Islamic glazed wares that probably originated somewhere in the Persian Gulf area or were trans-shipped in that area. Although the types of ware changed with the passage of time, and the places from which they came also changed to some degree, such Islamic glazed wares continued to be imported till well after Portuguese contact. In addition, from about the thirteenth century, Chinese ceramics began to arrive in Kilwa; indeed from about the fourteenth century onwards they equalled or exceeded the quantity of Islamic glazed wares. It is probably the occurrence of these Chinese products, both at Kilwa and at other East African coastal sites (at Shanga for instance they occur throughout the sequence), that has most profoundly convinced archaeologists of the extent of the long-distance trade of this coast. No doubt the Chinese material was usually trans-shipped several times but the distance involved is still most impressive. However, imports other than ceramics have also been found in East African coastal sites. At Kilwa, for instance, glass vessels and beads of glass, carnelian and other semi-precious stones occurred widely distributed through time. Copper kohl sticks (metal rods for the application to the eyelids of antimony as a cosmetic) were probably also imported. The carnelian beads and perhaps the glass beads may have come from western India, the other items probably from various parts of the Islamic world (Chittick 1974b; Davison and Clark 1974). Furthermore, this whole collection of trade-goods consists only of those which happen to have survived in the archaeological record. As was the case with the trans-Saharan trade discussed in Chapter 4 (p. 141), one wonders about the imports that have left no trace. For instance, it is thought that cloth would have been one of the principal imports, particularly high-quality cloth and coloured cloth (Chittick 1977: 216). Such a commodity could have been drawn from a very wide area indeed. So extensive and substantial was East Africa's international trade that Islamic, Indian, Sri Lankan and Chinese coinage reached the

Swahili coast and, to further facilitate commercial transactions, local rulers struck their own coins.

Why did overseas merchants supply so many things to the East African coast and islands? What did they get in return? Basically, they were tapping the natural resources of the African coast and interior, as has already been discussed when examining the available resources of East Africa (pp. 188–9). These primary products included ivory, rhinoceros horn, tortoiseshell, ambergris, gold, copper, iron, rock crystal, frankincense, myrrh, mangrove poles, ebony and other timbers, sandalwood and slaves, not to mention other commodities such as spices about which there is less certainty. Many of these exports would have come from deep in the African interior but the imported goods have not been found in the interior; with the notable exceptions of very small quantities of Chinese pottery of the type known as 'celadon', which reached the site of Great Zimbabwe in the fourteenth century, and of some later Chinese wares which have been found at other sites on and south of the River Zambezi (Chittick 1977: 216).

What sort of a trade could this have been that gathered so many African resources but gave nothing in exchange? The answer lies partly in the differential preservation of the archaeological evidence, for not only would imported cloth not have survived but we would know very little at all about the exports without historical sources. Nevertheless, this does not explain why imports that do survive in the archaeological deposits of the coastal sites, are not in general found in the interior: after all, Chinese ceramics are tough material. The only explanation that seems possible, is that the pattern of trade was more complex than a direct, simple exchange of overseas goods for products of the African interior. Chittick put his finger exactly on this problem, by distinguishing not two categories of goods that were traded, that is to say imports and exports, but four categories. These consisted of: (1) the African goods sought for export; (2) the goods imported for trade with the interior; (3) the goods imported for use in the coastal towns; (4) the goods produced in those towns for trade with the interior (Chittick 1977: 215). Thus, the East African coastal settlements were acting as entrepôts: that is to say as commercial centres of import, export, collection and distribution, at a more complex level than might be expected in a simple coastal trading town. Two sorts of imports arrived from overseas: cloth that could be traded into the interior and luxury goods that were sought by the more successful occupants of the coastal cities and towns for prestige purposes. These exotic manufactures, of which the ceramics and some other items are all that has survived, were probably restricted by both economic and social factors to the coastal elite. To trade with the peoples of the interior, the merchants of the coastal settlements used much of the cloth that had been imported from overseas but they also transported into the interior considerable quantities of cotton cloth manufactured in the coastal settlements. In addition, before the thirteenth century, beads of marine shell were manufactured on the coast and large numbers of cowrie shells collected. Both of these were probably used for the inland trade, although imported glass beads seem to have taken the place of the shell beads in later times (Chittick 1977: 216).

It is also likely that the coastal communities traded some of their agricultural surplus into the interior, just as inland riverine cultivators must have traded their surplus both to the coast and to more immediate neighbours. Nomadic pastoralists, residual groups of hunter-gatherers and even the farmers of the drier areas would probably have welcomed such additions to their diet. Very likely they would also have welcomed salt that was probably produced in substantial quantities on the coast. In return for these various commodities, recipients in the inland gave the primary products that the coastal merchants sought and which they, in turn, exported to the lands overseas. Some indication of the possible antiquity of such contacts between the coast and the inland is provided by the seated burial excavated at the site known as Murrapania IV, near Nampula, deep in the interior of Mozambique. Dated to the beginning of the first millennium AD, the burial was associated with an elephant tusk and with pottery decorated with marine-shell impressions (Sinclair 1991: 188).

It should be observed that a key factor in this somewhat complex pattern of trade was local input, of primary products and manufactures that originated from the coast itself. Environmental diversity and the consequent unevenness of resource distribution must have necessitated the early development of local exchange systems on the East African coast and between it and its hinterland. In particular, coastal trading in small vessels could be expected to have developed early on a coast that was generally suited to inshore navigation. Some indication of this local trade network was found at Kilwa, where stone vessels made of distinctive chlorite-schist appeared from about the eleventh to twelfth centuries onward. These are thought to have originated probably in Madagascar (Chittick 1974b: Vol. 1, 237). In addition, it was no doubt because of such a local, coastwise trading network that Kilwa was able to profit from the export of gold, from the Zimbabwe Plateau, by southern Mozambique coastal settlements. Indeed, it seems that the more successful of the coastal cities, like Kilwa, were successful not only because of their location on trade-routes connecting the interior to overseas markets but also because of their location on coastal trade-routes which enabled them to act as collecting points where local products could be bulked and as distribution points from which prestigious imports could be dispensed. Horton (1987b) wrote of what he called 'The Swahili Corridor', stressing movement of goods along the coast, but Sinclair (1995: 107) preferred the idea of a 'Swahili trading wheel', with its hub located in different places at different times, such as the Comoro Islands, Kilwa or Zanzibar. Such a circular trading network, or a series of such networks, may have linked the long East African coastal strip to the offshore islands and to

Madagascar, as well as to parts of the African interior such as the Zimbabwe Plateau, and then linked the whole complex system into the Indian Ocean trade.

Thus, it is probably not the case that the East African towns and cities resulted simply from the development of external trade with overseas markets. Certainly such trade had a substantial influence on their subsequent history but that trade was only part of a complex network involving local exchange systems that almost certainly pre-dated the overseas connections. As to the origins of these settlements, the situation was probably far more complicated than has sometimes been claimed. Trade was obviously a factor of some importance but to treat the settlements as alien trading colonies is to ignore the existence of a number of other factors that, as we have seen, suggest a basically indigenous origin.

Conclusion

The processes of urbanization and state formation on the East African coast and adjacent islands have sometimes been treated as though they resulted from a classic case of external stimulus. In particular, the larger settlements of this coast have been regarded as Islamic trading cities, founded by colonists who originated from the Persian Gulf area. Such a view has held that this coast was significant only as the edge of the wide Indian Ocean trading world, to which it supplied the products of the African interior and from which it received some of the products of the most sophisticated cultures of that time. Unfortunately, this interpretation has been arrived at by looking at the results rather than at the causes of the remarkable East African coastal developments.

Obviously external trade was extremely important to the settlements of this coast; no doubt there were some mercantile colonists from outside. But what was there that already existed on this coast to attract such attention? This question cannot be answered by excavating the more remarkable stone-built settlements of the thirteenth to fifteenth centuries, which is where so much of the archaeological field research on this coast has been concentrated. It is doubtful if it can even be answered by excavating the important settlement deposits of the ninth and tenth centuries, that are now commanding more attention. The answer must lie in the investigation of the coastal settlement archaeology of the last millennium BC and the first millennium AD, a task that archaeologists have only recently begun to tackle. In addition, the large coastal settlements of the first half of the second millennium AD would undoubtedly be better understood if they could be viewed in the context of the whole settlement pattern of which they formed a part: in short, archaeologists have to look for and investigate the smaller settlements that were contemporary with such places as Kilwa, or Gedi, or Shanga. Already there are indications that, when these things are done, it will be found that the indigenous contribution to cultural development on the East African coast was more substantial than previously thought and that the origins of the East African coastal culture were African not Asiatic. We have seen that there probably existed a strong subsistence base, capable of producing a surplus, encouraging complex local exchange networks. There is also the possibility that the introduction of the South-East Asian food plants had a catalytic effect on coastal cultural evolution. To these things should be added the existence of a sophisticated technology, that encouraged functional specialization, and there should also be added the possibility of complex population pressures within increasingly hierarchical societies, whose socio-economic order could be legitimized first by indigenous animism and later by Islam. As yet, the archaeological evidence is limited but surely it is significant that, during the second half of the first millennium AD, similar locally made pottery was in use both at widely separated coastal settlements and in parts of the interior? It is also significant that some early coastal sites show a gradual change from construction in mud, wood and thatch to stone and that some of the later coastal sites remained substantially settlements of mud, wood and thatch buildings, some of the less important ones almost entirely so. In addition, so widespread were these coastal and island settlements that a really massive immigration would have to be invoked if they are to be explained as alien foundations. It seems reasonable to conclude that the large settlements of the East African coast and islands were not merely the edge of an outside world but the centre of remarkable cultural developments that were of African origin, although subsequently incorporating substantial foreign elements.

Chapter 7

A question of context: Great Zimbabwe and related sites

Great Zimbabwe is one of the best-known and perhaps one of the most ill-used of the archaeological sites of Africa. Its fame is such that it has given its name to the country in which it is situated, the country formerly known as Rhodesia and before that as Southern Rhodesia. Its ill usage has had both intellectual and physical dimensions and started at the moment that it first became known to Europeans. The first such visitor was a German geologist, Carl Mauch, on 3 September 1871. After giving a careful account of the impressive stone ruins that he had seen, Mauch felt it necessary to explain their presence deep in the African interior and did so by associating them with King Solomon and the Queen of Sheba (Summers 1963: 19). Perhaps it is understandable that a nineteenth-century European, flushed with the excitement of something new and unexplained, should grasp at such an unlikely but respectable biblical explanation (which had already been used in the seventeenth century by the Portuguese writer João dos Santos, for stone ruins on Mount Fura in northern Zimbabwe (Theal 1964: Vol. 7, 275–6)). Unfortunately, however, the myth of alien origin for the Great Zimbabwe buildings was to survive for a long time, even surfacing as a political issue in the troubled period of the 1960s and 1970s (Garlake 1973: 209–10). This was probably because such a belief became psychologically essential for some of the European colonial settlers of this part of Africa. Perhaps the most damaging aspect of the whole African colonial experience was the attempted denial to African peoples of their own cultural heritage, of which the attribution of Great Zimbabwe to outside influence, without a shred of evidence, must be the classic example.

This is not the place to discuss the long controversy about whether the origins of Great Zimbabwe were exotic or indigenous. There was never any doubt about its African origins in the minds of those who really understood the archaeological evidence and the whole subject has, in any case, been discussed extensively by others (for example, Summers 1963; Garlake 1973; 1978a; Mahachi and Ndoro 1997). The controversy has been mentioned here because it has influenced so much of the research that has been conducted at this famous site. Intellectually, it has dictated the questions that have been asked by researchers; physically, it has sometimes occasioned both excavations and restoration work that were conducted in such a way as to destroy much of the archaeological evidence, without allowing it to yield the information that it must have contained. Excavations by Theodore Bent in

1891, by Richard Hall in 1902–4, by David Randall-MacIver in 1905 and by Gertrude Caton-Thompson in 1929 were all directed principally at the problem of who built the ruins and when (Bent 1896; Hall 1905; Randall-MacIver 1971; Caton-Thompson 1971). Even later excavations and survey work in 1958 were mainly concerned with the chronological sequence of occupation within the stone ruins (Robinson, Summers and Whitty 1961).

It was only in the latter part of the twentieth century that archaeologists began to ask themselves what the stone ruins of Great Zimbabwe and similar sites represented in social, economic and political terms. In particular, it was realized that the stone-walled enclosures of at least some of these sites were merely the central and most important features of quite large former settlements. At Great Zimbabwe, the recognition of extensive areas of huts densely packed together led to the revision of a population estimate put forward by Peter Garlake in 1973. Instead of an estimated 1000–2500 adults (Garlake 1973: 195), a later estimate gave a total of about 18,000 (Huffman 1986: 323; 1996: 125). It is most unfortunate, therefore, that archaeologists have been so obsessed by the stone structures at Great Zimbabwe and related sites that for a long time they virtually ignored other parts of these sites. To demonstrate this point, Sinclair calculated that of the estimated 600 square metres excavated and published from zimbabwe-tradition sites after the time of Randall-MacIver, all except about 20 square metres had been excavated in and immediately outside stone-walled enclosures (Sinclair 1984). Translated into human terms this could mean that 'at least at Great Zimbabwe over 90 per cent of archaeological effort has been focused upon 2 per cent of the population' (Morais and Sinclair 1980: 351). In short, attention concentrated on the elite and the commoners were ignored. However, changes in research orientation have been occurring, and Huffman's excavations of the early 1970s (p. 236), when fully published, will provide information about 1200 square metres of commoner areas (Huffman 1985a; 1996: 127).

Great Zimbabwe has indeed been ill-used. The only 'mystery' or 'riddle' connected with this site is why it should have taken archaeologists so long to recognize it for what it was. By the 1970s Huffman was calling it 'southern Africa's first town' (Huffman 1977) and others saw it as the capital of the earliest state in its area (for example, Randles 1972). Far more archaeological evidence will be needed before such interpretations can be more than interesting hypotheses, because we have very little documentary or oral traditional evidence that can inform us directly about sites of the Great Zimbabwe type. Nevertheless, it would seem likely that these sites on the Zimbabwe Plateau do indicate the presence of both urbanization and state formation during the first half of the second millennium AD. The real 'problem' of zimbabwe-type sites has been to explain why and how these developments took place. In particular, there has been the problem of the economic basis involved. What economic factors led to a growth in the size of some settlements and to increased centralization of authority? Furthermore, how did those factors change so that by the time of late-nineteenth-century European penetration there were merely ruins scattered through a rural landscape? Indeed, answering such economic questions is only part of the task of explaining the Great Zimbabwe phenomenon. In the end, both this and the related sites can only be understood by seeing them in their full context: chronological, geographical, economic and socio-cultural.

Geographical location and environmental factors

Most known sites of zimbabwe-type are located on the Zimbabwe Plateau, an area of high land much of which is over 1000 metres above sea-level. Situated between about 16° South and about 22° South, this plateau is bounded on the north by the valley of the Zambezi River, on the south by the valley of the Limpopo River, and on the east by an escarpment that runs down to the wide coastal plain of the Indian Ocean. To the west there is no clear boundary but the plateau merges gradually with the Kalahari Desert (Fig. 7.1). Described in this way, it might seem that the

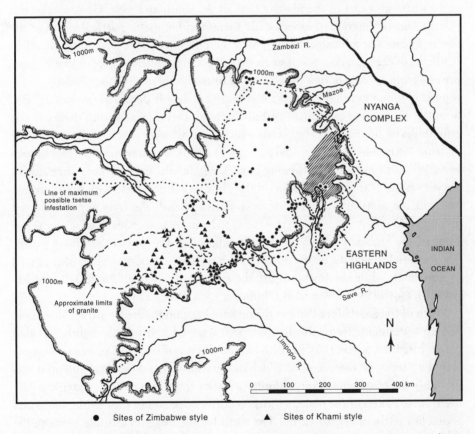

●   Sites of Zimbabwe style   ▲   Sites of Khami style

Fig. 7.1 Distribution of Zimbabwe and Khami style sites. After Garlake (1973: Figs. 25 and 26).

area consisted of a high inland plateau isolated from the rest of the world and, indeed, from the rest of Africa. From what we know of its past, however, this was not the case and the people of the Zimbabwe Plateau seem to have had contact, from time to time, with areas that are now in Zambia, southern Democratic Congo, the Transvaal and north-eastern Botswana, as well as with the Indian Ocean coast. Via this latter contact there were even remote connections with other parts of the world; in earlier times with the Persian Gulf and China, in later times with Western Europe. Contacts outside the plateau were made easier by the many river valleys which dissect its sides, particularly those of the various tributaries of the Save and Mazoe Rivers, and by the relatively open character of much of the upland country.

The Zimbabwe Plateau has a wet season from about November to about March and a dry season from about April to about October, although there can be a little winter drizzle during the dry season. Temperatures are highest late in the dry season, are slightly lower during the wet season and can fall below freezing-point during the winter months of the dry season. Rainfall tends in general to be heavier in the north and east of the plateau than in the south and west. Geologically, the plateau consists mainly of igneous and metamorphic rocks, particularly of granites and schists, amongst some of which there has been extensive mineralization (Collins 1965: 40–1). As a result of its overall geology, much of the landscape comprises gently rolling plains broken by granite inselbergs and by smooth, bare, rounded hills of granite. Parts of the plateau are deeply dissected by river valleys, however, leaving rugged ranges of hills between them. In addition, there are the mountains of the Eastern Highlands which contrast with much of the rest of the plateau. Variations in the detailed geology of the plateau have resulted in a variety of soil conditions, some soils being remarkably fertile, for instance, while others are very poor. Natural vegetation on the plateau varies a little with both altitude and soil but generally consists of savanna-woodland, the trees being scattered among wide grassy spaces. The trees tend to be more numerous in lower areas but some of the highest parts of the plateau consist of almost treeless grassy plains. The Eastern Highlands, on the other hand, have a variety of mountain trees as well as grassland, while the lowlands off the edge of the plateau are usually thickly wooded, mostly by *mopane* trees (Phimister 1976; Beach 1980).

Much of the Zimbabwe Plateau would have been undoubtedly attractive to early human settlement. Its relatively cool, well-watered and usually lightly wooded plains provided a generally healthy human environment. The plateau also possessed a variety of resources, of which its agricultural and pastoral potential was probably the most important, although varying from area to area. Extensive pasturage made parts of the plateau into classic livestock country for cattle, sheep and goats, but particularly for cattle. The considerable range in altitude between the plateau and the coastal plain offered the possibility of transhumant pastoralism for overcoming seasonal variations in pasture and other conditions. Suitable climate and soils also made cultivation important in some areas, however, and provided the staple foods of sorghum, millet, beans and squashes (Garlake 1978a: 73). The overall significance of food production amongst the plateau's resources was very clearly indicated by a Portuguese, Antonio Bocarro, writing in the seventeenth century about the Mwene Mutapa state, that seems to have been one of the successors of Great Zimbabwe even though it was situated on the northern not the southern fringes of the plateau. According to Bocarro the land 'abounds with ... millet, some rice, many vegetables, large and small cattle, and many hens . . . and the greater number of the Kaffirs are inclined to agricultural and pastoral pursuits, in which their riches consist' (Theal 1964: Vol. 3, 355).

There were, however, other riches amongst the resources of the plateau, of which gold was perhaps the most important and has certainly been the most discussed (Summers 1969; Swan 1994). This could be obtained both from alluvial deposits and from quartz reefs and became the basis of the long-distance trade of the Zimbabwe Plateau during the first half of the second millennium AD. In addition to gold, other metals could be obtained, including iron, copper and tin. Another resource of some importance was the granite, of which much of the plateau was made. This had the characteristic of continually exfoliating in thin layers from the many rock surfaces exposed to the marked daily changes of temperature. The thin, parallel-sided slabs of granite produced in this way collected as a scree around granite domes and inselbergs and could be readily broken up into rectangular blocks of uniform size. These provided an abundant building material that needed little or no further preparation. Indeed, supplies were virtually inexhaustible because exfoliation could be produced artificially by lighting fires on the rock surfaces and then quenching them with water (Garlake 1973). It was the ready availability of building stone in such a standard size and shape that gave many of the walls of Great Zimbabwe, and of some other sites, their unusually regular appearance. For though drystone building was widely practised in precolonial Africa, the neat, horizontal coursework of some of the zimbabwe-type ruins is unusual, if not unique. However, the resources of the plateau included other building materials as well as stone. Wood and grass were readily available for house construction and so were clays derived from decomposed granite, that formed the main ingredient of the 'mud' that was widely used in building. Known in this part of Africa as *daga*, this was sometimes of such high quality that it was used to produce free-standing structures that were able to survive considerable exposure. It is not surprising that some of the earlier excavators at Great Zimbabwe quite erroneously called this material 'cement' (Garlake 1973: 19). Also amongst the plateau's resources were clays suitable for potting and soapstone that could be carved. Finally, one should not overlook the importance of the wild fauna which not only provided ivory but could also supplement human food supplies.

Counterbalancing these various resources there were a number of environmental constraints that would have influenced the character of precolonial settlement on the Zimbabwe Plateau. Probably most important of these was the tsetse fly, particularly *Glossina morsitans*, whose presence tended to discourage human settlement both because of its danger to human health and because it rapidly killed the livestock on which so many human groups were dependent. Much of the plateau is free of tsetse fly, as Garlake showed (1978b: Fig. 1). However, Summers (1967) suggested that tsetse distribution could have expanded at times during the last two millennia, given slightly warmer and wetter conditions. Although Garlake doubted the evidence for such climatic changes, he showed nevertheless how the very location of zimbabwe-type sites might have been influenced by the practice of transhumant pastoralism, on the seasonally fluctuating boundaries of tsetse fly infestation (Garlake 1978b). At best it would seem that the plateau was a peninsula in a sea of tsetse, the limits of which constantly changed in response to a variety of ecological factors. Such circumstances were bound to affect the character of human settlement on the plateau itself.

Another constraint of importance was climatic variability, which often led to what the Shona (the principal inhabitants of the Zimbabwe Plateau) called *shangwa* (Beach 1980: 28–9). This was drought or some other comparable natural disaster. Thus the rains might arrive too late or fail completely or even be so abundant as to destroy the crops. Alternatively, locusts or other pests, whose appearance was climatically linked, might be similarly destructive. The result, according to Beach, was that although four years out of five might have normal rainfall, it was probable that the fifth would see some such disaster. The keeping of livestock (of which goats were the most numerous) was a major part of the strategy for surviving years of that sort, for not only could the animals be eaten during a famine but they could be exchanged for grain with neighbours who had not suffered so badly.

Variable soil fertility was also a constraining factor for plateau settlement. There were undoubtedly some areas of fertile red clay soil and some areas of fertile alluvial soil but large expanses of the plateau were covered by poor sandy soils developed on the granite (Sinclair 1987: 38–40). Thus it is probable that good land was limited and control of such land may have been one of the means by which rulers exerted economic control over their people (Sinclair 1984). Soil conditions affected not only cultivated crops, of course, but also the nutritional value of the pastures available for livestock. In addition, some parts of the land were agriculturally useless because they consisted of bare rock surfaces or because they were too steep to exploit. In the latter connection, however, the obvious solution was terracing and this was extensively employed in the Nyanga (formerly Inyanga) area of the Eastern Highlands from the sixteenth to the early nineteenth century AD. In that area not only were cultivation terraces constructed on hillsides but also stone-lined pits to house livestock within the stone-built homesteads, stone enclosures, so-called 'forts', hilltop 'ruin complexes', platforms for dwellings and channels to distribute water (Summers 1958; Soper 1994; 1996). However, it is thought that these structures were not related to those of the zimbabwe sites.

The complex interplay of environmental assets and constraints, that characterized the Zimbabwe Plateau, seems to have concentrated precolonial population around the main watershed between the middle Zambezi to the west and the lower Zambezi and Save-Limpopo rivers to the east. Both ethnohistorical and archaeological evidence show that there was a huge curved area of denser settlement, particularly to the east of this watershed, which David Beach has called 'The Great Crescent of population' (Beach 1994: 19–23). It was this area that was the scene of the remarkable socio-political developments associated with the zimbabwe-tradition sites.

Sources of information

Our knowledge of Great Zimbabwe and of comparable sites in the same area is heavily dependent on archaeological evidence. However, there are also both historical documentation and oral tradition that throw some light on the subject. Stone buildings on the Zimbabwe Plateau were certainly known to the Portuguese, who in the sixteenth and seventeenth centuries AD had trading posts along the Zambezi River and on adjacent parts of the plateau (Pikirayi 1990; 1993: 71–4). The Portuguese were interested in controlling the gold trade from this part of Africa and sought to do so by exerting their influence on the Mwene Mutapa, a ruler of part of an area of similar culture that covered most of the country from the Zambezi to the Limpopo and from the Kalahari to the Indian Ocean. Unfortunately, the Portuguese had little direct knowledge beyond the area of the Mwene Mutapa's own Karanga kingdom, on the northern end of the Zimbabwe Plateau. Nevertheless, it is thought probable that this kingdom was one of the successor states to the one which had been centred on Great Zimbabwe, on the southern part of the plateau. If this was the case, then the Portuguese descriptions of what they observed in the territories of the Mwene Mutapa must have some relevance for our understanding of Great Zimbabwe itself. In addition, the Portuguese actually seem to have been told about Great Zimbabwe, although they never visited the place themselves. One of them, João de Barros, published a secondhand account in 1552 (Theal 1964: Vol. 6, 267–8) and Garlake was of the opinion that the place being described was Great Zimbabwe, which had been virtually abandoned by that time. Although subsequent archaeological research has shown that it was still inhabited, it was clearly no longer the important settlement that it had been (Garlake 1973: 53; Huffman and Vogel 1991: 69).

The de Barros description is the nearest that historical documentation comes to providing us with details of any value about Great Zimbabwe but it was based on

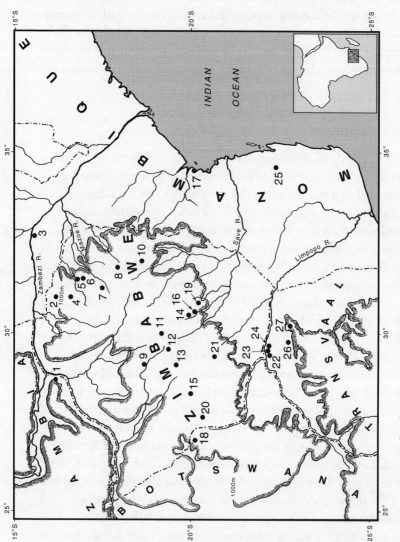

Fig. 7.2 Principal archaeological sites in the Zimbabwe region. Some of the sites mentioned in the text are too far south to appear on this map.

1: Ingombe Ilede. *2*: Kadzi. *3*: Songo Plateau. *4*: Zvongombe. *5*: Baranda. *6*: Ruanga. *7*: Nhunguza. *8*: Lekkerwater (Tsindi). *9*: Mtelegwa. *10*: Chipadze's Ruin (Harleigh Farm). *11*: Tebekwe Mine. *12*: Naletale. *13*: Danangombe (Dhlo Dhlo). *14*: Chivowa Hill. *15*: Khami. *16*: Montevideo Ranch. *17*: Sofala. *18*: Domboshaba. *19*: Great Zimbabwe. *20*: Leopard's Kopje. *21*: Chummungwa. *22*: Mapungubwe. *23*: Bambandyanalo. *24*: Schroda. *25*: Manyikeni (Manekweni). *26*: Machemma. *27*: Dzata. Note that the site of Bambandyanalo is also known as 'K2'.

information obtained at a time that was already too late to record the place during its heyday. To understand the economic, social and political organization of this place, it is necessary to draw heavily on later Portuguese accounts of the Mwene Mutapa and other states. Also it is necessary to turn to oral tradition but here again there are problems. Great Zimbabwe was at its most prosperous about 600 years ago, which is a long time for oral traditions to have any real value. In addition, it is probable that the Ngoni invasions of the 1830s, and other ethnic movements during the nineteenth century, caused something of a break in those traditions. Thus when Carl Mauch reached the site in 1871 he found people living there who seemed to know little about its history, significance and purpose. Nevertheless, sufficient oral traditions exist to demonstrate that Great Zimbabwe was built by the ancestors of the present Shona people, for whom it apparently formed an important political and religious centre. From these traditions it has been possible to reconstruct something of its religious significance (Garlake 1973), its social organization (Huffman 1981) and its position in Shona history as a whole (Beach 1980). Indeed, it has been claimed that oral and ethnohistorical evidence concerning the Venda, a people to the south of the Shona but said to be related to them, can also be used to reconstruct life in Great Zimbabwe (Huffman 1996). To simplify the argument greatly, this has been done by applying the Venda evidence to the layout of the seventeenth- to nineteenth-century site of Danangombe (formerly called Dhlo Dhlo), and then back to the fifteenth- to seventeenth-century site of Khami, and even further back to the thirteenth- to fifteenth-century site of Great Zimbabwe and its thirteenth-century predecessor at Mapungubwe. The result is a stimulating picture of life at Great Zimbabwe and in other similar sites but one that is imposed on the physical evidence rather than generated from it, and it has understandably occasioned much discussion, some of it critical (Beach *et al.* 1997; Soper 1997; Beach 1998).

It is archaeological evidence, however, that has the greatest potential for informing us about Great Zimbabwe and similar sites (Fig. 7.2). Great Zimbabwe is the largest of an extensive group of stone ruins situated on the high granite country of the Zimbabwe Plateau. It has been estimated that about 150 ruins built in the Great Zimbabwe style, or in the later related Khami style, survive in this area (Fig. 7.1) and that perhaps as many as another fifty have been destroyed since the 1890s (Garlake 1970a: 497; 1973: 162). Outside of the area, similar sites have been located by fieldwork in north-eastern Botswana, northern Transvaal, and Mozambique, and both these and the sites in Zimbabwe should be seen as part of a widespread practice of drystone construction in southern Africa (for example, Walton 1956). The characteristic feature of the zimbabwe-style sites is the presence of single or multiple enclosures of drystone walls, which are usually free-standing and broad-based relative to their height. These walls are constructed either of regularly coursed, dressed masonry or of poorly coursed masonry and both types of walling are often found on the same site. Occasionally the walls are decorated with courses of stonework set in a chevron, herring-bone or other pattern, or with courses of darker stone. Other typical architectural features are also to be found, including rounded 'bastions', stepped platforms and upright monoliths. The walls are usually built of granite blocks but on sites where granite was not available they are constructed of whatever stone was to hand. These stone-walled enclosures were evidently intended as 'containers', for apparently they usually sheltered small groups of circular huts with solid *daga* walls and thatched roofs. Alternatively on occasions they may have sheltered granaries (Huffman 1981: 6) or even groups of religious emblems (for example the Eastern Enclosure of the Hill Ruin at Great Zimbabwe).

Sites of this type have come to be called 'zimbabwe' (*madzimbabwe* is the more correct plural form) because this is what the Shona themselves called them. This word has been said to be a contraction of *dzimba dza mabwe*, meaning 'houses of stone' and has also been claimed to be derived from *dzimba woye*, meaning 'venerated houses', a phrase usually used to describe chiefs' houses or graves (Garlake 1978b: 479; 1973: 11). Shona linguists, however, regard both these interpretations as erroneous and point out that *dzimbahwe* itself means court, home or grave of a chief (Huffman 1985a). Most of these sites are situated on the Zimbabwe Plateau and within the modern state of Zimbabwe. To avoid confusion, it has become customary amongst archaeologists and others to refer to the largest and most researched of these sites as 'Great Zimbabwe'. However, sites of the same type do occur in more distant locations and there may well be more examples of this sort than have yet been reported. The most studied of such sites is Manyikeni (formerly known as Manekweni) situated on the coastal plain of Mozambique, only 50 kilometres from the Indian Ocean and some 270 kilometres from the nearest other known zimbabwe. This small site is dated principally to the thirteenth to fifteenth centuries and consists of a single stone enclosure built of poorly coursed limestone blocks. The enclosure is subdivided by internal walls and contains traces of occupation in the form of an eroding hut floor of *daga* and two middens. Outside of the stone ruin there is extensive evidence of habitation consisting of low mounds, most of which are middens, and house-floor remains. In addition, there is an overall scatter of broken pottery, defining the site limits at approximately 368 by 264 metres, and the population has been estimated at 150–200 (Garlake 1976a; Sinclair 1987: 91–9). Another outlying site of zimbabwe-type, although probably of a later date, has been found on the Songo Plateau, near the Cabora-Bassa Dam in central Mozambique (Ramos 1980; Macamo and Duarte 1996). Also a number of stone ruins of either the Zimbabwe or Khami complex are known to exist in northeastern Botswana, of which Domboshaba has been dated to the fifteenth to sixteenth centuries (Denbow 1986: 25–6). Furthermore, some of the numerous precolonial stone structures in the Transvaal show similarities with zimbabwe sites, notable examples being Dzata and Machemma in the Zoutpansberg (Walton 1956: 123, 125; Mason 1969: 414; Huffman and Hanisch 1987; Huffman 1996: 40, 75).

Nevertheless, Great Zimbabwe is by far the most outstanding of these sites. It consists of two main areas of stone ruins: a group of enclosures clustered around the boulders at the top of a precipitous granite hill and another group of enclosures on the far slope of an adjacent valley. Much of the 'Hill Ruin', as it has been called, consists of small enclosures separated by narrow twisting passages, but at one end is the large 'Western Enclosure', which is bounded by walls over 9 metres high, that are capped by turrets and monoliths. This enclosure contained deposits over 4 metres in depth, made up of the remains of a succession of *daga* structures, and had room for about fourteen dwelling huts. At the other end of the Hill Ruin is the 'Eastern Enclosure', which is much smaller than the Western Enclosure, and is bounded on one side by a high stone wall that was originally capped by two courses of decorative stonework. The ground inside this enclosure slopes steeply upwards, it was originally terraced and supported groups of stone platforms in which were set some of the large number of monoliths that have been found in this enclosure, including some of soapstone which were surmounted by carved birds (on the soap-stone birds from Great Zimbabwe, see Huffman 1985b; Matenga 1998). The most remarkable of the ruins in the valley is a large stone enclosure with a maximum diameter of 89 metres, which has been variously called the 'Temple', the 'Circular Ruin', the 'Great Enclosure' and the 'Elliptical Building'. Garlake, who preferred the last of these names, described its outer wall as 'by far the largest single prehis-toric structure in sub-Saharan Africa' (Garlake 1973: 27). This wall is 244 metres long and, at its greatest, 5 metres thick and 10 metres high. It has been estimated to contain 5151 cubic metres of stonework. Parts of the wall consist of exceptionally sophisticated drystone masonry, comprising the most regular coursing achieved at Great Zimbabwe and with the top of the wall capped by monoliths and a decorative frieze. Within this enclosure, the space is subdivided by other walls, many of which appear to belong to an earlier period than the outer wall. There is also a large conical tower, about 5.5 metres in diameter and over 9 metres high, built of solid drystone masonry and in itself constituting one of Africa's most remarkable pre-colonial structures. Spreads of *daga* within the enclosure suggest that parts of its interior were originally occupied by *daga* structures, most of them probably huts. The remainder of the ruins in the valley at Great Zimbabwe consist of a series of small enclosures, a number of which were formerly named after early European vis-itors. Thus there was the 'Mauch Ruin', the 'Renders Ruin', the 'Posselt Ruin', the 'Philips Ruin' and the 'Maund Ruin'. Others had names such as the 'East Ruin', the 'No.1 Ruin', the 'Ridge Ruins', the 'Camp Ruin' and the 'Outspan Ruin' (Garlake 1973: 25–30). Although these appear to have been renamed, the Posselt, Philips and Maund Ruins, for instance, becoming respectively the Western, Central and

Eastern Valley Enclosures (Collett, Vines and Hughes 1992), their former names are common in the older literature.

Investigations at Great Zimbabwe and at other zimbabwe sites have been both architectural and archaeological. Architecturally, it was shown that there was an indigenous evolution of masonry techniques, at Great Zimbabwe, from poorly coursed (P) to regularly coursed (Q) stonework, which finally devolved into uncoursed, loosely piled (R) walling (Robinson, Summers and Whitty 1961). Radiocarbon dating subsequently confirmed the sequence from P to Q masonry but showed that R stonework was contemporary with them rather than belonging to a separate late phase (Huffman and Vogel 1991: 69). Architectural studies at Great Zimbabwe have also identified a number of distinctive features in the zimbabwe style of building. Thus the poorly coursed, early walls were frequently built among and over boulders, which were incorporated into their fabric (Fig. 7.3). Regularly coursed, later walls, on the other hand, were usually built on level ground free of boulders. Doorways in these later walls were particularly distinctive, having rounded sides and high thresholds that frequently had curved steps; each successive step curved more sharply into the doorway, so that the greatest breadth of the threshold was at the centre of the doorway and it gradually merged into the walls at the sides. Pairs of semi-circular projections, often called 'bastions', are to be found inside most doorways and passages in later walls and these

Fig. 7.3 Stonework in the Hill Ruin at Great Zimbabwe. Note the skill with which the masonry has been built around the natural outcrops of granite. Photographed 1994.

have the effect of making entrances narrower and longer. Slots in the sides of many of these bastions and in other locations may originally have held upright stone slabs (but see Huffman 1984: 597–8; 1996) and similar slabs were also set upright as monoliths, either in the ground, or grouped on low *daga* platforms, or along the tops of some of the walls. Other features associated with the regularly coursed later walling are stepped, curved platforms, perhaps intended either as seats or as display stands for ceremonial objects, and small stone turrets, either on the ground within enclosures or on the tops of the walls (Garlake 1973: 21–5).

Archaeological investigations of Great Zimbabwe and at related sites have tended to concentrate on the questions of the date of the stone structures and of the identity of their builders. A considerable amount of attention has also been given to the question of why these structures were built. It appears that building in stone at Great Zimbabwe belongs mainly to the period from AD 1275 to 1450, with a late period from 1450 to 1550 (Huffman and Vogel 1991: 68). The builders may have been descendants of earlier occupants of the site during the first millennium AD, a people whose culture was related to that of cattle-oriented groups in south-eastern Zimbabwe (Huffman 1982). In particular, Great Zimbabwe seems eventually to have inherited the role of Mapungubwe, a hilltop settlement on the south side of the Limpopo Valley, which has been described as 'the first Zimbabwe Culture capital' (Huffman 1982: 146) and seems to have been at its most important in the thirteenth century AD. Thus the site of Zimbabwe already had a considerable history of occupation before the earliest stone walls were constructed. According to Huffman and Vogel (1991: 69), continuity in the pottery at Great Zimbabwe from the twelfth century onwards 'definitely establishes a Shona identity' for the builders, but why were the walls constructed? Archaeological opinion seems agreed that all zimbabwe-type stone structures were intended to be indicators of status for the dwelling places of the elite. In short, their first appearance may be regarded as a sign of considerable social and political change. That being the case, it is unfortunate that so much archaeological attention has been given to the stone ruins and so little to the rest of the settlement of which each ruin must have formed a part. As a result, not only has most attention been concentrated on a very small part of the population of these settlements, as Morais and Sinclair claimed (p. 224), but the impressive character of the stone ruins at Great Zimbabwe has led to a concentration of work on that site while inadequate attention has been given to other zimbabwe sites. Indeed, so single-minded were the earliest excavators that between them they virtually destroyed the archaeological deposits within the main stone-walled enclosures at Great Zimbabwe. However, both Randall-MacIver (1971) and Caton-Thompson (1971) recognized the necessity to excavate at other sites also, if they were ever to understand Great Zimbabwe itself. In addition, both of these excavators realized that the stone structures at Great Zimbabwe and similar sites were only part of the story. Thus Randall-MacIver wrote in 1906 that: 'It is, properly speaking, the huts which constitute the really essential part of the ruin in every case; the stone wall which the visitor so much admires is only the skin, the huts are the flesh and bone' (Randall-MacIver 1971: 84). Caton-Thompson went further by demonstrating, with her excavations in 1929 at the Maund Ruin (now called the Eastern Valley Enclosure) at Great Zimbabwe (Fig. 7.4), how an incomprehensible jumble of stone walls made sense when one included in their plan the *daga* huts, of which they were the courtyard walls (Caton-Thompson 1971: Plate 57; Garlake 1973: Fig. 3; Collett, Vines and Hughes 1992: Figs. 2 and 3 show the same for the Western and Central Valley Enclosures but from surface evidence alone). Even as late as 1973, Garlake remarked of the Maund Ruin excavation that 'this was the first and only time that area excavation was to be undertaken at Great Zimbabwe and it promised an insight into the function of the enclosures and the social organization of their inhabitants' (Garlake 1973: 81). It was only in the 1970s at Great Zimbabwe that attention was once again turned to area excavation and that interest at long last focused on the whole settlement, of which the enclosures and their inhabitants formed only a part.

As a result of field surveys and excavation conducted during the 1970s by Thomas Huffman, it was realized that the stone enclosures at Great Zimbabwe were only the central structures within an extensive settlement of *daga* huts. This work has never been published in detail but for the first time it provided a plan (Fig. 7.5) of the entire settlement (Huffman 1981: Fig. 1) and there was some preliminary discussion of the work (Huffman 1977). Indeed Beach (1980: 86) published an oblique aerial photograph of Huffman's that showed an area excavation of densely packed round huts at Great Zimbabwe. These were described in the caption as 'urban housing sites' and readers should note that the photograph was printed upside-down! As mentioned in the introduction to the present chapter (p. 224), this work led to a revision of the population estimate of Great Zimbabwe made by Garlake in 1973. Instead of a population of 1000–2500 adults (Garlake 1973: 195), it was suggested that the population may have numbered perhaps 5000 adults (Sinclair 1984) and also that the total population was 10,000 (Morais and Sinclair 1980: 351) and may have been as high as 11,000 (Huffman 1977: 13) or even 18,000 (Huffman 1986: 323; 1996: 125). The conclusion was inescapable: Great Zimbabwe had a concentration of population sufficient for it to be called a town or even a city. Beach even provided us with a description of what it may have been like:

> The effect of having so many people on a single site may easily be imagined: this was urban living. Inside the wall that enclosed the main site, the huts were so close together that their eaves must have been nearly touching. Judging from more modern settlements of the Shona, Zimbabwe must have had an appearance and atmosphere far different from that of today. A great deal of the valley, now green, must have been trampled bare by the passage of feet. From cockcrow to evening, the noise must have been tremendous. In certain weather conditions the smoke from hundreds if not thousands of cooking fires would have created conditions approaching that of smog. And, since so far there is no

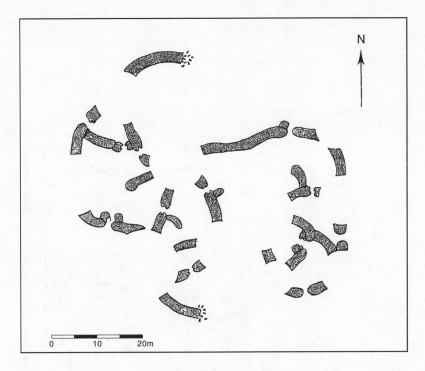

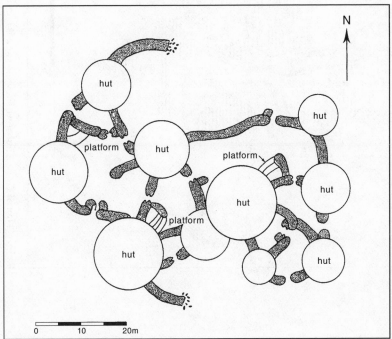

Fig. 7.4 Great Zimbabwe: the Maund Ruin. Above, plan of stone walls only. Below, plan of stone walls and *daga* huts as revealed by excavation. After Garlake (1973: Fig. 3).

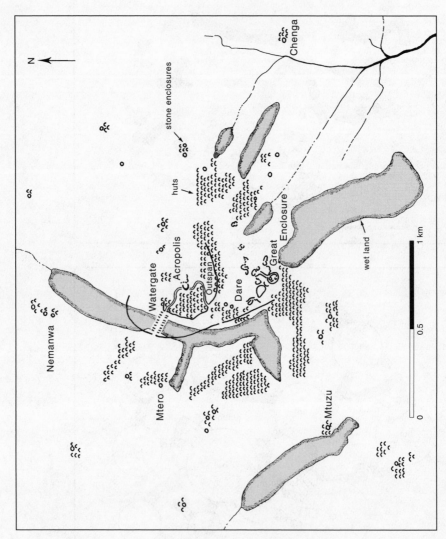

Fig. 7.5 Plan of Great Zimbabwe showing stone structures and areas of *daga* huts. After Huffman (1981: Fig. 1).

evidence for more elaborate arrangements, the people cannot have gone very far to defe-
cate, with the result that disease may have been as much a factor at Zimbabwe as in some
of its European counterparts. Zimbabwe has often been viewed through an aura of
romance, but perhaps a cloud of smoke and flies would be more appropriate from a
standpoint of archaeological accuracy. The contrast between the ruler and the ruled must
have been quite striking. (Beach 1980: 46)

Years later, Beach (1994: 85, 88) was almost apologetic for having taken his 'historian's imagination into a field usually dominated by the cooler intellects of
archaeologists'! Nevertheless, his analogy with London or Paris at a similar date
was a salutary reminder of the urban environment that might have existed at Great
Zimbabwe. The problem for archaeological investigators of such matters has
always been that the sheer size of an urban site makes it difficult to get an overall
picture. This is what makes the investigations of Sinclair so important. Soil
samples were collected at random from over 600 hectares, allowing geophysical
analysis, measurement of soil colour and geochemical analysis of phosphate concentrations to be carried out over the whole of the Great Zimbabwe site. In addition, more than 200 cores each of 50 millimetres in diameter were drilled from
across the centre of the site, covering an area of about 20 hectares. To all of this
data were added observations from field walking, local informants, and the records
of previous archaeological investigations, resulting in a series of maps that showed
the developmental history of Great Zimbabwe, covering both its growth and its
subsequent decline, from the fourth century AD to the nineteenth century (Fig. 7.6).
This work has provided a broad picture that would have taken many years of excavation to obtain, and has provided it with minimal impact on the archaeological
deposits at the site (Sinclair *et al*. 1993: 710, 712–13).

Yet if Great Zimbabwe was the scene of an urban development on the scale
which is now suggested, then the question arises of how it related to the other,
smaller zimbabwe sites. Insufficient attention has been given to these sites by
archaeologists but general fieldwork and the excavation of a number of sites has
begun to throw some light on this problem. Chipadze's Ruin at Harleigh Farm near
Rusape, for instance, seems to have been the earlier of two ruins at this site and it
has been shown by excavation that it comprised a small settlement with cultural
affinities to Great Zimbabwe. Occupied from about AD 1300 to some time after AD
1500, and with an apparent emphasis on cattle-keeping, this settlement consisted
of stone screening walls enclosing areas within which were massive *daga* huts
(Robins and Whitty 1966). It is difficult to avoid the conclusion that what the excavators investigated were the dwellings of a small political or religious elite and that
somewhere nearby must have been the rest of the settlement in which lived the ordinary people who supported that elite.

A similar impression is gained from the most extensively published of the other
zimbabwe sites that have been excavated. Thus both Nhunguza Ruin and Ruanga

Ruin are small sites, dated to about the fifteenth century AD, where stone screening walls enclosed only a small number of *daga* huts. Garlake was of the opinion that the adult population of such enclosures could never have been more than thirty and was probably more often nearer ten (Garlake 1973: 164). Several pieces of evidence at the Nhunguza and Ruanga sites reinforce the impression that the occupants of the stone-walled enclosures were merely an elite section of a larger settlement. First, at Nhunguza the largest hut seems to have been designed as a

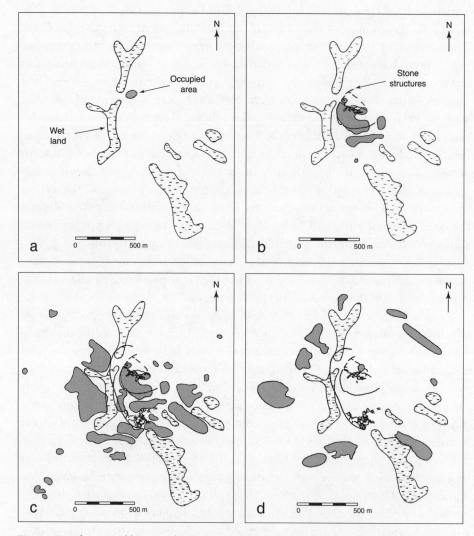

Fig. 7.6 Developmental history of Great Zimbabwe. *a:* Period 1, c.300–900 (early farming community). *b:* Period 3, c.1150–1300 (expansion of stone-building, having started in Period 2, c.1000). *c:* Period 4, c.1300–1450 (full development, after c.1450 followed by partial occupation only). *d:* Period 5, after c.1700 (latest occupation). After Sinclair *et al.* (1993: Fig. 43.2).

place for a person of authority to sit in audience, backed by the symbols of that authority which were housed in an adjacent, secluded room. Second, at both Nhunguza and Ruanga the pottery consisted of a limited range of vessels and excluded cooking-vessels and bowls for eating and serving. This characteristic, which has also been observed at other zimbabwe sites, is interpreted as indicating that food was prepared outside the stone enclosures, then brought into them and the vessels later removed. Third, at both these sites there is a suggestion that there were other habitations outside of the stone enclosures. At Ruanga it is possible that people of a lesser status than the inhabitants of the enclosure were living on the Lower Platform, while at Nhunguza the remains of at least six small huts were found outside of the enclosure but were not investigated (Garlake 1972). It is from the zimbabwe site of Manyikeni (Manekweni), however, that has come some of the best evidence for social differentiation in sites of this type. Here there is extensive surface evidence for occupation outside of the stone enclosure (Garlake 1976a: 29) and excavation has confirmed the presence of huts in this peripheral area (Morais and Sinclair 1980: 352; Sinclair 1987: 91–9). In addition, analysis of the faunal remains from this site has indicated that whereas cattle dominated the meat diet of the people living in the central enclosure and immediately around it, sheep or goat and game dominated that of the people living on the periphery of the site (Barker 1978).

The elite status of those who lived within zimbabwe structures, or the special function of those structures, is also suggested by excavations at the sites of Lekkerwater (officially known as Tsindi) and Zvongombe. At Lekkerwater a small number of *daga* huts nestled within stone enclosures on the top of a bare granite hill, one of them with an internal dividing wall like that in the largest hut at Nhunguza and two of them with finely moulded *daga* features, such as benches, post-bases and a hearth, some with complex relief decoration. Material culture, economy and occupation from the tenth to the nineteenth century clearly associate the site with the overall zimbabwe complex (Garlake 1973: Plates XVII and 99; Rudd 1984; Turner 1984). Like Nhunguza and Ruanga, the two zimbabwe sites at Zvongombe show that this complex extended also to the northern part of the Zimbabwe Plateau, where it seems to have been imposed on the unrelated Musengezi and Harare traditions, suggesting an expansion from a core area in the south (Pwiti 1996: Fig. 42, Table 20b). It is uncertain whether these two sites, known as Zvongombe North and Zvongombe South (Fig. 7.7), were contemporary, although both appear to have belonged to the fifteenth century AD. Again a small number of *daga* huts were located within the stone enclosures, and internal dividing walls and moulded *daga* features were present (Soper and Pwiti 1992). As with other similar sites, the number of occupants of the Zvongombe enclosures seems to have been small.

It has, in fact, become apparent that just as the stone structures at Great Zimbabwe can only be understood in the context of the substantial number of

241

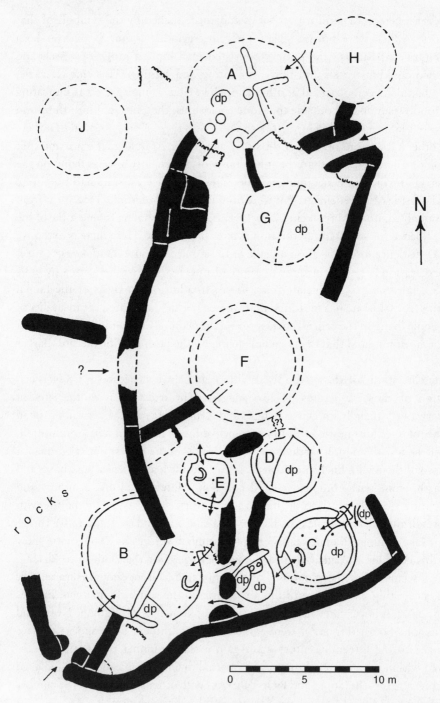

Fig. 7.7 Zvongombe South, in Zimbabwe, reconstructed layout. Stone walls are shown solid, *daga* huts in outline. *dp: daga* platform, small circles in A represent pots, small black dots are postholes, and arrows indicate entrances. After Soper and Pwiti (1992: Figs. 3 and 4).

people who lived outside of them, so also the associated smaller zimbabwe sites scattered over the landscape need to be examined in the context of the overall set-tlement pattern of which they formed a part. Indeed, it has been found that on the Zimbabwe Plateau there are some sites that are culturally and chronologi-cally related to the zimbabwe sites but which do not have any zimbabwe-type stone structures. It is possible that such sites are numerous but few have as yet been identified or investigated. Two relevant sites that have been excavated are Chivowa Hill (that has very little stone walling) and Montevideo Ranch (that has no walling), both quite near to Great Zimbabwe itself. These sites yielded evi-dence of communities that engaged in both pastoralism and (probably) sorghum and millet cultivation and for whom cattle seem to have been particularly impor-tant. They would appear to have been rural peasant communities that were con-temporary with the various zimbabwe sites (Sinclair 1984; 1987: 99–109). A similar situation was also revealed on part of the northern Zimbabwe Plateau, when a random stratified sampling strategy was applied to an area of approxi-mately 12 by 10 kilometres around Zvongombe. The 'Centenary Survey', as this fieldwork project was called, showed that whereas the zimbabwe stone structures of the area tendered to cluster, there were 'unwalled sites ceramically related to the zimbabwes' (and contrasting with other sites in the vicinity) that were more widely scattered (Soper 1990: 73). It was concluded that the evidence suggested 'a group of more important GZ [Great Zimbabwe] communities, perhaps a "polit-ical elite" though this may entail an unacceptable level of supposition, supported by a network of small subordinate settlements' (Soper 1990: 74). Subsequently, Soper (1992) discussed the socio-political status of the zimbabwe sites on the northern Zimbabwe Plateau, where they appear to represent a cultural intrusion from the south, but found that the evidence was still inadequate for any confident inferences to be made. However, the overall evidence from the various sites that are thought to be culturally related to Great Zimbabwe would suggest that there existed a graded series of settlements, from capital city to regional centre to rural village. If this was the case, then it seems likely that a formally organized state did exist on the Zimbabwe Plateau during the second quarter of the second millen-nium. By one means or another a small elite had acquired power over the rest of the population.

Radiocarbon dating and imports from the East African coast, of which ceramics are the most significant, have enabled archaeologists to piece together a reasonably consistent chronology for the zimbabwe sites. This indicates that they had ceased to be important by the end of the fifteenth century and indeed that Great Zimbabwe had declined sharply, at least as an urban centre, by the middle of that century. It used to be thought that the site was virtually abandoned at that time but it seems more likely that it continued to be inhabited until the nineteenth century, although it had lost both its economic and political importance and most of its population (Garlake 1968; 1970b; Huffman and Vogel 1991: 69; Collett, Vines and Hughes 1992: 157–8; Sinclair *et al.* 1993: Fig. 43.2).

Documentary and oral sources indicate that the kingdom of the Mwene Mutapa, on the northern end of the Zimbabwe Plateau, was the immediate successor of the state that had been centred on Great Zimbabwe, and archaeological research has provided some support for this probability. In an interesting and important piece of fieldwork in the Mount Fura area, Innocent Pikirayi has investigated sites which he identifies with the Mutapa state. During the sixteenth and seventeenth centuries the Portuguese had trading posts in this area, attracted, it would appear, by its gold resources. It is no surprise, therefore, that excavations at the large settlement site of Baranda produced imports of those and later dates, including glazed ceramics from the Near East, the Far East and Europe, as well as large quantities of Indian glass beads, and other imported glass. However, indigenous burnished graphite pottery was far more abundant than imported wares and is similar to pottery from zimbabwe sites at the time of their maximum development. Smaller sites in the same locality told a similar story, although less imported material was present, but there was no indication of building in stone at any of these sites. Sites of possibly later date and different cultural tradition, located on hills in the vicinity, do have stone-built enclosures that contain evidence of occupation and which in some cases are provided with loopholes, perhaps for the use of firearms, but these are said to be quite different from the stone structures of zimbabwe sites. Thus, some sites in this area do seem to have inherited parts of the zimbabwe cultural tradition but sophisticated building in stone was not one of them (Pikirayi 1992; 1993; Sinclair *et al.* 1993: 725–31; Soper 1999).

Actually, it was in the south-western part of the plateau, not its north, that the zimbabwe tradition of building in stone was to survive and indeed develop. The sites of Khami, Danangombe (Dhlo Dhlo) and Naletale are particularly remarkable examples of this phenomenon. These and a number of less well-known, similar sites belong to the period from the fifteenth to the nineteenth century AD. The stone structures typical of this later period consist mainly of revetment walls for building-platforms, on which *daga* huts were erected. These walls made considerable use of decorative features (Garlake 1973: 166–8, Plates XVI and 103). The most extensively investigated of these sites is the fifteenth- to seventeenth-century site of Khami, where Keith Robinson (1959) excavated parts of a group of elite buildings, some of which were approached by underground passages and many of which were provided with 'drains of a rather advanced type' (1959: 105). Khami is thought to have been the capital of the Torwa state, where many people may have moved after the decline of Great Zimbabwe. For this reason, Huffman (1981: 15–16) used the settlement pattern at Khami to throw light on the earlier one at Great Zimbabwe and in doing so provided us with a plan of the Khami site (Fig. 7.8). This demonstrates that Khami, like Great Zimbabwe, consisted in the main

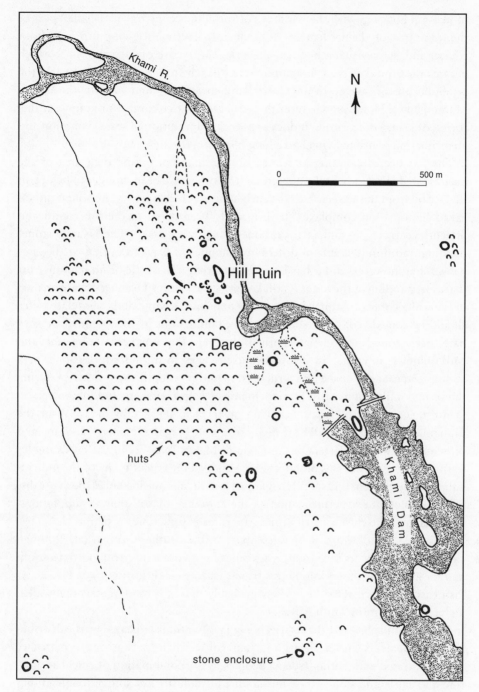

Fig. 7.8 Plan of Khami, in Zimbabwe, showing stone structures and areas of *daga* huts. After Huffman (1981: Fig. 13).

245

of peasant housing, with the buildings of the elite occupying only a small part of the total area of the settlement. Subsequently, Huffman (1996) also used both Khami and the seventeenth- to nineteenth-century site of Danangombe, which became the capital of the Changamire state (Beach 1994: 120), to help explain the symbolic use of space within Great Zimbabwe itself and even in the earlier Mapungubwe. However, whatever the actual level of cultural continuity over this period of some six centuries, it does appear that a tradition of state formation and an inclination to urban living had a long history in the area.

The practice of building in stone also continued in the Nyanga area of the Eastern Highlands, where the numerous structures have been thought to belong to the period from the sixteenth to the early nineteenth century AD, although the so-called hilltop 'ruin complexes' have recently been dated to the fourteenth and fifteenth centuries (Summers 1958; Soper 1994; 1996; 1999). The Nyanga stone-building tradition (pp. 228–9) differs in a number of ways from that of the zimbabwe sites, however, and it has been claimed that it has little or no relevance for the understanding of the latter (Garlake 1973: 172). Nevertheless, it does form part of the wider context within which Great Zimbabwe, Khami, and their related sites should be considered. As has already been pointed out (p. 232), zimbabwe sites have been found in north-eastern Botswana, the northern Transvaal and Mozambique, as well as in Zimbabwe itself. They form, indeed, part only of a widespread usage of stone as a structural material in south-eastern Africa during the second millennium AD. The settlements of Klipriviersberg and Olifantspoort (Mason 1969) and of Site 2628 CA1 near Heidelberg (Taylor 1984) in the Transvaal, of OND 3 and OU 1 (Maggs 1972: 178–9) in the Orange Free State, and of many places in the Tugela Basin in Natal (Maggs 1984) are just a few examples to show how extensive this practice was. Although the size of many of the individual walled settlement units is often relatively small, in some instances the dense distribution of these structures suggests the existence of substantial populations. Furthermore, the clustering of stone structures is sometimes urban in character: for example Molokwane, near Rustenburg in the southern Transvaal, although called a 'village' by its investigator, stretches for 3 kilometres from north to south and for an average of 1.5 kilometres from east to west (Pistorius 1992: Fig. 2). As Pistorius (1992: 17) remarked: 'This probably makes it the largest stone-walled archaeological site in South Africa.'

The economic basis of the relatively high populations indicated by the distribution of settlements with stone walling, many of which in South Africa seem to have been associated with Sotho-Tswana peoples, was a combination of cereal agriculture and cattle and small stock husbandry. Ethnohistorical sources confirm that urban development was in progress in some places: Truter and Somerville in 1801, for instance, estimated the number of huts at the Thlaping settlement of Old Lithako (which lacked stone structures), in north-eastern Cape Province, to be between 2000 and 3000 and the population between 10,000 and 15,000 (Walton 1956: 52). Furthermore, in 1835 Gardiner reckoned the number of inhabitants at the Zulu capital of Mgungundlovu, in Natal, at 5500 (Parkington and Cronin 1979: 136), and the later Zulu capital of Ondini is thought to have housed up to 5000 people at times during the 1870s (Watson and Watson 1990: 34), neither of these places possessing stone structures. Many of these societies lived south of the Tropic of Capricorn and are, therefore, technically not relevant in a book concerned with tropical Africa. However, the developments on the Zimbabwe Plateau that produced the zimbabwe and associated sites need to be seen in the context of the wider picture of socio-economic change in south-eastern Africa over the last millennium or so. These were societies in which cattle became wealth and their possession gave power; cattle even determined the layout of settlements and the symbolic use of space within them (Kuper 1980; 1982; Evers 1984). The 'Bantu Cattle Pattern', as it has been called, can be discerned in many sites, including the Toutswe settlements of eastern Botswana, which date from about AD 600 to about 1300 and show evidence of a graded settlement hierarchy based on the possession of large herds of cattle (Denbow 1984; 1986). Similar developments also took place in the Limpopo Valley from the ninth century onwards, eventually giving rise to the important centre of Mapungubwe, which by the thirteenth century had grown powerful and wealthy from its participation in long-distance trade with the Indian Ocean coast. At the peak of its power, 3000–5000 people are thought to have lived at Mapungubwe, making it 'the largest urban settlement in Southern Africa in its time' (Huffman 1996: 184). In conjunction with a number of associated sites, it also seems likely that Mapungubwe became one of the earliest identifiable states in the area (Hall 1987: 74–90). In such matters, the zimbabwe sites appear to have been the successors to Mapungubwe and, as Huffman (1996) has demonstrated, they need to be seen in the broader context which gave rise to such developments.

Part of that broader context is provided by another important source of archaeological evidence that should not be forgotten. This consists of the traces of precolonial mining, particularly for gold, which from time to time have been found on the Zimbabwe Plateau. These 'ancient workings', as they have often been called, have been associated with the builders of the zimbabwe sites and it was formerly suggested that the distribution of workings and ruins was similar (Summers 1969: 137–41). Summers (1969: 105) was able to list 1267 ancient workings, most of which resulted from gold-mining. Both alluvial and quartz reef gold was mined, stopes, shafts and sometimes adits being used to exploit the latter. The miners rarely penetrated deeper than about 25 metres, because of the harder rocks met at depth, as well as ventilation or drainage problems (Phimister 1976). Nevertheless, it has been claimed that of the 3041 kilometres of gold reef pegged by European miners by August 1894, some 611 kilometres were covered by 'ancient workings'

(Mennell and Summers 1955). The mining of placer deposits, both alluvial and eluvial, seems also to have been important and they were comparatively easy to exploit. It has, indeed, been suggested that the location of Great Zimbabwe was influenced by the presence of placer deposits in the vicinity (Phimister 1974). However, the main difficulty in discussing the archaeological evidence for precolonial mining on the Zimbabwe Plateau, which included mining for copper and iron as well as gold, is that so many of the old workings were destroyed by modern mining early in the twentieth century. Because of this, the work of Lorraine Swan, looking at changes through time in the proximity of settlements to gold mines (but excluding alluvial workings), has been particularly useful (Swan 1994). Although gold production seems to have peaked from the twelfth to the early fifteenth centuries (Phimister 1976: 16), she found 'a close relationship' between mines and first-millennium sites in the north-east of the Zimbabwe Plateau, and indications of a movement of sites towards the mines in the south-west between the seventh and ninth centuries (Swan 1994: 125). She also showed that mining was the work of a lower-status population living near the mines, while smelting was carried out at the elite zimbabwe sites, from which have come most of the gold artefacts that have been found. Furthermore, Swan was able to excavate a rare surviving portion of backfill in a stope at the Tebekwe Mine, in central Zimbabwe (Swan 1994: 103–16). This provided information on hard-rock mining techniques, and was dated by radiocarbon to the mid-fifteenth to mid-seventeenth centuries. Huffman (1974a) argued that gold-mining, at least, did not develop on the plateau until the eleventh century AD at the earliest and that the rise of the Great Zimbabwe state was a direct consequence of that mining and of the gold trade with the East African coast that it supported. Swan's work, and the presence of marine shells and beads in early- to mid-first-millennium contexts on the Zimbabwe Plateau (Swan 1994: 72–3), suggest that gold-mining actually began during the first millennium AD. Nevertheless, the greater part of the production of 7 to 9 million ounces that Phimister (1976: 16–17) estimated for the period from the late tenth century to the nineteenth does seem to have been produced during the time of greatest building activity at Great Zimbabwe (Chipunza 1994: 77) and the significance of gold-mining for the zimbabwe phenomenon seems incontrovertible.

Subsistence economy

The archaeological evidence that has been reviewed above is deficient in many respects but it does provide us with some idea of how urbanization originated on the Zimbabwe Plateau and how states developed there. For instance, we have relatively little information about the all-important subsistence base but it is nevertheless possible to outline in general terms the nature of the economy that supported these developments. The archaeological evidence indicates that livestock husbandry was particularly important and that cattle dominated this husbandry. Consider, for example, the remarkable results of an analysis of a large quantity of animal bones excavated from a midden on the lower slopes of the hill at Great Zimbabwe, on the top of which is located the so-called Hill Ruin. It was estimated that this collection consisted of about 140,000 pieces of bone. Of these, 15,298 were selected as easily recognizable and on examination it was found that all except 218 pieces came from cattle. The bones remaining after this selection consisted of fragmentary material but a random sample of 5061 fragments showed that only forty-five of them came from animals other than cattle. Amongst the other animals represented in the more recognizable material, domesticated sheep or goat was the most common but domesticated dog and a limited range of wild animals were also represented. The more recognizable material was also analysed for skeletal part, bone treatment and fragmentation, and minimum number of individuals. It was concluded that the food remains of the occupants of the Hill Ruin were dominated by cattle and that more than 75 per cent of the 1330 animals represented were immature when killed. It was also concluded that the cattle had been butchered on the hilltop rather than elsewhere (Brain 1974).

Evidence of a similar emphasis on cattle has been found at other sites. Thus at Ruanga Ruin the animal bones excavated by Garlake indicated that mature domestic cattle were the main source of meat, although smaller animals, either domestic sheep, goats or small buck, were also eaten (Garlake 1972: 134). Cattle were also the most common animal at Harleigh Farm (Robins and Whitty 1966), Sinclair found the same thing at Chivowa Hill and Montevideo Ranch (Sinclair 1984; 1987: 102, 108) and Turner the same thing at Lekkerwater (Tsindi) (Turner 1984). At all these sites sheep or goat and wild animals were also present but of considerably less importance. So far as it is possible to tell, the cattle seem to have been of the Sanga type, which are still kept by the Shona people of the area today. In an important and stimulating paper, Garlake suggested that transhumant pastoralism for the intensive production of beef was a major factor in the location of zimbabwe-type settlements, many of which were situated on the edge of the tsetse-free highlands so as to be able to exploit lowland grazing when it was relatively tsetse-free during the dry seasons. Indeed, Garlake argued that such specialist pastoralism is as likely to have formed part of the basis for the rise of Great Zimbabwe and its associated sites as gold-mining and long-distance trade, to which the development has so often been solely attributed (Garlake 1978b). Although his transhumance model has since been questioned (Thorp 1995: 73), there seems little doubt about the important role of cattle in the economy.

Perhaps those immature cattle bones at the base of the hill at Great Zimbabwe should make us pause, however. If the Hill Ruin was occupied by an elite group, or if the ethnohistorical evidence for cattle sacrifice collected by Carl Mauch in 1871 has any bearing on the practices of 400–600 years earlier (Brain 1974: 308–9), then the bones from the hill midden may not constitute reliable evidence for the role of cattle in the overall subsistence economy. Indeed, there is a general danger that faunal evidence from within or near stone structures at zimbabwe sites will only throw light on the diet or rituals of the elite. A comparison by Carolyn Thorp, of the age of cattle represented by the bones from the hill midden at Great Zimbabwe, with the age of cattle represented by bones from an area of commoners' houses in the valley, showed that the former indicated the killing of a significantly larger number of young animals (Thorp 1995: 73). Furthermore, it was found at Manyikeni (p. 241) that whilst those people within and near the stone enclosure mainly ate beef, those living on the edge of the site ate mainly sheep or goat and game (Barker 1978). In addition, a sample of faunal material from Khami contained not only a preponderance of cattle but also a wide variety of other species, some of which are not likely to have been used as food and may indicate the activities of a traditional healer (Thorp 1984). Nevertheless, at the rural villages of Chivowa Hill and Montevideo Ranch cattle were still the most common animals (Sinclair 1984; 1987: 102, 108) and it is difficult to avoid the conclusion that cattle were at least a very important element of the pastoralism practised by the occupants of zimbabwe and related sites.

Both the location and the apparently continuous occupation of the zimbabwe sites suggest that pastoralism was only a part of the subsistence economy and perhaps not the most important part. Direct archaeological evidence is limited but ethnohistorical evidence suggests that it was grain cultivation, particularly of sorghum and millet, that provided the basic staple foods. In addition, there was probably a wide range of vegetables cultivated. Carbonized seeds from Great Zimbabwe and from related sites of the Leopard's Kopje Tradition (Robinson, Summers and Whitty 1961: 170; Huffman 1974b: 120; 1977: 13) confirm that sorghum was grown, as well as finger millet (*Eleusine coracana*), pearl millet (*Pennisetum americanum*) and a variety of beans (*Voandzeia subterranea*) and peas (*Vigna* spp.). Furthermore, two grains of finger millet were recovered from deposits dated to the second half of the first millennium at the site of Kadzi, in the middle Zambezi Valley, north of the Zimbabwe Plateau (Pwiti 1996: 132). It is also relevant that far to the south, where organic remains tend to be better preserved, sites in Natal of a similar date have produced grains of *Eleusine coracana*, *Pennisetum typhoides* and *Sorghum* sp., together with evidence for the growing of pulses and cucurbits (Maggs 1995: 172). The role of livestock in such mixed farming economies was largely to cushion the effect of crop failure in bad years (p. 228) and, particularly in the case of cattle, to provide a means of amassing wealth in a negotiable form, wealth that could form the basis of power. Overall, the strength of the subsistence economy of the Zimbabwe Plateau by the first half of the second millennium AD was probably substantial. It seems likely that Bocarro (p. 227) was not exaggerating in the seventeenth century when he claimed that most of the people in this area were 'inclined to agricultural and pastoral pursuits, *in which their riches consist*' (my emphasis).

Technology

Archaeological evidence from zimbabwe and related sites indicates the existence of considerable technological expertise. The aspect of this that remains most obvious is the practice of building in stone. The construction of free-standing, drystone walls, especially on the scale and of the quality of some of those at Great Zimbabwe, requires skill, as those of us who have tried our hand at even quite modest drystone work have quickly realised. Admittedly the tabular nature of the exfoliated granite provided an almost limitless supply of superb building material but the builders also knew how best to use it within their own technological limitations. Although they never seem to have grasped fully the importance of bonding, either between courses or between separate walls, their building technique, at its best, exhibited remarkable sophistication. Walls were broad-based to spread their load and tapered to their tops. They were rubble-filled, to economise on labour, but the faces of the walls, so vital to the success of such a technique, were constructed with great care. Sharp corners and rectangular layouts were avoided and plans consisted of random curved forms. This emphasis on curves is also evident in the distinctive architectural features that were constructed. Overall, the stone structures of the zimbabwe sites, and of Great Zimbabwe particularly, imply remarkable technological skill; anyone doubting that should consider the details of the conical tower at Great Zimbabwe (p. 233). These structures also indicate the development, from an indigenous drystone walling tradition, of what Garlake called 'an architecture that is unparalleled elsewhere in Africa or beyond' (Garlake 1973: 50).

However, the stone walls of the zimbabwe sites were merely one component of a building technology, a component for which evidence happens to have survived. Somewhat fragmentary evidence from a number of sites suggests that building in *daga* (or 'mud') was just as important as building in stone, if not more so. Indeed, it seems that originally much of the impressive stonework at Great Zimbabwe that we so much admire would have been plastered with *daga* up to a height of some 2 metres above the ground (Garlake 1973: 20). This highly plastic material was used for a variety of constructional purposes, including floors and other internal fittings, and was skilfully moulded into decorative patterns, as well as being beautifully finished to a hard, smooth, almost polished surface. The craftsmanship suggested by the remnants of *daga* that have survived should also serve to remind us of other building skills of which we have no direct evidence, such as wood-working and thatching. For instance, by the early nineteenth century, if not before, it is apparent that huts in settlements in the Orange Free State and the Transvaal were even provided with the sophistication of sliding doors (Maggs 1993).

Another important aspect of the technology of the Zimbabwe Plateau during the first half of the second millennium AD comprised the related fields of mining and metallurgy. Archaeological evidence (pp. 247–8) indicates that mining was a widespread activity conducted on a considerable scale, although in the case of gold-mining at least it was limited in depth, and recovery methods were inefficient (Phimister 1976: 15). The complete range of metals that were produced probably consisted of iron, copper, gold and tin, and Great Zimbabwe has yielded evidence of metal-working in all of these. Iron-working seems to have been particularly well developed, producing a range of hoes, axes, spearheads, arrowheads, knives and other things. Copper, bronze and gold, on the other hand, were used mainly for decorative purposes, often in the form of wire made with the assistance of iron tongs and drawplates but also as sheet or cast metal (Garlake 1973: 113–16). The gold-covered rhinoceros figurine and other objects found in twelfth-century burials at Mapungubwe (Phillipson 1993a: 230–1) are a sad reminder of the objects that must have been lost to looters, particularly during the period 1895–1900 when more than 2000 ounces (62,200 grams) of gold were estimated to have been taken from ruin sites (Swan 1994: 70).

Other crafts indicated by the archaeological evidence from the zimbabwe sites included the manufacture of pottery, much of which had polished and graphited exteriors. In addition, spinning, presumably of cotton, is suggested by the large number of perforated discs of potsherd which have been found, although there are other uses to which these might have been put (Garlake 1973: 116–17). If they were spindle-whorls, which is quite likely, then the presence of spinning would presumably suggest that weaving was also taking place and we could assume that textile manufacture was of some significance (Davison and Harries 1980). Also amongst local crafts, it is worth noting the carving of soapstone, most of the evidence for which has come from Great Zimbabwe itself. Ritual bird figures, monoliths, flat-bottomed dishes, figurines and open moulds for casting cross-shaped ingots of copper were all carved from this soft, easily worked and locally available stone. The manner in which the soapstone has been carved suggests a familiarity with wood-carving and is a reminder of the many crafts in perishable materials that must have existed also at the zimbabwe settlements, but for which we have no evidence (Garlake 1973: 119–23, 130–1). There are, however, examples of ivory-carving and bone-working from the site of Bambandyanalo (also known as K2) and from nearby Mapungubwe, dating from the end of the first millennium and the beginning of the second millennium AD (Hall 1987: 80–1). More durable are the many remarkable pottery figurines of humans and animals, recovered from more than 200 sites and dating from about the third century AD to the end of the nineteenth century (Matenga 1993).

From what is known of the technology associated with the zimbabwe and related settlements, it would seem that there existed a varied range of craftsmanship. It is quite likely that by the second quarter of the second millennium AD there had, as a result, already developed a degree of functional specialization within the society to which these settlements belonged.

Social system

Great Zimbabwe and its associated sites provide many indications of social and economic stratification. The very stone structures that characterize most of these sites are symbols of privilege and power. They have no obvious practical role, such as defence. Rather, they seem to have been intended as containers, behind whose high walls could be hidden away both the living and the ceremonial areas of a ruling elite. Indeed, the walls themselves demonstrate the power of such a ruling group, able to spend its surplus wealth on such items of conspicuous consumption and able to exert the necessary control over substantial bodies of skilled and unskilled labour (although the work actually extended over some three centuries, a British drystone building contractor has estimated that the structures at Great Zimbabwe would take eighty-four men, working six days a week, two years to complete (Reader 1997: 338)). Furthermore, some of the items recovered from within these stone-walled compounds seem to confirm the elevated status of their occupants. Thus there are objects of gold, of copper or bronze and of soapstone; there are also exotic objects such as glass beads and, at Great Zimbabwe itself, glass vessels and Islamic and Chinese ceramics: all these the products of long-distance trade via the East African coast. Moreover, there are some significant absences from the artefacts found in zimbabwe-type stone enclosures. Garlake remarked on the 'extraordinarily limited range' of pottery, for instance, comprising, it would seem, drinking and brewing/storage vessels but lacking open bowls for cooking, serving and eating, and lacking pots suitable for fetching water. Garlake saw this evidence as suggesting that only a limited range of domestic activities took place within the enclosures and pointed out that there is also an almost complete absence of grindstones from the enclosures (Garlake 1973: 112–13). Add to all this the impression that many of the stone enclosures contained huts with finely finished solid *daga* walls, at least one of which (at Nhunguza) seems to have been an 'audience hut', and the elite nature of the occupants of these enclosures is almost certainly established. If a clincher is needed, then perhaps it can be found in the remarkably small populations that the enclosures are thought to have housed. Garlake estimated the total population of the enclosures at Great Zimbabwe as between 100 and 200 adults and the population of all the other known zimbabwes at any one time as about 750 adults (Garlake 1973: 195–6).

Only in the 1970s did archaeologists begin to ask questions about the rest of the population of these settlements. As has already been discussed (p. 236), evidence became available that the stone enclosures were merely central structures within more extensive settlements, which in the case of Great Zimbabwe may have had a total population of 18,000 people. With some justification, Huffman referred to Great Zimbabwe as 'southern Africa's first town' (Huffman 1977). The ordinary townspeople lived in cramped conditions (Fig. 7.9), at a density of about three times that of the elite (Huffman 1977: 12) and, judging from the evidence at Manyikeni (p. 241), they did not eat so well. However, there was probably already social differentiation amongst the townspeople themselves, with functional specialization giving a special status to craftsmen such as blacksmiths and builders in stone.

At Great Zimbabwe, at least, urbanization was already in progress. Furthermore, if this site is examined in the context of all the other zimbabwe sites and all the other sites that are culturally and chronologically related, then it is possible to discern a graded series of settlements that suggests the existence of a formally organized state (p. 243). At one end of the scale was the capital at Great Zimbabwe, with its large population controlled by a powerful elite; at the other end were the rural villages with their peasant communities. In between were regional centres: smaller towns, each of which was controlled by its own elite group which probably owed some sort of allegiance to that of the capital. It also seems highly probable that the occupants of all these settlements shared a similar worldview, originating from

Fig. 7.9 Remains of commoner's hut excavated at Great Zimbabwe. Scale in feet. Reproduced by permission of Thomas Huffman.

Kuper's 'Bantu Cattle Pattern' (p. 247) but developing into something quite distinctive. The attempt by Huffman (1996) to reconstruct the symbolism that shaped the material record at zimbabwe and related sites provides a stimulating picture of how society may have been organized, although it remains difficult to verify.

Population pressures

Spatial analysis (Fig. 7.10) of the distribution of zimbabwe and related sites on the Zimbabwe Plateau (bearing in mind that this may reflect the distribution of research rather than of sites) has demonstrated the existence of a settlement

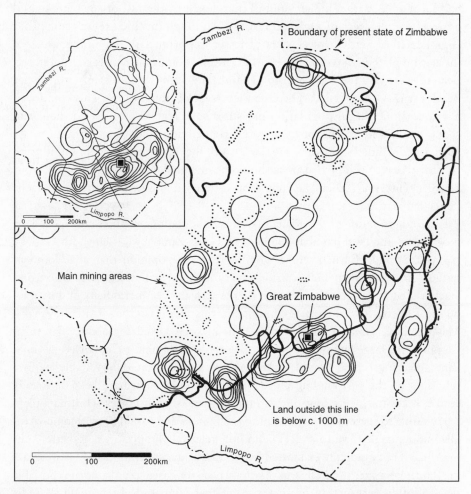

Fig. 7.10 Spatial analysis maps of zimbabwe sites. Large map: 50 km clustering level; inset map: 155 km clustering level and Garlake's (1978b) Thiessen polygon study. After Sinclair and Lundmark (1984: Fig. 5).

pattern in which the population showed a marked tendency to cluster. A similar analysis of Khami sites again shows obvious clustering but with a different location (Sinclair and Lundmark 1984; Sinclair 1987: 123–4). These clusters, which are thought to indicate the areas, respectively, of the Great Zimbabwe and the Torwa state, presumably resulted from the operation of those environmental constraints which have already been discussed (p. 228). Tsetse fly, climatic variability and differences in soil fertility must all have played a part in making some areas more attractive to human settlement than others. Thus there was a marked preference amongst zimbabwe sites for settlement on the southern edge of the plateau, which was high enough to be tsetse-free, within easy reach of lowland grazing that could only be exploited during its relatively tsetse-free dry season, had local areas with a higher rainfall than much of the rest of the plateau and possessed some areas of high soil fertility. Although this picture was somewhat complicated by settlement clusters of lesser importance in the mining areas of the central plateau, it would appear that the places most attractive to human settlement were relatively limited. In general they seem to have lain within what Beach (1994: 19–23) called 'The Great Crescent of population'. This could well have occasioned local population pressures sufficient to give rise to the social changes inherent in the processes of urbanization and state formation. As Sinclair concluded: 'pressure on land and the accompanying possibility to control access to productive areas should be included in the analysis of relations between élite and others and even of differentiation within the élite itself' (Sinclair 1987: 144).

Some confirmation of the existence of local population pressures may, indeed, be provided by the eventual abandonment of Great Zimbabwe itself. Both Garlake (1973: 198) and Huffman (1972: 365) were of the opinion that abandonment resulted from environmental deterioration brought on by the large population, and Sinclair (1987: 114, 116) thought that there was a 200 year periodicity in the sociopolitical history of the area resulting from this factor, so that Bambandyanalo-Mapungubwe, Great Zimbabwe and Khami each lasted for about that time. Certainly the large number of people that are now thought to have lived in Great Zimbabwe must have placed a tremendous demand on the available natural resources of the surrounding area. Firewood would soon have become locally scarce, necessitating its transport from ever-increasing distances (Huffman 1977: 13), wildlife to serve as a supplement to the human diet would have become virtually unobtainable (Brain 1974: 309), and the relatively limited areas of better soils must have been gradually exhausted by too frequent a cultivation and by overgrazing (Huffman 1972: 365). Thus, as may have been the case with Aksum, it is possible that one of the very factors that gave rise to Great Zimbabwe also brought about its destruction. Without fundamental changes in technology and agricultural system, it was fated to destroy itself.

Ideology

Religion seems to have permeated many aspects of Shona life, as is suggested by the numerous pottery figurines from Zimbabwe, widespread in space and time, which have been discussed by Matenga (1993). Therefore, it is probable that it was a contributory factor in the rise of Great Zimbabwe and of the state which it seems to have controlled. Indeed, one of the two main schools of thought concerning the origins of these developments has seen religion as the *major* factor in their initiation (Huffman 1972: 353). The problem is that our knowledge of Shona religion is drawn from oral tradition and ethnography and from such sources it is difficult to estimate the exact role of religion in changes that took place some seven centuries ago, although Huffman (1996) made a bold attempt to do so. According to Garlake (1973: 184), 'Great Zimbabwe was very probably always a major religious centre', where *Mwari*, the Shona supreme god, was particularly reverenced and where cults of the *mhondoro*, spirits associated with the ruling dynasties, also flourished (1973: 174). Certainly there are archaeological features and artefacts at Great Zimbabwe that suggest religious and ancestral associations – particularly the monoliths, some surmounted by carved birds, most of which originally stood in the Eastern Enclosure of the Hill Ruin. However, there is no archaeological evidence to support Garlake's assumption that religion was 'probably the most important single factor in bringing about the first steps towards the cohesion, organization and stratification of the society', and Garlake himself recognized this (1973: 184). Indeed, although Shona religion may have been very important as a means of reinforcing the authority of a ruling elite, the hypothesis that the rise of Great Zimbabwe and its associated sites was due to a religious minority, of either migrant or local origin, is unconvincing. The alternative school of thought to this religious hypothesis is the trade hypothesis, which 'maintains that Zimbabwe was a result of surplus wealth from the East African gold trade' (Huffman 1972: 353). This, at least, is an hypothesis that is susceptible to archaeological evaluation.

External trade

Both Arabic and early Portuguese documentary sources mention the existence of trade between the Sofala area (p. 188), on what is now the southern coast of Mozambique, and the interior. That area seems only to have been a clearing-house, where trade goods from the Islamic world and from India and China were imported for onward transmission to the interior, which in turn exported primary products via the same area. Most sought-after of those products was gold, although at the time of the first Portuguese contact ivory was another important export and it is probable that other commodities, including copper, were also handled. The imports, according to the Portuguese, were principally cloth, beads and glazed ceramics. The source of the gold that passed through the Sofala area was said by ibn Battuta, early in the fourteenth century, to be Yufi in the land of the Limiin, one month's march from the coast (Freeman-Grenville 1975: 31), and it has been suggested that the land of the Limiin was the Zimbabwe Plateau and that Yufi was Great Zimbabwe itself (Huffman 1972: 361–2). A number of questions arise from this. First: does the archaeological evidence at the various zimbabwe sites throw any light on this trade? Second: to what extent was this trade unusual and to what extent was it merely part of a complex network of external trade that involved both long-distance and inter-regional exchange? Third and most important: what role, if any, did this trade play in the rise of Great Zimbabwe and its associated sites? Is it really possible to claim, as has been done (Huffman 1977: 9), that 'The Zimbabwe Culture can be described as an indigenous reaction to an external stimulus – the East Coast gold trade'?

Without doubt there is archaeological evidence for the existence of trade between the Zimbabwe Plateau and the East African coast. This evidence is particularly abundant for the sixteenth and seventeenth centuries AD, when the Portuguese had trading posts in the Zambezi Valley and on the northern part of the plateau (Pikirayi 1993). For the earlier periods, of more relevance to the present discussion, there is less evidence but it is nonetheless remarkable. Some of the earliest comes from the site of Schroda, near the confluence of the Shashi and Limpopo Rivers, occupied between the eighth and tenth centuries and containing imported glass beads as well as indications that ivory was being worked and presumably traded. In the same area the eleventh-century site of Bambandyanalo (also known as K2) has produced similar evidence and, by the twelfth century, glass beads and gold-covered objects from Mapungubwe indicate that trade in gold with the East Coast, as well as ivory, was already occurring (Hall 1987: 75–85; Phillipson 1993a: 195, 230–1; Huffman 1996: 175–80). Perhaps the most important evidence for trade, however, comes from the so-called 'Renders Ruin' at Great Zimbabwe itself, where a hoard of material included a glazed Persian bowl of thirteenth- or fourteenth-century date. With it were a number of Chinese celadon dishes, some sherds of a Chinese stoneware vessel, another glazed Persian bowl and fragments of engraved and painted Near Eastern glass, all of about the same date. In addition there were a piece of coral, an iron spoon, an iron lamp holder with a copper suspension chain, a copper box, two copper finger rings and (nearby) two small bronze bells. There were also several tens of thousands of glass beads, some brass wire and a quantity of cowrie shells. This hoard was excavated by Hall in 1903 but in 1941 a further collection of some 30,000 beads was found in another part of the same ruin by E. Goodall (Garlake 1973: 131–3). This extraordinary assortment of exotic objects demonstrates that about the fourteenth century Great Zimbabwe was in direct contact with the trading cities of the East African coast. These objects from the Renders Ruin have often been interpreted as part of the stock of a visiting

Arab trader, but the diverse nature of the goods and their location within what has been thought to be part of the royal wives' living area make it more likely that they were part of the contents of a royal repository (Huffman 1981: 6). In addition, the unique character of this collection suggests that it must have had considerable prestige value to its owner. However, it should not be considered in isolation, for as late as the beginning of the sixteenth century imported Chinese porcelain was still reaching Great Zimbabwe (Collett, Vines and Hughes 1992: 139, 157–8).

Another remarkable piece of archaeological evidence for trading contacts between the Zimbabwe Plateau and the coast consists of a coin minted in Kilwa probably in the early fourteenth century. This coin was excavated at Great Zimbabwe itself and appears to be the only one ever recovered from a scientific context at that site (Huffman 1972: 362 and Plate 1). Of more use as evidence for trade with the coast, because they are more common, are the large numbers of glass beads recovered both from Great Zimbabwe and from many other zimbabwe sites. The ultimate origin of these beads is unknown but they are similar to beads found in the East Coast cities and like them they came from the Indian Ocean trade. Indeed, beads from the earlier sites of Bambandyanalo and Mapungubwe have been shown by rare earth element analysis to have been made at al-Fustat in Egypt (Saitowitz, Reid and van der Merwe 1996). Cowries are also very occasionally found at other zimbabwe sites, as well as at Great Zimbabwe. Otherwise, evidence of imports from the coast is limited, although the appearance at zimbabwe sites of spindle-whorls, that are absent from earlier sites, has been interpreted as an indication that the craft of spinning spread from the coast as a result of trading contacts (Huffman 1971; Garlake 1973: 117). It should perhaps be no surprise that a trade in which textiles and gold were the most important commodities has left relatively little archaeological evidence. Nevertheless, there is strong circumstantial evidence for the importance of trading between the Zimbabwe Plateau and the coast. There was a sudden and considerable increase in building activity at Great Zimbabwe during the fourteenth century, at the same time that equally sudden and considerable expansion was taking place in the cities of the East African coast, particularly in Kilwa in the south. Equally, the fortunes of both Great Zimbabwe and the coastal cities declined at about the same time during the fifteenth century. The most likely explanation for such a coincidence of prosperity must be that there was a 'close economic connection' (Garlake 1976b: 224). Sutton (1997) has suggested that depression in the coastal economy actually began in the second half of the fourteenth century, following a fall in the international price of gold, possibly resulting from the Black Death of 1346–9. Thus one of the factors in the decline of Great Zimbabwe may have been a reduced demand for gold on the 'world' market.

The second question that was asked concerned the extent to which this overseas trade was part of a more general network of long-distance and inter-regional exchange. In addition to items that must have derived from the East Coast trade, the Renders Ruin hoard contained a large quantity of material that suggests the existence of a substantial internal African trade. Thus there were about 30 kilograms of iron wire and about 100 kilograms of iron hoes, axes and chisels. With them were 'cakes of copper', ivory, two unusual spearheads, three iron gongs and three iron rods that were probably strikers for the gongs. There were also a soapstone dish, twenty small pieces of perforated gold sheathing, some gold wire and a handful of gold beads (Garlake 1973: 133). The gongs are bell-shaped and were made of two sheets of iron welded together round the flanges, although neither sheet metalwork nor welding seem to have been local techniques. Seven other similar gongs have been found at Great Zimbabwe and single examples have been found at Chumnungwa Ruins and Danangombe (Dhlo Dhlo) Ruins. Such gongs are characteristic of parts of Zambia, the Zaïre (Congo) Basin and West Africa, and it has been suggested that their distribution indicates contact between different African states (Vansina 1969). Indeed, two of the burials at the remarkable Zambezi Valley site of Ingombe Ilede were accompanied by gongs of this type (Fagan, Phillipson and Daniels 1969: 92–4) and their presence at Great Zimbabwe would presumably indicate trading connections in the Ingombe Ilede area. This probability is reinforced by the discovery of single examples of cross-shaped copper ingots, of a characteristic Ingombe Ilede form, at the zimbabwe-type site of Chumnungwa and at another ruin site in the Great Zimbabwe area. Three similar ingots have also been found in the Mtelegwa Ruin. It seems that during the fourteenth and fifteenth centuries the Ingombe Ilede people were mining copper on some scale, and as there are salt deposits in their area and a lack of such deposits on the Zimbabwe Plateau, it is likely that they traded salt as well as copper in that direction. In exchange they probably took gold beads and ornaments, and iron tools and weapons. The comparatively few glass beads at Ingombe Ilede sites suggest that the trade was with other internal African communities rather than with the East Coast (Garlake 1976b: 224). Furthermore, this Ingombe Ilede–Zimbabwe Plateau trade was probably just one small part of a complex internal trading network, of which the rest has left little evidence that has yet been identified. As Brian Fagan demonstrated for the region north of the Zimbabwe Plateau, the demand for raw materials, particularly iron, copper and salt, ensured the growth of such networks (Fagan 1969). As in other parts of Africa, it is likely that internal trading of this sort substantially pre-dated long-distance external trade. If this was the case, then the East Coast gold trade quite probably took advantage of an existing trading network, rather than creating something new.

The third and final question concerned the role of the East Coast trade in the rise of Great Zimbabwe and the other zimbabwe sites. The quick answer is that it was probably very important, but that its role in the social and economic changes that led to urbanization and state formation was to facilitate rather than to originate. The cause of these developments was deeper and more complex than a mere trade in luxuries, but without doubt that trade provided the elite with prestige goods and with a form of wealth that could be used to enhance their authority.

Conclusion

Great Zimbabwe and its related sites comprise the archaeological evidence for social and political developments that took place on the Zimbabwe Plateau during the first half of the second millennium AD. The stone structures that have so dominated archaeological research housed a small ruling elite, who governed settlements varying in size from the capital city of Great Zimbabwe itself, with a population of perhaps 18,000 people, to smaller regional towns. The authority of this elite probably extended also to rural villages that were too small and too unimportant to justify their own elite residences. The size of Great Zimbabwe would suggest that urbanization was already in process, at the very least at this place. The presence of comparable elite structures in so many of the other settlements would suggest that some progress had also been made towards the formation of a state. Why and how had all this happened?

The most basic reason was almost certainly the successful subsistence agriculture of this area. A generally healthy environment that was tsetse-free and with access to other areas that were seasonally tsetse-free, it supported a mixed farming economy in which grain, vegetables and livestock – particularly cattle – all played a part. This combination of cultivation and livestock would have helped to even out the effects of bad years and must inevitably have led to an increase in the population. However, good soils were limited and it is very probable that the tsetse boundaries fluctuated. Thus some areas must have been more productive than others and those who controlled such areas, or could gain control of them, must in time have come to control the less fortunate members of an expanding population.

However, there were some alternatives to agriculture: mining, trade and crafts of various sorts. The development of these activities provided some escape from the problem of limited productive land. They also provided the emerging elite with further sources of wealth that could be controlled and which were more negotiable than land or cattle. In particular, it is likely that a far-reaching and complex network of inter-regional trade in raw materials had developed within south central Africa, before Indian Ocean merchants were able to benefit from it. How could the latter have known that there was gold to be had from the relatively remote Zimbabwe Plateau, unless that gold was already reaching the coast? Nevertheless, the gold trade with the East Coast must in time have become extremely important in creating surplus wealth, that further enhanced the power of the Zimbabwe Plateau elite. Even the most conservative estimate suggests that between 7 and 9 million ounces of gold was made available for trade and internal consumption before the end of the nineteenth century (Phimister 1976: 16–17). It is not difficult to imagine the impact on Plateau society of the volume of goods (particularly cloth and beads) that must have been obtained in exchange for the portion of this quantity that was traded prior to the middle of the second millennium AD. It seems unlikely that the gold trade 'caused' the rise of Great Zimbabwe but nevertheless it must have had a great effect on it.

The apparent reasons for the decline and abandonment of Great Zimbabwe and its associated sites consist of a reversal of the factors that gave rise to their growth. The gold trade declined, probably because of falling world prices and the depletion of the more easily worked deposits on the Zimbabwe Plateau. More important, however, the environment around Great Zimbabwe collapsed: overcropped, overgrazed, overhunted, overexploited in every essential aspect of subsistence agriculture, it ceased to be able to carry the very concentration of people that it had given rise to. To begin to understand this episode of growth and decay, it is essential to see it in the broadest possible context, in space, time, and social, economic and political circumstances. Great Zimbabwe was only ever a mystery when viewed in isolation.

Chapter 8

In the heart of Africa: the Upemba Depression and the Interlacustrine Region

Previous chapters have presented a series of case-studies of archaeological evidence for urbanization and state formation in precolonial, tropical Africa. The choice of the areas which have been discussed has been mainly dictated by the character of the archaeological evidence and by the extent of archaeological research, resulting in an incomplete picture. Not only have the individual case-studies given somewhat lopsided impressions of developments in the selected areas, but also there were numerous precolonial cities and states in tropical Africa that are known to us from the evidence of ethnohistory or oral tradition, that have not been included at all. The main reason for this omission is that archaeological evidence for such entities is either totally absent or so limited that its discussion is hardly worthwhile.

The basic problem is one of archaeological visibility. Some manifestations of early urbanization and state formation in Africa are of such a character that their archaeological investigation is peculiarly difficult. For instance, the capital city of Buganda (Gutkind 1963), a state near Lake Victoria, was described in 1889 as 'one of the great capitals of Africa' (Ashe 1889: 52), but it was constructed totally of grass, wood and other organic materials and it moved frequently, particularly on the death of the *Kabaka*, the ruler of Buganda (Gutkind 1960: 29). The sites of these large settlements are, therefore, unlikely to have much depth of deposit or structural remains and no archaeological investigation of them has ever been attempted (in fact the last two of them are covered by modern Kampala). Thus there is no archaeological information about a settlement that John Hanning Speke, its first European visitor, described as 'a magnificent sight. A whole hill was covered with gigantic huts such as I had never seen in Africa before' (Speke 1863: 283). It is indeed fortunate that such travellers left descriptions and illustrations of what they saw. Henry Morton Stanley's picture of the capital of Buganda in 1875, when it was at Rubaga, shows how much archaeology may be missing (Stanley 1878: Vol. 1).

There is, however, no reason why archaeology should not be able to investigate such short-lived settlements of ephemeral materials, as has been done, for example, at the South African site of Mgungundlovu (Parkington and Cronin 1979). Provided that subsequent activity or erosion has not destroyed the inevitably shallow evidence, survey and excavation techniques do exist that enable information to be obtained from sites of this type. Nevertheless, they have been seldom applied in Africa and a lack of sophistication in research design has led to the excavation of many larger African settlement sites with structures of stone, fired brick or mud, while sites with less substantial structural remains have often been ignored. Although this situation is now changing, there are large areas of tropical Africa where political and economic problems make it difficult, and sometimes impossible, to conduct archaeological field research, so that there has not yet been sufficient opportunity to demonstrate what could be done with sites of supposed low archaeological visibility. In short, it may be that the low archaeological visibility of the sites in question is to some extent more apparent than real.

This could apply to many parts of tropical Africa but it is particularly relevant to a huge area of the continent extending across the modern states of the Congo Republic, Democratic Congo, Angola, Zambia, Rwanda, Burundi, Uganda and western Tanzania. This area straddles the Equator, although situated mostly to its south. Ethnohistorical and oral traditional evidence indicate that it was the location of a succession of cities and states from at least the sixteenth century AD onwards. Some of these, like the Kingdom of Kongo in the sixteenth century, or the state of Buganda in the nineteenth century, clearly impressed European visitors. The latter were often particularly interested in the cities that they came across and Dapper (1686) left us a remarkable illustration of the seventeenth-century equatorial city of Loango, in what is now the Congo Republic (Fig. 8.1). Even making allowance for considerable artistic licence, this appears to have been a settlement of both considerable size and organization. Nevertheless, archaeology has contributed relatively little to our knowledge of precolonial cities and states in this part of Africa. At its southern margin, for instance, the Lozi Kingdom is known from oral history not archaeology (Prins 1980). Furthermore, for all periods in the enormous area covered by equatorial rainforest there is only 'a meager scattering of excavated archaeological sites' (Vansina 1990: 8). In such circumstances, the little archaeological work that has been done on the origins of social complexity in Central Africa is particularly important.

To begin with the Kingdom of Kongo itself, there is the site of its capital city, Mbanza Kongo (São Salvador), in northern Angola (Fig. 8.2) but it has never been excavated (de Maret 1982: 80). Indeed, the only excavated evidence relevant to the Kongo state is a cemetery at Mbanza Mbata, where elite graves produced clear evidence of European trading contacts during the seventeenth and eighteenth centuries (de Maret 1982: 82). This is not very much for a state for which we have both contemporary accounts (e.g. Pigafetta 1591) and modern historical studies (e.g. Randles 1968). Further to the north, the city of Concobela (Ngombela) has been identified with the site of Kingabwa, near Kinshasa, but has since been destroyed by clay digging and covered by a garbage dump (de Maret 1982: 83). Similarly, the mounds of Mashita Bansa (meaning 'the city of the heaps'), a site situated in south-central Democratic Congo, can tell us little as yet, although test excavations were carried out there in 1984 (de Maret 1982: 84; de Maret and Clist 1985). Even the excavation of some of the royal tombs of Rwanda was of rather limited value, as the three graves investigated contained burials of the late nineteenth and early twentieth centuries. One of these, however, was of Cyirima Rujugira, a king who had been dead since the seventeenth or eighteenth century and was only buried in 1930 or 1931! This burial was accompanied by numerous grave-goods which had also remained unburied until the twentieth century and these are of some interest because they included items symbolic of royalty (Van Noten 1972). A similar problem of limited time-depth exists for the site of Ryamurari, the old capital of the Ndorwa Kingdom in Rwanda. Remains of circular mud walls indicate the king's enclosure, and there are also cattle kraals built of cattle dung and garbage, but excavation has produced radiocarbon dates of the eighteenth and twentieth centuries (Van Noten 1982: 75).

All this seems little enough but fortunately there are two areas in Central Africa where archaeological research has contributed significantly to our knowledge of socio-economic and political developments over the last millennium or so. One of these is the Upemba Depression, in south-east Democratic Congo, and the other is the Interlacustrine Region, particularly that part of it situated in Uganda (Fig. 8.2).

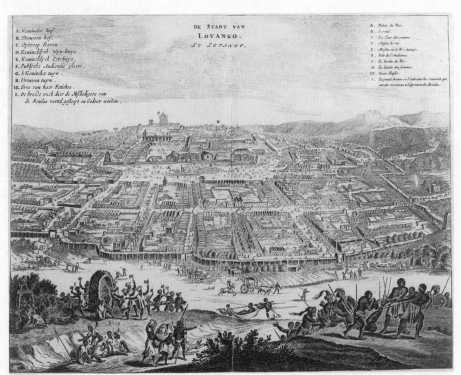

Fig. 8.1 The city of Loango (in what is now the Congo Republic) in the seventeenth century. From Dapper (1686: 320–1).

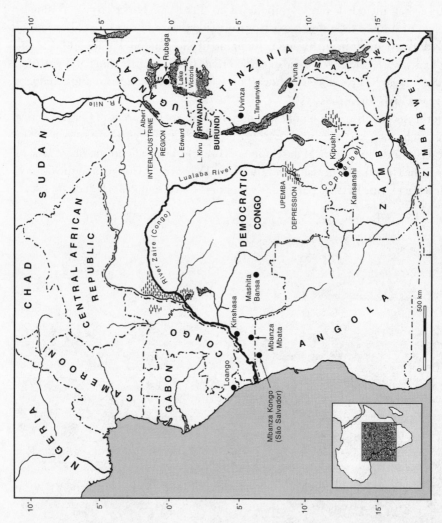

Fig. 8.2 Archaeological sites in Central Africa. Note the locations of the Upemba Depression and the Interlacustrine Region, for which see Figs. 8.3 and 8.5.

The first has shed light on the origins of the Luba state, which is known to have existed by the eighteenth and nineteenth centuries (Reefe 1981: 60–1); the second has provided information on the antecedents and early phases of several states which oral tradition suggests may have developed by about the middle of the second millennium AD (Sutton 1993). Situated in the heart of Africa, the relative isolation of these areas from influences originating outside of the continent makes it particularly likely that increasing social complexity was the result of indigenous rather than external factors. For this reason, it is especially important to examine the developments that took place, recollecting in doing so that the Upemba Depression and the Interlacustrine Region are merely representative of a huge region for much of which there is little or no relevant archaeological evidence.

Geographical location and environmental factors

Situated roughly 1000 kilometres apart, the two areas have many similarities but also some marked differences (Winterbotham, Smith and Longland 1944; Connah 1996). Both lie within the savanna that fringes the equatorial rainforest, the Interlacustrine Region actually straddling the Equator, the Upemba Depression over 8° south of it. This gives both areas an annual rainfall that in many places is of about 1000 millimetres and which tends to fall in two wet seasons each year. However, climatic conditions are modified by altitude, much of the Interlacustrine Region being over 1000 metres above sea level and even the Upemba Depression lying above 500 metres. In addition, there is a considerable altitudinal range within each area: the northern one being bordered by both the Western Rift Valley and the Ruwenzori Mountains, and the southern by the Hakansson Mountains to its north-west and the Mitumba Mountains to its south-east. The resulting environmental diversity of both areas is made even more complex by the presence of major bodies of water: the Victoria Nile and Lakes Victoria, Kyoga, Albert, George, Edward and Kivu in the one case, and the River Lualaba (the Upper Zaïre [Congo]) and Lakes Upemba and Kisale in the other. The Interlacustrine Region, however, is much larger than the Upemba Depression, with a greater variety of environments, although only relatively small scattered parts of the area have been investigated archaeologically. In addition, the Upemba Depression is dominated by a vast floodplain through which runs the Lualaba and to which archaeological research has so far been confined. Contrasting with the relatively dispersed natural resources of the Interlacustrine Region, those of the Upemba Depression are markedly concentrated.

Compared with much of the African savanna, both these areas provided environments rich in resources and attractive to human settlement. In the Upemba Depression fish were particularly important, being the main export of the area when Europeans first visited it (de Maret 1982: 90). However, fertile, well-watered, alluvial soils and access to mountain grasslands permitted a mixed agricultural economy, to which hunting of the prolific local game also made a significant contribution. Maize, cassava, groundnuts and sweet potatoes seem to have been the main crops in recent times but these were of course introductions from the Americas since the sixteenth century, and African millets and sorghum were also important. In addition, bananas, originally from South-East Asia, were grown, as were indigenous beans and cowpeas. Domesticated animals consisted mainly of chicken and goats (Vansina 1966: 21, 23). In the Upemba Depression itself, farmers controlled water levels with dams, and canoe channels were maintained to give fishermen access to open water (Reefe 1983: 163). So successful was the human exploitation of the area that for centuries a 'high population density supported by the richness of the ecosystem, appears to have strongly contrasted with neighboring less-populated areas' (de Maret 1997: 499). Not surprisingly the Upemba Depression seems to have become the heartland of the Luba people. Occupants of the Interlacustrine Region, however, may have been even more fortunate, although Peter Robertshaw (1999) has questioned the claim by John Reader (1997: 326) that 'The Great Lakes region was perhaps the largest, most richly endowed, most developed and most densely populated of indigenous agricultural systems in Africa.' A generally good rainfall, equatorial temperatures moderated by altitude, and relatively fertile soils, enabled the growing of a range of crops that now include, amongst other things, finger millet, cassava, sweet potatoes, beans, and above all bananas. Many varieties of the latter have been grown in the area for a long time, particularly the vegetable banana known as *matooke*, which in its cooked form has become a staple food for large numbers of people. Given adequate rainfall, moderate heat all year round and suitable soil, bananas need only modest inputs of land and labour, will yield within ten to eighteen months of planting, and can produce for thirty years or more (Wrigley 1989). Furthermore, in the drier parts of the Interlacustrine Region were some of Africa's best grasslands, often free of tsetse, which supported extensive pastoralism, particularly of cattle. In addition, the lakes and rivers of the area yielded important supplies of fish, and until recent times there were also substantial resources of wild game. Overall, this range of subsistence choices, especially those based on bananas or cattle (Schoenbrun 1993), not only supported local concentrations of population but also provided the basic source of the wealth and power that brought about socio-political changes leading to the emergence of the interlacustrine kingdoms.

As well as an exceptional subsistence base, however, both of these areas possessed other resources of considerable importance. In the case of the Upemba Depression, to its south-east lies one of the richest and largest copper deposits in the world, that extends some 400 kilometres from the extreme south-east of Democratic Congo into northern Zambia (Winterbotham, Smith and Longland 1944: 401–2). There are also sources of iron ore and salt in the area (Reefe 1983:

162) and, like the Interlacustrine Region, there would formerly have been substantial supplies of ivory. For this latter region, however, it was iron and salt that were the most important commodities (e.g. Tosh 1970: 104–6), iron having been smelted in Rwanda, Burundi and north-west Tanzania for well over 2000 years (Woodhouse 1998: 181) and salt having been produced at both Katwe on Lake Edward and Kibiro on Lake Albert probably for much of the second millennium AD (Connah 1996). Given such resources, and given the transport potential of the rivers and lakes as well as the relatively easy conditions of overland routes, both areas are likely to have played an important part in the development of trading networks within Central Africa, an activity that must have further stimulated socio-political changes.

Nevertheless, there were constraints, as even Winston Churchill realized in 1908 when eulogizing Uganda as 'a fairy-tale', 'a wonderful new world', 'from end to end one beautiful garden' (Churchill 1962: 59–60). Over the relatively short period for which written records have been kept, both human and animal diseases have had major demographic impacts, and it seems quite possible that the same could have been the case in the remoter past. As in much of Africa where there are substantial bodies of water, malaria, schistosomiasis, filariasis and other scourges must have long been a problem. In addition, as population densities increased in some parts of the areas concerned, so did the likelihood of disease transmission, particularly of gastrointestinal infections and intestinal parasites (Patterson 1993: 448). It was sleeping-sickness, however, that most impressed Churchill in the early years of the twentieth century, by the end of 1905 killing 'considerably more than two hundred thousand persons' in parts of Uganda, out of a population estimated at not more than 300,000 (Churchill 1962: 67). In the area between Lakes George and Edward, an especially nightmarish situation developed. In 1891 rinderpest swept through this country and most of the cattle and much of the game died. As a result the amount of thicket increased with the reduction of grazing, creating suitable environments for tsetse flies, that in turn spread trypanosomiasis that killed more of the cattle, and sleeping-sickness that killed large numbers of people. By 1912 the area was so badly affected that the British colonial authorities removed much of the remaining population, as was also done at about the same time in other areas along the eastern side of Lake Albert and along the lower Victoria Nile, and to this day large parts of these areas remain game reserves and national parks with very few human inhabitants (Good 1972: 571–7; Uganda National Parks n.d.). Admittedly these historical epidemics were triggered by colonial intervention causing movements of livestock and people: rinderpest, for instance, having been brought to Africa with infected cattle imported to Massawa in Eritrea to feed Italian troops in 1889 (Reader 1997: 624). It seems likely that previously a degree of ecological balance must have been maintained between disease vectors, animals and humans. However, even the threat of trypanosomiasis and sleeping-sickness must have constituted a long-term constraint on the distribution and density of human population in these areas.

Nevertheless, a final constraint in these areas could have resulted from the very population densities that the exceptional subsistence base, and other resources, sometimes and in some places gave rise to. At times the two areas here considered may have supported some of the densest populations in tropical Africa, particularly in Rwanda, Burundi and parts of Uganda. Increasing pressure on resources, especially competition for productive land, may well have produced intergroup violence in the absence of major epidemics, substantial emigration or fundamental technological change. Although compounded by the socio-political dislocation of the colonial and postcolonial experience, the explosion of violence in Rwanda in 1994 is a reminder of the potential for self-destruction within dense human populations. An estimated 500,000 to 850,000 people were killed over a period of about three months, more than 10 per cent of the population, and another 30 per cent were forced into exile (Reader 1997: 717–19). Political scientists, anthropologists and others may agonize for years about the precise reasons for this appalling series of events but one thing is clear enough: human beings can become a major constraint to other human beings.

Sources of information

For both the Upemba Depression and the Interlacustrine Region historical documentation is of limited time-depth. In the case of the former, it became known to the outside world only towards the end of the nineteenth century, and accounts of the latter area begin only in the 1860s with the visits of Speke, Grant and Baker (Winterbotham, Smith and Longland 1944: Fig. 36; Connah 1996: 1). It was indeed these writers who first brought some of the interlacustrine states to international attention, providing us with important accounts of Karagwe, Buganda and Bunyoro before the impact of European colonial ambitions. They, and other late-nineteenth-century and early-twentieth-century European visitors, officials, soldiers, traders, missionaries and scientists, not only left writings that have become a rich source of ethnohistorical data for the Upemba and Interlacustrine areas but also made some of the earliest records of their oral traditions, an important source of information for pre-contact periods. However, for the Luba area, 'individual tales yield only an occasional, tantalising glimpse of what happened before about AD 1700' (Reefe 1983: 165) and for the interlacustrine states, attempts to interpret the traditions about the supposed former state of Kitara and the Bacwezi dynasty have generated an extensive but inconclusive literature (Sutton 1993). It seems probable that these latter sources refer to about the middle of the second millennium AD and concern the antecedents of the states first visited by Europeans in the 1860s, but interpretations have ranged from seeing the Bacwezi as the rulers of an early pastoral state (Oliver 1953) to arguing that they were merely mythical figures (Wrigley 1958), and from suggesting that their origins lay in the first millennium AD (Schmidt 1978; Berger 1980) to concluding that they belonged to the fourteenth and fifteenth centuries (Steinhart 1981: 118). Collectively, the documentary and oral records seem unlikely to throw much light on socio-political developments in these areas of Central Africa before, at best, the last four or five centuries. A source of information with rather greater potential lies in the study of historical linguistics, particularly concerning cultivated plants and domesticated animals. Schoenbrun (1993), for instance, by setting his linguistic evidence in a broad interdisciplinary context, has been able to suggest that banana farming and pastoralism were already established in the Interlacustrine Region by the beginning of the second millennium. He has also examined the possible social dimensions of those agricultural developments (Schoenbrun 1995). This has provided a useful set of hypotheses for future testing but, to non-specialists at least, the chronological validity of the evidence remains uncertain. Much the same may be said for another potentially important source of information, the genetic history of the plants and animals themselves. For example, it is largely on the basis of such evidence, as well as linguistics, that De Langhe, Swennen and Vuylsteke (1995) have been able to propose that plantains had reached the Interlacustrine Region, from the other side of the Indian Ocean, by 2500 years ago. In all such matters, in the end we need some physical evidence, particularly evidence that can be subjected to absolute dating. This brings us to consider the archaeological knowledge of the areas in question, which at present provides a somewhat limited insight into the socio-political developments that concern us but nevertheless holds substantial promise for the future.

In the case of the Upemba Depression (Fig. 8.3), archaeological evidence provides a complete cultural sequence from the fifth century AD to the beginning of the nineteenth century and indicates the emergence of an hierarchical society by the end of the first millennium (de Maret 1979). The sequence is supported by more than fifty radiocarbon dates (de Maret 1997: 499) and constitutes one of the most successful pieces of archaeological research concerning the last two millennia in Central Africa. Unfortunately, however, the available evidence consists entirely of burials, clustered in cemeteries in the Upemba Depression, particularly on the banks of Lake Kisale on the upper Lualaba River. Settlement sites are known but appear to have only shallow deposits that have been extensively disturbed by continuous occupation or cultivation. As a result, they have not been excavated, but a total of over 265 graves have been. These were situated at the sites of Sanga, Katongo, Kamilamba, Kikulu and Malemba Nkulu (de Maret 1982: 89).

The Upemba Depression sequence can, therefore, tell us very little about early urbanization in this area but it is quite informative on the subject of social evolution and early state emergence. This first became apparent after the excavations of

Jacques Nenquin at Sanga in 1957 and Jean Hiernaux in 1958, which produced evidence of a remarkably sophisticated material culture during a period dated from the seventh to ninth century AD. Called by Nenquin the 'Kisalian', this culture was characterized by finely made and distinctive pottery, by skilful metal-working in both iron and copper and by graves containing evidence of accumulated wealth (Nenquin 1963; Hiernaux, Longrée and De Buyst 1971). Later excavations at Sanga by Pierre de Maret (de Maret 1977) and at other sites by the same researcher (de Maret 1979; 1982; 1992) revised Nenquin's dating and placed the Kisalian in its chronological context. The sequence thus established commenced in the fifth century AD with the Kamilambian tradition, which was replaced by the Early Kisalian tradition at the end of the eighth century. This, in turn, was succeeded by the Classic Kisalian tradition in the eleventh century, that was followed by the Kabambian tradition that appeared at the end of the fourteenth century. The Kabambian has been divided into Kabambian A and B, the latter ending at the

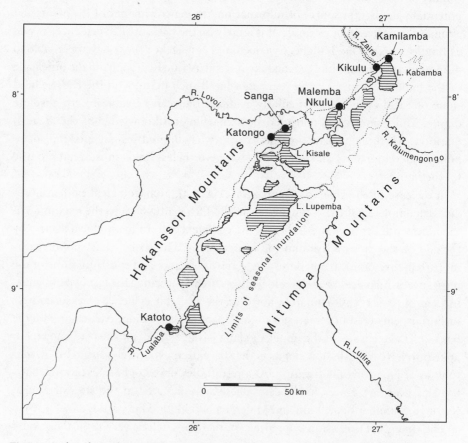

Fig. 8.3 Archaeological sites in the Upemba Depression, Democratic Congo. After de Maret (1992: Fig. 48).

beginning of the nineteenth century. The latest of the archaeological evidence is, indeed, comparable with the material culture of the Luba as studied in recent times. Thus, as de Maret claimed, 'It becomes apparent that in establishing an Iron Age sequence in the Upemba rift one is actually studying the emergence of the Luba Kingdom' (de Maret 1979: 234).

Anthropometric studies of the Sanga skeletons and of the present-day Luba, which are said to show strong affinities between the two, would seem to support this idea. In addition, the archaeological evidence suggests the gradual development of social stratification, political organization and functional specialization. For example, as far back as the Early Kisalian, ceremonial iron axes were placed in graves. These had handles decorated with nails, and were much like those later used by the Luba as symbols of authority. In one such Early Kisalian grave, the deceased had also been buried with an iron anvil, another symbol of power among Bantu-speaking peoples (Fig. 8.4). Iron bells found in graves of this period may have been indicative of authority (Vansina 1969). At Katoto, a cemetery in the southern part of the Upemba Rift belonging to a tradition approximately contemporaneous with the Kisalian, the richest graves included not only ceremonial axes and anvils but also evidence of child sacrifices. Social stratification was further indicated in the Classic Kisalian by the unequal distribution of grave-goods between the various burials. It was observed that the few graves that contained an unusually large number of pots also contained uncommon things like cowries and ivory pendants. Furthermore, such wealth appeared to be partly hereditary, since some children's graves were among the wealthiest (de Maret 1979; 1982).

Following Bisson (1975), it seems possible that the development of political organization in the Luba area can be inferred from the archaeological evidence for the use of copper. This metal was particularly valued in much of Africa during pre-colonial times, being variously used as a medium of exchange, for personal adornment, for status symbols and for cult objects (Herbert 1984). In the Upemba Depression sequence (de Maret 1979) there is no evidence of copper in the Kamilambian and its first appearance is in the Early Kisalian when there were a few copper objects, mainly in the form of hammered bangles. It is very common, however, in the Classic Kisalian, when it was used both for a wide range of personal ornaments and for some functional objects. Thus far it would appear that the role of copper was principally as an indicator of wealth, prestige and status. With the Kabambian came a marked change; distinctive copper *croisettes* (little crosses) appeared, probably originally as ingots but later used as currency. As time went by, these crosses grew smaller and more uniform in shape (de Maret 1981), and it is thought that they may have first been used as a special-purpose currency (for buying wives for instance) but gradually evolved into a general-purpose unit of exchange. Thus the smaller, later crosses could have been used for a variety of small purchases. The use of these crosses as a form of money is further suggested

Fig. 8.4 Early Kisalian burial at Kamilamba, Democratic Congo. Note ceremonial iron axe at left centre and iron anvil to left of skull. Reproduced by permission of Pierre de Maret.

by the fact that at Sanga they were often found in or near the hands of the deceased and that one grave that contained 140 of the smallest crosses had them tied up into groups of five (Bisson 1975: 287). The use of such a currency would imply the existence of a certain level of political sophistication.

The level of craftsmanship, indicated by the archaeological evidence for the Kisalian, suggests the attainment of some degree of functional specialization by the early part of the second millennium AD. The skilful handling of iron, copper, ivory, bone and pottery hints at the presence of professional artisans. The range of metalwork alone is one of the most impressive in tropical Africa: including (for the Kisalian) iron hoes, knives, axes, spears, arrows, harpoon heads, fish-hooks, necklaces, pendants and chain, together with copper artefacts, such as belts, necklaces, bangles, bracelets, small knives, spearheads and fish-hooks. Basket-weaving was also practised and there may well have been specialist traders bringing copper from the Copperbelt, some 200 kilometres to the south-east (de Maret 1979).

The relative proximity of one of the richest sources of copper in Africa must, indeed, have played a part in the developments in south-east Democratic Congo. From Kansanshi and Kipushi, in northern Zambia, Bisson (1976) obtained precolonial evidence for both mining and smelting of copper. It is apparent that exploitation of the Kansanshi deposits commenced possibly as early as the fourth century AD and there is also evidence that copper was being smelted at a similar date in the Lubumbashi region of south-east Democratic Congo (Anciaux de Faveaux and de Maret 1984; de Maret 1985: 138). The Kansanshi evidence led Bisson to reject the hypothesis sometimes advanced, that Arab or Swahili traders were responsible for both the origin of states and the start of large-scale copper-mining in this part of Africa. Similarly, de Maret argued that the Kisalian evidence for an hierarchical society as early as the end of the first millennium AD ruled out long-distance trade as a possible cause of this development. Rather, he saw a combination of fishing, hunting and agriculture as permitting a high population density that 'led to a need for political integration' (de Maret 1979: 234). Certainly, the evidence for the Classic Kisalian is suggestive of some form of early state, and this in an area where throughout the archaeological sequence the only indication of any contact with the outside world consists of a few glass beads and a small number of marine shells from the Indian Ocean coast (Hiernaux, Longrée and De Buyst 1971: 55; Hiernaux, Maquet and De Buyst 1972: 154–5; de Maret 1992: 170). Nevertheless, the possible role of internal trading networks should not be forgotten, and local exchanges of copper, iron and salt were probably particularly important (Fagan 1969). The people of the Classic Kisalian may well have participated in such networks by trading dried fish from the lakes and rivers of the Upemba Depression, as was still occurring when Europeans first entered the area (de Maret 1982: 90).

Although extremely important, the archaeological evidence from the Upemba Depression provides only a relatively small island of information amidst a sea of uncertainty. In the case of the Interlacustrine Region the situation is rather better, in that we have a number of such islands, admittedly somewhat scattered but covering a larger geographical area and providing a more varied selection of data (Fig. 8.5). Uganda, in particular, has had a long and distinguished record of archaeological research, although interrupted by periods of political instability during parts of the 1970s and 1980s. One of the most important of the nineteenth-century

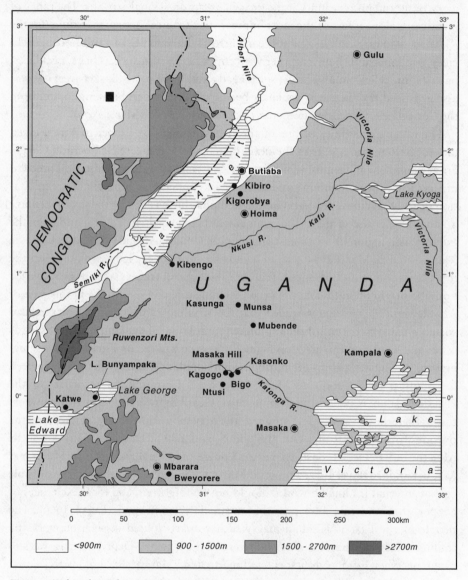

Fig. 8.5 Archaeological sites in the Ugandan part of the Interlacustrine Region. After Connah (1996: Fig. 2.2).

276

states in this area was Buganda (from which the modern state of Uganda takes its name) and although there is no archaeological evidence to throw light on the development of Bugandan urbanization (p. 263), Oliver (1959a) was able to make a preliminary study of the royal tombs and of their associated human jaw-bone shrines. However, rather more archaeological work has been carried out on Ankole, another one of the interlacustrine states. As with that of Buganda, the capital of Ankole moved many times, but careful use of oral tradition enabled Oliver (1959b) to identify a number of capital sites in the field, which were re-examined nearly thirty years later by Andrew Reid and Peter Robertshaw (1987). Bweyorere, seemingly the largest, was excavated by Merrick Posnansky (1968), demonstrating the difficulties of extracting useful information from this type of site. It consists of a series of low banks on the top of a hill, forming irregular, incomplete enclosures. The banks seem to be mainly of cattle dung and there are also several hollows that may have been cisterns. Posnansky excavated thirty-one interrupted, staggered trenches into the site and was able to identify the remains of the palace, a circular building of organic material over 15 metres in diameter, that had been destroyed by fire. The deposit was shallow, however, and no other habitation structures were found, although pottery and bones were generally distributed. Oral tradition indicated occupation of this site at three different periods: in the seventeenth century, in the eighteenth century and in the nineteenth century. Radiocarbon dating was in general agreement with this overall time-span. Animal bones from the site indicated the importance of cattle to its occupants but also suggested that hunting was common. Glass beads and fragments of pottery smoking-pipes probably belonged to the latter part of the sequence. Posnansky concluded that Bweyorere represented 'a large pastoral settlement with evidence of a palace site far larger than those encountered by the nineteenth century European travellers to Ankole' but which had a population of 'probably no more than a few hundred people', 'was not a town' and had 'no trace of the practice of any crafts' (Posnansky 1968: 165, 173). Indeed, Reid and Robertshaw quite reasonably pointed out that, as the traditions say that the site was occupied on several occasions, not all of it is likely to have been occupied at the same time, so that this relatively large site 'may be simply a palimpsest of several small sites, but admittedly with some substantial mounds'. They concluded that further excavation of such sites was unlikely to throw new light on 'the establishment and organization of the Ankole state . . . particularly in view of the poor state of preservation of most of them' (Reid and Robertshaw 1987: 87–8).

Of rather more value for the archaeological investigation of socio-political change in western Uganda is a series of large earthwork enclosures to the north of Ankole, extending from the Katonga River towards the south-eastern part of Lake Albert, of which the best known are Kibengo, Munsa and Bigo (Lanning 1953). The most investigated of these is Bigo, one of the most famous sites in east Central Africa. It consists of some 10 kilometres of ditches and banks, enclosing an area of

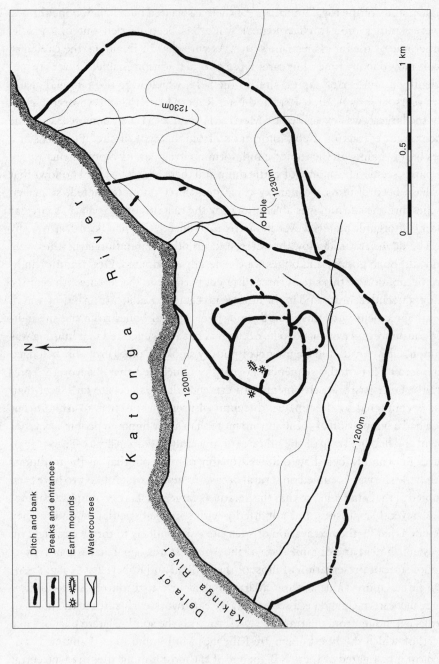

Fig. 8.6 Plan of earthworks at Bigo, Uganda. After Wayland (1934).

about 5 square kilometres (Fig. 8.6). The earthworks form two main enclosures, within the larger of which is a central group of smaller enclosures. The height and width of bank and ditch vary greatly, the greatest height from the bottom of the ditch to the top of the bank being over 7 metres. Situated within and around the central enclosures are three large mounds. Bigo was first described in 1909, was first mapped properly in 1921, and has been the subject of considerable published discussion. Rather tenuous oral tradition ascribes the site to the so-called Bacwezi dynasty, whose uncertain historical status has already been mentioned (p. 270). The site is associated with two smaller earthwork enclosures, Kagogo to its north-west and Kasonko to its north-east, and with the large open settlement site at Ntusi some 15 kilometres to its south-west, which is discussed below (pp. 280–3). All four of these sites are situated within an area less than 20 kilometres across (Wayland 1934; Shinnie 1960; Posnansky 1969).

Bigo itself has been excavated on two occasions; once by Shinnie in 1957 (Shinnie 1960) and once by Posnansky in 1960 (Posnansky 1969). These excavations indicated that there was settlement at Bigo prior to the construction of the bank and ditch system and radiocarbon dates suggested an overall occupation date in the fifteenth and sixteenth centuries AD. Although very few traces of timber structures were found, Posnansky claimed to be able to identify the location of a royal enclosure (Posnansky 1969: 135) and Shinnie was of the opinion that 'there was considerable human occupation at the centre of the complex' (Shinnie 1960: 27). The excavated animal bones, however, revealed an emphasis on cattle and it seems possible that the outer enclosures were intended for penning cattle rather than for defence. Some support for this idea is gained from the fact that more attention seems to have been given to the digging of the ditch than to the construction of the bank, but Robertshaw (1999) thinks that the protection of agricultural fields is more likely. Furthermore, as Posnansky has suggested (1969: 145), it is also possible that the immensity of the earthworks was intended to bestow prestige on those who lived there. Certainly they may be regarded as a form of monumental construction: in one place Shinnie found the rock-cut ditch to be nearly 4 metres deep, when he excavated a section across it (Shinnie 1960: 17), and Posnansky (1969: 144) estimated that more than 200,000 cubic metres of earth and rock had been removed in making the ditches as a whole. The size and direction of the labour force necessary to accomplish such work, together with the presence at this site of a royal enclosure, would imply the existence of some degree of political centralization. It would appear that Bigo was a settlement of considerable importance, the centre perhaps of an emerging state.

Such an assumption fails to make sufficient allowance for 'the ability of non-stratified societies to produce feats of construction over long periods of time' (Reid 1996: 621) but inevitably Bigo and the other earthwork sites have been interpreted as archaeological evidence of a Bacwezi-ruled Kitara state, such a view finding a place in modern politics even as archaeologists abandoned it (Robertshaw and Kamuhangire 1996). Of the other sites, only Munsa and Kibengo have been subjected to archaeological investigation, first by E.C. Lanning (1955; 1960) and later by Peter Robertshaw (Robertshaw 1997; Robertshaw *et al.* 1997). It now appears that the earthworks at these sites were probably constructed in about the fifteenth and sixteenth centuries AD, at roughly the same time as those at Bigo, although there is evidence of occupation at Munsa as early as around the tenth century and at Kibengo from the late thirteenth to the mid-seventeenth century. Like Bigo, the faunal remains at Munsa are dominated by cattle but Kibengo showed more variation and like Bigo lacked the evidence for smelting and iron-working present at Munsa. These and other differences between the sites have led Robertshaw *et al.* (1997: 75) to suggest that these places may have acted as 'the centres of three peer polities', rather than being 'the product of a single polity'. In further pursuit of the latter, excavations have also been conducted at shrine sites associated with the Bacwezi at both Mubende and Kasunga, but the former produced 'only the remains of a small village' (Robertshaw and Kamuhangire 1996: 740) dating to the late thirteenth or fourteenth century (Robertshaw 1988: 38), and the latter, which yielded both occupation and burial evidence, may date to as late as the seventeenth century (Robertshaw *et al.* 1997: 74; British Institute in Eastern Africa 1998: 14–17). At Masaka Hill there is another Bacwezi shrine site with the potential to throw light on this matter but this site remains unexcavated (Kamuhangire, Meredith and Robertshaw 1993).

In fact it is the site of Ntusi, that has neither earthworks nor a clearly demonstrated association with the Bacwezi traditions, that has proved most informative so far as socio-political changes in the first half of the second millennium are concerned (Reid 1990; 1996; Sutton 1993; Reid and Meredith 1993). Lanning (1970: 39) described it as 'an ancient capital site' and, indeed, survey and excavations conducted by Andrew Reid in the late 1980s and early 1990s showed that this open settlement site has archaeological material scattered over approximately 100 hectares and was occupied between the eleventh and fifteenth centuries AD (Fig. 8.7). Excavation of two large midden mounds and of an area associated with some of the low banks that characterize the site produced large quantities of broken pottery, a faunal assemblage dominated by young cattle, numerous grindstones, curved iron knives thought to have been for cereal harvesting, burnt grain which appeared to be sorghum, storage pits probably for grain, evidence of iron-working, fragments of ivory of which some were worked, ostrich eggshell beads, traces of circular houses dated to the fourteenth to fifteenth century (Fig. 8.8), and glass and cowrie shell beads indicating contact with the Indian Ocean coast by about the thirteenth century. Thus Ntusi was first occupied at an earlier date than Bigo, whose dates have been revised to the period from the thirteenth to sixteenth

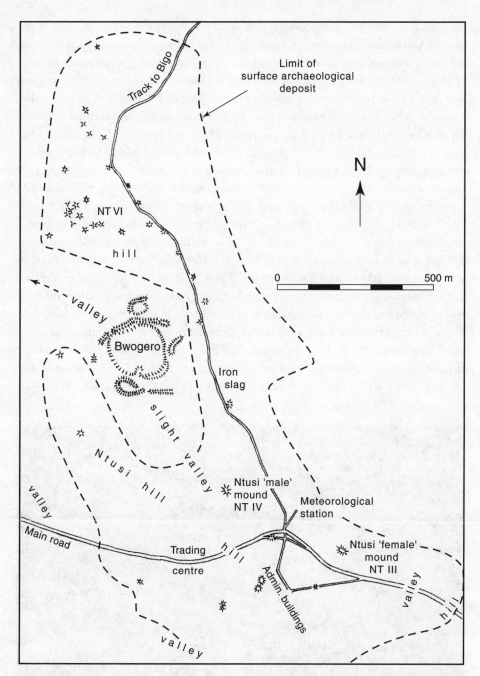

Fig. 8.7 Plan of Ntusi, Uganda. After Sutton (1993: Fig. 4) based on a survey by Andrew Reid in 1987–9.

century, but they apparently overlapped. Reid wisely conducted a survey of 5 per cent of 560 square kilometres around Ntusi and Bigo and located over fifty more sites of second-millennium date, of which several when excavated revealed faunal remains overwhelmingly dominated by cattle. However, these sites were in general less than half a hectare in area and the lack of sites of intermediate size, together with the other evidence, suggests that by the fourteenth and fifteenth centuries Ntusi was a chiefdom based on cattle pastoralism and sorghum cultivation rather than a centralized state. A social hierarchy based on cattle had perhaps not yet emerged, but the fifteenth-century abandonment of Ntusi and the construction of the Bigo earthworks may indicate that developments in that direction occurred subsequently. It might also be that Bigo, bordered on one side by the Katonga River, offered a more viable centre for cattle than the dry grassland area of Ntusi. The existence near the latter site of the huge artificial depression and associated mounds and banks known as the *Bwogero*, sometimes called the Ntusi 'dams', suggests that this may indeed have been so (Fig. 8.7). Reid has described this rather suspect feature as 'functionally ambiguous' (1996: 623), which is an archaeological way of admitting that he does not know what it is, but Sutton (1985: 174) suggested that it resulted from scraping away the deposits down to the water-table in order to provide water for cattle. If he is correct, then the scale of the feature (Reid thought that almost 30,000 cubic metres of material had been removed) would suggest that this activity continued for some centuries and that the pressure on the supply was

Fig. 8.8 Traces of circular houses at Ntusi. Reproduced by permission of Andrew Reid.

extreme. In such circumstances it would hardly be surprising if Ntusi was abandoned in favour of Bigo, particularly if cattle rather than a balance of pastoralism
and cultivation were becoming economically dominant. Unfortunately, however,
the *Bwogero* remains undated and its association with the site of Ntusi has never
been demonstrated.

Comparable with Reid's survey of the area around Ntusi and Bigo was
Robertshaw's series of investigations of the country south and west of Munsa.
Some 130 archaeological sites were recorded, which all appeared to belong to the
second millennium AD. By comparing the sizes and locations of these sites and
grouping them on the basis of a statistical analysis of the pottery found on them,
Robertshaw was able to suggest how the state of Bunyoro had developed in this
area prior to the nineteenth century. Early settlements tended to be small but it
appears that a hierarchy of site sizes existed from about the fourteenth century,
some of the larger being protected by earthworks by the fourteenth and fifteenth
centuries. This period of 'competing polities' (Robertshaw 1994: 127) between
about the fourteenth and sixteenth centuries may eventually have led to collapse,
which the Babito dynasty, the rulers of Bunyoro when the first Europeans arrived
on the scene, were able to exploit. Thus Bunyoro may only have emerged as such
during the seventeenth or eighteenth century but the socio-political changes that
gave rise to it could have originated in the earlier part of the second millennium
(Robertshaw 1991; 1994). Some support for this model came from my excavations
of the settlement site at Kibiro on the eastern shore of Lake Albert, the salt production of which was so important to the economy of nineteenth-century Bunyoro.
The exploitation of this resource could also be traced back to the early second millennium (Connah 1991; 1996). Furthermore, evidence from the surface of other
sites adjacent to the north-eastern part of Lake Albert and along the lower part of
the Victoria Nile suggests widespread cultural homogeneity in this area over the
last thousand years and gives some idea of the background of Bunyoro's development (Connah 1997).

Control of salt production and trading was probably of considerable importance in the rise of Bunyoro but in the case of both this and other interlacustrine
states the smelting and exchange of iron must also have been of great significance. In Uganda this subject has not yet been given the attention by archaeological research that it merits but in the Buhaya area, in north-west Tanzania,
important work by Peter Schmidt has shown that iron-smelting was already
being practised over 2000 years before European visitors came across the states of
that area (Schmidt 1978; Schmidt and Avery 1996). Given its probable socio-
economic role, it is hardly surprising that iron also took on political and religious
symbolic meaning, so that iron anvils were amongst the royal insignia of the
states of Karagwe (now part of Tanzania), Ankole, Buganda and Rwanda
(Sassoon 1983).

Subsistence economy

The extent to which the two areas that have been discussed are really representative of Central Africa as a whole is unknown. Nevertheless, at least in their case there is archaeological evidence for growing social complexity over the last millennium. It is surely significant that in both these instances there seems to have been a subsistence economy that was markedly stronger and more flexible than that to be found in surrounding savanna regions. A mixed farming tradition, relying on the cultivation of cereal and other crops as well as on the herding of domestic animals, was supplemented by fishing and hunting. In the Upemba Depression fishing was particularly important but fertile alluvial soils which were inundated seasonally provided a highly productive agricultural base. The limitation of archaeological evidence to burials and the lack of information from settlement sites make it difficult to assess the subsistence economy in detail but clearly it was a highly successful one that supported a substantial population. Direct evidence is sparse but oil-palm nuts (*Elaeis guineensis*), grain that was very probably finger millet (*Eleusine* [*coracana?*]), and the bones of goats and chicken were found in various contexts, as well as numerous fish bones, mollusc shells and bones from wild animals (de Maret 1992: 157, 170, 239–43).

In the Interlacustrine Region the available evidence is somewhat greater, with probable sorghum at Ntusi in the fourteenth to fifteenth century, finger millet from an approximately fourteenth-century context at Kibiro, cattle dominating the faunal evidence at Ntusi, Bigo, Munsa and other sites, and sheep or goats apparently as important as cattle at Kibiro (Posnansky 1969; Reid and Meredith 1993; Reid 1996; Connah 1996; Robertshaw *et al.* 1997). It is evident that, in the more fertile areas with higher rainfall, cereal cultivation was supplemented by banana growing, although bananas are only just beginning to be identified in the archaeological record (Robertshaw 1999 reports banana phytoliths from Kasunga). It is also apparent that cattle herding so successfully exploited the drier grasslands that it came to be socio-politically if not economically dominant. It may be concluded that both these areas had a highly successful subsistence base that was capable of producing a surplus that could be accumulated: in the form of grain or dried fish or, indeed, of cattle and small stock. It seems quite likely that some parts of these areas were able to support locally dense populations.

Technology

Archaeological evidence from the Upemba Depression and from the Interlacustrine Region indicates the existence of a sound technological base in both areas. Because the former consists of grave-goods, in which a high incidence of intact artefacts can be expected, and the latter of material from settlement sites, where items are normally fragmented, the technology of the Upemba area, particularly during the Classic Kisalian phase, appears to be one of the most remarkable in early-second-millennium tropical Africa. This impression is also heightened by the brilliant quality of the illustrations, especially the drawings, in the relevant Belgian publications. Metal-working, of both iron and copper, was clearly sophisticated, producing weapons, tools and items of personal adornment, by hammering and wire-drawing techniques. The carving of ivory and bone and the making of high-quality pottery also indicate the existence of considerable craftsmanship, while evidence for basket-making is a reminder of the probable skills using a variety of organic materials of which evidence has not survived.

Because of the different character of the archaeological evidence, for the Interlacustrine Region we have almost more information on processes than on finished products. Thus numerous sites indicate skill in iron-smelting and smithing and, indeed, relevant sites in north-west Tanzania have been claimed to show the use of such advanced techniques as a preheated air blast and a direct steel process, although it seems that these claims need some qualification (Killick 1996; Woodhouse 1998). Similarly the evidence from Kibiro demonstrates the existence, from early in the second millennium, of a possibly unique salt-making technique that implies an understanding of the sun's capillary action on waterlogged deposits and is capable of producing a salt of 97.6 per cent purity (Connah 1996). Salt was also made at Katwe, on Lake Edward, and at Lake Bunyampaka, near Lake George, by the more conventional solar evaporation technique that still needed considerable expertise, although it is unknown for how long this had been done prior to its being first recorded in the nineteenth century (Connah 1998a). In contrast, the making of pottery was already well established by the first millennium AD, and during the second millennium was producing an impressive range of vessel forms and sizes, on the basis of coil-building and clamp firing. Because there is so much broken pottery on so many of the interlacustrine sites it is easy to overlook the skills required for its production, which relatively late in the Kibiro sequence included the application of a graphite slip to some high-status items, a slip that required the mining of graphite for which evidence was found at Kigorobya nearby (Connah 1996: 129, 180). The pottery is also technologically informative in other ways: acquiring suitable clay and tempers needed an understanding of surface geology, knotting and twisting the flexible roulettes used in decoration required a knowledge of suitable plant fibres, and the making of the finely carved wooden roulettes also used in decoration suggests the existence of wood-carving skills. Finally, perhaps the most impressive aspect of the technology of the Interlacustrine Region is indicated by the existence of the earthwork sites, of which Bigo is the best known. Requiring the excavation of earth, the quarrying of rock, and the construction of substantial banks of these materials, something more than massed hoes and copious sweat was needed. Civil engineering skills were involved, just as must also have been the case with the creation of the so-called Ntusi 'dams'. Overall, the technology of the two Central African areas that have been discussed was apparently well developed.

Social system

In both the Upemba Depression and the Interlacustrine Region there is archaeological evidence that suggests the emergence of a social hierarchy. As already mentioned, some of the Upemban burials were accompanied by more grave-goods than others, some even by child sacrifices, and the existence of wealthy children's graves suggested that wealth was partly hereditary. Large numbers of high-quality pots, iron and copper artefacts, items of ivory, even glass beads and cowrie shells from the Indian Ocean coast, were probably indicative of the existence of one or more elite groups. Furthermore, some graves contained probable symbols of power, such as an iron axe, an anvil or a bell, suggesting that the individuals with whom they were buried were actually invested with political or sacred authority. Indeed, the eventual use of copper *croisettes* as a form of currency suggests that a political structure of some sophistication gradually developed. It seems likely that a society of cultivators, herdsmen and fishermen was ruled by several small, privileged groups that had attained at least chieftain status, one of which by the eighteenth century was able to found the Luba state. The diverse technological skills indicated by the artefactual assemblage would suggest that some degree of functional specialization also developed.

In the Interlacustrine Region the evidence is rather different. In this case it is the construction of large earthworks, with all that this implies in terms of control of resources, planning and direction of labour, that suggests the existence of powerful elites whose wealth was accumulated in the form of cattle, the bones of which appear to be so numerous at these and related sites. In addition, at both Bigo and Bweyorere the sites of supposed elite structures were found and it is possible that the two large midden mounds at Ntusi were associated with the dwellings of sociopolitical leaders. That some members of society were wealthier and perhaps more powerful than others is also suggested by several approximately eleventh-century burials excavated at Munsa, that were accompanied by the earliest glass beads found in the area as well as by bracelets of iron and one of copper (Robertshaw 1997: 13–14; Robertshaw *et al.* 1997: 73). Furthermore, the roughly fourteenth-century female burial found at Kibiro, that had iron and copper jewellery with it as well as glass beads and beads of freshwater shell, suggests that women as well as men were among the elite (Connah 1996: 90–2). From the evidence of Robertshaw's survey south and west of Munsa (Robertshaw 1994) and from Reid's research in and around Ntusi (Reid 1996), it seems likely that the process of sociopolitical change followed much the same course as in the Upemba Depression, with separate chiefdoms gradually giving way to a number of interlacustrine states by the eighteenth century at the latest. At the same time the archaeological evidence for iron-working, salt-making and perhaps some other activities suggests that at least some functional specialization was also occurring. Finally, although the Upemba Depression lacks evidence from settlement sites that could throw light on the matter in that area, at least in the Interlacustrine Region the beginnings of urbanization were apparent. For example, by the fifteenth century Ntusi was an extensive settlement, probably covering much of its approximately 100 hectares; round about the sixteenth century the massive enclosures at Bigo may at times have sheltered large numbers of people and their cattle (although Robertshaw 1999 questions this); and in 1894 Kibiro was described as 'the only manufacturing town in [B]Unyoro', consisting 'of about a thousand grass huts closely huddled together' (Thruston 1900: 143). One may conclude that both of the areas that have been discussed had already attained a substantial level of social complexity before the advent of sustained contact with the outside world.

Population pressures

An important causative factor in these changes may have been localized population pressures, that resulted in competition for some particularly important but limited part of the resource base. In the Upemba Depression this could have been access to prime fishing areas, or to fertile alluvial soils in an environment where 'Dense populations had to compete for the few stretches of land not inundated during the annual flood' (Reefe 1983: 163). In the Interlacustrine Region it is more likely to have been access to dryland grazing rights and to the more fertile cultivable soils in higher rainfall areas, but water supplies for livestock and sources of salt, iron ore, and even charcoal, are also possibilities. It seems that exceptional natural resources may have promoted population growth in areas that were so endowed but that such growth inevitably led to competition for control of the best of those very resources. Those who succeeded in gaining that control could then accumulate a surplus in one form or another and use this as a means of establishing authority over larger and larger numbers of the less fortunate members of the population. However, these propositions have yet to be adequately tested with relevant archaeological evidence, and Parker Shipton argued that in agrarian East Africa it was areas of low population pressure not high population pressure that were characterized by the development of political hierarchy (Shipton 1984).

Ideology

The archaeological evidence for the role of religion in the socio-political changes that took place in the Upemba Depression and the Interlacustrine Region is limited, although both oral tradition and the ethnohistorical record suggest that it must have been an important contributory factor. In both areas, but particularly the former, the placing of valuable and sometimes numerous items as grave-goods in burials indicates a concern with the spirit world, and the remarkable collection of both secular and sacred objects placed with the 1930/1 burial of the seventeenth- or eighteenth-century Rwandan king Cyirima Rujugira suggests that this was particularly the case with state rulers (Van Noten 1972: Fig. 8; 1982: Fig. 36). Evidence of the association of kingship and the sacred is also provided by the large number of royal tombs in both Bunyoro and Buganda, that were still maintained and venerated during the twentieth century (Uganda 1967: 71). Indeed in these states it was customary to remove the mandible from the deceased and house it in a separate 'jaw-bone shrine', specifically because it represented part of the credentials of his successor (Oliver 1959a). It is possible that these various tombs and shrines extend back as far as the fifteenth century but other shrines associated with the supposed earlier Bacwezi rulers could well have been developments subsequent to the existence of the possibly mythical figures that they revere. This could be the case at Mubende, Kasunga and Masaka Hill, and certainly is the case at Bigo where such a shrine seems to have appeared only in the 1990s (Robertshaw and Kamuhangire 1996: 741). Nevertheless, it does seem very likely that those who ruled emergent states in Central Africa based their power on the spiritual world as well as on material resources.

External trade

It has often been assumed that until late in the second millennium, Central Africa remained so remote from the world outside of the continent that external long-distance trade cannot have played a part in processes of political integration and population aggregation (e.g. Connah 1996: 1, 213). The archaeological evidence indicates that such changes were already in progress at an earlier date. Nevertheless, such a view may need some modification, particularly because of its apparent origin in nineteenth-century Eurocentric ideas about intrepid European explorers ending the timeless isolation of the remotest parts of Africa. Can they have been previously so completely isolated, when nineteenth-century European visitors found American crops such as maize, cassava, sweet potatoes and groundnuts already growing there? Furthermore, tobacco was also being grown and was being smoked in pottery pipes that were generally similar in form to pipes found in other parts of Africa and beyond (Shaw 1960). It might be countered that none of these introductions is likely to pre-date the sixteenth century, by which time the Portuguese were already present in the Kingdom of Kongo. However, there is also the problem of bananas to explain, for it has been proposed that they were introduced to Central Africa, from the other side of the Indian Ocean, by 2500 years ago

(De Langhe, Swennen and Vuylsteke 1995). Indeed, a small amount of archaeological evidence does suggest that contacts with the outside world go back to early in the second millennium. Such is the approximate date of a few glass beads and a small number of marine shells (from the Indian Ocean coast) that were found at the site of Katoto in the Upemba Depression (Hiernaux, Maquet and De Buyst 1972: 154–5), while glass and cowrie shell beads were excavated from a roughly thirteenth-century context at Ntusi (Reid 1990: 27), and glass beads from a grave of about the fourteenth century at Kibiro (Connah 1996: 90–2). In addition, glass beads were also recovered from several approximately eleventh-century burials at Munsa (Robertshaw 1997: 13–14; Robertshaw *et al.* 1997: 73). In short, Central Africa was not totally isolated from the rest of the world but it has to be admitted that the evidence for long-distance trade from outside the continent before the middle of the second millennium AD is tenuous. Surface collections from no less than thirty-six sites in the Ugandan part of the Western Rift Valley, for instance, produced only seven glass beads (Connah 1996: 213).

In such circumstances, although isolation was clearly not total, external trade is still hardly likely to have been an important factor in the development of social complexity. On the other hand, internal African trading networks, particularly in salt, iron and copper, could have played a significant role in these developments. Salt, for instance, is known to have been produced at Uvinza, in western Tanzania, from the middle of the first millennium AD (Sutton and Roberts 1968); at Ivuna, also in western Tanzania, from early in the second millennium (Fagan and Yellen 1968); at Kibiro, in Uganda, from a similar date (Connah 1996); and from Katwe, also in Uganda, from an unknown date prior to the nineteenth century (Connah 1998a). Iron production was clearly important in the Interlacustrine Region, and one of the world's great copper deposits was already being exploited in south-east Democratic Congo and northern Zambia. In addition, it is probable that numerous other commodities were traded widely in Central Africa, such as dried fish, millet, sorghum, charcoal, bark cloth, wild animal skins, ivory, and other things that we can only guess at. With landscapes over which movement was relatively easy, many trade goods could have travelled long distances as head-loads, but it should not be forgotten that this is a land of lakes and rivers in which there is ethnohistorical evidence for substantial development of water transport. In the course of a thousand years or more a vast and complex series of overlapping trading networks could have developed, of which we still know very little. It was possibly these that spread the bananas and the other new crops, as well as the occasional glass beads and marine shells, all of them picked up at the periphery of the networks from international sources. It may also have been these internal trading networks that generated concentrations of wealth in particular areas, brought disparate groups of people into contact with one another, and stimulated competition and conflict — by these and other means contributing to the social, political and economic transformations that took place in some parts of Central Africa.

Conclusion

The relative isolation of much of Central Africa from influences external to the continent, until the middle of the second millennium AD, makes it particularly important to understand the processes that led in some places to state emergence and/or the growth of larger, denser settlements. Explanation of such developments in this context might help us to comprehend similar socio-political changes that took place in other parts of tropical Africa, and perhaps even elsewhere in the world. Unfortunately, however, a relatively low level of archaeological visibility, that may be more apparent than real, and a very uneven distribution of archaeological research given the huge area involved, make it virtually impossible to draw any general conclusions. Nevertheless, for the relatively small Upemba Depression and the much larger but still limited Interlacustrine Region, there is sufficient archaeological evidence to throw a little light on the matter, assuming that they can to at least some extent be taken as representative of the Central African situation. Both of these areas were distinguished by potentially highly productive environments, with access to other major resources. In spite of the constraints of periodic disease and human conflict, both of them could have supported locally dense populations sustained by cereal, banana and other cultivation, pastoralism, fishing and hunting, and with a varied metallurgy-based technology. The archaeological evidence also suggests that increasingly hierarchical social systems were developing during the first half of the second millennium, stimulated by competition for prime resources as population pressures increased in some areas. Elite individuals were able to manipulate larger and larger groups of people, legitimizing their position by assumption of sacred status but basing their power on economic control. The growth of extensive trading networks within Central Africa are also likely to have played an important contributory part in these developments, with only attenuated input from outside the continent. Many commodities were probably involved, but the importance of salt (so keenly sought for both human and livestock use), iron (the very basis of the technology on which society depended) and copper (such a valued symbol of status and means of exchange) can hardly be exaggerated. It is apparent that all of these factors helped to shape the complex socio-political landscape, that so impressed nineteenth-century European explorers deep in the heart of Africa.

Chapter 9
What are the common denominators?

The examples of African precolonial urbanization and state formation that have been discussed in Chapters 2–8 come from a wide range of environments. In general terms these include: river valley, in such cases as Kerma on the Nile or Jenné-jeno on the Niger; mountain plateau, for example Aksum in Ethiopia or Great Zimbabwe in the country now called after it; savanna plain, for instance Koumbi Saleh or Kano in West Africa; rainforest, such as Ife or Benin in Nigeria; and coastal fringe as with Kilwa or Gedi in East Africa. The geographical locations of these developments within the continent are equally diverse. The middle Nile was so positioned that it had substantial and long-standing contacts with Egypt and the eastern Mediterranean. Aksum was situated beside a major trade route between the Mediterranean world and the lands of the Indian Ocean and directly on a trade route from the Red Sea to the Nile Valley near Meroë. The West African savanna, on the other hand, was separated from the outside world by one of the greatest deserts on earth, the traversal of which delayed and attenuated the influence of external factors. This was even more the case for the West African forest, situated far to the south of the desert margins and backed by the empty Atlantic Ocean that for many centuries was a more effective barrier than the Sahara. Different again were the cities and towns of the East African coast, which looked out on the Indian Ocean that provided links with a number of distant but technologically sophisticated cultures. More remote from such contacts but still in touch with them was the Zimbabwe Plateau, while the Upemba Depression and the Interlacustrine Region, in the heart of Africa, had relatively little contact with the outside world until quite late. Such environmental and geographical diversity would suggest that we must look elsewhere for any common factors that might explain the appearance of social complexity in some parts of the African continent and, equally, its failure to appear in other parts.

Nevertheless, when considering the details of the environments that have been discussed, it is apparent that each area had its own characteristic environmental advantages. True, in every case there were also environmental constraints but the ingenuity of human culture partly mitigated their impact. Nowhere is this more starkly illustrated than on the middle Nile; on the one hand the river offered life but on the other hand parts of the surrounding environment were so dry as to be scarcely habitable. Yet, by means of a combination of irrigation, rainfed cultivation and pastoralism, human populations were able to exploit both the river and the adjacent savanna and desert margins. So successfully were the environmental constraints overcome that this area was the scene of some of tropical Africa's earliest states and cities and of the longest succession of such developments. A similar interplay of environmental advantage, environmental constraint and human culture can be discerned (to varying extents) in each of the cases that have been considered. This interplay was a dynamic one and clearly its outcome in each case was normally very much in favour of the human inhabitants, except when episodic imbalance threatened collapse of the often delicately balanced system. However, this does not go very far in explaining the emergence of social complexity in Africa; obviously, human beings thrive better in some places than in others, but this is no reason why they should build cities or create states.

In the cases under review, however, it is the numbers of people who thrived that may be significant. The population densities of such areas seem to have been rather higher than was usual in this generally thinly populated continent. All of the areas discussed had a strong subsistence base with a potential for producing a storable, transportable surplus. All the people concerned were agriculturalists, growing a range of food plants suited to the local environments and in all cases keeping livestock, even though this was severely limited by trypanosomiasis in the case of the West African forest. The importance of pastoralism (Smith 1992) can hardly be overstated: herds of cattle and flocks of sheep and goats converted grass into wealth during good years and could provide relief from starvation when crops failed in bad years. Of course, the farmers and the pastoralists were often different groups of people, interacting one with the other; but from this symbiosis came strength, just as weakness resulted from their periodic conflicts. In addition, there are signs that in some areas there was an intensification of agricultural strategy and this in a continent where agricultural systems have tended to be extensive rather than intensive. Thus, on the middle Nile more efficient irrigation was achieved by introducing the ox-driven waterwheel; in the Inland Niger Delta of Mali recessional cultivation of rice was developed to a sophisticated level; in the Ethiopian Highlands slopes were terraced and water-storage dams constructed. Developments of this sort would suggest that populations in such areas were indeed increasing, creating a demand for more food and for more labour to produce it. It is surely significant that people became such a persistent trade commodity in some parts of Africa.

In each of the cases considered, the exploitation of resources was accomplished not only by means of a mixed agricultural strategy but also by the application of a varied and sometimes sophisticated metallurgically based technology. Most of the societies with which we are concerned seem to have been particularly proficient in the working of iron, and iron technology has been extremely important in Africa as an enabling and intensifying agent during the last two millennia or so. Without iron, the farmers of the West African forest could not have exploited their heavily vegetated environment as successfully as they did, nor could the occupants of Bigo in Uganda have dug such impressive rock-cut ditches. Iron provided both the tools to exploit available resources and the weapons to discourage others who coveted them. In addition to iron-working and other metallurgical skills, the technology of the various groups of people discussed in this book covered a range of abilities. Although engineering knowledge of the sort indicated by the Aksumite stelae seems to have been unusual, there was, nevertheless, a widespread understanding of building techniques, in stone, in fired brick, in mud-brick, in coursed mud, in wood, in grass, and in other organic materials. Building technology was both accomplished and diverse. Furthermore, there appear to have been other crafts, usually including such things as pottery-making, wood-working, textile production and leather-working. In some instances, however, there must have been people with technological skills specific to the region, such as boatbuilders and sailors on the middle Nile or on the East African coast, and scribes in Meroë or in Aksum where indigenous alphabets were developed. One is led to the conclusion that specialist artisans were involved in at least some of these activities. When it is considered that a number of the cases studied also have evidence suggesting the existence of religious functionaries, government officials and specialist traders, it becomes apparent that some degree of functional specialization was probably present in all of the areas examined.

Inevitably, some resources were more limited than others and, as Haas (1982: 151) claimed, it is control of resources that gives rulers their power (p. 6). All of the case studies examined in this book show unmistakable signs of the emergence of an elite who told other people what to do. The question is, what were the vital resources that they controlled? Most commonly this has been answered by pointing to the existence of raw materials such as gold, ivory and other things which commanded a high price on the world market. Control of these meant control of long-distance overseas trade and control of such trade provided prestige and wealth. Thus appeared the African elites; thus developed the cities and the states. The problem with this explanation is not that it is basically incorrect but that it is wrongly timed. Looking at the archaeological evidence on the middle Nile, in the Ethiopian Highlands or along the East African coast, it is obvious that external long-distance trade did sometimes play a major role in African urbanization and state formation, but it seems likely that this was as an intensifier rather than as an originator. Thus we now have evidence that suggests an indigenous origin for the development of social complexity on the East African coast; the earliest urbanization in the West African savanna pre-dates the growth of large-scale trans-Saharan trade; and in central Africa there are signs of increasing social complexity at a time before there was any substantial long-distance trade with the outside world. Furthermore, neither Zimbabwe nor the West African forest has evidence for early long-distance trade on a large scale, and even in the middle Nile and the Ethiopian Highlands the origins of socio-political changes seem to have pre-dated such a development.

If external long-distance trade was merely an intensifier of changes that had already commenced, then the question remains of what started them. There seem to be two possibilities. The first is that extensive *internal* trading networks pre-existed external trading contacts and that African elites first gained power by controlling resources that were important in such internal exchange systems. Copper, iron and salt are likely to have been amongst these resources but there could have been many more, including the gold and the ivory that subsequently became so vital to the overseas trade. Indeed, the earliest commodities to be exchanged by internal trade were probably foodstuffs and other plant and animal resources. The ecological diversity of much of Africa makes this likely and, in fact, the movement of such commodities has remained significant down to modern times. Thus shea-butter has been exported from northern Nigeria to the south of that country, whilst kola nuts travelled in the opposite direction (Shaw 1984: 156) and Africa has many similar examples of resource exchange. Although archaeology tends to be silent on perishable goods of this sort, there is some indication that early internal trading networks really did exist, particularly in Central Africa, West Africa and Ethiopia. This being the case, it seems likely that external long-distance trade merely plugged into the extant circuitry of the internal networks.

A second possible explanation is that elite power was first acquired by the control of land, not of any land but of land with an unusually high production potential. The role of this factor is, indeed, seen as possibly complementary to that of internal trade, rather than as alternative to it. Given the relatively poor quality of many African soils, together with their often moisture-stressed condition, and given situations of expanding populations in some places, the greatest area of competition was very likely to be around land which was more highly productive. In all of the case-studies examined, it is possible to find indications that such land may have existed. Thus, in the middle Nile area, fertile silts which could be reached by the available irrigation technology were limited and the proportion of each year for which they could be watered varied with position. As a result, some areas of land must have been more productive than others. On the north-eastern Ethiopian plateau, some soils were more fertile than others and more suitable for plough cultivation of cereals, and periodic drought must have given irrigated land a particularly significant role during resulting episodes of famine. The generally water-stressed environment of the West African savanna gave the limited areas available for recessional cultivation, such as parts of the Inland Niger Delta, a particular importance. In the West African forest, it seems to have been the upper interfluves and the forest–savanna ecotonal areas that provided the best farmlands and again these were limited. For the East African coast it was a matter of fertile soils and water availability, some areas being better provided for than others. On the Zimbabwe Plateau, it was again a matter of soils, where some soils were particularly fertile in an otherwise rather rocky area with granite soils of indifferent or poor fertility. For the Upemba Depression it was access to seasonally inundated fertile alluvium and to the most productive fishing-grounds. In the Interlacustrine Region it was control of the best soils for cultivation in areas of good rainfall and of the best grazing lands for cattle in the drier areas.

Thus it is possible that the crucial common factor underlying the emergence of African elites was access to, and control of, more highly productive land. If this was the case, then we have a purely indigenous explanation for the origin of social complexity in some parts of tropical Africa. Doubtless, local trading networks also played an important role, and clearly, external long-distance trade eventually came to act as an intensifying agent of considerable significance. Nevertheless, this 'productive land hypothesis', as it might be called, does provide an originating agent, within each locality, of the developments that we are seeking to understand. It also provides an hypothesis that is testable, as field research progresses.

With the emergence of an elite in the societies that have been discussed, social stratification became inevitable. All of the archaeological examples that have been examined show signs of such social differentiation to a greater or lesser degree. There were clearly those few who were in charge and those masses who did what they were told. Less easy to recognize are the people in the middle, who acted on behalf of the elite but were neither of their ranks nor of those of the labouring majority. Whatever the details of the hierarchy, however, in each of the cases reviewed in this book it was legitimized and reinforced by one form or another of religious ideology. In all instances, the earliest manifestations of this were indigenous, presumably animistic, religions but in cases where there was prolonged contact with the outside world these were eventually replaced or overlaid by Christianity or Islam. Whatever its form, however, it does seem that in each case the spiritual came to the aid of the material. That, perhaps, is to understate the importance of African indigenous religions, particularly during the earlier phases of the processes with which this book has been concerned. Such religions were often a means of manipulating the forces believed to control fertility, in all senses of that word, and therefore gave power to those who were thought to be able to do this. In that case, the role of religion could have been much more than merely validating the authority of those who had acquired power by other means: African power-holders were nearly always priests *themselves*. As such, they could indeed have claimed control of the best land or of the internal exchange systems or even, eventually, of their end of external long-distance trade networks, and who would have been prepared to deny them?

This book has been more concerned with archaeological evidence than with theoretical matters but any attempt to identify some of the main factors that gave rise to the cities and states of precolonial Africa has theoretical implications. It appears that the power theory of state formation advocated by Haas (see p. 6) does help to understand the African situation and therefore does have some explanatory value. Furthermore, it seems that Lonsdale (see p. 9) was correct in concluding that state formation in Africa was a very slow process, involving the coercive centralization of power, and resulting from local politics, not from external ideas. This being the case, one is inclined to agree with Renfrew (see p. 7) that the division into 'pristine' and 'secondary' states, which has so often been made, is a meaningless exercise.

Clearly the development of cities and the formation of states in Africa were not aspects of a single process; not all cities were capitals of significant states and not all states had large, static centres of population. Nevertheless, they were both important manifestations of precolonial complex societies and it is sometimes difficult to discuss them in isolation. Centralization of power, social stratification, functional specialization, these and other related developments, together with population growth, are phenomena that can be associated with both the appearance of cities and the emergence of states. Furthermore, their separate identification in the archaeological record can be particularly difficult. In some cases we do have physical evidence for the existence of settlements in which relatively large numbers of people were congregated: whether they are called large villages, towns or even cities hardly matters, the important point is that they were relatively dense aggregations of population, recalling Mabogunje's straightforward definition of urbanization (see p. 8). More ambiguous, however, are the instances of archaeological evidence that might suggest the extension of political authority, or at least some commonality of culture, over a substantial geographical area. Indeed, even in the minds of some of the African people involved, it seems that the ideas of city and state may at times have been inextricably associated. Thus, in 1893, Lugard found it necessary to emphasize the close association of state, ruler and city in the case of Buganda: 'The Waganda consider their country to be where the King is, and if no Kabaka of the Royal blood is installed in Mengo [the capital], the result would be a break-up of the people' (Lugard 1893: 36). It is with the overall process of the coming together of people in tropical Africa that this book has been concerned.

In the African case this coming together occurred in a diversity of forms. Varied in their indigenous origins, states were also variously influenced by Pharaonic Egypt, by the Christian world, by Islamic North Africa, by Indian Ocean traders, and by each other. Urban centres also showed considerable variety: some densely occupied for long periods, some only briefly occupied, some completely mobile, some with transient residence from season to season and year to year, some with dispersed settlement covering immense areas. Such diversity would suggest that the physical evidence for African social complexity would merit far more attention from archaeologists than it has yet had and might have a far greater role in the formation of social theory than has yet been the case.

Bibliography

Abungu, G.H.O. 1990. *Communities on the River Tana, Kenya: an archaeological study of relations between the delta and the river basin, 700–1890 AD.* (PhD thesis, University of Cambridge), National Museums of Kenya, Nairobi.

    1995. Agriculture and settlement formation along the East African coast. *Azania* 29–30, 248–56.

Abungu, G.H.O. and Mutoro, H.W. 1993. Coast–interior settlements and social relations in the Kenya coastal hinterland. In *The archaeology of Africa: food, metals and towns,* ed. T. Shaw, P. Sinclair, B. Andah and A. Okpoko, 694–704. Routledge, London and New York.

Adams, R.McC. 1981. *Heartland of cities: surveys of ancient settlement and land use on the central floodplain of the Euphrates.* University of Chicago Press, Chicago and London.

Adams, W.Y. 1961. The Christian potteries at Faras. *Kush* 9, 30–43.

    1966. The vintage of Nubia. *Kush* 14, 262–83.

    1974. Sacred and secular polities in ancient Nubia. *World Archaeology* 6(1), 39–51.

    1976. Meroitic north and south. A study in cultural contrasts. *Meroitica* 2, 11–26.

    1977. *Nubia: corridor to Africa.* Allen Lane, London. (Reprinted 1984.)

    1981. Ecology and economy in the Empire of Kush. *Zeitschrift für Ägyptische Sprache* 108, 1–12.

    1982. Qasr Ibrim: an archaeological conspectus. In *Nubian studies: proceedings of the Symposium for Nubian Studies, Selwyn College, Cambridge, 1978,* ed. J.M. Plumley, 25–33. International Society for Nubian Studies, Aris and Phillips, Warminster.

    1984. The first colonial empire: Egypt in Nubia, 3200–1200 BC. *Comparative Studies in Society and History* 26(1), 36–71.

    1996. *Qasr Ibrim: the Late Mediaeval period.* Egypt Exploration Society, Excavation Memoir 59, London.

Adams, W.Y., Alexander, J.A. and Allen, R. 1983. Qasr Ibrim 1980 and 1982. *Journal of Egyptian Archaeology* 69, 43–60.

Addo-Fening, R. 1976. The gold mining industry in Akyem Abuakwa c.1850–1910. *Sankofa* 2, 33–9.

Adelaar, K.A. 1996. Malagasy culture-history: some linguistic evidence. In *The Indian Ocean in Antiquity,* ed. J. Reade, 487–500. Kegan Paul International, London and New York.

Africanus, Leo. 1896. *The history and description of Africa,* 3 vols., ed. R. Brown. Hakluyt Society, London.

Agbaje-Williams, B. 1990. Oyo ruins in NW Yorubaland, Nigeria. *Journal of Field Archaeology* 17(3), 367–73.

Bibliography

Ahmed, K.A. 1984. *Meroitic settlement in the Central Sudan.* BAR International Series 197, Oxford.

Ajayi, J.F.A. and Smith, R. 1971. *Yoruba warfare in the nineteenth century,* 2nd edn. Cambridge University Press, Cambridge.

Alagoa, E.J. 1970. Long-distance trade and states in the Niger Delta. *Journal of African History* 11(3), 319–29.

Alexander, J. 1988. The Saharan divide in the Nile Valley: the evidence from Qasr Ibrim. *African Archaeological Review* 6, 73–90.

    1993a. Beyond the Nile: the influence of Egypt and Nubia in Sub-Saharan Africa. *Expedition* 35(2), 51–61.

    1993b. The salt industries of West Africa: a preliminary study. In *The archaeology of Africa: food, metals and towns,* ed. T. Shaw, P. Sinclair, B. Andah and A. Okpoko, 652–7. Routledge, London and New York.

    1995. The Turks on the Middle Nile. *Archéologie du Nil Moyen* 7, 15–35.

Ali, A.M. 1972. Meroitic settlement of the Butana (central Sudan). In *Man, settlement and urbanism,* ed. P.J. Ucko, R. Tringham and G.W. Dimbleby, 639–46. Duckworth, London.

Allen, J. de V. 1974. Swahili culture reconsidered: some historical implications of the material culture of the northern Kenya coast in the eighteenth and nineteenth centuries. *Azania* 9, 105–38.

    1979. The Swahili house: cultural and ritual concepts underlying its plan and structure. In *Swahili houses and tombs of the coast of Kenya,* ed. J. de V. Allen and T.H. Wilson. Art and Archaeology Research Papers, London.

    1980. Settlement patterns on the East African coast, c.AD 800–1900. In *Proceedings of the 8th Panafrican Congress of Prehistory and Quaternary Studies, Nairobi, 5 to 10 September 1977,* ed. R.E. Leakey and B.A. Ogot, 361–3. The International Louis Leakey Memorial Institute for African Prehistory, Nairobi.

    1982. The 'Shirazi' problem in East African coastal history. In *From Zinj to Zanzibar: studies in history, trade and society on the eastern coast of Africa (Paideuma 28),* ed. J. de V. Allen and T.H. Wilson, 9–27.

    1983. Shungwaya, the Mijikenda, and the traditions. *International Journal of African Historical Studies* 16(3), 455–85.

    1993. *Swahili origins: Swahili culture and the Shungwaya phenomenon.* James Currey, London.

Allibert, C., Argant, A. and Argant, J. 1990. Le site de Dembeni (Mayotte, Archipel des Comores) Mission 1984. *Etudes Océan Indien* 11. *Archéologie des Comores: I: Maore & Ngazidja,* 63–172. Institut des Langues et Civilisations Orientales, Paris.

Allibert, C. and Vérin, P. 1996. The early pre-Islamic history of the Comores Islands: links with Madagascar and Africa. In *The Indian Ocean in Antiquity,* ed. J. Reade, 461–70. Kegan Paul International, London and New York.

Allison, P.A. 1962. Historical inferences to be drawn from the effect of human settlement on the vegetation of Africa. *Journal of African History* 3(2), 241–9.

al-Sa'di. 1964. *Tarikh es-Soudan,* texte Arabe édité et traduit par O. Houdas. Adrien-Maisonneuve, Paris.

Anciaux de Faveaux, E. and de Maret, P. 1984. Premières datations pour la fonte du cuivre au Shaba (Zaïre). *Bulletin de la Société Royale Belge d'Anthropologie et de Préhistoire* 95, 5–20.

Andah, B.W. 1976. An archaeological view of the urbanization process in the earliest West African states. *Journal of the Historical Society of Nigeria* 8(3), 1–20.

1982. Urban origins in the Guinea Forest with special reference to Benin. *West African Journal of Archaeology* 12, 63–71.

Andrews, F.W. 1948. The vegetation of the Sudan. In *Agriculture in the Sudan*, ed. J.D. Tothill, 32–61. Oxford University Press, London.

Anfray, F. 1963. La première campagne de fouilles à Matara, près de Sénafé (Novembre 1959–Janvier 1960). *Annales d'Ethiopie* 5, 87–166.

1967. Matara. *Annales d'Ethiopie* 7, 33–88.

1968. Aspects de l'archéologie éthiopienne. *Journal of African History* 9(3), 345–66.

1972a. Fouilles de Yeha. *Annales d'Ethiopie* 9, 45–64.

1972b. L'archéologie d'Axoum en 1972. *Paideuma* 18, 60–78.

1973. Nouveaux sites antiques. *Journal of Ethiopian Studies* 11(2), 13–27.

1974. Deux villes Axoumites: Adoulis et Matara. *IV Congresso Internazionale di Studi Etiopici (Roma, 10–15 aprile 1972)*. Tomo 1, 745–65 and Planche I–VI. Accademia Nazionale dei Lincei, Rome.

1981. The civilization of Aksum from the first to the seventh century. In *General History of Africa*, Vol. 2, *Ancient civilizations of Africa*, ed. G. Mokhtar, 362–80. Heinemann, University of California, Unesco; London, Berkeley, Paris.

1990. *Les Anciens Ethiopiens: siècles d'histoire*. Armand Colin, Paris.

Anfray, F. and Annequin, G. 1965. Matara, deuxième, troisième et quatrième campagnes de fouilles. *Annales d'Ethiopie* 6, 49–85.

Annequin, G. 1965. Château de Gouzara. *Annales d'Ethiopie* 6, 22–5.

Anquandah, J. 1982. *Rediscovering Ghana's past*. Longman and Sedco; Harlow and Accra.

1993a. Urbanization and state formation in Ghana during the Iron Age. In *The archaeology of Africa: food, metals and towns*, ed. T. Shaw, P. Sinclair, B. Andah and A. Okpoko, 642–51. Routledge, London and New York.

1993b. The Kintampo complex: a case study of early sedentism and food production in sub-Sahelian West Africa. In *The archaeology of Africa: food, metals and towns*, ed. T. Shaw, P. Sinclair, B. Andah and A. Okpoko, 255–60. Routledge, London and New York.

Ashe, R.P. 1889. *Two Kings of Uganda*. Sampson Low, London.

Babayemi, S.O. 1974. The Upper Ogun and Old Oyo Game Reserve. *Nigerian Field* 39(1), 4–12.

Bard, K.A. and Fattovich, R. 1993. The 1993 excavations at Ona Enda Aboi Zague (Aksum, Tigray). *Nyame Akuma* 40, 14–17.

Bard, K.A., Fattovich, R., Manzo, A. and Perlingieri, C. 1997. Archaeological investigations at Bieta Giyorgis (Aksum), Ethiopia: 1993–1995 field seasons. *Journal of Field Archaeology* 24(4), 387–403.

Barker, G. 1978. Economic models for the Manekweni Zimbabwe, Mozambique. *Azania* 13, 71–100.

Barth, H. 1857–8. *Travels and discoveries in North and Central Africa: being a journal of an expedition undertaken under the auspices of H.B.M.'s Government in the years 1849–1855*, 5 vols. Longman, Brown, Green, Longmans, and Roberts, London.

Bascom, W. 1955. Urbanization among the Yoruba. *The American Journal of Sociology* 60(5), 446–54.

1959. Urbanism as a traditional African pattern. *Sociological Review* (NS) 7, 29–43.

Beach, D. 1980. *The Shona and Zimbabwe 900–1850*. Heinemann, London.

1994. *The Shona and their neighbours*, Blackwell, Oxford.

1998. Cognitive archaeology and imaginary history at Great Zimbabwe. *Current Anthropology* 39(1), 47–72.

Beach, D., Bourdillon, M.F.C., Denbow, J., Hall, M., Lane, P., Pikirayi, I., Pwiti, G. and Huffman, T.N. 1997. Review feature: *Snakes and crocodiles: power and symbolism in ancient Zimbabwe*, by Thomas N. Huffman. *South African Archaeological Bulletin* 52, 125–43.

Beaujeu-Garnier, J. and Chabot, G. 1967. *Urban geography*, trans. G.M. Yglesias and S.H. Beaver. Longmans, London.

Bedaux, R.M.A., Constandse-Westermann, T.S., Hacquebord, L., Lange, A.G. and van der Waals, J.D. 1978. Recherches archéologiques dans le Delta Intérieur du Niger (Mali). *Palaeohistoria* 20, 19–220.

Bellamy, C.V. 1904. A West African smelting house. *Journal of the Iron and Steel Institute* 66, 99–126.

Bent, J.T. 1893. *The sacred city of the Ethiopians*. Longmans, Green, and Co., London.

1896. *The ruined cities of Mashonaland*, new edition (reissue; 1st edn 1892). Longmans, London.

Berger, I. 1980. Deities, dynasties, and oral tradition: the history and legend of the Abacwezi. In *The African past speaks: essays on oral tradition and history*, ed. J.C. Miller, 60–81. Dawson, Folkestone.

Bernus, S. and Cressier, P. 1991. *La Région d'In Gall-Tegidda-n-Tesemt (Niger). IV. Azelik-Takadda et l'implantation sédentaire médiévale*. Etudes Nigériennes 51, Niamey.

Berthier, S. 1997. *Recherches archéologiques sur la capitale de l'empire de Ghana: étude d'un secteur d'habitat à Koumbi Saleh, Mauritanie. Campagnes II–III–IV–V (1975–1976)–(1980–1981)*. Cambridge Monographs in African Archaeology 41, BAR International Series 680, Oxford.

Binger, Capitaine. 1892. *Du Niger au Golfe de Guinée*, 2 vols. Hachette, Paris.

Bisson, M.S. 1975. Copper currency in central Africa: the archaeological evidence. *World Archaeology* 6(3), 276–92.

1976. The prehistoric coppermines of Zambia. PhD thesis, University of California, Santa Barbara. University Microfilms International.

Bivar, A.D.H. and Shinnie, P.L. 1962. Old Kanuri capitals. *Journal of African History* 3(1), 1–10.

Blake, J.W. 1942. *Europeans in West Africa, 1450–1560*, 2 vols. Hakluyt, London.

Blench, R. 1993. Ethnographic and linguistic evidence for the prehistory of African ruminant livestock, horses and ponies. In *The archaeology of Africa: food, metals and towns*, ed. T. Shaw, P. Sinclair, B. Andah and A. Okpoko, 71–103. Routledge, London and New York.

Bloch, M.R. 1963. The social influence of salt. *Scientific American* 209, 88–98.

Boisragon, A. 1897. *The Benin Massacre*. Methuen, London.

Bonnet, C. 1982. Les fouilles archéologiques de Kerma (Soudan). *Genava* 30, 29–70.

1992. Excavations at the Nubian royal town of Kerma: 1975–91. *Antiquity* 66, 611–25.

Bonnet, C. (ed.) 1990. *Kerma, royaume de Nubie*. Mission archéologique de l'Université de Genève au Soudan, Geneva.

Bonnet, C., Chaix, L., Honegger, M. and Simon, C. 1995. Les fouilles archéologiques de Kerma (Soudan), 1993–1995. *Genava* (NS) 43, 31–64 (English translation, pp. i–xv).

Bosman, W. 1967. *A new and accurate description of the coast of Guinea*, 4th edn. Cass, London (1st English edn 1705).

Bourriau, J. 1991. Relations between Egypt and Kerma during the Middle and New Kingdoms. In *Egypt and Africa: Nubia from prehistory to Islam*, ed. W.V. Davies, 129–44. British Museum Press, London.

Bovill, E.W. 1968. *The golden trade of the Moors*, 2nd edn. Oxford University Press, London.

Bowdich, T.E. 1966. *Mission from Cape Coast Castle to Ashantee*, 3rd edn. Cass, London (1st edn 1819).

Bradbury, R.E. 1959. Chronological problems in the study of Benin history. *Journal of the Historical Society of Nigeria* 1(4), 263–87.

  1973. *Benin studies*. Oxford University Press, London.

Bradley, R.J. 1982. Varia from the city of Meroë. *Meroitica* 6, 163–70.

Brain, C.K. 1974. Human food remains from the Iron Age at Zimbabwe. *South African Journal of Science* 70, 303–9.

Breunig, P. 1996. The 8000-year-old dugout canoe from Dufuna (NE Nigeria). In *Aspects of African archaeology: papers from the 10th Congress of the PanAfrican Association for Prehistory and Related Studies*, ed. G. Pwiti and R. Soper, 461–8. University of Zimbabwe, Harare.

Breunig, P., Neumann, K. and Van Neer, W. 1996. New research on the Holocene settlement and environment of the Chad Basin in Nigeria. *African Archaeological Review* 13(2), 111–45.

British Institute in Eastern Africa 1998. *Annual report 1997–1998*. BIEA, London.

Broberg, A. 1995. New aspects of the medieval towns of Benadir in southern Somalia: topography, climate and population. In *Islamic art and culture in Sub-Saharan Africa*, ed. K. Ådahl and B. Sahlström, 111–22. Acta Universitatis Upsaliensis, Figura Nova Series 27, Uppsala.

Brooks, G.E. 1998. Climate and history in West Africa. In *Transformations in Africa: essays on Africa's later past*, ed. G. Connah, 139–59. Leicester University Press, London and Washington.

Brown, H. 1996. The coins. In *Shanga: the archaeology of a Muslim trading community on the coast of East Africa*, ed. M. Horton, 368–75. British Institute in Eastern Africa, Memoir 14, London.

Buchanan, K.M. and Pugh, J.C. 1955. *Land and people in Nigeria: the human geography of Nigeria and its environmental background*. University of London Press, London.

Budge, E.A.W. 1907. *The Egyptian Sudan: its history and monuments*, Vol. 2. Kegan Paul, Trench, Trübner and Co., London.

Bulliet, R.W. 1975. *The camel and the wheel*. Harvard University Press, Cambridge, MA.

Butzer, K.W. 1976. *Early hydraulic civilization in Egypt: a study in cultural ecology*. University of Chicago Press, Chicago.

  1981. Rise and fall of Axum, Ethiopia: a geo-archaeological interpretation. *American Antiquity* 46(3), 471–95.

Buxton, D.R. 1947. The Christian antiquities of Northern Ethiopia. *Archaeologia* 92, 1–42.

  1970. *The Abyssinians*. Thames and Hudson, London.

1971. The rock-hewn and other medieval churches of Tigré Province, Ethiopia. *Archaeologia* 103, 33–100.

Buxton, D.R. and Matthews, D. 1974. The reconstruction of vanished Aksumite buildings. *Rassegna di Studi Etiopici* 25, 53–77 and figs. 1–31.

Calvocoressi, D. and David, N. 1979. A new survey of radiocarbon and thermoluminescence dates for West Africa. *Journal of African History* 20(1), 1–29.

Camps, G. 1982. Le cheval et le char dans la préhistoire nord-africaine et saharienne. In *Les chars préhistoriques du Sahara*, ed. G. Camps and M. Gast, 9–22. Université de Provence, Aix-en-Provence.

Caney, R.W. and Reynolds, J.E. 1976. *Reed's marine distance tables*, 3rd edn. Reed, London.

Carneiro, R.L. 1970. A theory of the origin of the state. *Science* 169, 733–8.

Carter, P.L. and Flight, C. 1972. A report on the fauna from the sites of Ntereso and Kintampo Rock Shelter Six in Ghana: with evidence for the practice of animal husbandry during the second millennium BC. *Man* 7(2), 277–82.

Carter, P.L. and Foley, R. 1980. A report on the fauna from the excavations at Meroë, 1967–1972. Appendix B in *The capital of Kush 1: Meroë excavations 1965–1972* (*Meroitica* 4), ed. P.L. Shinnie and R.J. Bradley, 298–312. Akademie-Verlag, Berlin.

Casey, J. 1998. The ecology of food production in West Africa. In *Transformations in Africa: essays on Africa's later past*, ed. G. Connah, 46–70. Leicester University Press, London and Washington.

Casson, L. 1989. *The Periplus Maris Erythraei: text with introduction, translation, and commentary*, Princeton University Press, Princeton.

Caton-Thompson, G. 1971. *The Zimbabwe culture: ruins and reactions*, 2nd edn. Cass, London (1st edn 1931).

Chami, F.A. 1994. *The Tanzanian coast in the first millennium AD: an archaeology of the iron-working, farming communities*. Studies in African Archaeology 7, Societas Archaeologica Upsaliensis, Uppsala.

1995. The first millennium AD on the East Coast: a new look at the cultural sequence and interactions. *Azania* 29–30, 232–7.

1999a. Graeco-Roman trade link and the Bantu migration theory. *Anthropos: Internationale Zeitschrift für Völker- und Sprachenkunde* 94(1/3), 205–15.

1999b. Roman beads from the Rufiji Delta, Tanzania: first incontrovertible archaeological link with the *Periplus*. *Current Anthropology* 40(2), 237–41.

Chami, F.A. and Msemwa, P.J. 1997. A new look at culture and trade on the Azanian coast. *Current Anthropology* 38(4), 673–7.

Chandler, T. and Fox, G. 1974. *3000 years of urban growth*. Academic Press, New York and London.

Chikwendu, V.E., Craddock, P.T., Farquhar, R.M., Shaw, T. and Umeji, A.C. 1989. Nigerian sources of copper, lead and tin for the Igbo-Ukwu bronzes. *Archaeometry* 31(1), 27–36.

Childe, V.G. 1950. The urban revolution. *The Town Planning Review* 21, 3–17.

1951. *Social evolution*. Watts, London.

1957. Civilization, cities and towns. *Antiquity* 31, 36–8.

Chipunza, K.T. 1994. *A diachronic analysis of the architecture of the Hill Complex at Great Zimbabwe*. Studies in African Archaeology 8, Societas Archaeologica Upsaliensis, Uppsala.

Chittick, N. 1965. The 'Shirazi' colonization of East Africa. *Journal of African History* 6(3), 275–94.

1966. Six early coins from near Tanga. *Azania* 1, 156–7.

1967. Discoveries in the Lamu Archipelago. *Azania* 2, 37–67.

1971. The coast of East Africa. In *The African Iron Age*, ed. P.L. Shinnie, 108–41. Clarendon Press, Oxford.

1974a. Excavations at Aksum, 1973–4: a preliminary report. *Azania* 9, 159–205.

1974b. *Kilwa: an Islamic trading city on the East African coast*, 2 vols. British Institute in Eastern Africa, Memoir 5, Nairobi.

1975. An early salt-working site on the Tanzanian coast. *Azania* 10, 151–3.

1977. The East Coast, Madagascar and the Indian Ocean. In *The Cambridge history of Africa*, ed. R. Oliver, Vol. 3, 183–231. Cambridge University Press, Cambridge.

1980. Sewn boats in the western Indian Ocean, and a survival in Somalia. *International Journal of Nautical Archaeology and Underwater Exploration* 9(4), 297–309.

1981. The *Periplus* and the spice trade. *Azania* 16, 185–90.

1984. *Manda: excavations at an island port on the Kenya coast*, British Institute in Eastern Africa, Memoir 9, Nairobi.

Churchill, W.S. 1962. *My African journey* (first published 1908). Heron Books.

Claessen, H.J.M. and Oosten, J.G. (eds.) 1996. *Ideology and the formation of early states*. Brill, Leiden.

Claessen, H.J.M. and Skalník, P. (eds.) 1978. *The early state*. Mouton, The Hague.

Claessen, H.J.M. and van de Velde, P. (eds.) 1987. *Early state dynamics*. Brill, Leiden.

Clarke, S. 1912. *Christian antiquities in the Nile Valley: a contribution towards the study of the ancient churches*. Clarendon Press, Oxford.

Cohen, R. and Service, E.R. (eds.) 1978. *Origins of the state: the anthropology of political evolution*. Institute for the Study of Human Issues, Philadelphia.

Collett, D.P., Vines, A.E. and Hughes, E.G. 1992. The chronology of the Valley Enclosures: implications for the interpretation of Great Zimbabwe. *African Archaeological Review* 10, 139–61.

Collins, M.O. (ed.) 1965. *Rhodesia: its natural resources and economic development*. M.O. Collins, Salisbury, Rhodesia.

Connah, G. 1972. Archaeology in Benin. *Journal of African History* 13(1), 25–38.

1975. *The archaeology of Benin*. Oxford University Press, Oxford.

1981. *Three thousand years in Africa: man and his environment in the Lake Chad region of Nigeria*. Cambridge University Press, Cambridge.

1985. Agricultural intensification and sedentism in the firki of N.E. Nigeria. In *Prehistoric intensive agriculture in the tropics*, ed. I.S. Farrington, 765–85. BAR International Series 232, Oxford.

1987. *African civilizations: precolonial cities and states in tropical Africa: an archaeological perspective*. Cambridge University Press, Cambridge.

1991. The salt of Bunyoro: seeking the origins of an African kingdom. *Antiquity* 65, 479–94.

1996. *Kibiro: the salt of Bunyoro, past and present*, British Institute in Eastern Africa, Memoir 13, London.

1997. The cultural and chronological context of Kibiro, Uganda. *African Archaeological Review* 14(1), 25–67.

1998a. Resource exploitation and population aggregation: the case of Kibiro. In *The development of urbanism from a global perspective*, ed. P. Sinclair. Department of Archaeology and Ancient History, Uppsala University. Electronic publication (http://www.arkeologi.uu.se/afr/projects/BOOK/contents.htm).

2000. African city walls: a neglected source? In *Africa's urban past*, ed. D.M. Anderson and R. Rathbone. James Currey, Oxford.

in press. Contained communities in tropical Africa. In *City walls: the urban enceinte in global perspective*, ed. J. Tracy. Cambridge University Press, New York.

Connah, G. (ed.) 1998b. *Transformations in Africa: essays on Africa's later past.* Leicester University Press, London and Washington.

Conrad, D.C. 1994. A town called Dakajalan: the Sunjata tradition and the question of ancient Mali's capital. *Journal of African History* 35(3), 355–77.

Coursey, D.G. 1980. The origins and domestication of yams in Africa. In *West African culture dynamics: archaeological and historical perspectives*, ed. B.K. Swartz and R.E. Dumett, 67–90. Mouton, The Hague.

Craddock, P.T. 1991. Man and metal in ancient Nigeria. *British Museum Magazine* 6, 9.

Craddock, P.T., Ambers, J., Hook, D.R., Farquhar, R.M., Chikwendu, V.E., Umeji, A.C. and Shaw, T. 1997. Metal sources and the bronzes from Igbo-Ukwu, Nigeria. *Journal of Field Archaeology* 24(4), 405–29.

Craddock, P.T. and Picton, J. 1986. Medieval copper alloy production and West African bronze analyses – Part II. *Archaeometry* 28(1), 3–32.

Crawford, O.G.S. 1951. *The Fung kingdom of Sennar.* John Bellows, Gloucester.

Crosby, A.W. 1986. *Ecological imperialism: the biological expansion of Europe, 900–1900.* Cambridge University Press, Cambridge.

Crossland, L.B. 1976. Excavations at Nyarko and Dwinfuor sites of Begho – 1975. *Sankofa* 2, 86–7.

Curtin, P.D. 1973. The lure of Bambuk gold. *Journal of African History* 14(4), 623–31.

Dahalani, S.A. 1992. Itsandramdjini: espace et société. In *Urban origins in Eastern Africa: proceedings of the 1991 workshop in Zanzibar*, ed. P.J.J. Sinclair and A. Juma, 180–6. Swedish Central Board of National Antiquities, Stockholm.

Dalziel, J.M. 1937. *The useful plants of west tropical Africa.* Crown Agents for the Colonies, London.

Damir, B.A. 1988. The Comores proposal. In *Urban origins in Eastern Africa: project proposals and workshop summaries*, ed. P.J.J. Sinclair and S. Wandibba, 23–34. Central Board of National Antiquities, Stockholm.

Daniel, G. 1968. *The first civilizations: the archaeology of their origins.* Thames and Hudson, London.

Dapper, O. 1686. *Description de l'Afrique . . . traduite du Flamand.* Chez Wolfgang, Waesberge, Boom and van Someren, Amsterdam.

Dark, P.J.C. 1973. *An introduction to Benin art and technology.* Clarendon Press, Oxford.

Darling, P.J. 1974. The earthworks of Benin. *Nigerian Field* 39(3), 128–37.

1976. Notes on the earthworks of the Benin Empire. *West African Journal of Archaeology* 6, 143–9.

1982. Ancient linear earthworks of Benin and Ishan, Southern Nigeria, 2 vols. PhD thesis, University of Birmingham.

1984. *Archaeology and history in southern Nigeria*, 2 vols. Cambridge Monographs in African Archaeology 11, BAR International Series 215(i) and (ii), Oxford.

1988. Emerging towns in Benin and Ishan (Nigeria) AD 500–1500. In *State and society: the emergence and development of social hierarchy and political centralization*, ed. J. Gledhill, B. Bender and M.T. Larsen, 121–36. Unwin Hyman, London.

1998. A legacy in earth – ancient Benin and Ishan, southern Nigeria. In *Historical archaeology in Nigeria*, ed. K.W. Wesler, 143–97. Africa World Press, Trenton and Asmara.

Datoo, B.A. 1970. Rhapta: the location and importance of East Africa's first port. *Azania* 5, 65–75.

Davidson, B. 1959. *Old Africa rediscovered*. Gollancz, London.

1970. *The lost cities of Africa*. Little, Brown and Co., Boston. (Originally published 1959 as *Old Africa rediscovered*, Gollancz, London.)

Davison, C.C. and Clark, J.D. 1974. Trade wind beads: an interim report of chemical studies. *Azania* 9, 75–86.

Davison, P. and Harries, P. 1980. Cotton weaving in south-east Africa: its history and technology. *Textile History* 11, 175–92.

de Contenson, H. 1961. Les fouilles à Ouchatei Golo, près d'Axoum, en 1958. *Annales d'Ethiopie* 4, 3–14.

1962. Les monuments d'art Sud-Arabe découverts sur le site de Haoulti (Ethiopie) en 1959. *Syria: Revue d'Art Oriental et d'Archéologie* 39, 64–87.

1963a. Les fouilles de Haoulti en 1959: rapport préliminaire. *Annales d'Ethiopie* 5, 41–86.

1963b. Les fouilles à Axoum en 1958: rapport préliminaire. *Annales d'Ethiopie* 5, 1–40.

1981. Pre-Aksumite culture. In *General history of Africa*, Vol. 2, *Ancient civilizations of Africa*, ed. G. Mokhtar, 341–61. Heinemann, University of California, Unesco; London, Berkeley, Paris.

De Langhe, E., Swennen, R. and Vuylsteke, D. 1995. Plantain in the early Bantu world. *Azania* 29–30, 147–60.

de Maret, P. 1977. Sanga: new excavations, more data, and some related problems. *Journal of African History* 18(3), 321–37.

1979. Luba roots: the first complete Iron Age sequence in Zaïre. *Current Anthropology* 20(1), 233–5.

1981. L'évolution monétaire du Shaba Central entre le 7e et le 18e siècle. *African Economic History* 10, 117–49.

1982. The Iron Age in the west and south. In *The archaeology of Central Africa*, ed. F. Van Noten, 77–96. Akademische Druck- und Verlagsanstalt, Graz, Austria.

1985. Recent archaeological research and dates from Central Africa. *Journal of African History* 26, 129–48.

1992. *Fouilles archéologiques dans la vallée du Haut-Lualaba, Zaïre III: Kamilamba, Kikulu, et Malemba-Nkulu, 1975*. Musée Royal de l'Afrique Centrale, Tervuren, Belgium.

1997. Savanna states. In *Encyclopedia of precolonial Africa: archaeology, history, languages, cultures, and environments*, ed. J.O. Vogel, 496–501. AltaMira Press, Walnut Creek, CA.

de Maret, P. and Clist, B. 1985. Archaeological research in Zaïre. *Nyame Akuma* 26, 41–2.

Denbow, J.R. 1984. Cows and kings: a spatial and economic analysis of a hierarchical Early Iron Age settlement system in eastern Botswana. In *Frontiers: southern African archaeology today*, ed. M. Hall, G. Avery, D.M. Avery, M.L. Wilson and A.J.B. Humphreys, 24–39. Cambridge Monographs in African Archaeology 10, BAR International Series 207, Oxford.

    1986. A new look at the later prehistory of the Kalahari. *Journal of African History* 27, 3–28.

Denham, D., Clapperton, H. and Oudney, W. 1826. *Narrative of travels and discoveries in Northern and Central Africa, in the years 1822, 1823, and 1824*. Murray, London.

Denyer, S. 1978. *African traditional architecture*. Heinemann, London.

Desplagnes, L. 1903. Etude sur les Tumuli du Killi, dans la région de Goundam. *L'Anthropologie* 14, 151–72.

    1951. Fouilles du tumulus d'El Oualedji (Soudan); annoté par R. Mauny. *Bulletin de l'IFAN*, Dakar, 13(4), 1159–73.

Devisse, J. (ed.) 1983. *Tegdaoust III: Recherches sur Aoudaghost (Campagnes 1960–1965)*. ADPF, Paris.

Dewar, R.E. 1996. The archaeology of the early settlement of Madagascar. In *The Indian Ocean in antiquity*, ed. J. Reade, 471–86. Kegan Paul International, London and New York.

Dobrowolski, J. 1991. The first church at Site 'D' in Old Dongola (Sudan). *Archéologie du Nil Moyen* 5, 29–40.

Donley, L.W. 1982. House power: Swahili space and symbolic markers. In *Symbolic and structural archaeology*, ed. I. Hodder, 63–73. Cambridge University Press, Cambridge.

    1987. Life in the Swahili town house reveals the symbolic meaning of spaces and artefact assemblages. *African Archaeological Review* 5, 181–92.

Donley-Reid, L.W. 1990. A structuring structure: the Swahili house. In *Domestic architecture and the use of space: an interdisciplinary cross-cultural study*, ed. S. Kent, 114–26. Cambridge University Press, Cambridge.

Doresse, J. 1959. *Ethiopia*, trans. E. Coult. Elek Books, London.

Dualeh, A. 1996. *The origins and development of Mogadishu AD 1000 to 1850: a study in urban growth along the Benadir coast of southern Somalia*. Studies in African Archaeology 12, Uppsala.

Duarte, R.T. 1993. *Northern Mozambique in the Swahili world: an archaeological approach*. Studies in African Archaeology 4, Central Board of National Antiquities, Sweden, Eduardo Mondlane University, Mozambique, and Uppsala University, Uppsala.

Dumett, R.E. 1979. Precolonial gold mining and the state in the Akan region: with a critique of the Terray Hypothesis. *Research in Economic Anthropology* 2, 37–68.

Dunham, D. 1950. *The royal cemeteries of Kush*, Vol. 1, *El Kurru*. Harvard University Press, Cambridge, MA.

    1955. *The royal cemeteries of Kush*, Vol. 2, *Nuri*. Museum of Fine Arts, Boston, MA.

Dunham, D. and Macadam, M.F.L. 1949. Names and relationships of the royal family of Napata. *Journal of Egyptian Archaeology* 35, 139–49.

Eades, J.S. 1980. *The Yoruba today*. Cambridge University Press, Cambridge.

Earle, T. 1997. *How chiefs come to power: the political economy in prehistory*. Stanford University Press, Stanford, CA.

Edwards, D.N. 1989. *Archaeology and settlement in Upper Nubia in the 1st millennium AD.* Cambridge Monographs in African Archaeology 36, BAR International Series 537, Oxford.

    1996. *The archaeology of the Meroitic state: new perspectives on its social and political organisation.* Cambridge Monographs in African Archaeology 38, BAR International Series 640, Tempus Reparatum, Oxford.

    1999. Letter to author dated 18 February 1999.

Effah-Gyamfi, K. 1979. Bono Manso archaeological research project. *West African Journal of Archaeology* 9, 173–86.

    1985. *Bono Manso: an archaeological investigation into early Akan urbanism.* University of Calgary Press, Calgary.

    1986. Ancient urban sites in Hausaland. *West African Journal of Archaeology* 16, 117–34.

Egharevba, J. 1968. *A short history of Benin*, 4th edn. Ibadan University Press, Ibadan.

Ehret, C. 1979. On the antiquity of agriculture in Ethiopia. *Journal of African History* 20, 161–77.

    1998. *An African Classical Age: Eastern and Southern Africa in world history, 1000 BC to AD 400.* University Press of Virginia, Charlottesville, and James Currey, Oxford.

Eisenstadt, S.N., Abitbol, M. and Chazan, N. (eds.) 1988. *The early state in African perspective: culture, power and division of labor.* Brill, Leiden.

Ellis, W. 1859. *Three visits to Madagascar during the years 1853–1854–1856. Including a journey to the capital. With notices of the natural history of the country and of the present civilisation of the people.* John Murray, London.

Emery, W.B. 1938. *The royal tombs of Ballana and Qustul*, 2 vols. Government Press, Cairo.

    1948. *Nubian treasure: an account of the discoveries at Ballana and Qustul.* Methuen, London.

    1965. *Egypt in Nubia.* Hutchinson, London.

Ethiopian Mapping Authority. 1988. *National atlas of Ethiopia.* Ethiopian Mapping Authority, Addis Ababa.

Evers, T.M. 1984. Sotho-Tswana and Moloko settlement patterns and the Bantu Cattle Pattern. In *Frontiers: southern African archaeology today*, ed. M. Hall, G. Avery, D.M. Avery, M.L. Wilson and A.J.B. Humphreys, 236–47. Cambridge Monographs in African Archaeology 10, BAR International Series 207, Oxford.

Eyo, E. 1974. Odo Ogbe Street and Lafogido: contrasting archaeological sites in Ile-Ife, Western Nigeria. *West African Journal of Archaeology* 4, 99–109.

Fagan, B.M. 1969. Early trade and raw materials in south central Africa. *Journal of African History* 10(1), 1–13.

Fagan, B.M., Phillipson, D.W. and Daniels, S.G.H. 1969. *Iron Age cultures in Zambia (Dambwa, Ingombe Ilede and the Tonga)*, Vol. 2. Chatto and Windus, London.

Fagan, B.M. and Yellen, J.E. 1968. Ivuna: ancient salt-working in southern Tanzania. *Azania* 3, 1–43.

Fage, J.D. and Verity, M. 1978. *An atlas of African history*, 2nd edn. Edward Arnold, London.

Fagg, W. 1963. *Nigerian images.* Lund Humphries, London.

Fairman, H.W. 1938. Preliminary report on the excavations at Sesebi (Sudla) and Amarah West, Anglo-Egyptian Sudan, 1937–8. *Journal of Egyptian Archaeology* 24, 151–6.

Fattovich, R. 1987. Some remarks on the origins of the Aksumite stelae. *Annales d'Ethiopie* 14, 43–69.

1990a. The problem of Punt in the light of recent field work in the Eastern Sudan. *Studien zur Altägyptischen Kultur*, Beiheft 5, 257–72.

1990b. Remarks on the Pre-Aksumite Period in northern Ethiopia. *Journal of Ethiopian Studies* 23, 1–33.

1991. At the periphery of the empire: the Gash Delta (Eastern Sudan). In *Egypt and Africa: Nubia from prehistory to Islam*, ed. W.V. Davies, 40–8. British Museum Press, London.

Filipowiak, W. 1966. Expédition archéologique Polono-Guinéenne à Niani (Guinée). *Africana Bulletin* 4, 116–27.

1969. L'expédition archéologique Polono-Guinéenne à Niani, en 1968. *Africana Bulletin* 11, 107–17.

Fletcher, R. 1995. *The limits of settlement growth: a theoretical outline*. Cambridge University Press, Cambridge.

1998. African urbanism: scale, mobility and transformations. In *Transformations in Africa: essays on Africa's later past*, ed. G. Connah, 104–38. Leicester University Press, London and Washington.

Flight, C. 1975. Gao, 1972: first interim report: a preliminary investigation of the cemetery at Sané. *West African Journal of Archaeology* 5, 81–90.

1976. The Kintampo Culture and its place in the economic prehistory of West Africa. In *Origins of African plant domestication*, ed. J.R. Harlan, J.M.J. de Wet and A.B.L. Stemler, 211–21. Mouton, The Hague.

Forman, W., Forman, B. and Dark, P. 1960. *Benin art*. Hamlyn, London.

Freeman-Grenville, G.S.P. 1960. East African coin finds and their historical significance. *Journal of African History* 1(1), 31–43.

1975. *The East African coast: select documents from the first to the earlier nineteenth century*, 2nd edn. Collings, London.

Fried, M.H. 1967. *The evolution of political society: an essay in political anthropology*. Random House, New York.

Gallay, A., Huysecom, E., Honegger, M. and Mayor, A. 1990. *Hamdallahi, capitale de l'Empire peul du Massina, Mali. Première fouille archéologique, études historiques et ethnoarchéologiques*. Sonderschriften des Frobenius-Instituts 9, Franz Steiner, Stuttgart.

Gallay, A., Pignat, G. and Curdy, P. 1982. Mbolop Tobé (Santhiou Kohel, Sénégal): contribution à la connaissance du mégalithisme sénégambien. *Archives Suisses d'Anthropologie Générale* (Geneva) 46(2), 217–59.

Garlake, P.S. 1966. *The early Islamic architecture of the East African coast*. British Institute in Eastern Africa, Memoir 1, Oxford University Press, London.

1968. The value of imported ceramics in the dating and interpretation of the Rhodesian Iron Age. *Journal of African History* 9(1), 13–33.

1970a. Rhodesian ruins — a preliminary assessment of their styles and chronology. *Journal of African History* 11(4), 495–513.

1970b. The decline of Zimbabwe in the fifteenth century. *Rhodesian Prehistory* 5, 6–8.

1972. Excavations at the Nhunguza and Ruanga Ruins in northern Mashonaland. *South African Archaeological Bulletin* 27, 107–43.

1973. *Great Zimbabwe*. Thames and Hudson, London.

1974. Excavations at Obalara's Land, Ife: an interim report. *West African Journal of Archaeology* 4, 111–48.

1976a. An investigation of Manekweni, Mozambique. *Azania* 11, 25–47.

1976b. Great Zimbabwe: a reappraisal. In *Proceedings of the Panafrican Congress of Prehistory and Quaternary Studies: 7th Session, Addis Ababa, December 1971*, ed. B. Abebe, J. Chavaillon and J.E.G. Sutton, 221–6. Provisional Military Government of Socialist Ethiopia, Ministry of Culture, Addis Ababa.

1977. Excavations on the Woye Asiri Family Land in Ife, Western Nigeria. *West African Journal of Archaeology* 7, 57–96.

1978a. *The kingdoms of Africa*. Elsevier–Phaidon, Oxford.

1978b. Pastoralism and Zimbabwe. *Journal of African History* 19(4), 479–93.

Garlake, P.S. and Garlake, M. 1964. Early ship engravings of the East African coast. *Tanganyika Notes and Records* 63, 197–206.

Garrard, T.F. 1982. Myth and metrology: the early trans-Saharan gold trade. *Journal of African History* 23(4), 443–61.

Garstang, J., Sayce, A.H. and Griffiths, F.W. 1911. *Meroë, the city of the Ethiopians*. Oxford University Press, Oxford.

Gerster, G. 1970. *Churches in rock: Early Christian art in Ethiopia*, trans. R. Hosking. Phaidon, London.

Geus, F. 1991. Burial customs in the upper main Nile: an overview. In *Egypt and Africa: Nubia from prehistory to Islam*, ed. W.V. Davies, 57–73 and plates 4 and 5. British Museum Press, London.

Ghaidan, U. (ed.) 1976. *Lamu: a study in conservation*. East African Literature Bureau, Nairobi.

Gibbon, E. 1952. *The decline and fall of the Roman Empire*, 2 vols. Encyclopaedia Britannica, Inc., Chicago.

Godlewski, W. 1990. The Northern Church in Old Dongola. *Archéologie du Nil Moyen* 4, 37–62.

1991. Old Dongola 1988–1989: House PCH 1. *Archéologie du Nil Moyen* 5, 79–101.

Godlewski, W. and Medeksza, S. 1987. The so-called mosque building in Old Dongola (Sudan): a structural analysis. *Archéologie du Nil Moyen* 2, 185–205.

Good, C.M. 1972. Salt, trade, and disease: aspects of development in Africa's northern Great Lakes Region. *International Journal of African Historical Studies* 5(4), 543–86.

Goodwin, A.J.H. 1957. Archaeology and Benin architecture. *Journal of the Historical Society of Nigeria* 1(2), 65–85.

1963. A bronze snake head and other recent finds in the old palace at Benin. *Man* 63, 142–5.

Goody, J. 1971. *Technology, tradition and the state in Africa*. Oxford University Press, London.

Green, M.M. 1947. *Ibo village affairs: chiefly with reference to the village of Umueke Agbaja*. Sidgwick and Jackson, London.

Griffith, F.Ll. 1922. Oxford excavations in Nubia. *Annals of Archaeology and Anthropology* 9, Liverpool Institute of Archaeology, Liverpool University Press, Liverpool.

Grove, A.T. 1978. *Africa*, 3rd edn. Oxford University Press, Oxford.

Grzymski, K. 1984. Population estimates from Meroitic architecture. *Meroitica* 7, 287–9.

Gutkind, P.C.W. 1960. Notes on the kibuga of Buganda. *Uganda Journal* 24(1), 29–43.
   1963. *The royal capital of Buganda*. Mouton, The Hague.

Gwynne, M.D. 1975. The origin and spread of some domestic food plants of Eastern Africa. In *East Africa and the Orient: cultural syntheses in pre-colonial times*, ed. N. Chittick and R.I. Rotberg, 248–71. Africana Publishing Company, New York and London.

Haas, J. 1982. *The evolution of the prehistoric state*. New York University Press, New York.

Håland, R. 1980. Man's role in the changing habitat of Mema during the old kingdom of Ghana. *Norwegian Archaeological Review* 13, 31–46.

Haaland, R. 1995. Dakawa: an early Iron Age site in the Tanzanian hinterland. *Azania* 29–30, 238–47.

Hall, M. 1987. *The changing past: farmers, kings and traders in southern Africa, 200–1860*. David Philip, Johannesburg.

Hall, R.N. 1905. *Great Zimbabwe*. Methuen, London.

Harlan, J.R. and Pasquereau, J. 1969. Décrue agriculture in Mali. *Economic Botany* 23(1), 70–4.

Harris, D.R. 1976. Traditional systems of plant food production and the origins of agriculture in West Africa. In *Origins of African plant domestication*, ed. J.R. Harlan, J.M.J. de Wet and A.B.L. Stemler, 311–56. Mouton, The Hague.

Hassan, F.A. 1997. Holocene palaeoclimates of Africa. *African Archaeological Review* 14(4), 213–30.

Herbert, E.W. 1973. Aspects of the use of copper in pre-colonial West Africa. *Journal of African History* 14(2), 179–94.
   1984. *Red gold of Africa: copper in precolonial history and culture*. University of Wisconsin Press, Madison.

Herring, R.S. 1979. Hydrology and chronology: The Rodah Nilometer as an aid in dating interlacustrine history. In *Chronology, migration and drought in interlacustrine Africa*, ed. J.B. Webster, 39–86. Longman, London.

Hiernaux, J., de Longrée, E. and De Buyst, J. 1971. *Fouilles archéologiques dans la vallée du Haut-Lualaba. I Sanga 1958*. Musée Royal de l'Afrique Centrale, Tervuren, Belgium.

Hiernaux, J., Maquet, E. and De Buyst, J. 1972. Le cimetière protohistorique de Katoto (Vallée du Lualaba, Congo-Kinshasa). In *Congrès panafricain de préhistoire, Dakar 1967: Actes de 6e session*, ed. H.J. Hugot, 148–58. Les Imprimeries Réunies de Chambéry, Chambéry.

Hinkel, F.W. 1997. Meroitic architecture. In *Sudan: ancient kingdoms of the Nile*, ed. D. Wildung, 392–416, 421. Flammarion, Paris and New York.

Hintze, F. 1959. Preliminary report of the Butana Expedition 1958, made by the Institute for Egyptology of the Humboldt University, Berlin. *Kush* 7, 171–96.

Hodgkin, T. 1975. *Nigerian perspectives*, 2nd edn. Oxford University Press, Oxford.

Hofmann, I. 1991. Der Wein- und Ölimport im Meroitischen Reich. In *Egypt and Africa: Nubia from prehistory to Islam*, ed. W.V. Davies, 234–45. British Museum Press, London.

Hogendorn, J. and Johnson, M. 1986. *The shell money of the slave trade*. Cambridge University Press, Cambridge.

Holl, A. 1985. Background to the Ghana Empire: archaeological investigations on the transition to statehood in the Dhar Tichitt region (Mauritania). *Journal of Anthropological Archaeology* 4, 73–115.

1993. Late Neolithic cultural landscape in southeastern Mauritania: an essay in spatiometrics. In *Spatial boundaries and social dynamics: case studies from food-producing societies*, ed. A. Holl and T.E. Levy, 95–133. International Monographs in Prehistory, Ann Arbor, MI.

1996. Genesis of central Chadic polities. In *Aspects of African archaeology: papers from the 10th Congress of the PanAfrican Association for Prehistory and Related Studies*, ed. G. Pwiti, and R. Soper, 581–91. University of Zimbabwe, Harare.

Home, R. 1982. *City of Blood revisited: a new look at the Benin expedition of 1897*. Collings, London.

Horton, M. 1980. *Shanga 1980: an interim report of the National Museums of Kenya archaeological project at Shanga, during the summer of 1980, as part of the work of Operation Drake*. Operation Drake, London.

1983. Personal communication.

1986. Asiatic colonization of the East African coast: the Manda evidence. *Journal of the Royal Asiatic Society* 2, 201–13.

1987a. Early Muslim trading settlements on the East African coast: new evidence from Shanga. *Antiquaries Journal* 67, 290–323.

1987b. The Swahili Corridor. *Scientific American* 257(3), 76–84.

1991. Africa in Egypt: new evidence from Qasr Ibrim. In *Egypt and Africa: Nubia from prehistory to Islam*, ed. W.V. Davies, 264–77. British Museum Press, London.

1996. *Shanga: the archaeology of a Muslim trading community on the coast of East Africa*. British Institute in Eastern Africa, Memoir 14, London.

Horton, M., Brown, H.M. and Oddy, W.A. 1986. The Mtambwe hoard. *Azania* 21, 115–23 and plate 1.

Horton, M. and Mudida, N. 1993. Exploitation of marine resources: evidence for the origin of the Swahili communities of east Africa. In *The archaeology of Africa: food, metals and towns*, ed. T. Shaw, P. Sinclair, B. Andah and A. Okpoko, 673–93. Routledge, London and New York.

Huffman, T.N. 1971. Cloth from the Iron Age in Rhodesia. *Arnoldia* (Rhodesia) 5, 1–19.

1972. The rise and fall of Zimbabwe. *Journal of African History* 13(3), 353–66.

1974a. Ancient mining and Zimbabwe. *Journal of the South African Institute of Mining and Metallurgy* 74, 238–42.

1974b. *The Leopard's Kopje Tradition*. Museum Memoir No. 6, Trustees of the National Museums and Monuments of Rhodesia. Salisbury, Rhodesia.

1977. Zimbabwe: southern Africa's first town. *Rhodesian Prehistory* 7(15), 9–14.

1981. *Snakes and birds: expressive space at Great Zimbabwe*. Inaugural lecture, University of Witwatersrand, Johannesburg. Witwatersrand University Press, Johannesburg. (Also published in 1981 in *African Studies* 40(2), 131–50.)

1982. Archaeology and ethnohistory of the African Iron Age. *Annual Review of Anthropology* 11, 133–50.

1984. Expressive space in Zimbabwe culture. *Man* (NS) 19, 593–612.

1985a. Letter to author dated 5 September 1985.

1985b. The soapstone birds from Great Zimbabwe. *African Arts* 18(3), 68–73, 99–100.

1986. Iron Age settlement patterns and the origins of class distinction in southern Africa. *Advances in World Archaeology* 5, 291–338.

1996. *Snakes and crocodiles: power and symbolism in ancient Zimbabwe.* Witwatersrand University Press, Johannesburg.

Huffman, T.N. and Hanisch, E.O.M. 1987. Settlement hierarchies in the northern Transvaal: zimbabwe ruins and Venda history. *African Studies* 46, 79–116.

Huffman, T.N. and Vogel, J.C. 1991. The chronology of Great Zimbabwe. *South African Archaeological Bulletin* 46, 61–70.

Hull, R.W. 1976a. *African cities and towns before the European conquest.* Norton, New York.

1976b. Urban design and architecture in precolonial Africa. *Journal of Urban History* 2(4), 387–414.

Hunwick, J. 1971. Songhay, Bornu and Hausaland in the sixteenth century. In *History of West Africa*, Vol. 1, ed. J.F.A. Ajayi and M. Crowder, 202–39. Longman, London.

1973. The mid-fourteenth century capital of Mali. *Journal of African History* 14(2), 195–206.

Iliffe, J. 1995. *Africans: the history of a continent.* Cambridge University Press, Cambridge.

Insoll, T. 1995. A cache of hippopotamus ivory at Gao, Mali; and a hypothesis of its use. *Antiquity* 69, 327–36.

1996a. *Islam, archaeology and history: Gao region (Mali) ca. AD 900–1250.* Cambridge Monographs in African Archaeology 39, BAR International Series 647, Tempus Reparatum, Oxford.

1996b. Settlement and trade in Gao, Mali. In *Aspects of African archaeology: papers from the 10th Congress of the PanAfrican Association for Prehistory and Related Studies*, ed. G. Pwiti and R. Soper, 663–9. University of Zimbabwe, Harare.

Insoll, T. and Shaw, T. 1997. Gao and Igbo-Ukwu: beads, interregional trade, and beyond. *African Archaeological Review* 14(1), 9–23.

Jahadhmy, A.A. 1981. *Learner's Swahili–English, English–Swahili Dictionary.* Evans, London.

Jakobielski, S. 1982. Polish excavations at Old Dongola in 1976 and 1978. In *Nubian studies: proceedings of the Symposium for Nubian Studies, Selwyn College, Cambridge 1978*, ed. J.M. Plumley, 116–26. International Society for Nubian Studies, Aris and Phillips, Warminster, UK.

Johnson, M. 1970a. The cowrie currencies of West Africa, Part I. *Journal of African History* 11(1), 17–49.

1970b. The cowrie currencies of West Africa, Part II. *Journal of African History* 11(3), 331–53.

Johnson, S. 1921. *The history of the Yorubas.* Routledge, London.

Joire, J. 1943. Archaeological discoveries in Senegal. *Man* 43, 49–52.

1955. Découvertes archéologiques dans la région de Rao (Bas-Sénégal). *Bulletin de l'IFAN*, Dakar, 17(B), 249–333.

Jones, E. 1966. *Towns and cities.* Oxford University Press, London.

Jones, E.W. 1956. Ecological studies on the rain forest of southern Nigeria, IV, part II. *Journal of Ecology* 44, 83–117.

Juma, A.M. 1996. The Swahili and the Mediterranean worlds: pottery of the late Roman period from Zanzibar. *Antiquity* 70, 148–54.

Kamuhangire, E.R., Meredith, J. and Robertshaw, P. 1993. Masaka Hill revisited. *Nyame Akuma* 39, 57–60.

Keay, R.W.J. 1959. *Vegetation map of Africa south of the Tropic of Cancer*. Oxford University Press, London.

Kendall, T. 1991. The Napatan palace at Gebel Barkal: a first look at B1200. In *Egypt and Africa: Nubia from prehistory to Islam*, ed. W.V. Davies, 302–13. British Museum Press, London.

1997. *Kerma and the Kingdom of Kush 2500–1500 BC: the archaeological discovery of an ancient Nubian empire*. Smithsonian Institution, Washington.

Kiéthéga, J.-B. 1983. *L'or de la Volta Noire: archéologie et histoire de l'exploitation traditionnelle (Région de Poura, Haute-Volta)*. Karthala, Paris.

Killick, D. 1996. On claims for 'advanced' ironworking technology in precolonial Africa. In *The culture and technology of African iron production*, ed. P.R. Schmidt, 247–66. University Press of Florida, Gainesville.

Killick, D. and Bocoum, H. 1998. Metals and metallurgy in the Middle Senegal River Valley. Unpublished abstracts from Society of Africanist Archaeologists 14th Biennial Conference, Syracuse University, Syracuse, New York, May 20–24, 1998, 39.

Kirkman, J.S. 1952. The excavations at Kilepwa. An introduction to the medieval archaeology of the Kenya coast. *Antiquaries Journal* 32, 168–84.

1954. *The Arab city of Gedi: excavations at the Great Mosque. Architecture and finds*. Oxford University Press, London.

1959. Mnarani of Kilifi: the mosques and tombs. *Ars Orientalis* 3, 95–112.

1960. *The tomb of the dated inscription at Gedi*. Royal Anthropological Institute of Great Britain and Ireland, Occasional Paper 14, London.

1963. *Gedi: the Palace*. Mouton and Co., The Hague.

1964. *Men and monuments on the East African coast*. Lutterworth Press, London.

1966. *Ungwana on the Tana*. Mouton and Co., The Hague.

1975a. Some conclusions from archaeological excavations on the coast of Kenya, 1948–1966. In *East Africa and the Orient: cultural syntheses in pre-colonial times*, ed. N. Chittick and R.I. Rotberg, 226–47. Africana Publishing Company, New York and London.

1975b. *Gedi*, 8th edn. National Museums of Kenya, Nairobi.

Kirwan, L.P. 1972. The Christian topography and the Kingdom of Axum. *Geographical Journal* 138(2), 166–77.

Kluckhohn, C. 1960. The moral order in the expanding society. In *City invincible: a symposium on urbanization and cultural development in the ancient Near East*, ed. C.H. Kraeling and R.M. Adams, 391–404. Chicago University Press, Chicago.

Kobishchanov, Y.M. 1979. *Axum*, trans. L.T. Kapitanoff, ed. J.W. Michels. Pennsylvania State University Press, University Park and London.

Kobish[ch]anov, Y.M. 1981. Aksum: political system, economics and culture, first to fourth century. In *General history of Africa*, Vol. 2, *Ancient civilizations of Africa*, ed. G. Mokhtar, 381–400. Heinemann, University of California, Unesco; London, Berkeley, Paris.

Krapf-Askari, E. 1969. *Yoruba towns and cities*. Clarendon Press, Oxford.

Krencker, D. 1913. *Deutsche Aksum-Expedition*, Band II. Georg Reimer, Berlin.

Kuper, A. 1980. Symbolic dimensions of the Southern Bantu homestead. *Africa* 50(1), 8–23.

1982. *Wives for cattle: bridewealth and marriage in southern Africa*. Routledge and Kegan Paul, London.

Kuper, L. and Smith, M.G. (eds.) 1969. *Pluralism in Africa*. University of California Press, Berkeley and Los Angeles.

Lacovara, P. 1991. The stone vase deposit at Kerma. In *Egypt and Africa: Nubia from prehistory to Islam*, ed. W.V. Davies, 118–28. British Museum Press, London.

Lanning, E.C. 1953. Ancient earthworks in western Uganda. *Uganda Journal* 17(1), 51–62.

1955. The Munsa earthworks. *Uganda Journal* 19(2), 177–82.

1960. The earthworks at Kibengo, Mubende District. *Uganda Journal* 24(2), 183–96.

1970. Ntusi: an ancient capital site in western Uganda. *Azania* 5, 39–54.

LaViolette, A. 1996. Report on excavations at the Swahili site of Pujini, Pemba Island, Tanzania. *Nyame Akuma* 46, 72–83.

Law, R. 1978. Slaves, trade, and taxes: the material base of political power in pre-colonial West Africa. *Research in Economic Anthropology* 1, 37–52.

1980a. Wheeled transport in pre-colonial West Africa. *Africa* 50(3), 249–62.

1980b. *The horse in West African history*. Oxford University Press, Oxford.

Lawal, B. 1973. Dating problems at Igbo-Ukwu. *Journal of African History* 14(1), 1–8.

Leclant, J. 1973. Glass from the Meroitic necropolis of Sedeinga (Sudanese Nubia). *Journal of Glass Studies* 15, 52–68.

Lenoble, P. 1989. 'A new type of mound-grave' (continued): le tumulus à enceinte d'Umm Makharoqa, près d'el Hobagi (AMS NE-36-0/7-0-3). *Archéologie du Nil Moyen* 3, 93–120.

Lenoble, P. and Sharif, N.M. 1992. Barbarians at the gates? The royal mounds of El Hobagi and the end of Meroë. *Antiquity* 66, 626–35.

Levtzion, N. 1973. *Ancient Ghana and Mali*. Methuen, London.

Liesegang, G. 1972. Archaeological sites on the Bay of Sofala. *Azania* 7, 147–59.

Livingstone, F.B. 1967. The origin of the sickle-cell gene. In *Reconstructing African culture history*, ed. C. Gabel and N.R. Bennett, 139–66. Boston University Press, Boston.

Lonsdale, J. 1981. States and social processes in Africa: a historiographical survey. *African Studies Review* 24(2 and 3), 139–225.

Lovejoy, P.E. 1986. *Salt of the desert sun: a history of salt production and trade in the central Sudan*. Cambridge University Press, Cambridge.

Lucas, A. and Harris, J.R. 1962. *Ancient Egyptian materials and industries*, 4th edn. Edward Arnold, London.

Lugard, F.D. 1893. In British Parliamentary Papers. Africa. No. 2 (1893). c.–6848, 1–102.

1903. *Northern Nigeria: report for 1902*. Colonial Reports: Annual, No. 409, His Majesty's Stationery Office, London.

Mabogunje, A.L. 1962. *Yoruba towns*. Ibadan University Press, Ibadan.

1968. *Urbanization in Nigeria*. University of London Press, London.

Macamo, S.L. and Duarte, R.T. 1996. Oral tradition and the Songo Ruins. In *Aspects of African archaeology: papers from the 10th Congress of the PanAfrican Association for Prehistory and Related Studies*, ed. G. Pwiti and R. Soper, 561–3. University of Zimbabwe, Harare.

MacDonald, K.C. 1995. Analysis of the mammalian, avian, and reptilian remains. In *Excavations at Jenné-jeno, Hambarketolo, and Kaniana (Inland Niger Delta, Mali), the 1981 season*, ed. S.K. McIntosh, 291–318. University of California Press, Berkeley and Los Angeles.

1998. Before the Empire of Ghana: pastoralism and the origins of cultural complexity in the Sahel. In *Transformations in Africa: essays on Africa's later past*, ed. G. Connah, 71–103. Leicester University Press, London and Washington.

1999a. Letter to author dated 15 March 1999.

1999b. More forgotten tells of Mali: an archaeologist's journey from here to Timbukti. *Archaeology International* 1, 40–2.

MacDonald, K.C. and MacDonald, R.H. 1999. The origins and development of domesticated animals in arid West Africa. In *The origins and development of African livestock*, ed. R.M. Blench and K.C. MacDonald. University College London and Routledge, London.

McIntosh, R.J. 1983. Floodplain geomorphology and human occupation of the upper Inland Delta of the Niger. *Geographical Journal* 149(2), 182–201.

1998. *The peoples of the Middle Niger: the Island of Gold*. Blackwell, Oxford.

McIntosh, R.J. and McIntosh, S.K. 1981a. The Inland Niger Delta before the Empire of Mali: evidence from Jenné-Jeno. *Journal of African History* 22, 1–22.

1981b. West African prehistory. *American Scientist* 69, 602–13.

1983. Forgotten tells of Mali: new evidence of urban beginnings in West Africa. *Expedition* 25, 35–46.

1988. From *Siècles Obscurs* to revolutionary centuries on the Middle Niger. *World Archaeology* 20(1), 141–65.

McIntosh, R.J., Sinclair, P., Togola, T., Petrèn, M. and McIntosh, S.K. 1996. Exploratory archaeology at Jenné and Jenné-jeno (Mali). *Sahara* 8, 19–28.

McIntosh, S.K. 1994. Changing perceptions of West Africa's past: archaeological research since 1988. *Journal of Archaeological Research* 2(2), 165–98.

McIntosh, S.K. (ed.) 1995. *Excavations at Jenné-jeno, Hambarketolo, and Kaniana (Inland Niger Delta, Mali), the 1981 season*. University of California Press, Berkeley and Los Angeles.

1999. *Beyond chiefdoms: pathways to complexity in Africa*. Cambridge University Press, Cambridge.

McIntosh, S.K. and McIntosh, R.J. 1979. Initial perspectives on prehistoric subsistence in the Inland Niger Delta (Mali). *World Archaeology* 11(2), 227–43.

1980. *Prehistoric investigations in the region of Jenné, Mali*, 2 vols. Cambridge Monographs in African Archaeology 2, BAR International Series 89(i) and (ii), Oxford.

1983. Current directions in West African prehistory. *Annual Review of Anthropology* 12, 215–58.

1984. The early city in West Africa: towards an understanding. *African Archaeological Review* 2, 73–98.

1986a. Archaeological reconnaissance in the region of Timbuktu, Mali. *National Geographic Research* 2(3), 302–19.

1986b. Recent archaeological research and dates from West Africa. *Journal of African History* 27, 413–42.

1988. From stone to metal: new perspectives on the later prehistory of West Africa. *Journal of World Prehistory* 2(1), 89–133.

1993a. Cities without citadels: understanding urban origins along the middle Niger. In *The archaeology of Africa: food, metals and towns*, ed. T. Shaw, P. Sinclair, B. Andah and A. Okpoko, 622–41. Routledge, London and New York.

1993b. Field survey in the tumulus zone of Senegal. *African Archaeological Review* 11, 73–107.

McIntosh, S.K., McIntosh, R.J. and Bocoum, H. 1992. The Middle Senegal Valley Project: preliminary results from the 1990–91 field season. *Nyame Akuma* 38, 47–61.

McLeod, M.D. 1981. *The Asante*. British Museum, London.

McWhirter, N. 1980. *Guinness book of records*. Guinness Superlatives Ltd, London.

Maggs, T. 1972. The Iron Age of the Orange Free State. In *Congrès panafricain de préhistoire, Dakar 1967: Actes de 6e session*, ed. H.J. Hugot, 175–81. Les Imprimeries Réunies de Chambéry, Chambéry.

1984. Iron Age settlement and subsistence patterns in the Tugela River Basin, Natal. In *Frontiers: southern African archaeology today*, ed. M. Hall, G. Avery, D.M. Avery, M.L. Wilson and A.J.B. Humphreys, 194–206. Cambridge Monographs in African Archaeology 10, BAR International Series 207, Oxford.

1993. Sliding doors at Mokgatle's, a nineteenth century Tswana town in the central Transvaal. *South African Archaeological Bulletin* 48, 32-6.

1995. The Early Iron Age in the extreme south: some patterns and problems. *Azania* 29–30, 171–8.

Mahachi, G. and Ndoro, W. 1997. The socio-political context of southern African Iron Age studies with special reference to Great Zimbabwe. In *Caves, monuments and texts: Zimbabwean archaeology today*, ed. G. Pwiti, 89–107. Studies in African Archaeology 14, Department of Archaeology and Ancient History, Uppsala University, Uppsala.

Maliphant, G.K., Rees, A.R. and Roese, P.M. 1976. Defence systems of the Benin empire — Uwan. *West African Journal of Archaeology* 6, 121–30.

Manson-Bahr, P.E.C. and Apted, F.I.C. 1982. *Manson's tropical diseases*, 18th edn. Baillière Tindall, London.

Mason, R. 1969. *Prehistory of the Transvaal: a record of human activity* (1st edn 1962). Witwatersrand University Press, Johannesburg.

Matenga, E. 1993. *Archaeological figurines from Zimbabwe*. Studies in African Archaeology 5, Uppsala University, Sweden, and Queen Victoria Museum, Zimbabwe.

1998. *The soapstone birds of Great Zimbabwe: symbols of a nation*. African Publishing Group, Harare.

Matthews, D. and Mordini, A. 1959. The monastery of Debra Damo, Ethiopia. *Archaeologia* 97, 1–58.

Mauny, R. 1961. *Tableau géographique de l'Ouest Africain au Moyen-Age d'après les sources écrites, la tradition et l'archéologie*. Mémoires de l'IFAN 61, Dakar.

1970. *Les siècles obscurs de l'Afrique noire: histoire et archéologie*. Fayard, [Paris].

1978. Trans-Saharan contacts and the Iron Age in West Africa. In *The Cambridge history of Africa*, Vol. 2, ed. J.D. Fage, 272–341. Cambridge University Press, Cambridge.

Mayor, A. 1995. Hamdallahi, capital of the Fulani empire of Macina (Mali): from excavations to interpretations with pluridisciplinarity. Unpublished abstracts from the 10th Congress of the PanAfrican Association for Prehistory and Related Studies, 18–23 June 1995, Harare, Zimbabwe, 54–5. University of Zimbabwe in association with National Museums and Monuments of Zimbabwe.

1996. Hamdallahi, capital of the Fulani empire of Macina, Mali: a multidisciplinary approach. In *Aspects of African archaeology: papers from the 10th Congress of the PanAfrican Association for Prehistory and Related Studies*, ed. G. Pwiti and R. Soper, 671–80. University of Zimbabwe, Harare.

Meillassoux, C. 1991. *The anthropology of slavery: the womb of iron and gold*. Athlone Press, London.

Mennell, F.P. and Summers, R. 1955. The 'ancient workings' of Southern Rhodesia. *Occasional Papers of the National Museum of Southern Rhodesia* 20, 765–78.

Meyboom, P.G.P. 1995. *The Nile Mosaic of Palestrina: early evidence of Egyptian religion in Italy*. Brill, Leiden.

Michels, J.W. 1988. The Axumite kingdom: a settlement archaeology perspective. In *Proceedings of the Ninth International Congress of Ethiopian Studies, Moscow, 26–29 August 1986*, ed. An.A. Gromyko, Vol. 6, 173–83. Nauka Publishers, Central Department of Oriental Literature, Moscow.

1990. Review article: Excavations at Aksum. *African Archaeological Review* 8, 177–87.

1994. Regional political organization in the Axum–Yeha area during the Pre-Axumite and Axumite eras. In *Etudes éthiopiennes I. Actes de la Xe conférence internationale des études éthiopiennes*, ed. C. Lepage, 61–80. La Société français pour les études éthiopiennes, Paris.

Miller, J.I. 1969. *The spice trade of the Roman Empire, 29 BC to AD 641*. Oxford University Press, London.

Momin, K.N. 1989. Urban Ijebu Ode: an archaeological, topographical, toponymical perspective. *West African Journal of Archaeology* 19, 37–49.

Monod, T. 1969. Le 'Ma'den Ijâfen': une épave caravanière ancienne dans la Majâbat Al-Koubrâ. In *Actes du Ier Colloque international d'archéologie africaine, 1966*, Fort-Lamy, 286–320.

Moody, H.L.B. 1967. Ganuwa — the walls of Kano City. *Nigeria Magazine* 92, 19–38.

n.d. [1970]. *The walls and gates of Kano City*. Department of Antiquities, Nigeria.

Morais, J. and Sinclair, P. 1980. Manyikeni, a Zimbabwe in Southern Mozambique. In *Proceedings of the 8th Panafrican Congress of Prehistory and Quaternary Studies, Nairobi, 5 to 10 September 1977*, ed. R.E. Leakey and B.A. Ogot, 351–4. The International Louis Leakey Memorial Institute for African Prehistory, Nairobi.

Morton-Williams, P. 1972. Some factors in the location, growth and survival of towns in West Africa. In *Man, settlement and urbanism*, ed. P.J. Ucko, R. Tringham and G.W. Dimbleby, 883–90. Duckworth, London.

Mumford, L. 1961. *The city in history: its origins, its transformations, and its prospects*. Secker and Warburg, London.

Munro-Hay, S. 1980. Ezana (Ezana/Ezanas): some numismatic comments. *Azania* 15, 109–19.

1982. The foreign trade of the Aksumite port of Adulis. *Azania* 17, 107–25.

1989a. *Excavations at Aksum: an account of research at the ancient Ethiopian capital directed in 1972–74 by the late Dr Neville Chittick*. British Institute in Eastern Africa, Memoir 10, London.

1989b. The British Museum excavations at Adulis, 1868. *Antiquaries Journal* 69(1), 43–52 and plates III–VI.

1990. The rise and fall of Aksum: chronological considerations. *Journal of Ethiopian Studies* 23, 47–53.

1991. *Aksum: an African civilisation of late antiquity*. Edinburgh University Press, Edinburgh.

1996. Aksumite overseas interests. In *The Indian Ocean in Antiquity*, ed. J. Reade, 403–16. Kegan Paul International, London and New York.

Munson, P.J. 1976. Archaeological data on the origins of cultivation in the southwestern Sahara and their implications for West Africa. In *Origins of African plant domestication*, ed. J.R. Harlan, J.M.J. de Wet and A.B.L. Stemler, 187–209. Mouton, The Hague.

Murdock, G.P. 1959. *Africa: its peoples and their culture history*. McGraw-Hill, New York.

Mutoro, H.W. 1995. Tana ware and the *kaya* settlements of the coastal hinterland of Kenya. *Azania* 29–30, 257–60.

1998. Precolonial trading systems of the East African interior. In *Transformations in Africa: essays on Africa's later past*, ed. G. Connah, 186–203. Leicester University Press, London and Washington.

Negussie, C. 1994. *Aksum and Matara: a stratigraphic comparison of two Aksumite towns*. Department of Archaeology, Uppsala University, Sweden.

Nenquin, J. 1961. *Salt: a study in economic prehistory*. Dissertationes Archaeologicae Gandenses 6. De Tempel, Bruges.

1963. *Excavations at Sanga, 1957: the protohistoric necropolis*. Musée Royal de l'Afrique Centrale, Tervuren.

Neumann, K., Ballouche, A. and Klee, M. 1996. The emergence of plant food production in the West African Sahel: new evidence from northeast Nigeria and northern Burkina Faso. In *Aspects of African archaeology: papers from the 10th Congress of the PanAfrican Association for Prehistory and Related Studies*, ed. G. Pwiti and R. Soper, 441–8. University of Zimbabwe, Harare.

Nzewunwa, N. 1980. *The Niger Delta: aspects of its prehistoric economy and culture*. Cambridge Monographs in African Archaeology 1, BAR International Series 75, Oxford.

O'Connor, D. 1991. Early states along the Nubian Nile. In *Egypt and Africa: Nubia from prehistory to Islam*, ed. W.V. Davies, 145–65. British Museum Press, London.

1993. *Ancient Nubia: Egypt's rival in Africa*. University of Pennsylvania, Philadelphia.

O'Fahey, R.S. and Spaulding, J.L. 1974. *Kingdoms of the Sudan*. Methuen, London.

Ojo, G.J.A. 1966a. *Yoruba culture*. University of London Press, London.

1966b. *Yoruba palaces*. University of London Press, London.

Okafor, E.E. 1993. New evidence on early iron-smelting from southeastern Nigeria. In *The archaeology of Africa: food, metals and towns*, ed. T. Shaw, P. Sinclair, B. Andah and A. Okpoko, 432–48. Routledge, London and New York.

Okpoko, A.I. 1998. Archaeology and the study of early urban centres in Nigeria. *African Study Monographs* (Center for African Area Studies, Kyoto University) 19(1), 35–54.

Oliver, P. (ed.) 1971. *Shelter in Africa*. Praeger, New York.

Oliver, R. 1953. A question about the Bachwezi. *Uganda Journal* 17(2), 135–7.

1959a. The royal tombs of Buganda. *Uganda Journal* 23(2), 124–33.

1959b. Ancient capital sites of Ankole. *Uganda Journal* 23(1), 51–63.

1993. *The African experience* (1st edn 1991). Pimlico, London.

Oliver, R. and Fage, J.D. 1962. *A short history of Africa*. Penguin, Harmondsworth.

Onwuejeogwu, M.A. and Onwuejeogwu, B.O. 1977. The search for the missing links in dating and interpreting the Igbo-Ukwu finds. *Paideuma: Mitteilungen zur Kulturkunde* 23, 169–88.

Oxford English Dictionary, 1933. Vol. 10, Clarendon Press, Oxford (1970 reprint).

Ozanne, P. 1969. A new archaeological survey of Ife. *Odu* (NS) 1, 28–45.

Pankhurst, R. 1961. *An introduction to the economic history of Ethiopia from early times to 1800*. Lalibela House, distributed by Sidgwick and Jackson, London.

1979. Ethiopian medieval and post-medieval capitals: their development and principal features. *Azania* 14, 1–19.

Paribeni, R. 1907. Ricerche nel luogo dell'antica Adulis (Colonia Eritrea). *Monumenti Antichi, Reale Accademia dei Lincei* 18, 437–572 and plates I–XI.

Parkington, J. and Cronin, M. 1979. The size and layout of Mgungundlovu 1829–1838. *South African Archaeological Society Goodwin Series* 3, 133–48.

Patterson, K.D. 1993. Disease ecologies of Sub-Saharan Africa. In *The Cambridge world history of human disease*, ed. K.F. Kiple, 447–52. Cambridge University Press, Cambridge.

Phillipson, D.W. 1977a. *The later prehistory of eastern and southern Africa*. Heinemann, London.

1977b. The excavation of Gobedra rock-shelter, Axum: an early occurrence of cultivated finger millet in northern Ethiopia. *Azania* 12, 53–82.

1993a. *African archaeology*, 2nd edn. Cambridge University Press, Cambridge.

1993b. The antiquity of cultivation and herding in Ethiopia. In *The archaeology of Africa: food, metals and towns*, ed. T. Shaw, P. Sinclair, B. Andah and A. Okpoko, 344–57. Routledge, London and New York.

1994. The significance and symbolism of the Aksumite stelae. *Cambridge Archaeological Journal* 4(2), 189–210.

1995. Excavations at Aksum, Ethiopia, 1993–4. *Antiquaries Journal* 75, 1–41.

1996. The 1993–94 excavations at Aksum, Ethiopia. In *Aspects of African archaeology: Papers from the 10th Congress of the PanAfrican Association for Prehistory and Related Studies*, ed. G. Pwiti and R. Soper, 601–9. University of Zimbabwe, Harare.

1998a. *Ancient Ethiopia. Aksum: its antecedents and successors*. British Museum Press, London.

1998b. Personal communication.

1999. Letter to author dated 25 February 1999.

Phillipson, D.W. (ed.) 1997. *The monuments of Aksum* (based on the work of the Deutsche Aksum-Expedition of 1906). Addis Ababa University Press and British Institute in Eastern Africa, Addis Ababa and London.

Phillipson, D.W. and Reynolds, A. 1996. BIEA excavations at Aksum, Northern Ethiopia, 1995. *Azania* 31, 99–147.

Phillipson, L. 1999. Letter to author dated 20 July 1999.

Phimister, I.R. 1974. 'Ancient' mining near Great Zimbabwe. *Journal of the South African Institute of Mining and Metallurgy* 74, 233–7.

1976. Pre-colonial gold mining in southern Zambezia: a reassessment. *African Social Research* 21, 1–30.

Pigafetta, F. 1591. *A report of the Kingdom of Congo*, trans. M. Hutchinson, 1881. Murray, London.

Pikirayi, I. 1990. The Portuguese phase of the Later Iron Age of Zimbabwe. In *Urban origins in Eastern Africa: proceedings of the 1989 Madagascar workshop*, ed. P.J.J. Sinclair and J.-A. Rakotoarisoa, 187–97. Central Board of National Antiquities, Stockholm.

    1992. Loopholed stone structures in a regional and local context: towards a definition of an archaeological tradition in northern Zimbabwe. In *Urban origins in Eastern Africa: proceedings of the 1991 workshop in Zanzibar*, ed. P.J.J. Sinclair and A. Juma, 120–39. Swedish Central Board of National Antiquities, Stockholm.

    1993. *The archaeological identity of the Mutapa state: towards an historical archaeology of northern Zimbabwe*. Studies in African Archaeology 6, Societas Archaeologica Upsaliensis, Uppsala.

Pirenne, J. 1970. Haoulti, Gobochela (Melazo) et le site antique. *Annales d'Ethiopie* 8, 117–27.

Pistorius, J.C.C. 1992. *Molokwane: an Iron Age Bakwena village: early Tswana settlement in the western Transvaal*. Perskor, Johannesburg.

Pitt Rivers, Lieutenant-General. 1900. *Antique works of art from Benin*. Printed privately, London.

Plant, R. 1985. *Architecture of the Tigre, Ethiopia*. Ravens Educational and Development Services, Worcester.

Portères, R. 1970. Primary cradles of agriculture in the African continent. In *Papers in African prehistory*, ed. J.D. Fage and R.A. Oliver, 43–58. Cambridge University Press, Cambridge. (Originally published in 1962 in French in *Journal of African History* 3(2), 195–210.)

Posnansky, M. 1968. The excavation of an Ankole capital site at Bweyorere. *Uganda Journal* 32(2), 165–82.

    1969. Bigo bya Mugenyi. *Uganda Journal* 33(2), 125–50.

    1973. Aspects of early West African trade. *World Archaeology* 5(2), 149–62.

    1975. Connections between the lacustrine peoples and the coast. In *East Africa and the Orient: cultural syntheses in pre-colonial times*, ed. N. Chittick and R.I. Rotberg, 216–25. Africana Publishing Company, New York and London.

    1976. Archaeology and the origins of the Akan society in Ghana. In *Problems in economic and social archaeology*, ed. G. de G. Sieveking, I.H.Longworth and K.E.Wilson, 49–59. Duckworth, London.

    1980. Trade and the development of the state and town in Iron Age West Africa. In *Proceedings of the 8th Panafrican Congress of Prehistory and Quaternary Studies, Nairobi, 5 to 10 September 1977*, ed. R.E. Leakey and B.A. Ogot, 373–5. The International Louis Leakey Memorial Institute for African Prehistory, Nairobi.

    1987. Prelude to Akan civilization. In *The Golden Stool: studies of the Asante center and periphery*, ed. E. Schildkrout, 14–22. Anthropological Papers of the American Museum of Natural History, New York, Vol. 65, Part 1.

Posnansky, M. and McIntosh, R. 1976. New radiocarbon dates for Northern and Western Africa. *Journal of African History* 17(2), 161–95.

Powell, J.E. (trans.) 1949. *Herodotus*, 2 vols. Clarendon Press, Oxford.

Price, B.J. 1978. Secondary state formation: an explanatory model. In *Origins of the state: the anthropology of political evolution*, ed. R. Cohen and E.L. Service, 161–86. Institute for the Study of Human Issues, Philadelphia.

Prins, A.H.J. 1982. The *mtepe* of Lamu, Mombasa and the Zanzibar sea. In *From Zinj to Zanzibar: studies in history, trade and society on the eastern coast of Africa* (*Paideuma* 28), ed. J. de V. Allen and T.H. Wilson, 85–100.

Prins, G. 1980. *The hidden hippopotamus: reappraisal in African history: the early colonial experience in western Zambia.* Cambridge University Press, Cambridge.

Pullan, R.A. 1974. Farmed parkland in West Africa. *Savanna* 3(2), 119–51.

Pwiti, G. 1996. *Continuity and change: an archaeological study of farming communities in northern Zimbabwe AD 500–1700.* Studies in African Archaeology 13, Department of Archaeology, Uppsala University, Uppsala.

Radimilahy, C. 1992. Travaux de reconnaissance archéologique à Mahilaka en 1989–1990: rapport préliminaire. In *Urban origins in Eastern Africa: proceedings of the 1991 workshop in Zanzibar*, ed. P.J.J. Sinclair and A. Juma, 222–9. Swedish Central Board of National Antiquities, Stockholm.

1998. *Mahilaka: an archaeological investigation of an early town in northwestern Madagascar.* Studies in African Archaeology 15, Department of Archaeology and Ancient History, Uppsala University.

Rakotoarisoa, J.-A. 1998. *Mille ans d'occupation humaine dans le Sud-Est de Madagascar: Anosy, une île au milieu des terres.* Editions L'Harmattan, Paris.

Ramos, M. 1980. Une enceinte (Monomotapa?) peu connue du plateau du Songo, Mozambique. In *Proceedings of the 8th Panafrican Congress of Prehistory and Quaternary Studies, Nairobi, 5 to 10 September 1977*, ed. R.E. Leakey and B.A. Ogot, 373–5. The International Louis Leakey Memorial Institute for African Prehistory, Nairobi.

Randall-MacIver, D. 1971. *Mediaeval Rhodesia*, 1st edn 1906. Cass, London.

Randles, W.G.L. 1968. *L'ancien royaume du Congo.* Mouton, Paris.

1972. Pre-colonial urbanization in Africa south of the Equator. In *Man, settlement and urbanism*, ed. P.J. Ucko, R. Tringham and G.W. Dimbleby, 891–7. Duckworth, London.

Rathje, W.L. 1971. The origin and development of lowland Maya classic civilization. *American Antiquity* 36, 275–85.

1972. Praise the gods and pass the metates: a hypothesis of the development of lowland rainforest civilizations in Mesoamerica. In *Contemporary archaeology*, ed. M.P. Leone, 365–92. Southern Illinois University Press, Carbondale.

Ravenstein, E.G. (trans. and ed.) 1898. *A journal of the first voyage of Vasco da Gama, 1497–1499.* Hakluyt Society, London.

Reader, J. 1997. *Africa: a biography of the continent.* Hamish Hamilton, London.

Redman, C.L. 1978. *The rise of civilization: from early farmers to urban society in the ancient Near East.* Freeman, San Francisco.

Reefe, T.Q. 1981. *The rainbow and the kings: a history of the Luba Empire to 1891.* University of California Press, Berkeley.

1983. The societies of the eastern savanna. In *History of Central Africa*, ed. D. Birmingham and P.M. Martin, Vol. 1, 160–204. Longman, London and New York.

Reid, A. 1990. Ntusi and its hinterland: further investigations of the Later Iron Age and pastoral ecology in southern Uganda. *Nyame Akuma* 33, 26–8.

1996. Ntusi and the development of social complexity in southern Uganda. In *Aspects of African archaeology: Papers from the 10th Congress of the PanAfrican Association for*

Prehistory and Related Studies, ed. G. Pwiti and R. Soper, 621–7. University of Zimbabwe, Harare.

Reid, A. and Meredith, J. 1993. Houses, pots, and more cows: the 1991 excavation season at Ntusi. *Nyame Akuma* 40, 58–61.

Reid, A. and Robertshaw, P. 1987. A new look at Ankole capital sites. *Azania* 22, 83–8.

Reisner, G.A. 1923. *Excavations at Kerma*, Parts I–III, Parts IV–V, Harvard African Studies 5 and 6. Peabody Museum of Harvard University, Cambridge, MA.

Renfrew, C. 1972. *The emergence of civilization: the Cyclades and the Aegean in the third millennium BC.* Methuen, London.

1983. The emergence of civilization. In *The encyclopedia of ancient civilizations*, ed. A. Cotterell, 12–20. Macmillan, London.

Richards, P.W. 1952. *The tropical rain forest: an ecological study.* Cambridge University Press, Cambridge.

Ricks, T.M. 1970. Persian Gulf seafaring and East Africa: ninth–twelfth centuries. *African Historical Studies* 3(2), 339–57.

Robert, D. 1970. Les fouilles de Tegdaoust. *Journal of African History* 11, 471–93.

Robert, D., Robert, S. and Devisse, J. (eds.) 1970. *Tegdaoust: recherches sur Aoudaghost*, Vol. 1. Arts et Métiers Graphiques, Paris.

Robert, S. and Robert, D. 1972. Douze années de recherches archéologiques en République Islamique de Mauritanie. *Annales de la Faculté des Lettres et Sciences Humaines, Université de Dakar* 2, 195–233.

Robert-Chaleix, D. 1989. *Tegdaoust V: une concession médiévale à Tegdaoust: implantation, évolution d'une unité d'habitation.* Editions Recherche sur les Civilisations, ADPF, Paris.

Robertshaw, P. 1988. The Interlacustrine Region: a progress report. *Nyame Akuma* 30, 37–8.

1991. Recent archaeological surveys in western Uganda. *Nyame Akuma* 36, 40–6.

1994. Archaeological survey, ceramic analysis, and state formation in western Uganda. *African Archaeological Review* 12, 105–31.

1997. Munsa earthworks: a preliminary report on recent excavations. *Azania* 32, 1–20.

1999. Letter to author dated 25 February 1999.

Robertshaw, P. and Kamuhangire, E.R. 1996. The present in the past: archaeological sites, oral traditions, shrines and politics in Uganda. In *Aspects of African archaeology: Papers from the 10th Congress of the PanAfrican Association for Prehistory and Related Studies*, ed. G. Pwiti and R. Soper, 739–43. University of Zimbabwe, Harare.

Robertshaw, P., Kamuhangire, E.R., Reid, A., Young, R., Childs, S.T. and Pearson, N. 1997. Archaeological research in Bunyoro-Kitara: preliminary results. *Nyame Akuma* 48, 70–7.

Robins, P.A. and Whitty, A. 1966. Excavations at Harleigh Farm, near Rusape, Rhodesia. *South African Archaeological Bulletin* 21, 61–80.

Robinson, K.R. 1959. *Khami ruins: report on excavations undertaken for the Commission for the Preservation of Natural and Historical Monuments and Relics, Southern Rhodesia, 1947–1955.* Cambridge University Press, Cambridge.

Robinson, K.R., Summers, R. and Whitty, A. 1961. *Zimbabwe excavations 1958.* The National Museums of Southern Rhodesia, Occasional Papers, 3(23A), 157–332.

Roese, P.M. 1981. Erdwälle und Gräben im ehemaligen Königreich von Benin. *Anthropos* 76, 166–209.

Roth, H.L. 1903. *Great Benin: its customs, art and horrors.* King, Halifax.

Rowley-Conwy, P. 1988. The camel in the Nile Valley: new radiocarbon accelerator (AMS) dates from Qasr Ibrim. *Journal of Egyptian Archaeology* 74, 245–8 and Plate XXXV.

1989. Nubia AD 0–550 and the 'Islamic' agricultural revolution: preliminary botanical evidence from Qasr Ibrim, Egyptian Nubia. *Archéologie du Nil Moyen* 3, 131–8.

1991. Sorghum from Qasr Ibrim, Egyptian Nubia, c.800 BC–AD 1811: a preliminary study. In *New light on early farming: recent developments in palaeoethnobotany*, ed. J.M. Renfrew, 191–212. Edinburgh University Press, Edinburgh.

Rudd, S. 1984. Excavations at Lekkerwater Ruins, Tsindi Hill, Theydon, Zimbabwe. *South African Archaeological Bulletin* 39, 83–105.

Ryder, A.F.C. 1969. *Benin and the Europeans, 1485–1897.* Longmans, London.

Saitowitz, S.J., Reid, D.L. and van der Merwe, N.J. 1996. Glass bead trade from Islamic Egypt to South Africa c.AD 900–1250. *South African Journal of Science* 92, 101–4.

Saliège, J.F. *et al.* 1980. Premières datations de tumulus pré-islamiques au Mali: site mégalithique de Tondidarou. *C.R. Acad. Sc. Paris Série D* 291, 981–4.

Sassoon, H. 1980. Excavations at the site of early Mombasa. *Azania* 15, 1–42.

1983. Kings, cattle and blacksmiths: royal insignia and religious symbolism in the interlacustrine states. *Azania* 18, 93–106.

Säve-Söderbergh, T. 1960. The paintings in the tomb of Djehuty-hetep at Debeira. *Kush* 8, 25–44.

Sayce, A.H. 1911. Part II — The historical results. Second interim report on the excavations at Meroë in Ethiopia. *Annals of Archaeology and Anthropology* 4, Liverpool Institute of Archaeology, Liverpool University Press, Liverpool.

Schmidt, P.R. 1978. *Historical archaeology: a structural approach in an African culture.* Greenwood Press, Westport, Connecticut.

Schmidt, P.R. and Avery, D.H. 1996. Complex iron smelting and prehistoric culture in Tanzania. In *The culture and technology of African iron production*, ed. P.R. Schmidt, 172–85. University Press of Florida, Gainesville.

Schoenbrun, D.L. 1993. Cattle herds and banana gardens: the historical geography of the western Great Lakes region, *ca* AD 800–1500. *African Archaeological Review* 11, 39–72.

1995. Social aspects of agricultural change between the Great Lakes, AD 500 to 1000. *Azania* 29–30, 270–82.

Sergew, H.S. 1972. *Ancient and medieval Ethiopian history to 1270.* United Printers, Addis Ababa.

Service, E.R. 1975. *Origins of the state and civilization: the process of cultural evolution.* Norton, New York.

Shaw, T. 1960. Early smoking pipes: in Africa, Europe, and America. *Journal of the Royal Anthropological Institute* 90(2), 272–305 and Plates 1–9.

1970. *Igbo-Ukwu*, 2 vols. Faber and Faber, London.

1973. A note on trade and the Tsoede Bronzes. *West African Journal of Archaeology* 3, 233–8.

1975a. Why 'darkest' Africa? Archaeological light on an old problem. The University Lectures 1974, Ibadan University Press, Ibadan.

1975b. Those Igbo-Ukwu radiocarbon dates: facts, fictions and probabilities. *Journal of African History* 16(4), 503–17.

1977. *Unearthing Igbo-Ukwu*. Oxford University Press, Ibadan.

1978. *Nigeria: its archaeology and early history*. Thames and Hudson, London.

1980. New data on the pre-European civilizations of southern Nigeria. In *Proceedings of the 8th Panafrican Congress of Prehistory and Quaternary Studies, Nairobi, 5 to 10 September 1977*, ed. R.E. Leakey and B.A. Ogot, 376–8. The International Louis Leakey Memorial Institute for African Prehistory, Nairobi.

1984. Archaeological evidence and effects of food-producing in Nigeria. In *From hunters to farmers: the causes and consequences of food production in Africa*, ed. J.D. Clark and S.A. Brandt, 152–7. University of California Press, Berkeley.

1993. Further light on Igbo-Ukwu, including new radiocarbon dates. In *Proceedings of the 9th Congress of the Pan-African Association of Pre-history and Related Studies: Jos, 11–17 December 1983*, ed. B.W. Andah, P. de Maret and R. Soper, 79–83. Rex Charles, Ibadan.

Shaw, T. and Daniels, S.G.H. 1984. Excavations at Iwo Eleru, Ondo State, Nigeria. *West African Journal of Archaeology* 14, 1–269.

Shaw, T., Sinclair, P., Andah, B. and Okpoko, A. (ed.) 1993. *The archaeology of Africa: food, metals and towns*. Routledge, London and New York.

Shepherd, G. 1982. The making of the Swahili: a view from the southern end of the East African coast. In *From Zinj to Zanzibar: studies in history, trade and society on the eastern coast of Africa (Paideuma 28)*, ed. J. de V. Allen and T.H. Wilson, 129–47.

Shinnie, M. 1965. *Ancient African Kingdoms*. Arnold, London.

Shinnie, P.L. 1955. *Excavations at Soba*. Sudan Antiquities Service, Occasional Papers No. 3, Khartoum.

1960. Excavations at Bigo, 1957. *Uganda Journal* 24(1), 16–28.

1967. *Meroë: a civilization of the Sudan*. Thames and Hudson, London.

1989. The culture of Meroë and its influence in the central Sudan. *Sahara* 2, 21–30.

1996. *Ancient Nubia*. Kegan Paul, London and New York.

Shinnie, P.L. and Bradley, R.J. 1980. *The capital of Kush 1: Meroë excavations 1965–1972 (Meroitica 4)*. Akademie-Verlag, Berlin.

Shinnie, P.L. and Kense, F.J. 1982. Meroitic iron working. *Meroitica* 6, 17–28, 43–9.

1989. *Archaeology of Gonja, Ghana: excavations at Daboya*. University of Calgary Press, Calgary.

Shinnie, P.L. and Shinnie, M. 1978. *Debeira West: a mediaeval Nubian town*. Aris and Phillips, Warminster.

Shipton, P.M. 1984. Strips and patches: a demographic dimension in some African land-holding and political systems. *Man* (NS) 19, 613–34.

Siddle, D.J. 1968. War-towns in Sierra Leone: a study in social change. *Africa* 38(1), 47–56.

Simoons, F.J. 1965. Some questions on the economic prehistory of Ethiopia. *Journal of African History* 6(1), 1–12.

Sinclair, P.J.J. 1982. Chibuene — an early trading site in southern Mozambique. In *From Zinj to Zanzibar: studies in history, trade and society on the eastern coast of Africa (Paideuma 28)*, ed. J. de V. Allen and T.H. Wilson, 149–64.

1984. Some aspects of the economic level of the Zimbabwe state. In *Papers presented in honour of Miss G. Caton-Thompson (Zimbabwea 1)*, National Museums and Monuments of Zimbabwe, 48–53.

1987. *Space, time and social formation: a territorial approach to the archaeology and anthropology of Zimbabwe and Mozambique c.0–1700 AD*. Aun 9, Societas Archaeologica Upsaliensis, Uppsala.

1991. Archaeology in Eastern Africa: an overview of current chronological issues. *Journal of African History* 32, 179–219.

1995. The origins of urbanism in East and southern Africa: a diachronic perspective. In *Islamic art and culture in Sub-Saharan Africa*, ed. K. Ådahl and B. Sahlström, 99–109. Acta Universitatis Upsaliensis, Figura Nova Series 27, Uppsala.

Sinclair, P.J.J. and Lundmark, H. 1984. A spatial analysis of archaeological sites from Zimbabwe. In *Frontiers: southern African archaeology today*, ed. M. Hall, G. Avery, D.M. Avery, M.L. Wilson and A.J.B. Humphreys, 277–88. Cambridge Monographs in African Archaeology 10, BAR International Series 207, Oxford.

Sinclair, P.J.J., Pikirayi, I., Pwiti, G. and Soper, R. 1993. Urban trajectories on the Zimbabwean plateau. In *The archaeology of Africa: food, metals and towns*, ed. T. Shaw, P. Sinclair, B. Andah and A. Okpoko, 705–31. Routledge, London and New York.

Sjoberg, G. 1960. *The preindustrial city*. Free Press of Glencoe, Illinois.

Smith, A.B. 1992. *Pastoralism in Africa: origins and development ecology*. Hurst, London.

Smith, M.C. and Wright, H.T. 1988. The ceramics from Ras Hafun in Somalia: notes on a classical maritime site. *Azania* 23, 115–41.

Smith, R. 1970. The canoe in West African history. *Journal of African History* 11(4), 515–33.

Soper, R. 1990. Great Zimbabwe tradition sites in local context: the Centenary Survey. In *Urban origins in Eastern Africa: proceedings of the 1990 workshop, Harare and Great Zimbabwe*, ed. P.J.J. Sinclair and G. Pwiti, 67–76. Central Board of National Antiquities, Stockholm.

1992. Observations on the sociopolitical status of Great Zimbabwe tradition sites in northern Mashonaland. In *Urban origins in Eastern Africa: proceedings of the 1991 workshop in Zanzibar*, ed. P.J.J. Sinclair and A. Juma, 140–5. Swedish Central Board of National Antiquities, Stockholm.

1993. The palace at Oyo Ile, western Nigeria. In *Imprints of West Africa's past: Forum on West African Archaeology at the Conference in Honour of Thurstan Shaw, Founding Editor of WAJA*, ed. B.W. Andah, C.A. Folorunso and I.A. Okpoko, 295–311. Special Book Issue, *West African Journal of Archaeology* 22. Wisdom Publishers, Ibadan.

1994. Ancient fields and agricultural systems: new work on the Nyanga Terrace Complex. *Nyame Akuma* 42, 18–21.

1996. The Nyanga terrace complex of eastern Zimbabwe: new investigations. *Azania* 31, 1–35.

1997. Review of *Snakes and crocodiles: power and symbolism in ancient Zimbabwe* by Thomas N. Huffman, Witwatersrand University Press, Johannesburg, 1996. *Azania* 32, 123–7.

1999. Letter to author dated 1 March 1999.

Soper, R. and Darling, P. 1980. The walls of Oyo Ile. *West African Journal of Archaeology* 10, 61–81.

Soper, R. and Pwiti, G. 1992. Excavations at Zvongombe, Centenary District, Northern Zimbabwe. In *Urban origins in Eastern Africa: proceedings of the 1991 workshop in Zanzibar*, ed. P.J.J. Sinclair and A. Juma, 146–60. Swedish Central Board of National Antiquities, Stockholm.

Sowunmi, M.A. 1993. The Quaternary in West Africa: vegetational evidence. In

Proceedings of the 9th Congress of the Pan-African Association of Pre-history and Related Studies: Jos, 11–17 December 1983, ed. B.W. Andah, P. de Maret and R. Soper, 12–16. Rex Charles, Ibadan.

Spear, T.T. 1978. *The Kaya Complex: a history of the Mijikenda peoples of the Kenya coast to 1900.* Kenya Literature Bureau, Nairobi.

Speke, J.H. 1863. *Journal of the discovery of the source of the Nile.* Blackwood, London.

Stahl, A.B. 1993. Intensification in the West African Late Stone Age: a view from central Ghana. In *The archaeology of Africa: food, metals and towns*, ed. T. Shaw, P. Sinclair, B. Andah and A. Okpoko, 261–73. Routledge, London and New York.

Stanley, H.M. 1878. *Through the Dark Continent*, 2 vols. and maps. Sampson Low, Marston, Searle and Rivington, London.

Staudinger, P. 1889. *Im Herzen der Haussaländer.* Landsberger, Berlin. Trans. J. Moody 1990 as *In the heart of the Hausa states*, 2 vols. Ohio University Center for International Studies, Athens, Ohio.

Steinhart, E.I. 1981. Herders and farmers: the tributary mode of production in Western Uganda. In *Modes of production in Africa: the precolonial era*, ed. D. Crummey and C.C. Stewart, 114–55. Sage Publications, Beverly Hills.

Stiles, D. 1992. The ports of East Africa, the Comoros and Madagascar: their place in Indian Ocean trade from 1–1500 AD. *Kenya Past and Present* 24, 27–36.

Summers, R. 1958. *Inyanga: prehistoric settlements in Southern Rhodesia.* Cambridge University Press, Cambridge.

1963. *Zimbabwe: a Rhodesian mystery.* Nelson, Johannesburg.

1967. Archaeological distributions and a tentative history of tsetse infestation in Rhodesia and the Northern Transvaal. *Arnoldia* (Rhodesia) 3(13), 1–18.

1969. *Ancient mining in Rhodesia and adjacent areas.* Museum Memoir 3, Trustees of the National Museums of Rhodesia, Salisbury, Rhodesia.

Sutton, J.E.G. 1982. Archaeology in West Africa: a review of recent work and a further list of radiocarbon dates. *Journal of African History* 23(3), 291–313.

1985. Ntusi and the 'dams'. *Azania* 20, 172–5.

1991. The international factor at Igbo-Ukwu. *African Archaeological Review* 9, 145–60.

1993. The antecedents of the interlacustrine kingdoms. *Journal of African History* 34, 33–64.

1997. The African lords of the intercontinental gold trade before the Black Death: al-Hasan bin Sulaiman of Kilwa and Mansa Musa of Mali. *Antiquaries Journal* 77, 221–42.

Sutton, J.E.G. and Roberts, A.D. 1968. Uvinza and its salt industry. *Azania* 3, 45–86.

Swan, L. 1994. *Early gold mining on the Zimbabwean Plateau: changing patterns of gold production in the first and second millennia AD.* Studies in African Archaeology 9, Societas Archaeologica Upsaliensis, Uppsala.

Szumowski, G. 1957. Fouilles au nord du Macina et dans la région de Ségou. *Bulletin de l'IFAN*, Dakar, 19(B), 224–58.

Taddesse, T. 1972. *Church and state in Ethiopia 1270–1527.* Clarendon Press, Oxford.

Tainter, J.A. 1988. *The collapse of complex societies.* Cambridge University Press, Cambridge.

Tarekegn, A. 1996. Aksumite burial practices, the 'Gudit Stelae Field', Aksum. In *Aspects of African archaeology: Papers from the 10th Congress of the PanAfrican Association for Prehistory and Related Studies*, ed. G. Pwiti and R. Soper, 611–19. University of Zimbabwe, Harare.

Taylor, M.O.V. 1984. Southern Transvaal stone walled sites — a spatial consideration. In *Frontiers: southern African archaeology today*, ed. M. Hall, G. Avery, D.M. Avery, M.L. Wilson and A.J.B. Humphreys, 248–51. Cambridge Monographs in African Archaeology 10, BAR International Series 207, Oxford.

Theal, G.M. (ed.) 1964. *Records of south-eastern Africa*, 9 vols. Printed for the Government of the Cape Colony, 1898–1903; facsimile reprint, Struik, Cape Town.

Thilmans, G. and Descamps, C. 1974. Le site mégalithique de Tiékène-Boussoura (Sénégal): fouilles de 1973–1974. *Bulletin de l'IFAN*, Dakar, 36(B), 447–96.

1975. Le site mégalithique de Tiékène-Boussoura (Sénégal): fouilles de 1974–1975. *Bulletin de l'IFAN*, Dakar, 37(B), 259–306.

Thomassey, P. and Mauny, R. 1951. Campagne de fouilles à Koumbi Saleh. *Bulletin de l'IFAN*, Dakar, 13(1), 438–62.

1956. Campagne de fouilles de 1950 à Koumbi Saleh (Ghana?). *Bulletin de l'IFAN*, Dakar, 18(B), 117–40.

Thompson, H.N. 1910–11. The forests of Southern Nigera. *Journal of the African Society* 10 (38), 121–45.

Thorp, C.R. 1984. A cultural interpretation of the faunal assemblage from Khami Hill Ruin. In *Frontiers: southern African archaeology today*, ed. M. Hall, G. Avery, D.M. Avery, M.L. Wilson and A.J.B. Humphreys, 266–76. Cambridge Monographs in African Archaeology 10, BAR International Series 207, Oxford.

1995. *Kings, commoners and cattle at Zimbabwe Tradition sites*. National Museums and Monuments of Zimbabwe, Harare.

Thruston, A.B. 1900. *African incidents: personal experiences in Egypt and Unyoro*. John Murray, London.

Thurman, C.C.M. 1979. The textiles. In *Ancient textiles from Nubia: Meroitic, X-Group, and Christian fabrics from Ballana and Qustul*, C.C.M. Thurman and B. Williams, 36–46. The Art Institute of Chicago, Chicago.

Togola, T. 1996. Iron Age occupation in the Méma region, Mali. *African Archaeological Review* 13(2), 91–110.

Török, L. 1992. Ambulatory kingship and settlement history: a study on the contribution of archaeology to Meroitic history. In *Etudes Nubiennes: Conférence de Genève, Actes du VIIe Congrès international d'études nubiennes 3–8 septembre 1990*, ed. C. Bonnet, Vol. 1, 111–26. Geneva.

1997. *Meroe city: an ancient African capital: John Garstang's excavations in the Sudan*, Parts 1 and 2. Egypt Exploration Society, London.

Tosh, J. 1970. The northern Interlacustrine Region. In *Pre-Colonial African trade: essays on trade in Central and Eastern Africa before 1900*, ed. R. Gray and D. Birmingham, 102–18. Oxford University Press, London.

Trigger, B.G. 1965. *History and settlement in Lower Nubia*. Yale University Publications in Anthropology No. 69, New Haven.

1969a. The myth of Meroë and the African Iron Age. *African Historical Studies* 2(1), 23–50.

1969b. The social significance of the diadems in the royal tombs at Ballana. *Journal of Near Eastern Studies* 28(4), 255–61.

327

1970. The cultural ecology of Christian Nubia. In *Kunst und Geschichte Nubiens in Christlicher Zeit*, ed. E. Dinkler, 347–79. Aurel Bongers, Recklinghausen.

1973. Meroitic language studies: strategies and goals. In *Sudan im Altertum*, ed. F. Hintze. Internationale Tagung für meroitische Forschungen in Berlin 1971. *Meroitica* 1, 243–72. Akademie-Verlag, Berlin.

1982. Reisner to Adams: paradigms of Nubian cultural history. In *Nubian studies: proceedings of the Symposium for Nubian Studies, Selwyn College, Cambridge, 1978*, ed. J.M. Plumley, 223–6. International Society for Nubian Studies, Aris and Phillips, Warminster.

Turner, G. 1984. Vertebrate remains from Lekkerwater. *South African Archaeological Bulletin* 39, 106–8.

Uganda, 1967. *Atlas of Uganda*, 2nd edn. Department of Lands and Surveys, Uganda.

Uganda National Parks, n.d. *Queen Elizabeth National Park (North Sector)*, guide leaflet, Kampala. (Acquired 1990.)

Ullendorff, E. 1960. *The Ethiopians: an introduction to country and people*. Oxford University Press, London.

Vanacker, C. 1979. *Tegdaoust II: recherches sur Aoudaghost: fouille d'un quartier artisanal*. Institut Mauritanien de la Recherche Scientifique No. 2.

van Beek, G.W. 1967. Monuments of Axum in the light of South Arabian archeology. *Journal of the American Oriental Society* 87(2), 113–22.

van der Veen, M. 1991. The plant remains. In *Soba: archaeological research at a medieval capital on the Blue Nile*, ed. D.A. Welsby and C.M. Daniels, 264–73. British Institute in Eastern Africa, Memoir 12, London.

Van Noten, F.L. 1972. *Les tombes du Roi Cyirima Rujugira et de la Reine-Mère Nyirayuhi Kanjogera: description archéologique*. Musée Royal de l'Afrique Centrale, Tervuren.

1982. The Iron Age in the north and east. In *The archaeology of Central Africa*, ed. F.L. Van Noten, 69–76. Akademische Drück- und Verlagsanstalt, Graz, Austria.

Vansina, J. 1966. *Kingdoms of the savanna*. University of Wisconsin Press, Madison.

1969. The bells of kings. *Journal of African History* 10(2), 187–97.

1973. *Oral tradition: a study in historical methodology* (first published in French 1961). Penguin, Harmondsworth.

1990. *Paths in the rainforests: toward a history of political tradition in Equatorial Africa*. James Currey, London.

Vantini, G. 1970. *The excavations at Faras, a contribution to the history of Christian Nubia*. Nigrizia, Bologna.

Vercoutter, J. 1959. The gold of Kush: two gold-washing stations at Faras East. *Kush* 7, 120–53.

1962. Un palais des 'Candaces', contemporain d'Auguste (fouilles à Wad-ban-Naga 1958–1960). *Syria: Revue d'Art Oriental et d'Archéologie* 39, 263–99.

Vérin, P. 1976. The African element in Madagascar. *Azania* 11, 135–51.

1986. *The history of civilisation in north Madagascar*, trans. D. Smith. Balkema, Rotterdam.

Vogel, J.O. (ed.) 1997. *Encyclopedia of precolonial Africa: archaeology, history, languages, cultures, and environments*. AltaMira Press, Walnut Creek, CA.

von Endt, D.W. 1978. Was civet used as a perfume in Aksum? *Azania* 13, 186–8.

Waller, H. 1874. *The last journals of David Livingstone, in Central Africa, from 1865 to his death* . . ., 2 vols. Murray, London.

Walton, J. 1956. *African village*. Van Schaik, Pretoria.

Watson, E.J. and Watson, V. 1990. 'Of commoners and kings': faunal remains from Ondini. *South African Archaeological Bulletin* 45, 33–46.

Wayland, E.J. 1934. Notes on the Biggo bya Mugenyi: some ancient earthworks in northern Buddu. *Uganda Journal* 2(1), 21–32.

Weeks, K.R. 1967. *The Classic Christian townsite at Arminna West*. Publications of the Pennsylvania–Yale Expedition to Egypt, No. 3, New Haven and Philadelphia.

Welsby, D.A. 1996. *The Kingdom of Kush: the Napatan and Meroitic Empires*. British Museum Press, London.

  1998. *Soba II: renewed excavations within the metropolis of the Kingdom of Alwa in Central Sudan*. British Institute in Eastern Africa, Memoir 15, and British Museum Press, London.

Welsby, D.A. and Daniels, C.M. 1991. *Soba: archaeological research at a medieval capital on the Blue Nile*. British Institute in Eastern Africa, Memoir 12, London.

Wiesmüller, B. 1998. Stages of pottery development in the south of Lake Chad from 1000 BC up to historical times. Unpublished abstracts from Society of Africanist Archaeologists 14th Biennial Conference, Syracuse University, Syracuse, New York, May 20–24, 1998, 57–8.

Wildung, D. 1997. Meroitic ceramics. In *Sudan: ancient kingdoms of the Nile*, ed. D. Wildung, 342–68. Flammarion, Paris and New York.

Wilks, I. 1962. A medieval trade-route from the Niger to the Gulf of Guinea. *Journal of African History* 3(2), 337–41.

Willett, F. 1966. On the funeral effigies of Owo and Benin and the interpretation of the life-size bronze heads from Ife, Nigeria. *Man* (NS) 1(1), 34–45 and Plates 1–4.

  1967. *Ife in the history of West African sculpture*. Thames and Hudson, London.

  1977. *Baubles, bangles and beads; trade contacts of mediaeval Ife*. Thirteenth Melville J. Herskovits Memorial Lecture, Edinburgh University.

Willett, F. and Fleming, S.J. 1976. A catalogue of important Nigerian copper-alloy castings dated by their thermoluminescence. *Archaeometry* 18(2), 135–46.

Wilson, T.H. 1978. *The monumental architecture and archaeology north of the Tana River*. National Museums of Kenya, Xerox.

  1979. Swahili funerary architecture of the north Kenya coast. In *Swahili houses and tombs of the coast of Kenya*, ed. J. de V. Allen and T.H. Wilson. Art and Archaeology Research Papers, London.

  1980. *The monumental architecture and archaeology of the central and southern Kenya coast*, National Museums of Kenya, Xerox.

  1982. Spatial analysis and settlement patterns on the East African coast. In *From Zinj to Zanzibar: studies in history, trade and society on the eastern coast of Africa* (*Paideuma* 28), ed. J. de V. Allen and T.H. Wilson, 201–19.

Wilson, T.H. and Lali Omar, A. 1997. Archaeological investigations at Pate. *Azania* 32, 31–76.

Winterbotham, H.S.L., Smith, E.G. and Longland, F. 1944. *The Belgian Congo*. Geographical Handbook Series, Naval Intelligence Division, Oxford.

Wittfogel, K.A. 1957. *Oriental despotism*. Yale University Press, New Haven.

Woodhouse, J. 1998. Iron in Africa: metal from nowhere. In *Transformations in Africa: essays on Africa's later past*, ed. G. Connah, 160–85. Leicester University Press, London and Washington.

Woolley, C.L. 1911. *Karanòg: the town*, Eckley B. Coxe Junior Expedition to Nubia, Vol. 5. University Museum, University of Pennsylvania, Philadelphia.

Woolley, C.L. and Randall-MacIver, D. 1910. *Karanòg: the Romano-Nubian cemetery*, Eckley B. Coxe Junior Expedition to Nubia, Vols. 3 and 4. University Museum, University of Pennsylvania, Philadelphia.

Wright, H.T. 1984. Early seafarers of the Comoro Islands: the Dembeni Phase of the ixth–xth centuries AD. *Azania* 19, 13–59.

  1992. Early Islam, oceanic trade and town development on Nzwani: the Comorian Archipelago in the xith–xvth centuries AD. *Azania* 27, 81–128.

  1993. Trade and politics on the eastern littoral of Africa, AD 800–1300. In *The archaeology of Africa: food, metals and towns*, ed. T. Shaw, P. Sinclair, B. Andah and A. Okpoko, 658–72. Routledge, London and New York.

Wright, H.T. and Johnson, G.A. 1975. Population, exchange, and early state formation in southwestern Iran. *American Anthropologist* 77, 267–89.

Wright, H.T. and Rakotoarisoa, J.-A. 1990. The archaeology of complex societies in Madagascar: case-studies in cultural diversification. In *Urban origins in Eastern Africa: proceedings of the 1989 Madagascar workshop*, ed. P.J.J. Sinclair and J.-A. Rakotoarisoa, 21–31. Central Board of National Antiquities, Stockholm.

Wright, H.T., Vérin, P., Ramilisonina, Burney, D., Burney, L.P. and Matsumoto, K. 1996. The evidence of settlement systems in the Bay of Boeny and the Mahavavy River Valley, north-western Madagascar. *Azania* 31, 37–73.

Wrigley, C.C. 1958. Some thoughts on the Bacwezi. *Uganda Journal* 22(1), 11–17.

  1989. Bananas in Buganda. *Azania* 24, 64–70.

Ylvisaker, M. 1982. The ivory trade in the Lamu area, 1600–1870. In *From Zinj to Zanzibar: studies in history, trade and society on the eastern coast of Africa (Paideuma 28)*, ed. J. de V. Allen and T.H. Wilson, 221–31.

York, R.N. 1973. Excavations at New Buipe. *West African Journal of Archaeology* 3, 1–189.

Zabkar, L.V. 1975. *Apedemak, lion god of Meroë: a study in Egyptian-Meroitic syncretism*. Aris and Phillips, Warminster.

Index